Lenses:
Perspectives on Literature

SECOND EDITION

Editors

Abigail Browning

Melissa Ridley Elmes

HAYDEN
HM
McNEIL

Hayden-McNeil Sustainability

Hayden-McNeil's standard paper stock uses a minimum of 30%
post-consumer waste. We offer higher % options by request,
including a 100% recycled stock. Additionally, Hayden-McNeil
Custom Digital provides authors with the opportunity to convert
print products to a digital format. Hayden-McNeil is part of a larger
sustainability initiative through Macmillan Higher Ed.
Visit http://sustainability.macmillan.com to learn more.

Printed in the United States of America

10 9 8 7 6 5 4 3 2 1

ISBN 978-0-7380-7007-0

Hayden-McNeil Publishing
14903 Pilot Drive
Plymouth, MI 48170
www.hmpublishing.com

Rifkin 7007-0 F14

Table of Contents

Table of Contents

Editorial and Advisory Board

Editors

Abigail Browning, MFA, and Melissa Ridley Elmes, MA

Editorial Assistant

Martha Hammer

Advisory Board

Poetry

Shawn Delgado, MFA

Kyla Sterling, MFA

Drama

Crystal Matey, MA

Christina Romanelli, PhD

Short Prose

Beckie Dashiell, MFA

Brendan Missett, MFA

Long Prose

Virginia Eudy, MA

Kellia Moore, MA

Acknowledgments

The *Lenses* editors want first and foremost to thank the writers who contributed so much time, talent, and expertise to this endeavor and without whom this textbook would, quite simply, not exist. It is impossible to over-praise the members of our advisory board for their work in providing thoughtful, constructive, and expert critical peer review for the major chapters on literary genres. We present heartfelt thanks and deepest gratitude to our editorial assistant, Martha Hammer, who went above and beyond the call of duty and handled every task with the grace and maturity of an old pro. We also wish to express gratitude to the incredible English department support staff: Lydia Howard, Alyson Everhart, Anna Tysor, and Sarah Foster. Dr. Amy Vines and Dr. Alexandra Moore supported our efforts by helping us to create and promote the *Lenses* internship so that we could provide undergraduate students with the chance to work on an academic editing and publishing project. Thanks to Chelsea Skelley and Cara Williams for helpful feedback on the introductory remarks for this book, and to Shawn Delgado for invaluable assistance in compiling the anthology section. Brenta Blevins stepped in at the ninth hour with formatting assistance, just in time to prevent us from pulling out our hair over column breaks, and we are grateful for her digital expertise. We believe that everyone who has worked on this project will agree with us that a nod to all of the families and friends of this book's contributors is not out of line, since they shared the journey to its completion. Finally, Dr. Mark Rifkin trusted us, encouraged us, and occasionally prodded us, to the finish line, and we have valued the opportunity to work with him towards the creation of this second edition of *Lenses: Perspectives on Literature*.

Notes on Contributors

Fausto Barrionuevo has published poems in several journals, including *Off the Coast: Maine's International Poetry Journal, decomP magazine, Rougarou,* and *Sliver of Stone,* and was nominated for a Pushcart prize in 2011 for his poem "Ground." He recently earned an MFA in poetry at the University of North Carolina, Greensboro. A native of Miami, Florida, he is concurrently working on his first full-length collection of poems and a feature-length screenplay.

Michael Bedsole holds master's degrees in both English and Library and Information Studies from the University of North Carolina, Greensboro, and is currently a fourth-year doctoral student in the English Department at UNCG. He has taught college writing and literature courses for a number of years, and before that taught high school English. His research interests include the construction and representation of subjectivity in modernist fiction and poetry, and his dissertation examines metaphors of exteriority in the work of T.S. Eliot.

Brenta Blevins is pursuing a doctorate in rhetoric and composition at the University of North Carolina, Greensboro. She has worked in the software industry, taught composition and literature courses, served as Assistant Director of the UNCG Digital ACT Studio, and has been a Fellow with the Digital Rhetoric Collaborative through the University of Michigan's Sweetland Center for Writing. Her research interests include digital rhetoric, pedagogy, and digital literacy.

Gregory Brown hails from Vancouver Island, in beautiful British Columbia. He is a graduate of the University of North Carolina, Greensboro MFA program for Fiction and Memorial University of Newfoundland's Master of Arts program in English Literature. He is the recipient of the Roy Daniels Memorial Essay Prize and his fiction and criticism have appeared in *Postcript* and *Paragon.* He currently teaches English Literature and College Writing at UNCG.

Abigail Browning received her MFA in Poetry at the University of North Carolina, Greensboro, in 2012. In addition to teaching English Literature and College Writing at her alma mater, Ms. Browning is contributing editor for the literary blog, *Tate Street High Society* (www.tatestreethighsociety.com), and has poems published in the *Yemassee Journal Online, The Greensboro Review, Linebreak,* and *RHINO Poetry.* She was honored to receive the Amon Liner Poetry Award (2012), the Noel Callow and Academy of American Poets' Prize (2012), and was a finalist for the Linda Flowers NC Arts Prize (2012).

Brian Butler specializes in Postcolonial Literature and Theory, World Literature, and Critical Theory. His research interests include: "Postcolonial" literatures and cultures; imperialism, nationalism, and anti-colonial resistance; modernization/capitalist modernity/modernism; globalization; literature of Empire; and modernist literature and theories of modernism.

Matthew Carter is a doctoral student in the University of North Carolina, Greensboro, English Department. He is a member of the Society of American Fight Directors (SAFD) and the American Marlowe Society (AMS). Matthew worked as a professional actor in Richmond, Virginia, before continuing his education in English Literature. His research deals with the ethnic, gendered, and racial encoding of weaponry on the early modern stage.

Jenny Dale is the English Liaison Librarian at the UNCG University Libraries. She has worked with English composition and literature courses at the University of North Carolina, Greensboro, since 2010 and provides research support to students and faculty in the English department. She received both her MS in Library Science and her BA in English and Creative Writing from the University of North Carolina at Chapel Hill.

Beckie Dashiell is a member of the Lenses Advisory Board. She received her MFA in Fiction at the University of North Carolina, Greensboro, in 2013 and is currently serving as a lecturer in the English department. She admires the work of the Canadian short story writer Alice Munro immensely, and tells anyone who will listen that they should give her a read. Seriously, if you meet her, she will tell you this, too.

Shawn Delgado earned his BS in Science, Technology, and Culture from the Georgia Institute of Technology and his MFA in Creative Writing from the University of North Carolina at Greensboro, where he currently is finishing the second year of his lectureship. He is the Layout Editor for Jeanne Duval Editions and the Editor of the Million Writers Award, which celebrates the best short stories published online.

Virginia Eudy is a recent MA graduate in English at the University of North Carolina, Greensboro, focusing in 18th-century British Poetry, specifically Thomas Gray and Robert Burns. Her other loves, however, include Edgar Allan Poe and Nathaniel Hawthorne.

Martha Hammer is on the Editorial Advisory Board and is also the Editorial Assistant for *Lenses: Perspectives on Literature*. She will graduate with a Bachelor of Arts, Concentration in English, in May of 2014. Ms. Hammer is also a member of the English Honor Society Sigma Tau Delta. With her experience working on *Lenses*, after college, she hopes to pursue a career in the print and editing field. Ms. Hammer's favorite books are Kate Chopin's *The Awakening* and Aldous Huxley's *Brave New World*.

Carrie Hart is a doctoral student in Educational Studies and Cultural Studies at the University of North Carolina, Greensboro. She graduated with an MA in Women's and Gender Studies from UNCG in 2011. She currently teaches courses in Educational Studies and Women's and Gender Studies, organizes a community group for LGBTQIA teens, and co-produces *KiQ*, a documentary web series about queerness. Her research interests include transnational feminisms, queer theory, visual literacies, and critical art pedagogy.

Courtney Hartnett is an MFA candidate in poetry at the University of North Carolina at Greensboro. She graduated from the University of Virginia in 2013 with a BA in Interdisciplinary Writing, and her poems and prose are published or are forthcoming in *Appalachian Journal, storySouth, Blood Lotus*, and *Dew on the Kudzu*. Courtney was a finalist for the *Crab Orchard Review*'s 2014 Allison Joseph Poetry Award.

Catherine Hawkins is a 2014 graduate of the University of North Carolina, Greensboro, MFA program in Fiction. She earned her undergraduate degree at Colby College in Waterville, Maine. She currently works as a lecturer in the English Department of UNCG.

Abigail Lee is an MFA student in poetry at the University of North Carolina, Greensboro. She spent time rebuilding homes in New Orleans after receiving her undergraduate degree from the University of Virginia. Her work has appeared or will appear in the *Evansville Review, Emry's Journal*, the *Aurorean, Amoskeag*, and other publications.

Kristine Lee received her BA in English from Mars Hill College (2007) and her MA in English and Comparative Literature from Hofstra University in 2008. She is currently a second-year doctoral student in the University of North Carolina, Greensboro, English department and is also pursuing the Women's and Gender

Studies graduate certificate. Kristine specializes in Victorian literature, with specific interests in working class poetry, gender, and class issues in the Victorian age. She has been delighted to teach at UNCG and contribute to this text!

Crystal Matey is pursuing a PhD in English, in addition to a graduate certificate in Women's and Gender Studies, at the University of North Carolina, Greensboro. Crystal has taught literature and composition for many years, and has served on the executive board for the English Graduate Student Association. She is on the Editorial Advisory Board for *Lenses* and authored the sections on "Long Prose" and "Symbolism." Her main research interests include the long eighteenth century, with specific concentrations in empiricism, the imagination, and genre studies. She is interested in speculative fiction, particularly science fiction and dystopian literature.

Meghan McGuire is a third-year doctoral student in the University of North Carolina, Greensboro, English department, specializing in twentieth-century British and Irish literature. In addition to authoring chapters on "Allusion" and "New Historicism" for *Lenses: Perspectives on Literature*, Meghan is also an assistant editor of *Rhetorical Approaches to College Writing*. Meghan has been teaching literature and composition at the college level since receiving her MA in English from Wake Forest University in 2006. She has also studied in Ireland at the Burren College of Art, Co. Clare and at the National University of Ireland in Galway.

Brendan Missett received his MFA in Fiction at the University of North Carolina, Greensboro, in 2014, and is working on a collection of short stories. He has served as the Fiction Editor at *The Greensboro Review*, and Editor for the *Oaxaca Times*. Originally from Connecticut, Brendan spent several years traveling in Asia and Mexico before arriving in North Carolina.

Kellia Moore hopes to continue working toward a doctorate in English Literature after finishing her MA at the University of North Carolina, Greensboro. She specializes in 18th- and 19th-century British literature and anything and everything about Jane Austen.

Melissa Ridley Elmes is a second-year doctoral student in the English and Women's and Gender Studies departments at the University of North Carolina, Greensboro. She has taught literature and composition for several years, and has served as assistant editor for *Hortulus: The Online Journal of Graduate Medieval Studies* and a reader for *Medieval Perspectives*. She has published on Chaucer and Arthuriana, and also researches and writes on monstrosity, gender, and magic. Her dissertation focuses on feasts and feasting in post-Conquest through

15th-century British literatures and cultures. Melissa is the recipient of the English Department's Graduate Student Essay prize (2013) and the Cloninger-Stout Award (2014).

Christina Romanelli specializes in Renaissance Literature and the theory of religion, ritual, and magic. As a doctoral student at the University of North Carolina, Greensboro, her dissertation focuses on early modern retellings of the Harrowing of Hell, or Christ's descent into hell between the crucifixion and the resurrection.

Shana Scudder is currently pursuing her doctorate in Rhetoric and Composition at the University of North Carolina, Greensboro, focusing on the intersection of embodied rhetoric, feminist theory, and dance studies.

Kyla Sterling received her MFA in Poetry at the University of North Carolina, Greensboro (2011) and is currently a lecturer in English at UNCG. She served on the Advisory Board for the current edition of *Lenses: Perspectives on Literature*. Her poetry appears in *Notre Dame Review, Cream City Review, Barrow Street Journal*, and *The Greensboro Review*.

Corrie Lynn White received her MFA in Poetry from the University of North Carolina, Greensboro, where she currently works as a lecturer in the English department. Her poems have appeared or are forthcoming in *Best New Poets 2013, The Greensboro Review, Mississippi Review, Grist: A Journal for Writers*, and *Yemassee*, among others. In 2013, she was named a finalist in the Mississippi Review Prize Contest and the winner of the Noel Callow Poetry Prize, sponsored by the Academy of American Poets. Corrie is the author of the chapter on "Metaphor, Simile, and Imagery" in *Lenses: Perspectives on Literature*.

April Williams is a third-year doctoral student at the University of North Carolina, Greensboro, specializing in nineteenth-century American literature. April's other scholarly interests include gender studies, environmental literature, children's literature, pedagogy, and rhetoric and composition theory. In addition to her ongoing role as a UNCG teaching assistant, April has also served as a research assistant for English Department professors Anthony Cuda, Jennifer Keith, and Hephzibah Roskelly. In 2012, she received the English Department's Graduate Student Essay Award.

Introduction

Abigail Browning and Melissa Ridley Elmes

Whether you were a straight-A student in English at the high-school level, or have not taken a literature course in years, the book you are now holding should prove to be a useful tool as you learn to critically read and think about literature. This second edition of *Lenses: Perspectives on Literature* has been designed to meet the needs of students enrolled in 100-level literature courses at the University of North Carolina, Greensboro, by providing a concise yet comprehensive introduction to the study of literature at the college level. With that in mind, we hope you will use *Lenses* as a starting point for actively exploring the texts that you encounter both in and outside of the classroom.

ORGANIZATIONAL APPROACH

Following this introduction, Abigail Browning and Shana Scudder start us off with an essay entitled, "To Read Is to Write: Strategies for Reading," in which they advise on how to read, question, remember, and interact critically with literature. From there, the book is divided into six sections: 1) an introduction to literary genres, 2) a discussion of literary elements, 3) an overview of theoretical lenses for interpreting texts, 4) advice on writing about literature, and 5) an anthology of texts, followed by 6) supplemental information in the form of a poetic forms appendix, a glossary of key terms, and finally, the index. While the book as a whole is designed as a continuous discussion, each individual chapter also stands on its own as a close examination of a single point in the study of literature, giving readers the agency to approach the book in the order that will most benefit their personal learning experience.

Reading chronologically, you will notice that Part I comprises the longer essays on literary genres: poetry, drama, short prose, and long prose. Each of these genre chapters was written and peer-reviewed by experts to ensure that we met our primary, two-fold concern: *Does this chapter sufficiently address the main points that an undergraduate literature student could reasonably be expected to know about that genre?* And, *Is this chapter accessible to a general audience?* With each chapter carefully crafted to introduce you to key terms and approaches to reading each genre, we think you will agree with us that the answer to both questions is a resounding "yes."

Starting with "Poetry," Fausto Barrionuevo provides a clear and engaging introduction to the world of verse, focusing on the foundational elements of structure, rhyme, meter, and scansion. Matthew Carter follows this with a chapter on "Drama" that takes us beyond the literary elements of a play text, into considerations of performance spaces and acting choices that can affect our interpretation as we read a play. Next, Gregory Brown offers a playful yet insightful discussion of "Short Prose," considering both fiction and nonfiction forms. This first section ends with Crystal Matey's thorough and accessible guide to "Long Prose," including an invaluable list of techniques for close reading.

In Part II, we move into the various literary elements you will be expected to know and use as you read critically for your literature course: plot, character, theme, point of view, voice, style, setting, atmosphere, metaphor, imagery, symbol, allusion, and irony. Each of these shorter essays focuses closely on one major element or a set of related elements, with several textual examples to help you learn to identify and use these elements for the purposes of literary interpretation and analysis. First, April Williams describes the difference between "story" and "plot," and Kristine Lee provides examples of some of the most common themes and character types in literature. Catherine Hawkins explains the sometimes tricky issues we can face as readers when it comes to a narrator's point of view. Courtney Hartnett and Abigail Lee show us how style, voice and tone, and setting, atmosphere, and mood all tend to work together to set up the backbone of a literary work; reading their essays together convinces us that it would be nearly impossible to understand the concepts in one without the context of the other. Corrie Lynn White provides an insightful explanation of metaphor, simile, and imagery, while Crystal Matey's chapter will help you understand and learn to identify symbols in literary analysis. In her chapter on allusion, Meghan McGuire explains how authors use references to historical events and figures, places, and other literary works to add depth to their texts. Finally, Michael Bedsole's chapter covers the four modes of literary irony. While reading, you will notice that the chapters in this section work together to enhance your understanding of the introductions to genre in Part I.

Part III provides carefully considered, introductory essays to four of the critical approaches most commonly used by scholars of literature: New Historicism, Postcolonialism, Feminism, and Queer Theory. Meghan McGuire explores the usefulness of New Historicism as a means of exploring the cultural contexts embedded within a text. Brian Butler presents a concise summary of the major thinkers and ideas associated with postcolonial theory, which analyzes and criticizes empire and imperialism by focusing on questions of subalterity and Otherness. In the final two chapters of this section, Carrie Hart provides a useful introduction to the distinct, yet often overlapping, lenses of Feminist and Queer Theory, which focus on the power dynamics associated with questions of gender, agency, identity, and sexuality.

Part IV provides you with some guidance for approaching the assignments in your literature classes. Melissa Ridley Elmes's essay provides a general overview of the most common types of essays assigned in literature courses here at UNCG, along with suggestions for how you might go about getting started, and a brief overview of the MLA citation method most commonly used in English classes. Brenta Blevins extends the discussion beyond the written essay to consider multimodal and multigenre assignments in the literature classroom. Finally, Jenny Dale, the Undergraduate Research Specialist at Jackson Library, graciously lends her expertise in a specially commissioned essay focusing on how to conduct library research for literature classes.

Part V comprises an anthology of texts selected to accompany the various chapters of this book. This anthology includes works from each literary genre in whole or excerpt form, with which you may practice using the techniques for close reading and literary analysis presented throughout the book.

GUIDING PRINCIPLES

The guiding principle underlying every chapter of this book is simple; our authors were asked to consider at every stage of chapter development: *Is this easily understood by a non-specialist? Can a student read this chapter and use the knowledge and skills presented within it in context?* To help ensure that this book meets the pedagogic needs of instructors and the learning needs of students, each literary genre, literary element, and theoretical chapter closes with "questions to consider" and an essay prompt, to give you the chance to practice the skills of close reading and literary analysis presented within the chapter. Key terms are bold printed when they are defined within the chapter, and glossed at the back of the book for your convenience. Finally, the index includes all key terms, major authors and thinkers, and titles of works mentioned in this book, to make it easy to cross-reference and look up materials you want to read more about. All of these tools should help you learn to engage actively with literature.

When we learn to read actively—that is, critically—with an understanding that the words we are reading perform work to convey an author's vision or message, we learn to engage more fully with a text. Active reading, in turn, opens us to the endless potential of written language. Therefore, the study of literature is also the study of language. Every written text is comprised of words organized in various ways—as phrases, lines, stanzas, dialogues, monologues, soliloquys, sentences, paragraphs, and chapters. Every word within every text is chosen because it performs some task, has some purpose to contribute towards the overall meanings and functions of a literary work. When we learn to use the techniques of literary interpretation and analysis to look for the myriad possibilities and inventions of written language in a text, and to discuss what we find with others, we read as a social act. We come to realize that whether we are reading "just for class," for ourselves, or for both, as the famous author and scholar C.S. Lewis said: "We read to know we are not alone."

We hope that you will find this book an invaluable guide as you learn to join this conversation.

Abigail Browning and Melissa Ridley Elmes

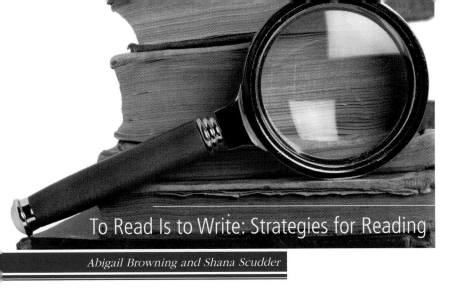

To Read Is to Write: Strategies for Reading

Abigail Browning and Shana Scudder

WHY DO WE READ?

We read daily for practical reasons—to apply for a job, to vote a person into office, to order a hot dog off a menu, to look up a doctor in our zip code. We derive pleasure from reading a friend's letter, a magazine, or a book that we'd been waiting to receive. We follow endless trails of information to read about the people, places, and things that pique our curiosity, and we read to connect ourselves with others in the world.

In an academic setting, how does the way we read change—or does it change at all? How is reading for pleasure different than reading for discovery or comprehension? Could you, right now, make the argument that pleasure and discovery are one and the same?

Skills derived from academic reading improve self-directed reading. The process of reading includes not just collecting information but especially questioning and challenging that information. Learning, especially, hinges on having the ability and confidence to question information, not simply remembering or being able to summarize the information. Reading is about actively asking questions, and this chapter offers some strategies for asking questions that can lead to a rewarding experience reading literary texts.

QUESTION EVERYTHING

Why, for example, is this chapter titled "To Read Is to Write"? It may be because the author simply liked the symmetry of the two infinitives. Perhaps it just sounds good. You might ask: *Is just sounding good enough of a reason to make it the title?*

Probably not. (In your notes above the title, you might jot down: "*Writing important to reading? Interesting. Why?*") Perhaps it is because the editor didn't like the plain title "Strategies for Reading," since a title is meant to be a miniature thesis (main argument). If the title, then, is a mini-argument, maybe the author is trying to challenge the view that reading and writing are separate activities.

By questioning the information you read—even the title of a chapter or essay—you are practicing the critical thinking skills that lead to a deeper sense of comprehension. By writing down a note about the title, you can continue to allow that question to penetrate the rest of the chapter. The title is the author's invitation for you to the essay, and your questioning it brings the reading conversation to life.

JUST TELL ME WHAT I NEED TO KNOW...

More and more, our culture relies on quickness—fast food, fast friends, fast cars—but reading is a process that is often at odds with this fast-paced lifestyle. If you're doing it well, thoroughly reading takes an investment of time. Just "knowing the plot" or the argument is not enough. Both are great beginning points, but your teachers and peers are going to expect more from you.

As a competent reader of any type of literature, one must not only read for the plot, characters, and basic meaning of the text (if you've gotten this far, you're only part of the way there). Your job is not even to figure out the "correct" interpretation of what the author "intended," as often essays, poems, short stories, plays, and other literary works are not so straightforward. In most cases, reading for the author's "intention" is a futile endeavor, since we may not know exactly what an author intended, and even if we do, such readings limit the possible range of interpretation. What, then, is your goal?

A successful reader's objective is to examine the poem, story, or essay at hand, and decipher, yes, the plot or meaning—but also to compare and contrast that piece of writing with other texts and think about how it follows or deviates from your expectations. What surprises you about the piece? What kinds of words (elevated language, colloquial, or mixed language) is the author using, and what does the diction say about the characters or the ideas? Does the form dictate the function? To better connect with the piece itself, you may also start by finding how your experience compares with (and either is different from or coincides with) the character, narrative, or idea in the text. In other words, just "understanding the plot" is not enough.

The chapters contained in this book will help you generate questions about the content and form of literary works, as well as the cultural and historical contexts in which they are read and produced. One primary goal of this book, then, will be to provide reading strategies that help you consider not only what a literary work says, but also how it says it. Here are some very basic questions to get you started:

■ What is the author writing about (the plot of the story)?

■ Who is the author? When was she/he born? What is his/her history? How does that influence the diction, tone, location, or ideas in the text?

■ Who do you think the author is writing for? Who is his/her audience?

The first question addresses the basic events of the story: *If you could summarize what happens in a few sentences, what would you include?* The second question asks about context: *How do you think the historical context/era in which the text was written affects its meaning?* The third question addresses who exactly the author had in mind when he/she was writing: *Can you determine social or cultural factors that influence the text through the content, style, and word choice (diction)?*

Through deciphering the overall picture of the message, speaker, and audience, you can start to piece together clues for understanding what you are reading at a deeper level. For example, if we use "Letter from a Birmingham Jail" by Martin Luther King, Jr. as our text, perhaps we'll start with the second question because we might happen to have more information about the speaker. Most of us learn at some point who Dr. King is—a famous reverend and African-American political activist during the Civil Rights Movement who wrote, spoke, and demonstrated for desegregation and equality in the United States.

Upon closer analysis, however, we might also examine Dr. King's letter through a range of literary lenses. We might consider him as a writer participating in a long tradition of writing about justice. For example, how does King's representation of justice compare, say, to Sophocles's *Antigone*, a play written over two-thousand years earlier? In contrast, we might look at the formal elements of his letter, and ask why he chose to use an epistolary form to reach his audience, or how he uses metaphors to convey his ideas. Finally, we might consider his own socio-historical context, considering how his text would have been received by various audiences during the Civil Rights era, and how our reaction to the text may vary from that of its original audience. Another consideration that shapes our reading practices is the genre of a literary work. Since Dr. King's letter is a nonfictional, historical document, there are some specific ways this text can be approached, as compared to a novel or a poem.

Each genre requires a different, sophisticated approach. For nonfiction short prose, although you might not know exactly when King was born, what you do know will make up the scaffolding of how you read the text. You can expect, say, that the voice in the text is meant to reflect Dr. King's own ideas, and that it will be speaking in favor of desegregation from a position of faith in the face of strong adversity. In the case of poetry or fiction, however, the literary voice cannot be assumed to be the same as the author's—an issue taken up in greater detail in Fausto Barrionuevo's section on "Author, Speaker, and Persona" and Catherine Hawkins' chapter on "Point of View." Nonetheless, if you have never heard of the author before, a good practice involves writing down some questions you'd like to know the answers to, and then doing a little research on your own. Having this background may prompt new questions that enrich your reading experience and lead to insightful analysis.

OK, so you've gotten the basics down. Several other chapters in this book give you more direction on formal considerations such as literary genres, characters, and voice, as well as a survey of critical theories on the cultural work of literature. You can practice the basic questions from this section—in terms of author, audience, and message—with each chapter as you gain more extensive and sophisticated knowledge about how to interpret what you read. However, retention is still something to grapple with as you are considering the content of complex works. Being prepared with a strategy for preserving your findings is the next step.

WRITING IS READING: THE MIGHTY PEN

Whether reading a play, a digital manuscript, a newspaper, a poem, or a 500-page novel, having a pen or pencil handy to record your thoughts is a must. With so many distractions in our culture, a pen is the perfect tool to focus your understanding of the text you are reading. Each time you transfer your thoughts from your mind to paper—as in raising or answering questions you have about the text—you are becoming more skilled in the art of retention and critical thinking. If you're reading with a pen or note-taking tool right now, give yourself a pat on the back.

Why read with a pen? Well, first off, people forget. You might know someone who loses her keys daily. It is difficult for even the most disciplined and intelligent readers to remember all the important details of a text. However, through jotting down the main ideas of each paragraph, there is less pressure to recall the information. And, since you have already practiced writing the information down, you will be more likely to be successful in writing similar answers in an exam situation. In addition, jotting down ideas or questions, or even marking important or intriguing passages in a work, provides reminders that can be useful in class discussion or in writing a literary analysis.

In many cases, writing notes on a separate sheet of paper or typing on the computer may be awkward or impractical. Instead, try writing short notes in the margin, as Crystal Matey suggests in the "active reading" section of the chapter on long prose. As you are leafing through the book later, you will have quick access to the reactions and questions you might have had while reading the text. Circle interesting details. Highlight introductions of new characters or ideas. Underline words you don't know. Look them up. Make your own code for understanding the text. Each of these strategies provides useful information about the text as well as your own reading practices. Over time, you will become so skilled at note-taking that it will become second nature.

You may be wondering: *What should I take notes on?* Your notes may be completely different from a colleague's or a professor's. Ultimately, it is wise to write down the main ideas from each paragraph of an essay or chapter of a story to keep you focused. In longer works of fiction or drama, you may have a hard time remembering character names or key events, so make a list that helps you find your way around a play or novel. You can keep them on an index card or sheet of paper for easy access, or write them in the blank pages near the front and back covers of your book. Sometimes it helps to write down the main events chronologically in a timeline, or make a list of chapters and quick summaries or plot points that occur. This can help you reference parts of the text later on, and also it is helpful in creating a study guide for exams, or a reference for research papers.

Additionally, feel free to write what you think and feel about passages in a work of literature. For example, how does the book relate to you and your life? Does an event in a novel remind you of a personal experience, or perhaps a current event that might be familiar to your classmates and instructor? What words are strange and interesting? The sooner you practice writing while reading, the sooner you will learn what information is most helpful.

BUILDING A VOCABULARY

It has been said that if you don't know the meaning of every single word that you read in a text, then there is no possibility that you can understand the meaning of the text as a whole. Many of us have learned to "speed-read" by skipping over difficult words and inferring meaning through context clues, but the methods of speed-reading and skimming do not allow for the kind of thoughtful engagement with the text that is necessary for class discussion and analysis. Instead, we must take the time to read carefully and consider the diction, or word choice, of a text.

A dictionary, then, is a necessary tool for engaged reading. If you find a word you do not know while reading, circle or highlight it, write it down in your notes, and immediately look it up. Even if you can understand the word's basic idea in context of the other words in the sentence, it's still a good idea to look it up and write down the definition along with the sentence in which you found the word. That way, if you still don't fully understand the definition, you can reread it in a sentence and try to create one of your own using the new word to integrate it into your bank of knowledge.

After all, it is difficult to understand a text if we don't precisely understand all of its words; this would be like trying to read a book that has periodic interjections of words in a foreign language. Some people like to keep an index card or sticky note in the book they're reading to make note of new words and the page numbers from which they gathered them. In fact, there is a glossary of key terms at the end of this book dedicated to helping you strengthen your knowledge of the literary terms throughout each chapter, and an index in which you can cross-reference those terms! Building a collection of words is a lifelong process, and the more words you truly understand, the easier and more fulfilling reading becomes. Not only that, you will become a better writer as you improve and expand your ability to communicate. Vocabulary is not "natural talent"—it is a skill that you can practice and improve every time you read.

TWICE IS NICE

Even those of us who consider ourselves voracious readers, lovers of books, and "well-read" people, still sometimes need to slow down when reading and really take the time to comprehend the words, the characters, and the intricacies of the argument, narrative, or poetic structure of a text. Those of us who find reading difficult might find that once we take the time to engage in these reading/writing strategies, reading becomes more fun because we are better able to grasp the meaning of the material.

Once we get a handle on the "details" of a reading, such as definitions of difficult words, character names, or the overall argument, then it's time to reread. This is when we get to just sit back and enjoy the writer's style, or to take a closer look at portions of a text that confused or intrigued us the first time around. Sometimes it is difficult to do all of these things at once, which is why multiple readings of texts are important.

It is also crucial to remember that even skilled readers, like many of you, as well as professors and professional writers, struggle with certain reading material and find it necessary to go back over it more than once. It is easy to feel discouraged or unintelligent when we don't understand a reading on the first pass. Don't worry: that is normal. The pleasure of reading lies in rereading (and sometimes even three-reading): that is when we can really get absorbed in a piece without worrying about keeping characters or plot points in order. In short, careful reading is rereading.

As Frank Herbert writes in his classic fantasy novel, *Dune*, "Fear is the mind killer." If you are uncomfortable reading, you will fear and even dread the task. It is actually normal to be afraid of not understanding what a book is about. However, it is also normal to not understand initially. In fact, one has to begin by not knowing in order to ask the questions that lead to learning, growth, and progress. Each time you look up a new word or question a text, you will have more confidence because you are closer to understanding. There is no true secret to reading; the secret is your own willingness to be curious about life—and the way we as humans try to communicate its deepest mysteries through writing.

I. Literary Genres

Fausto Barrionuevo

Poetry

INTRODUCTION

Key Terms
- **poetry**
- **poem**
- **verse**
- **oral tradition**

Many students assume that **poetry** is meant for the elite, or the well-read, but it is not. Poetry seeks to illuminate a single experience, to inspire or give insight into the human condition. Often, students mistake a poem's complexity—how difficult it is to understand—for its quality, and become intimidated. However, poetry does not have to be difficult in order to be enjoyable and meaningful, and even difficult poetry can become a pleasurable experience when we understand how to read it.

Poetry is meant to perform an infinite variety of functions, like inspire, confess love or hatred, deal with guilt, show the immeasurable power behind language, or simply share in the commodity of humanity. The American poet Robert Frost once stated that poetry occurs "when an emotion has found its thought and the thought has found words." Frost's quote acts as an intuitive definition of what a **poem** is, and is more helpful in understanding the motivation behind poetry than its common definition as a written or spoken composition in **verse**, or the emphasis on arranging words into a rhythmic pattern. Unlike any other literary genre, poetry is the root of language, originating in songs sung in the **oral tradition** and later evolving with written language into full manuscripts, books that have traveled the globe. Whether through song or poetry, this ancient tradition of communication in verse is something that continues to pervade our society today.

READING POETRY

In this chapter, we'll begin exploring basic elements of poetry like the line, stanza, rhythm, and voice; this will help us to build a vocabulary to use in analyzing and discussing poetry. Readers should pay attention to a poem's patterns and consistencies, and by doing this we realize that a poem can convey a variety of meanings beyond what is literally presented in the words on the page. To truly understand a poem, we have to consider both its formal elements *and* its content.

Like any other discipline, reading poetry is a skill that requires practice and persistence; in order to perform a poetic analysis, whether in class or for an essay, reading a poem multiple times is a must. Having a set of steps or even a checklist to follow while you read might help at first with narrowing down some of the connections between what is happening in the poem and what is being said in the poem beyond its immediate subject.

HOW TO START: A SUGGESTED BEGINNER'S APPROACH TO READING A POEM

Key Terms
- **title**
- **epigraph**
- **stanza**

Poems are comprised of several main parts—in order from top to bottom on the page, these are the title, epigraph (for some), and lines, often arranged in stanzas (which we will learn about later in the chapter). A **title** is often also a mini-thesis or introduction to a poem, or could indicate an important image or phrase to which the author is explicitly directing the reader. While not all poems have **epigraphs**, or brief citations alluding to other literary works and/or their writers, when present they serve to help provide context for the poem. Finally, **stanzas** contain the lines in which the poet conveys meaning.

Armed with this knowledge of the title, epigraph, and stanzas, how might one use these elements to go about reading a poem? Here are some possible first steps towards reading poetry. Make sure you have a pen in hand as you practice the following actions:

1. Starting with the title and epigraph (if there is one), read the whole poem aloud.

2. Read the poem to yourself, taking note of the visual shape of the poem on the page.

3. Read the whole poem aloud again as with the first step, taking note of the sounds or rhyme, if any. Circle, underline, or write your notes in the margin.

4. Read aloud again. What questions do you have about the poem? Write them down.

The more you practice reading poetry, the better you will become at understanding it. Practice the steps above with the following poem, "Fire and Ice," by Robert Frost:

FIRE AND ICE
Robert Frost

Some say the world will end in fire,
Some say in ice.
From what I've tasted of desire
I hold with those who favor fire.
But if it had to perish twice,
I think I know enough of hate
To say that for destruction ice
Is also great
And would suffice. (1915)

Note: As the questions we've asked you to consider above suggest, the goal of reading poetry at first is simply observational: *How long is the poem? What information does the title provide? What images do you notice immediately? What sounds repeat as you read?* You do not need to understand everything in a poem right away. Some poems are more straightforward than others in their presentation of images or narrative. However, as you read and write down notes in an attempt to answer these questions, you can also begin to make more confident analyses about the content of the poem.

You may have noticed that in the steps for reading that we've outlined, there is an emphasis on *reading aloud*. Since verse originated from oral traditions such as singing and storytelling, reading aloud is an integral means of accessing poetry. Robert Pinsky, former Poet Laureate of the United States, explains in an interview with *Tin House*, "…the medium of poetry is the column of breath rising from the diaphragm to be shaped into meaning sounds inside the mouth. That is, poetry's medium is the individual chest and throat and mouth of whoever undertakes to say the poem—a body, and not necessarily the body of the artist or an expert as in dance" (Downing and Kunitz). While the medium of dance is the dancer's body, Pinsky is observing that the way to fully perform poetry is with your own voice. As a reader, then, choosing to read a poem aloud allows you to access the poem in a way that is inherent to this medium.

PERSPECTIVE: AUTHOR, SPEAKER, AND PERSONA

Key Terms
- **perspective**
- **speaker**
- **persona**

Every poem is told from a **perspective**, or point of view, and this is how we receive the poem—either through the voice of a speaker, or of a persona. In poetry, a **speaker** performs the actions in the poem in conjunction with the world view presented by the poet. On the other hand, a **persona** is a role or mask through which the perspective of the poet is presented. In a persona poem, the author usually will state either in the title or through the text that the poem is being told by a specific person, as in Robert Browning's "My Last Duchess," a poem in which a Duke speaks about his deceased wife. Since Browning himself was not a Duke, as readers we can assume that the poem is in the voice of a persona.

Why is this distinction important?

The distinction between speaker and persona determines our response to a poem and its poet in important ways. If an author of fiction writes a story from the perspective of a serial killer, we should not, and usually do not, assume that the author must have been a criminal, too. Yet often with poetry we automatically assign the voice of the poem to its writer; when we do this, the poetic voice can be misinterpreted as the poet's actual voice or even as evidence of his or her personal experiences, which alters our response to the poem by skewing its intended meaning. This is why we have the distinction between speaker and persona. Even in the most confessional or autobiographical poetry, poets may only use one aspect of themselves from which to write. The choice of a speaker or persona is an important aspect of the poet's craft, and the chosen speaker or persona is central to the poem's meaning. When as readers we choose to ascribe the poetic voice automatically to the poet, we flatten any possible deeper meaning offered by the true voice of the poem. Therefore, as readers, we have to practice not confusing the poet as the voice of the poem.

THE LINE AND LINE BREAKS

Key Terms
- **line**
- **surface reading**
- **caesura**
- **enjambment**
- **end-stopped/end-blocked**

Let's continue with a basic structural element—the **line**. Even though a poetic line might look and read like an ordinary sentence, it has a greater function to a poem than a sentence does to a novel or short story. There are two key concepts to understand about a line's structure: 1) a line is a row of words in the poem, and 2) the poet, not the right-hand margin, has determined the length of the line—or where the line "breaks."

Depending on the poem, lines may be equal in length or vary drastically, and since poetry is a compressed form, the length of the lines is important: the poet has specifically selected line breaks to convey meaning. Let's look at the first four lines from Robert Browning's "My Last Duchess" (1842) and think about the function of these lines, and where line breaks occur:

> That's my last Duchess painted on the wall,
> Looking as if she were alive. I call
> That piece a wonder, now: Frà Pandolf's hands
> Worked busily a day, and there she stands.

Important details for the poem's context exist in the first line. Words like "my" and "last" point out a personal relationship between the speaker and one of the paintings, and the phrase "on the wall" suggests a setting, more than likely the speaker's home. In the second line, we understand that the woman ("my last Duchess") the speaker was close to has died ("looking *as if* she were alive") and that she is the subject of the painting. This is a **surface reading** of the poem—meaning that we have described what is happening literally, the scene the poet has painted for us.

Next, by reading carefully and paying close attention to how the line is broken, other poetic elements guide us through the poem's subtle contexts. At this point, we should pay attention to elements like **caesura**, the punctuation that occurs in the middle of a line and emphasizes important elements in the text. In the above Browning passage, the colon in the third line highlights the importance of the name that follows, so that, as readers, we will remember its significance later in the poem.

When an idea or phrase in a poem carries over from one line to the next with no punctuation, it is known as an **enjambment**. This technique emphasizes that line's (non-) ending, placing greater significance on a particular word or phrase. In the Browning passage, there is an enjambment between lines two and three: "I call / That piece a wonder." We are naturally drawn by this deliberate break to wonder why the poet has isolated "I call" from the rest of the line.

Lastly, when a line of poetry ends with a form of punctuation, such as a comma or period, that line is considered an **end-stopped or end-blocked** line, which happens in the final line of the passage. This tells us that the line contains a complete idea, which may or may not depend upon the lines immediately before or after it for meaning.

THE STANZA AND STANZA BREAKS

Key Terms

- **stanza**
- **couplet**
- **triplet/tercet**
- **quatrain**
- **cinquain/quintain/quintet**
- **sestet**
- **septet**
- **octave**
- **juxtaposition**

The **stanza**—an Italian word for "room"—is a set of lines in a poem that are intentionally grouped together. In many ways, a stanza *is* like a room, in that it is a self-contained space where the poet may discuss a particular issue or explore a specific image. Stanzas can also be viewed as functioning similarly to paragraphs in prose literary works—the lines that are grouped together work together to construct meaning.

Stanzas are identified by the number of lines they contain. Depending on how many lines it contains, we may refer to a stanza as a **couplet** (two lines), **triplet or tercet** (three lines), **quatrain** (four lines), **cinquain, quintain, or quintet** (five lines), **sestet** (six lines), **septet** (seven lines), and **octave** (eight lines). Bear in mind that not all poems make use of stanzas; many narrative poems, like Robert Frost's "Fire and Ice" and Robert Browning's "My Last Duchess," take the form of one long, continuous stanza.

Note that the order of the stanzas in a poem is important, as this order may indicate the passage of time, a shift in ideas, or even the poem's introduction or conclusion. We can see the importance of paying close attention to the order of stanzas in the following poem. In Maya Angelou's poem, "I Know Why the Caged Bird Sings" (1969), the first two stanzas—both septets but excerpted here as quintets—show the contrast of a free bird and a caged one:

> The free bird leaps
> on the back of the wind
> [...] and dips his wings
> in the orange sun rays
> and dares to claim the sky.
>
> But a bird that stalks
> down his narrow cage
> can seldom see through
> his bars of rage
> [...] so he opens his throat to sing. (ll. 1–14)

What is so important about the order of the stanzas here? In the first septet, Angelou makes the conscious effort to establish an atmosphere and the vivid imagery of her free bird such as "leaps/on the back of the wind" and "dares to claim the sky." However, Angelou uses the stanza break in order to distinguish between being free and a caged bird, which "can seldom see through/his bars of rage."

Many poems that you will encounter use the stanza break to show that time has passed or—as Angelou does above—to show a **juxtaposition** between ideas, imagery, symbols, settings, and poetic voices. This comparing and contrasting of images by placing them next to each other in corresponding stanzas often serves to highlight meaning.

Reading tip: *When doing a close reading of a poem, stanza breaks are good spots to summarize the previous stanza before continuing. They often provide a break in ideas.*

I. LITERARY GENRES

SOUND IMAGERY: RHYME

Key Terms

- **sound**
- **rhyme**
- **sound imagery**
- **rhyme scheme**
- **end rhymes**
- **near rhymes/slant rhymes**
- **internal rhyme**

- **assonance**
- **consonance**
- **alliteration**
- **onomatopoeia**
- **sonnet**
- **atmosphere**
- **imagery**

In any line of poetry, the line is made up of words, and when these words are strung together, they create **sound**. In terms of **rhyme**, syllables in a line repeat in various patterns to cause a particular type of musicality, or **sound imagery**, in a poem.

In order to determine a poem's **rhyme scheme**, or, the pattern of **end rhymes** found in the poem, we use a lettering system. The first line's end rhyme is always given the letter "A," and if the following line rhymes with the previous, it gets the same letter; if not, we use a different letter to signify a change in the rhyme scheme. Elizabeth Barrett Browning's "Sonnet 43" (1850) follows the rhyme scheme ABBAABBACDCDCD:

How do I love thee? Let me count the *ways*.	A
I love thee to the depth and breadth and *height*	B
My soul can reach, when feeling out of *sight*	B
For the ends of Being and ideal *Grace*.	A
I love thee to the level of *everyday's*	A
Most quiet need, by sun and candle-*light*.	B
I love thee freely, as men strive for *Right;*	B
I love thee purely, as they turn from *Praise*.	A
I love thee with the passion put to *use*	C
In my old griefs, and with my childhood's *faith*.	D
I love thee with a love I seemed to *lose*	C
With my lost saints,—I love thee with the *breath*,	D
Smiles, tears, of all my life!—and, if God *choose*,	C
I shall but love thee better after *death*.	D

You might have noticed while reading this poem that some of the end rhymes feature perfect matches of the final vowel and consonant sounds at the end of the word—like "height" and "sight" in lines 2–3. However, "faith" in line 10 is slightly different from "breath" and "death" in lines 12 and 14. Poets often use close rhymes like this—often called **near rhymes** or **slant rhymes**—as substitutes for exact rhymes to either fit a specific form (like the sonnet above), or to cause aural dissonance within the poem itself. In the case of poems written in English in the pre-modern era, many such words actually did rhyme before language shifts occurred.

While we often think of poetry as having lines that rhyme at the end (as in "height" and "sight" in lines 2–3 of "Sonnet 43") poets also use rhyming within the lines themselves. These types of patterns are sometimes seen as **internal rhyme**, rhyme that occurs from line to line not at the end but usually in the middle, and sometimes within parts of the words themselves.

Assonance is the repetition of identical vowel sounds closely grouped together, like the long "e" sound found in "d*ee*p gr*ee*n s*ea*." At the other end of the spectrum is **consonance**, which is when the consonant sounds are similar or even identical, like the "d" sound in "sha*d*ow mea*d*ow." When consonance occurs at the beginning of the word, like the "g" sound in "goodness gracious," it is called **alliteration**. Sounds can also mimic the action they are describing, and words like "buzz" and "slurp" are examples of this sound device, known as **onomatopoeia**.

Practice: *In the following poem, "Ozymandias" by Percy Bysshe Shelley (1792–1822), what end rhymes or internal rhymes do you notice? Identify the rhyme scheme, and then circle or underline words in the line that have assonance, consonance, or alliteration.*

OZYMANDIAS
Percy Bysshe Shelley

I met a traveller from an antique land
Who said: "Two vast and trunkless legs of stone
Stand in the desert . . . Near them, on the sand,
Half sunk, a shattered visage lies, whose frown,
And wrinkled lip, and sneer of cold command,
Tell that its sculptor well those passions read
Which yet survive, stamped on these lifeless things,
The hand that mocked them, and the heart that fed:
And on the pedestal these words appear:
'My name is Ozymandias, king of kings:
Look on my works, ye Mighty, and despair!'
Nothing beside remains. Round the decay
Of that colossal wreck, boundless and bare
The lone and level sands stretch far away." (1818)

There are many types of sound imagery within Shelley's poem. End rhymes alternate in lines one, three, and five, "land," "sand" and "command," following a derivation of the **sonnet** form. Notice, though, that in line three Shelley uses internal rhyme with "stand" and "sand." Then, in line five, assonance of the short "i" sounds in "wrinkled lip" actually makes us, as readers, wrinkle our lips into a sneer as we try to read the line aloud. Similarly, the consonance of the hard "c" and "d" sounds in "cold command" create a harshness to the sound in the line, like the harshness of the "sneer." As you read, you may notice that poets often use sound to create an **atmosphere** that matches the **imagery** in the lines of a poem, as Shelley does in "Ozymandias."

POETIC RHYTHM: METER AND SCANSION

Key Terms

- **syntax**
- **meter**
- **syllabic meter**
- **accentual meter**
- **unstressed syllable**
- **stressed syllable**
- **foot**
- **iamb/iambic**
- **trochee/trochaic**
- **anapest/anapestic**

- **dactyl/dactylic**
- **spondee/spondaic**
- **pyrrhic**
- **accentual-syllabic meter**
- **iambic pentameter**
- **blank verse**
- **scansion**
- **pattern(s)**
- **metrical variance**

Within the lines of a poem, **syntax**, or grammatical structure and punctuation, creates variations in rhythm. In verse, **meter** is the rhythmical patterns that make up each line of a poem, and hinges on syntax. Three common types are syllabic, accentual, and accentual-syllabic meter.

Thinking in Syllables

Syllabic meter describes poems that have lines devoted to a certain number of syllables, like the modern haiku form. In the haiku, each line has a set number of syllables: five for the first line, seven for the second line, and five syllables for the third line (5-7-5):

> The brook moves slowly
> Ripples circle and reflect
> The moon's silent gaze.

To practice, you can clap to count each syllable in the first line: The (1) brook (2) moves (3) slow (4) -ly (5). Counting each syllable in a line can give insight into the kind of rhythm that the poet is using. If you see a pattern—perhaps all of the lines in the poem have ten syllables—then you might note that the poem is using syllables as a defining characteristic of its meter.

Stressed? Or Unstressed?

Accentual meter, on the other hand, is based on how the pronunciation of each word affects the cadence of the line. Every word comprises a syllable or syllables, and each syllable is either **unstressed** or **stressed**. Usefully, this pattern of stressed and unstressed syllables can be likened to the rise and fall of a heartbeat. The various combinations of stressed and unstressed syllables within words and phrases create the natural rhythm of our language. The accentuated line becomes alive with each syllable of every word, sometimes contributing to the ambiance, the dialect of a speaker, and more often than not, the pacing of a poem.

Let's practice with a word like "today." The word *today* has two syllables: (*to*) and (*day*). The unstressed syllable is (to) because we naturally place less emphasis on its pronunciation than its counterpart (day) which we emphasize more strongly. If you aren't sure about which syllable is stressed when you read or pronounce it, just check the dictionary, as it highlights the stressed syllable in the word. You can also use the clapping technique we used with the haiku above; when you say a word out loud, you will naturally want to clap on its stressed syllable(s).

Any given combination of stressed and unstressed syllables in a line of poetry is called a **foot**. Metrical feet are identified with specific names, based on the placement of stresses. Iambic and trochaic feet are the most common rhythms in English. More complicated feet are anapests and dactyls, which consist of three syllables each. The rarer meters are the spondee and the pyrrhic. Note the following examples of each type of meter, with the "|" separating each foot:

- **Iamb:** a metrical foot of two syllables that follows an unstressed-stressed pattern, as in the word to**day**.

  Iambic lines from Paul Laurence Dunbar's "We Wear the Mask" (1872–1906):

  We **wear**| the **mask** |that **grins** |and **lies,**|
  It **hides** |our **cheeks**| and **shades**| our **eyes,**--|

- **Trochee:** a metrical foot of two syllables that follows a stressed-unstressed pattern: **play**ing

Trochaic lines from "The Tyger" by William Blake (1757–1827):

Tyger |**Tyger,**| **burn**ing |**bright**,
In the| **for**ests| **of** the| **night**;

- **Anapest:** a metrical foot of three syllables that follows an unstressed-unstressed-stressed pattern: inter**rupt**

  Also known as the "waltz meter" because it follows the pattern of a waltz in music, anapestic meter is used in the Christmas poem, "A Visit from St. Nicholas," by Clement Clarke Moore (1779–1863):

  'Twas the **night**| before **Christ**|mas, when **all**| through the **house**|
  Not a **crea**|ture was **stir**|ring, not **e**|ven a **mouse**;|

- **Dactyl:** a metrical foot of three syllables following a stressed-unstressed, unstressed pattern: **di**nosaur

  Unlike anapestic meter, dactylic meter tends to sound like galloping hooves, and has a different sense of urgency since the stress is at the beginning of the line, as seen in Alfred, Lord Tennyson's "The Charge of the Light Brigade" (1809–1892):

  Flashed all their| **sa**bres bare,|
  Flashed as they |**turned** in air|

- **Spondee:** a metrical foot of two syllables, stressed-stressed: **homemade**

- **Pyrrhic:** a metrical foot of two syllables, unstressed-unstressed: in a

  A pyrrhic foot often supports a spondaic foot. For example, Andrew Marvel's poem "The Garden" uses a combination of the two:

  To a| **green thought**| in a |**green shade**.|

  In the first stanza of a didactic poem written for his son, "Metrical Feet—A Lesson for a Boy" (1807; published in 1835), poet Samuel Taylor Coleridge provides a mnemonic device for remembering these metrical feet, using them in action to illustrate their sounds:

  Trochee|**trips** from| **long** to |**short**.|
  From **long**| to **long**,| in **sol**|emn **sort**,
  Slow Spond|ee **stalks**.| **Strong foot!** |**Yet ill**| able|
  Ever to| **come** up with| **Dac**tyl tri|**syll**able.|
  Iam|bics **march** |from **short** |to **long**.|
  With a **leap** |and a **bound** |the swift **an**|apests **throng!**|

In this poem Coleridge makes use of each common metrical foot in its corresponding line (although the second line, "From **long**| to **long**,| in **sol**|emn **sort**," is not a trochaic one, it is actually iambic). Reading the poem aloud, you may notice that each type of meter creates a different sensation as you are speaking. Because much poetry is meant to be read aloud, poets pay great attention to their use of rhythm; readers should therefore be attentive to metrical rhythm in poetry as an inherently important quality. Understanding its rhythmic patterns can give insight into the form, themes, mood, and even the characters of a poem.

Syllables and Stresses

When a poem's lines follow both patterns in syllables and in stresses, then its rhythm is considered a hybrid of the two: **accentual-syllabic meter**. How we refer to the line depends on two things: the meter (i.e., iambic, trochaic, dactylic, etc.) and how many feet of it are in each line. Based on the number of feet per line, we can identify more precisely the meter of the poem:

> One foot per line: *monometer*
> Two feet per line: *dimeter*
> Three feet per line: *trimeter*
> Four feet per line: *tetrameter*
> Five feet per line: *pentameter*
> Six feet per line: *hexameter*
> Seven feet per line: *heptameter*
> Eight feet per line: *octameter*

You may have heard the phrase "iambic pentameter" before in English classes; this phrase refers to poems that comprise five-foot lines of iambic meter, a particularly English metrical pattern found in the poetry of William Shakespeare—"My **mis** | tress' **eyes** |are **no** | thing **like** | the **sun**," for example. To precisely indicate the meter of a poem, then, all you need to do is to combine the name of the metrical foot ("iambic") with the number of feet in the line ("pentameter")—**iambic pentameter**. Notably, the most common metrical pattern in English is **blank verse**—unrhymed lines of iambic pentameter.

With this information, let's look at the first two lines of Dunbar's "We Wear the Mask" again:

> We **wear**| the **mask** |that **grins** |and **lies**,|
> It **hides** |our **cheeks**| and **shades**| our **eyes**,--|

Both lines consist of four sets—or feet—of iambs; therefore, these lines are *iambic tetrameter*. In fact, this pattern of iambic tetrameter continues throughout

"We Wear the Mask." By understanding how accentual and syllabic verse work together, you can begin to identify a poem's meter through scansion.

Scansion

To find the meter of a poem, we usually note the unstressed and stressed syllables, using markings such as (⌣) to indicate unstressed and (´) to indicate stressed syllables. The act of marking these metrical distinctions is called **scansion**, because you are *scanning* a line for the number of syllables, observing where the accents (or stresses) are, and how they comprise metrical feet. Performing scansion helps us to locate **patterns**—rhythmic repetitions of meter—in lines of poetry. Patterns can serve as important identifiers of poetic form [see Appendix].

Practice: *Let's look at lines 31–32 from Alfred, Lord Tennyson's poem "Ulysses" (1842). First, count the number of syllables of each line. Then, place the unstressed and stressed symbols above the corresponding syllable:*

To follow knowledge like a sinking star

Beyond the utmost bound of human thought.

As you can count, there are ten syllables per line. Also, with five unstressed syllables and five stressed syllables to each line, the pattern equally divides into five iambic feet: so, this poem is written in iambic pentameter.

Finally, bear in mind that while many poems follow a specific meter perfectly, some poems do not adhere entirely (or at all) to a specific or traditional accentual-syllabic meter pattern. When this is true, we say that the poem incorporates **metrical variance**. Consider, for example, Sir Philip Sidney's "Sonnet 61" from *Astrophil and Stella* (1591):

Oft[1] with true sighs, oft with uncalled tears,   *1. often*
Now with slow words, now with dumb eloquence[2]   *2. elegant or persuasive speaking*
I Stella's eyes assail[3], invade her ears;   *3. attack*
But this at last is her sweet breath'd defense:
5   That who indeed infelt[4] affection bears,   *4. heartfelt*
So captives to his saint both soul and sense,
That wholly hers, all selfness he forbears[5],   *5. does without*
Thence[6] his desires he learns, his life's course thence.   *6. from that place*

Now since her chaste[7] mind hates this love in me,   *7. pure, morally*

10 With chasten'd mind, I straight[8] must show that she   *8. immediately*

Shall quickly me from what she hates remove.

Oh Doctor Cupid, thou for me reply,

Driv'n else to grant by angel's sophistry[9],   *9. false or illogical reasoning*

That I love not, without I leave[10] to love.   *10. having the approval*

In this poem, Astrophil is giving up his desires and sense of self to become what Stella wants, yet knows that his approach for gaining her affection is illogical. Critics see the speaker's unsettled emotional state reflected in the uneven scansion of the poem's lines. A majority of the sonnet, specifically lines 3–8 of the octave and 9–13 of the sestet, adheres to iambic pentameter, making that the dominant meter of the poem. This is not entirely surprising, since the sonnet form traditionally makes use of iambic pentameter. However, you may have noticed that lines 1–2 sound a little different in comparison. Looking closer, one might consider that the first two lines have a more spondaic quality, especially if emphasis is also attributed to "**now with**" as it echoes "**oft with**" of the preceding line. Another point in the poem where one could argue metrical variance is in the spondaic foot "**Oh Doc**|tor" at the beginning of the mostly iambic line 12. And, notably, the first half of the final line could be scanned as spondaic while the second half is iambic: "**That I** |**love not** |with**out** |I **leave**| to **love**|." Having observed these changes in the meter, you might ask: *What does metrical variance contribute to a poem?*

A change in meter might reflect a change of mood of the speaker, which is why it is helpful to look more closely at which lines deviate from the dominant meter and try to identify a reason for that shift. In a poetic analysis, we might think of the metrical variance in Sidney's "Sonnet 61" as a mirror of the speaker's unsettled emotional state. One could argue that in that final line, the most important spondaic emphasis is "**love not**" because it guides our ears to focus on the unrequited nature of Astrophil's relationship to Stella.

Scansion takes practice, so do not be discouraged if you have difficulty at first. There are many poems with which you can practice in the anthology section at the end of this book.

POETIC FORM AND HISTORICAL AND LITERARY CONTEXT

Key Terms

- **form poetry**
- **narrative**
- **lyric**
- **free verse**
- **collection of poetry/poetry collection**

It's important to remember that **form poetry** will always follow a pattern or some consistencies from line to line. Traditional poetic forms (such as the sonnet, villanelle, pantoum, sestina, ghazal, ballad, heroic couplet, blank verse, elegy, ode, pastoral, and dramatic monologue, all of which are defined and discussed in detail in the appendix at the end of this book—starting on page 329) help readers identify themes and content based on the history of their evolution. Looking at several poems in the same form from different time periods can shed light on the kinds of themes and ideas commonly associated with those forms—in other words, it can help us to understand how the forms function as vehicles for particular modes of thought and address. Form poems for the most part will be either **narrative**—telling a story—or **lyric**—a meditation on a particular subject, feelings, or mood of the speaker—and at times, may even be both. Comparing the kinds of stories narrative form poems tell, or the kinds of ideas and moods in lyric poetry, across several generations and in light of their historical context—what was going on in a certain place and time in which each poem was written—can help us understand how poetic forms function as cultural memory.

Form poetry is usually identifiable through its conventional presentation—a set number of lines, for instance, as in the case of a sonnet, or a specific rhyme scheme, as in a ballad [see Appendix]. However, not all form poetry follows its standard structure entirely, and when we come across a form poem that diverges from the standard, just as with metrical variance, we may want to think about why the poet chose to deviate from a conventional presentation of that poetic form. In such cases, it might be especially important to think about the poem's historical or cultural context.

For example, Harlem Renaissance poet Claude McKay often chose to write sonnets. Why? Perhaps McKay wrote in sonnet form because it carried a tradition and technical quality that elevated the seriousness of his work, and he wanted to show that African-American authors were just as capable of writing in form as their Caucasian counterparts. While this is only one possibility, and does not fully take into consideration other reasons for which McKay may have deviated from the poetic form, it suffices as an example of the importance of questioning why poets would purposefully choose to conform to or deviate from a poetic form.

Modern and contemporary poetry evolves from traditional forms. In the case of free-verse poems, this can be difficult to see, since they don't seem to follow any poetic rules. However, while free verse poems do not follow traditional forms, this does not mean there is no structure to a free verse poem; in fact, the opposite is true. A poem that is written in **free verse** creates its own structure through various elements such as internal rhyme, line breaks, and word choice. In other words, although formless by traditional standards, a free verse poem forms its own set of rules through the employment of traditional poetic elements. A free verse poem's internal dynamic structure determines how the poem is read, sounds, and the way in which the meaning of the poem is relayed to its reader. A poet might choose to write a free verse poem because the poem's meaning or central idea will not benefit from the structure of a traditional form poem.

When looking at a free verse poem, instead of searching for rhyme or refrains, what might help give context to the author's chosen style are other poems in the collection in which said work appears. A **collection of poetry** is a book that compiles multiple poems by the same author. While it is true of any poem that looking at it in the context of other poems with which it is published is helpful in establishing its context and meaning, this is especially true in the case of a free verse poem that otherwise seems inaccessible to us as readers. Placing a free verse poem in the context of the other poems surrounding it in the collection and studying their similarities and differences can help us narrow down the poem's theme and meanings, and may even point to some poets' intentions with their work.

As this chapter has shown, poetry is a genre rich in form and function. With origins as ancient as human communication itself, poetry both written and in the form of music lyrics remains the most popular literary means by which we share our experiences and make meaning of the world around us.

SAMPLE POETIC ANALYSIS

As an example of how to put all of this together, let's look at a sample **poetic explication**, or analysis, of "My Last Duchess" by Robert Browning. While in a poetic explication you might choose to discuss any number of poetic elements (meter, sound imagery, form, stanza, persona), you will have to narrow the list to include a few specific aspects. In this case, the focus is on form (the dramatic monologue) and diction. As a reminder, the poem seems to take place within a large home, where our persona gazes upon the work done by Frá Pandolf, who has painted the last duchess on the wall.

When Robert Browning's "My Last Duchess" begins, the Duke, speaking to an unidentified Other, wanders up and down the halls of his castle and mentions to this unnamed companion that his "last" Duchess is on the wall. From this, we can infer that she is gone, and it seems likely that she has died. While the Duke initially seems harmless, and we naturally expect that he would be grieving for his absent duchess, we slowly realize that the Duke has most likely played a hand in her untimely demise. Notably, Robert Browning uses the form of the dramatic monologue to show the disconnect between what the Duke is literally saying and what he is implying.

Furthermore, Browning uses a persona—"the Duke"—to explore issues of jealousy, power, and love. Thus, in "My Last Duchess," although Browning never has the Duke overtly declare that he killed his wife, by analyzing the poem's form—a dramatic monologue, often used in plays to reveal one's secret thoughts or actions—use of tone, and diction, we understand that he has inadvertently revealed himself as her killer.

Throughout the poem, the Duke is addressing an unnamed companion, and he shows this companion around his castle. Once he reaches the portrait of his "last" Duchess, he stops his companion so that he can better draw attention to her portrait. He notes that she blushes in the portrait, but then seems to complain that "'Twas not / Her husband's presence only, called that spot / Of joy into the Duchess' cheek" (13–15). His tone here appears quite bitter, as he follows this statement with the presumption that it was the presence of "Frá Pandolf" that created "that spot of joy" (20). The fact that he calls it a "spot of joy" is important, as we automatically assume that the Duchess was infatuated with the painter, her "joy" the result of his presence.

It's important to remember, however, that we only get the Duke's perspective on the Duchess' nature. Not only does he complain that she blushes in her portrait, he also criticizes her for being nice to everyone, rather than only him: "A heart—how shall I say?—too soon made glad /Too easily impressed" (21–22). This fact is vital to understanding the poem, as it suggests that the Duchess was not a flirt, as the Duke would like us to believe, but rather, a genuinely pleasant woman who saw the best in others. While the Duchess spoke "approving speech" to all, she did not go out of her way to show her husband, in his mind, enough affection (27). As the Duke continues his speech, he again criticizes her for not appreciating enough the "gift of a nine-hundred-years'-old name" (30). We understand here that the Duke is both highly jealous and very arrogant, as he wanted the Duchess to show him affection commensurate with the worth of his title. Interestingly, this is the only thing that we know he has given her. He never reveals being kind to her; instead, he expects her to appreciate his wealth and title.

As the Duke continues his monologue, we eventually realize that the duchess has not merely died; she has been killed. He cryptically notes that once he realized that she smiled equally brightly towards everyone, he "gave commands; / Then all smiles stopped together" (42–43). Although he does not literally say that he had her killed, we understand that he's implying this through his word choices, or diction. Our understanding of who the Duke is shifts from originally thinking of him as arrogant and jealous, to perceiving him as a murderer. The use of a dramatic monologue makes this even more climactic because the Duke does not realize that we view him thusly as he unwittingly reveals himself to be a horrendous person. Furthermore, we realize at the end of the poem that his unnamed companion is arranging a new marriage for him in the lines: "The Count your master's known munificence / Is ample warrant that no just pretense / Of mine for dowry be disallowed" (46–48). The word "dowry" forces us to realize that he's talking to the very man who must arrange his next marriage. Thus, the Duke has revealed that he is a jealous, violent husband to the man he hopes will secure him a new wife.

By looking closely at poetic elements like the poem's persona form, tone, and diction, we can better understand the meaning of "My Last Duchess" not as an elegy for the dead wife, but as a dramatic monologue revealing the Duke's unconscious self-satisfaction at arranging her removal and replacement with a more suitable companion. The irony of the Duke exposing his true nature to the man arranging his future marriage is key to understanding that the Duke is incapable of assessing his own character.

At the end of the poem, we have little hope that the Duke will change his behavior with his next wife, as he cares so little for the first. While the Duke may want us to think of him as regal and worthy, by really analyzing his own words, we understand that he is arrogant and vile.

CONCLUSION

Remember that to comprehend and discuss any piece of literature is to be able to name and understand its parts—to explore every aspect of the text. Thus, by being knowledgeable about all the elements that help make a poem, we can further comprehend it. Yes, art is meant to entertain, enlighten, and evoke emotion. However, that does not mean that we should be afraid to question aspects of the poem, as this is the starting point for interpreting and analyzing the text.

Questions to Consider

1. Select one poem you've read for class. Does the poet use a speaker or a persona throughout the poem? How does the use of a speaker or persona shape your reading of the poem? Why do you think the poet chose this particular speaker/persona?

2. Many people believe that in order for a poem to *be* a poem, "it has to rhyme." In what way can this definition by rhyme be viewed as limited, and how do modern poetic forms such as free verse change this expectation? (Why, in other words, is a free verse poem still a poem?)

3. Examine the rhyme scheme of a poem and explain how the poet's use of sound imagery contributes to your understanding of the poem's tone in presenting its subject. In a broader sense, what conclusions can you make about the poet's use of end rhymes and/or internal rhyming as a tool to illuminate meaning in the poem?

4. What reasons might a poet have for deviating from a traditional poetic form? Can you think of any poems you've read where an author has done this? In those instances, what did altering the poem's form do for the poem as a whole?

Essay Prompts

1. Choosing a poem (or using a poem assigned to you by your instructor), perform a preliminary poetic explication, taking into consideration elements such as rhyme, rhythm, meter, figurative language, persona, diction, and symbol. Use these notes to write an essay in which you explain how the poet uses these elements to construct meaning.

2. Choose a poetic element (rhyme, meter, imagery, figurative language, *etc.*) and locate examples of its use in 2–3 poems. Write an essay explaining what the element is and how the poets use it in each of these poems.

Work Cited

Downing, Ben and Daniel Kunitz. "Robert Pinsky, The Art of Poetry No. 76." *Tin House*. 144 (Fall 1997). Web. 4 April 2014.

Drama

Matthew Carter

INTRODUCTION

Key Term
■ **play**

Imagine a marble statue of a famous warrior, colorfully painted and raised on a pedestal at the center of an ancient building. Over the centuries, the paint disintegrates, leaving only the white marble underneath. Eventually, the building around it begins to collapse, and after one of the statue's arms breaks off, the local citizenry decides to take the statue down and place it in a museum in order to protect it from further damage. Now you come to visit this museum and look at the statue. While the basic essence of the statue is there, you can't really understand what it once looked like. The paint is gone. The building and pedestal are gone. One of its arms is missing. You have an idea about what the statue looked like, but there is a lot now left to the imagination. You might have to do extra research, or at least draw on your outside knowledge, to reconstruct all the missing trappings. When we read a **play**, what we have—the text—is somewhat like the statue I just described. We know the words, more or less as they were spoken, but we don't see the actors, costumes, stage, or audience. We don't smell the smells, and there is no chance that we might miss the words because of other noises. The lights can't highlight or obscure the action. To try to access the original, you need to do a little textual archaeology.

This chapter treats reading a play like a work of archaeology. Your job is to try to reconstruct the missing elements that the text cannot replicate. Some of this will require extra work—simply reading the words isn't enough. While most literary forms develop certain images for you—for instance, the narrator of a novel might describe a river next to which the characters are talking—plays do not usually include such descriptions because the audience can see the set, or the characters might give the details through dialogue. This chapter will give you the tools you need to successfully excavate the missing pieces of a play. You will learn how to read a play text, the major dramatic genres, the major types of performance spaces, the nature of audience contact, and a little about technical theatre.

READING A PLAY TEXT

Key Terms
- **speech prefixes**
- **stage directions**
- **implied stage directions**

While the textual representation of a play may seem confusing at first, reading a play is no harder than reading a poem or novel. Like those genres of literature, plays have their own rules, and being unfamiliar with those rules can make them difficult to tackle. This section will prepare you for some of the mechanical challenges of reading a play.

The sample text. Throughout this chapter, most of the examples will come from William Shakespeare's *Othello* (1603), which I have chosen because of its familiarity and its complex staging (which will allow a variety of examples to come from the same text). In case you haven't read *Othello*, the play is about Othello, the moor of Venice ("moor" is an early modern term for a person of African or Middle Eastern descent), who receives a military promotion over the jealous Iago. The play shows Iago's schemes to ruin Othello by convincing him that his wife, Desdemona, is cheating on him with a fellow soldier (Michael Cassio). In the end, Othello murders his wife in a jealous rage, only to find out that Iago set him up. After killing Iago, he kills himself in shame.

The first thing you'll notice in comparison with other kinds of literature is the presence of speech prefixes in play texts. **Speech prefixes** are the way play texts identify the speaker, usually with the character's name, an abbreviated version of the name, or sometimes the character's function in the play (like "king" or "soldier"). In printed play texts, speech prefixes usually occur before the character's lines, but sometimes they are centered on the line above. Speech prefixes are important because they indicate which character speaks the lines.

Another concept with which you should be familiar in order to engage with the printed play text is the stage direction. **Stage directions** are unspoken sentences in a play text that tell the actor what to do in performance; for the reader, they describe something which physically occurs onstage. Many students read a play without paying attention to the stage directions, which can cause them not to understand the action of the play. Since the stage directions describe physical actions the characters perform, they are often not referenced in the spoken dialogue. You can see how this might make a reader confused. Let's take a look at a stage direction from *Othello* as an example:

> OTHELLO. It is too late.
> DESDEMONA. O Lord, Lord, Lord! (V.ii.92–93)

These lines could mean anything as printed above. What happens? Does a comet fall from the sky and kill the couple? Is Othello telling Desdemona that she has a terminal health condition? Without the stage direction, there is no way to know… and yet, many students would read right over the stage direction, pushing forward, and deciding that Shakespeare is confusing. Now, read the lines again, this time with the omitted stage direction:

> OTHELLO. It is too late.
> *He smothers her*
> DESDEMONA. O Lord, Lord, Lord! (V.ii.92–93)

With the stage direction in place, it is clear that Desdemona's plaintive cry of "O Lord, Lord, Lord" is a reaction to Othello, who is choking her to death. This is a simple example of why the stage directions are so important. As you can see, skipping those three words can change the scene from a murder to any number of confusing possible circumstances.

When they are imbedded in the dialogue, as they often are, stage directions can be easy to miss. For example, before Othello kills Desdemona, he starts kissing her:

> O balmy breath, that dost almost persuade
> Justice to break her sword! One more, one more.
> Be thus when thou art dead, and I will kill thee
> And love thee after. One more, and that's the last.
> *He kisses her* (V.ii.16–19)

While we have a printed stage direction at the end of the scene, we can infer from the lines that Othello actually kisses Desdemona at least three times during the speech. The comment "that's the last" in line 19 implies that Othello has already kissed her before. The repetition of "one more" suggests that he kisses Desdemona once, and then does so again. So, in total, he kisses her twice in line 17, then again when the script calls for it after line 19. When stage directions are implied from the spoken text in this way, we call them **implied stage directions** (Smith 173). This is a good example of why picturing the play in performance is so important to understanding as we read it. If we only notice the printed stage direction, Othello seems much less troubled about killing his wife. Seeing him try again and again to get *just one more kiss* from her before he kills her, we pick up on the conflict he experiences in becoming a murderer. As a result, we see Othello as a more complex character with this extra information at our disposal.

READING THE TEXT AS A WHOLE

Key Terms
- **dramatic action**
- **beats**
- **trigger**
- **heap**
- **motivation(s)**

One method of analyzing a text is to look for the dramatic action. **Dramatic action** is the series of cause-and-effect relationships that drive a play forward (Ball 9). If you think of novels, you talk about the story of a novel as the "plot." In plays, "plot" isn't often a good word to describe dramatic action, because it implies a continuity that doesn't usually exist in theatrical performance. After all, why do we call play theatre practitioners "actors"? They perform "actions." Instead of one continuous storyline, it can be helpful to think of a play as a linked series of actions, one action after another, each causing new things to happen because of what happened before, like a string of dominoes knocking each other over.

Dramatic action is subdivided into smaller units, often referred to as beats (Ball 10). **Beats** are specific actions that take place in the play. So, one beat consists of exactly one cause and one effect. Beats are further subdivided into triggers and heaps. The **trigger** is the thing that causes something to happen (imagine I pull the trigger of a gun), while the **heap** is what happens as a result (someone falls over in a heap, presumably dead) (Ball 11).

Most dramatic actions take place over the space of a few lines, sometimes even within the space of a few words. For instance, at the end of the play, we have a beat: "Othello stabs himself." He learns that he killed his wife for no reason (trigger), so he stabs himself (heap). We can see the connections between the beats as the play's dramatic action. The next beat is "Othello dies." Following the two beats in reverse, we get a sense of the cause-and-effect relationships between them. Why does Othello die? He dies because he stabbed himself. Why does he stab himself? He stabs himself because he learns that he killed Desdemona under false pretenses.

The difference between plot and dramatic action, then, boils down to the motivations of different characters. Have you ever heard an actor ask "what's my motivation?" This joke actually alludes to an important point in terms of interpreting a play. Once you know *what* happens in a play, you'll want to know *why* it happens—this is the motivation for the action. Knowing the dramatic action can help you figure out the *why*. If you read the dramatic action of a play backwards, as we did above, you can find the motivation for the characters' behaviors.

More clearly defined, **motivation** represents an attempt to explain why a character performs any specific action in a play, and is important for the purposes of character analysis. As fictional people, characters in a play do not have an interior life. As much as we might love the characters in a text, they exist only in our imaginations, or in the imaginations of the playwright or of the actors who perform them. That said, considering motivation allows us to learn about ourselves from reading the play, because our interpretation of a character's motivation is actually our *personal* interpretation of events. So, Shakespeare's Othello kills himself only because Shakespeare wrote the suicide into the play. Your personal Othello, however, is motivated by your thoughts. So, when you ask yourself the question, *Why does Othello kill himself?*, you're actually trying to figure out what might motivate you to do the same thing Othello does in the play. Maybe you wouldn't do it at all, but attempting to describe motivation allows you to process and internalize the dramatic action, which allows you to make sense of the play. Once you have some ideas about what may have motivated a character to act as s/he does, you can then go into the text to see if there is any evidence to support those possibilities. In this way, you can use your personal response, together with textual evidence, to construct meaning in ways that you wouldn't be able to do otherwise.

Performance art serves a social function. Ultimately, the idea behind all of this is that you, as the audience member/reader, can learn about yourself by trying to understand the character a little better. You can then use your own interpretation of the story as a starting point for reading the play for evidence to support your interpretation. Therefore, we see something acted onstage, or read it in a play text, and we interpret it with our own values and ideas, then corroborate that with proof from the play, itself. Our anxieties about our personal lives are hard to stomach in private. When we project them onto a play's characters, we find a safe place to examine our foibles, while keeping ourselves safe from scrutiny.

DRAMATIC GENRES

Key Terms

- **tragedy**
- **complex tragedy**
- **tragedy of suffering**
- **tragedy of character**
- **simple tragedy**
- **tragic flaw**

- **comedy**
- **burlesque**
- **farce**
- **tragicomedy**
- **history**

Just as with other forms of literature, there are different genres of plays, each of which can be defined according to certain specific features. It is important to note that plays are a product of their time. As a result, plays might not fit into standardized generic expectations, if the playwright needed to construct meaning differently for a specific audience. Very infrequently does a play easily fit into a single generic classification. That said, the most common play genres are tragedy, comedy, tragicomedy, and history.

Aristotle explains that **tragedy** is a dramatic genre which aims to "be an imitation of events that evoke fear and pity, since that is the distinctive feature of this kind of imitation" (20). We might think of the tragic genre as including any play that hopes to teach us something by representing loss, death, disruption, or destruction. Tragedy often focuses on the death or failure of royalty, as they have further to fall. Examples of famous tragedies include Sophocles' *Oedipus Rex*, Christopher Marlowe's *Doctor Faustus*, William Shakespeare's *Othello*, Joseph Addison's *Cato*, and Arthur Miller's *Death of a Salesman*. Tragedy comes in four subcategories. The first type is **complex tragedy**, which depends on "reversal and recognition," caused by the main character's failings (Aristotle 29). *Othello* is a good example of this type, as Othello learns too late that he was wrong about his wife, and this recognition has disastrous consequences. The next type of tragedy is the **tragedy of suffering**, which focuses on society's emotional or physical suffering. William W. Pratt's *Ten Nights in a Barroom* (1858), which shows a town falling apart because of a newly founded pub, is a good example. The third type is **tragedy of character**, which focuses on the pain of a specific person. Arthur Miller's *Death of a Salesman* (1949) might be considered a tragedy of character, because the play centers on the dissembling main character, Willie Loman, and his ultimate suicide. Last, but not least, is **simple tragedy**, in which events simply happen to a character for no discernible reason (Aristotle 29). You may also have heard of the **tragic flaw**, which refers to the character trait that leads to the hero's downfall in tragedy. Usually, the tragic flaw is a specific kind of personality flaw, like "greed" or "pride."

Comedy, according to Aristotle, is "…an imitation of inferior people"—which refers both to socially low-ranked people and morally corrupt people—behaving badly (lxii). In comedies, we laugh at the expense of others, often because they are unintelligent or silly. Unlike tragedy, comedy tends to focus on the common man, rather than the fall of kings. Typically, comedies end in events like marriage. In this sense, comedy is more depressing than tragedy. What I mean here is that, in tragedy, society learns something about itself at the expense of social upheaval, while comedy tends to return things to their original state—but few lessons, if any, are learned by the characters. Some famous comedies include Ben Jonson's *Every Man in His Humor* (1598), William Wycherly's *The Country Wife* (1675), and Richard Brinsley Sherridan's *The School for Scandal* (1777). A common subgenre of comedy is **burlesque**, or **farce**. While all the usual characteristics of comedy hold true for farce, this subgenre tends to include deliberately over-the-top buffoonery. An example of this subgenre is Moliere's *Tartuffe* (1664).

Somewhere between comedy and tragedy lies tragicomedy. **Tragicomedy** is a decidedly more modern genre than its two predecessors, because it denies a cosmic order to world events. As a result, the audience is expected to find humor in the suffering and pain of others. Tragicomedy has the aims of tragedy, in the sense that it shows suffering and heartache, but the results of comedy, in the sense that we revel and laugh over the characters' suffering (Greenwald, et al. 60). Important tragicomedies include Samuel Beckett's *Waiting for Godot* (1953), Eugene Ionesco's *The Bald Soprano* (1950), Jean-Paul Sartre's *No Exit* (1944), and Tom Stoppard's *Rozencrantz and Guildenstern are Dead* (1966).

History plays are fictional representations of historical events. They fall into their own category because the writer is often restrained, in terms of room for invention, by what *actually happened* to the characters. The aim of such plays tends to be educational or patriotic in nature. For instance, why do we need to see the actions of our famous forbears? Should we try to be more like them, or should we learn from their mistakes? Famous history plays include Christopher Marlowe's *Edward II* (1593), William Shakespeare's *Henry V* (1599?), Friedrich Schiller's *Mary Stuart* (1800), Bertolt Brecht's *Life of Galileo* (1943), and James Goldman's *The Lion in Winter* (1966). History plays tend to closely follow historical events. The farther the dramatic action strays from accepted history, the closer the plays come to falling into other categories. For instance, comedies can end however the writer deems best, but a history play about George Washington that ends in a space alien invasion might prove problematic for its audience. Consider, for the sake of example, Shakespeare's *Julius Caesar*. While the play dramatizes an actual Roman leader, the events are too similar to tragic conventions, and most scholars characterize it as a tragedy as a result.

TRADITIONAL LITERARY CONCEPTS IN PLAY TEXTS

Key Terms

- **linear plot**
- **inciting incident/point of attack**
- **complication**
- **climax**
- **denouement**
- **the three unities/classical unities**
- **dramatic irony**
- **verbal irony**

Linear Plot: Some plays follow a very linear, or traditional, plot structure. In such plays, it is easier to discuss plot in the traditional sense, alongside dramatic action. When discussing "plot" in association with a play text, what other genres call the **inciting incident** is called the **point of attack**. The "point of attack" refers to the "moment at which the play's principle conflict begins" (Greenwald, et al. 38). The **complication** refers to the "struggle between opposing forces through a series of crises, which move the action forward" (Greenwald, et al. 39). The **climax** is the late-play moment when the conflict we see in the complication is finally resolved (whether the resolution is happy or sad depends on the play). The climax leads to the **denouement**, or resolution, which finalizes any unresolved issues in the play (Greenwald, et al. 38). *Othello* is a linear play. The point of attack happens when Othello gets his promotion. The complication happens when Iago begins plotting with Roderigo to set him up. The climax happens when Othello finally decides to kill Desdemona. The denouement occurs when Iago, Othello, and Emilia die as a result of Othello's actions.

For more information on the subject of plot, refer to April Williams's chapter in this book.

The Three Unities: Another concept at work in some plays is that of the classical unities. This refers to the idea that a complete work of theatrical performance is consistent in *time* (there is a 1:1 ratio between how long the play takes and how long the represented action goes on), *action* (we only follow one story; there are no subplots), and *place* (there are no changes of setting). These unities are inspired by Aristotle's *Poetics*, in which he explains that, without these unities, drama will be unintelligible (13). Few of the plays you're likely to read in introductory literature classes actually follow this structure, however. Early Elizabethan dramas, some Victorian dramas, and early French drama (like that of Moliere) attempt to emulate it. Most plays, however, break at least one of the unities. Medieval drama, for instance, rarely maintains a unity of time; later Elizabethan plays almost always have one or more subplots, breaking the unity of action; and Restoration comedy almost always makes a point of moving from the hero's bedroom to the outside world within the first few minutes of the play, undermining the unity of place.

Irony: Dramatic irony, the most common type of irony in theatre, exists when the audience knows something the characters do not. Consider, for instance, Othello's decision to murder his wife for her infidelity. The **dramatic irony** of the situation is that the audience/reader knows that Iago actually fooled Othello into doubting Desdemona, who is innocent. **Verbal irony** is often closely connected to dramatic irony in plays, because the audience usually knows what makes the comment ironic, while the recipient may or may not recognize the same. An example of verbal irony in *Othello* occurs when Iago tells Othello that, "For Michael Cassio, / I dare be sworn I think that he is honest" (III.iii.129–130) in order to cause Othello to doubt that Cassio is trustworthy. This is ironic because Iago really knows that Cassio is honest, but he uses his own insistence to make Othello believe the opposite.

For more information on the different forms of irony, consult Michael Bedsole's essay, "On Irony" in this book.

THEATRE SPACES

Key Terms

- **thrust stage**
- **arena/theatre-in-the-round**
- **proscenium**
- **fourth wall**
- **trapdoor**
- **discovery space**

One of the most important elements in understanding how a play works in performance is to understand the staging conditions. Since every play is performed, every play has a performance space. For the purposes of this chapter, I'll focus on traditional performance spaces—that is, formal playhouses—but it's useful to remember that, any time someone does something while another person watches, a rudimentary form of theatre is taking place.

A **thrust stage** allows the audience to sit on three sides of the playing space. In this sense, the actors have "thrust" their way into the audience. This type of playing space was most notably used in the Elizabethan and Jacobean periods, and is again becoming popular. Shakespeare's Blackfriars and Globe theatres had thrust stages. Because the actors are surrounded on three sides, thrust theatres allow more direct contact with the audience. Often, audience members will sit on the stage in this configuration, and it is very common to see actors speak directly to—and sometimes, physically interact with—the audience. Thrust stages still have a backstage area, however, which allows actors to leave the audience's sight if need be (Carter 258).

An **arena** space allows the audience to sit on all sides of the actors, which means there is very little room on such stages for sets, as anything—even furniture—blocks the audience's view. The first arena stages were built in Ancient Rome: the Coliseum was a giant arena performance space. Some theatre practitioners also call arena spaces **"theatre-in-the-round"** (Carter 259). Today, the most common use of arena seating is in the world of sports. That's right! A football stadium is also a form of arena theatre!

The most well-known theatre structure today is the proscenium. A **proscenium** theatre features a contained staging area with the audience located entirely on one side of the stage. Generally, the walls of a proscenium space form a giant picture frame, within which the action of the play takes place. The audience is separated from the actors by an invisible line in proscenium spaces, which leads to the idea of a "fourth wall." The "**fourth wall**" is a fictional notion that the audience is seeing the play take place through an invisible wall, and is therefore separate—even alienated—from the action of the play (Clurman 61). Any floor space beyond the doors in the set walls and behind the "picture frame" of the proscenium's arch is the "backstage" area. In this area, set placement and costume changes can take place beyond the audience's vision. Any actor who is "backstage" is considered separate from the dramatic action happening onstage, but some plays, like those of Bertolt Brecht, call for actors to always be visible, even when they are offstage.

In addition to the overall structure of the stage, theatres often employ various structural elements to help enliven the performances. **Trapdoors** allow actors to enter the space from either above or below the stage, which often can convey important information about characters. For instance, in Elizabethan theatres, the trapdoor in the floor was known as the "Hell" door, while the one in the ceiling was known as "Heaven." A character entering from above would usually be a protagonist, while one entering from below would usually be an antagonist. Another versatile theatre space, most commonly found in thrust configurations, is the **discovery space**. This space serves the same function as a proscenium arch by separating the audience from the actors or props inside (Cohen 84).

Now, you may be wondering, *Why do I have to learn about theatre structures to read a play? Can't I just imagine it the same way I picture the action of a novel?*

Absolutely not! Novels are a completely different literary form—plays, as I have mentioned already, are the remains of a performance. If you read a play with performance in mind, you will be able to understand it the way it was written. Reading a play like a book is like watching a movie with your eyes closed! The reason we've spent so much time on theatre spaces is that we have to understand the most important part of theatre, performance, in order to read a play as the textual remnants of a production. The theatre spaces dictate the location of the audience, and being able to picture yourself in the audience allows you more easily to interpret the information plays do not relate textually. The theatre space also affects the aims and effects of specific forms of dramatic action, setting, and staging.

AUDIENCE CONTACT

Key Terms
- **monologue**
- **soliloquy**

Each theatre space allows for unique performance options. When you read a play, knowing when it was originally written and for what kind of space can allow you to imagine the circumstances under which it was performed. To demonstrate my point, let's look at how a performance of Act 5, Scene 2 of Shakespeare's *Othello* might be different if there were a change of venue. It only takes three lines to see how much this information can matter to our interpretation of the play. In Act V, scene ii, lines 1–3, Othello enters, preparing to murder his wife, and carrying a light. He finds her sleeping in bed and says, "It is the cause, it is the cause, my soul / Let me not name it to you, you chaste stars. / It is the cause" (V.ii.1–3). The "cause" he refers to is his plan to murder his wife.

Let's start by imagining the scene in a thrust staging, which was Shakespeare's only available option. The discovery space would probably hide Desdemona's bed, as moving the bed onstage would prove time-consuming and difficult. Since no one can turn off the sunlight (electric lights did not exist yet), everything on stage would be clearly visible, and the audience, sitting on the stage, would be part of the stage picture. Othello would enter carrying a candle to show that it is currently dark out. It would be up to the audience to imagine the darkness, rather than having technicians to replicate it for them. Because the audience has to imagine the darkness, they are helping make the play and are, therefore, slightly more responsible for Othello's behavior. As he talks to the audience, Othello pulls the curtain on the discovery space, which reveals Desdemona. It is at this moment that we see what Othello has come to do. When he calls out to the "chaste stars" (2), he most likely incorporates the audience in his conversation. Rather than imagining stars in the night, the audience members *are the stars*. When Othello tries to explain to them that "it is the cause" (3), he is apologizing to the audience, not waging a psychological war with himself. Because Othello is talking to the audience in this case, the speech becomes a **monologue**—that is, a conversation by one person delivered to an audience of listeners. A monologue differs from a soliloquy (discussed below) because in a monologue the speaker demonstrates awareness of his/her audience—whether this is the actual audience in the theater, or an imagined audience within the action of the play.

In a staging of this same scene in a proscenium space, a curtain might conceal the actors' setup prior to the scene. There would likely be a detailed set, since the backstage crew has the time required to set up a bedroom while the curtain shields them from the audience's view. When the curtain opens, we find Desdemona already asleep; Othello would enter from the backstage area, carrying his light with him. Since prosceniums came along after the invention of artificial lights, we might see a dark stage with a spotlight on Othello and Desdemona. When Othello petitions the "chaste stars" (2), he would likely be referring to stars in the sky, probably looking up into the darkness above him. Because proscenium stages illuminate the playing space, but not the audience, the audience is hidden, while the performers are visible. As a result, the scene would be isolating, and the audience could easily cast judgment on Othello's behavior. Because Othello is talking to himself, rather than to other actors or audience members, the speech is a soliloquy. A **soliloquy** is a speech that is not intended to be heard by others. Because plays, unlike novels, cannot show the thoughts of a character directly, soliloquies exist as a way of communicating the character's internal struggle. While the actor is actually speaking, we are generally expected to understand this speech as the character's thoughts, not an attempt to communicate with us.

If we set the play in an arena space, there would likely be no bed, as bedposts would obscure the audience's view, and it is very difficult to move large pieces of furniture into an arena space. The actress playing the sleeping Desdemona would most likely stretch out on the floor, and the audience might either imagine a bed, or simply decide that she sleeps on the floor. Because Desdemona is present from the outset, we know when we see Othello that he is coming for her, much like in the proscenium example. (Remember, in the thrust example, he has to enter and open up the curtain to the discovery space, so we actually see Othello *first.*) When Othello enters, with audience on all sides, he might come through a trapdoor in the floor, or else pass through the aisles, between the audience's seats. The trapdoor option sets Othello up as an ominous figure; he rises from the ground like a monster. The other option equalizes him with the audience, because he comes *from* the audience. Either way, the audience's attachment with Othello becomes stronger because the staging requires more imagination on the audience's part, and both options provide different, but equally strong, resonance for the watchers. In this case, we could again easily imagine the stars as audience members, since there is no backdrop—and the audience is once more clearly visible because of the proximity to the stage.

So, to summarize, the thrust configuration allows the audience to participate in the action to a mild degree, but still offers the actors a chance to leave the stage discreetly. The upside is the existence of optional audience interaction, while the downside is the potential for audience members to become disruptive or uncomfortable due to their proximity to the action. The proscenium separates the audience and the actors, which focuses on the performers, while downplaying the interaction with the audience. The upside is that the audience is more comfortable; the downside is that they are isolated from the action. The arena configuration offers no place for subtle entrances and exits, but produces the most possible immediacy between the actors and audience members. As these examples suggest, each of the staging options for a play presents us with different interpretive possibilities, and knowing what kind of performance space a playwright used enlightens us about their intent. Understanding the playwright's relationship with the audience informs our understanding of the purpose and function of the play.

CONSIDERING TECHNICAL THEATRE

Key Terms
- **properties/props**
- **set**

Another important aspect of theatre performance is all the technical work that goes into a production. Since play texts often exclude detailed descriptions of physical objects, the reader will need to do that imaginative work in order to get a more detailed picture of the play's action. This section will focus on two of those options—**properties** and **set**. I leave costumes out, as every production differs so variously in this regard that costume choices are too difficult to discuss in a single chapter. Furthermore, costumes, unless specifically described in the play text, are less frequently important to our ability to read the text.

Properties, or **props**, are any objects that appear onstage during a performance. They are often specifically prescribed in the play text and are therefore worthy of our consideration. How the characters interact with the physical world is a big part of our interpretation of a play. Props are defined by how they appear onstage. A costume prop (like Othello's sword) is worn on the actor's person. A hand prop (like his candle) is carried onstage in the actor's hand. A set prop (like Desdemona's bed) is used to decorate the set, but is not permanently attached to the stage. The use and distribution of props can affect our understanding of characters, and is therefore important to consider when imagining performance (Langley 131).

Set refers to the scenery that isn't part of the actual structure of the playhouse. For instance, the trapdoor I mentioned earlier is part of the stage, because it is actually part of the playhouse's structure, while the walls of the room are part of the set (in the proscenium example), because they are newly erected, and not part of the larger building. Arena stages don't allow for much set construction, because walls or columns can block the audience's view. Sets in these stages tend to be raised platforms, or even unembellished floors in many instances. By comparison, proscenium theatres allow for curtains to hide the actors, so sets can be much more elaborate—and even changed between acts or scenes behind the curtain—without spoiling the audience's view of the action. Thrust theatres tend only to use set props, as anything placed on the stage usually has to stay out for the duration of the show, unless it can be carried offstage through the discovery space. The set is a very important part of our understanding of plays, as it is linked to the types of performance spaces, and its presence and size affect our understanding of the world of the play. The set provides us with a sense of location, and serves the same function as setting in other literary forms.

CONCLUSION

Let's go back for a moment to the analogy with which this chapter opened. Reading a play text is different from reading other forms of literature because the printed play is a fragment of the complete product, while, in general, printed novels, short stories, and poems are complete in themselves. Like the remnants of the ancient statue we considered at the beginning of this chapter, reading a play requires the imaginary reconstruction of an incomplete object from the elements that remain, and this involves more work than simply reading through the text. Viewing the dramatic text, like our ancient statue, as the residue of something larger can enable the reading of a play to be an enriching experience like none other. Unlike novels, which define the experience of the reader through specificity, plays come alive through their lack of definition. Reading a play en- courages you to use your imagination in a more active way. What would this play have looked like on stage? How would the characters/actors have interacted with one another? How would the audience have reacted to the actors? What might change in the way we understand the play if we made different choices in staging or technical design?

Robert Edmond Jones says it best in *The Dramatic Imagination*, when he writes that "The loveliest and most poignant of stage pictures are those that are seen in the mind's eye [...] It is this delighted exercise of imagination, this heady joy, that the theatre has lost and is about to find once more" (139). When you read a play, I hope that you'll not *only* read the play. Don't think of yourself as simply a reader! Imagine you're an audience member, sitting there in the playhouse, watching the action take place. I hope you'll imagine yourself standing on the muddy ground of a medieval town square, pushing other audience members out of the way to get a better view of Abraham and Isaac while they teach you moral lessons. I hope you'll pretend you're in the middle of a rowdy Elizabethan playhouse, striv- ing to hear Othello sob over his dead wife's corpse over the calls of nut salesmen and prostitutes trying to sell you their wares. I hope you'll imagine what it might be like to lean over a Restoration-era balcony to shush the smart aleck on the bottom floor who is yelling abuse at the actors. I hope you'll try to picture what it would be like, sitting teary-eyed in a quiet, dark playhouse while Arthur Miller's poor salesman contemplates suicide. In short, because it can affect the ways we might interpret and understand the play as both actions and a social event, I hope you will read the play your teacher assigns not as a skeletal book, but as a frag- ment of a living, engaging performance.

Questions to Consider

1. After reading a play in your class, consider its original performance/publica- tion date. Based on this information, what type of theatre space was it likely performed in? What type of theatre would you choose if you could perform this play in any of the three types of houses, and why?

2. What are the benefits of taking the audience into consideration when reading a play? How is this different from simply picturing the story as though you were reading a novel?

3. In the past, have you paid attention to stage directions? If so, how has this helped you understand plays when you read them? If not, how might reading the stage directions affect your understanding of the plays you read?

4. Explain the differences between tragedy, comedy, tragicomedy, and history.

Group Activities

1. Divide into small groups. Consider a specific scene from a play (fewer than 20 lines). Each group offers a different suggestion for how to stage the section of text. After each group presents an option, discuss as a class how the meaning of the scene changes with different performance choices. The discussion should be about how the interpretation changes the scene, not about which was a "good" choice. (This activity helps us to understand dramatic action, performance spaces, and audience contact.)

2. (Students should prepare for this activity beforehand): While reading a play for class, write questions posed directly to a character, asking why s/he made the choice s/he did in a difficult situation. In class, one student pretends to be the character in question. Another student plays a prosecution lawyer and asks the questions generated by his or her classmates, trying to find out why the character did what s/he did. At the end, students can decide whether or not the character's account fits the evidence in the play. This activity helps us to understand dramatic action and motivation.

3. Your instructor will divide the class into three groups and assign the same section of a play to each group. One group will attempt to "stage" the scene in a proscenium configuration, one will do the same with a thrust configuration, and one will use arena seating. At the end, the other two groups must analyze the benefits and drawbacks of the performing group's seating configuration. (This activity helps with understanding performance spaces and audience contact.)

4. After reading a play, outline the dramatic action of the text. Then, either in a group or individually, create a new outline, using the same characters but rewriting the dramatic action within a different genre. So, if the play is a tragedy, rewrite the outline to show what needs to change to make it a comedy, a tragicomedy, or a history. (This activity helps us to understand genre and dramatic action.)

Essay Prompt

Using your understanding of genre, discuss the genre of a play you have read for class. In what way(s) is the genre it is written in an appropriate choice for the story? In what ways does the play fit the conventions of that genre? What would have to change to permit the play to fit into a different genre? How might a change in genre affect our fundamental understanding of the play?

Works Cited

Aristotle. *Poetics*. London: Penguin Books, 1996. Print.

Ball, David. *Backwards & Forwards*. Carbondale: Southern Illinois University Press, 1983. Print.

Carter, Paul. *Backstage Handbook*. Louisville: Broadway Press, 1994. Print.

Clurman, Harold. *On Directing*. New York: MacMillan, 1972. Print.

Cohen, Ralph Alan. *Shakesfear and How to Cure It*. Clayton: Prestwick House, 2007. Print.

Greenblatt, Stephen, et al., eds. *The Norton Shakespeare, Vol. 2*. New York: W.W. Norton, 2008. Print.

Greenwald, et al., eds. *The Longman Anthology of Drama and Theatre*. New York: Addison-Wesley Educational Publishers, Ltd., 2001. Print.

Jones, Robert Edmond. *The Dramatic Imagination*. New York: Routledge, 2004. Print.

Langley, Stephen. *Theatre Management and Production in America*. New York: Drama Publishers, 1990. Print.

Smith, Warren. "New Light on Stage Directions in Shakespeare." *Studies in Philology* 47.2. (1950): 173–181. *JSTOR*. Web.

Drama

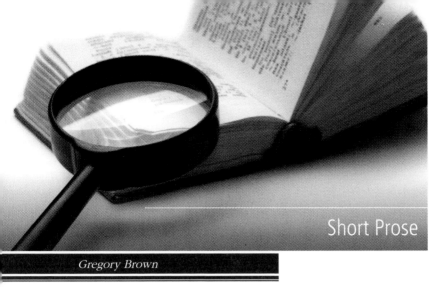

Short Prose

Gregory Brown

INTRODUCTION: WHAT IS SHORT PROSE?

Key Terms
- **short prose**
- **genre**

Short prose is a diverse category of written texts including both fiction and nonfiction genres. It is comprised of textual forms as diverse as myths, political speeches, riddles, short stories, personal essays, and fairy tales. As we'll see in this chapter, though these various **genres**, or types, of literary works share some common features, the primary similarity between them is their length. They are all—well, short! *How* short? Unfortunately, that question is not always easily answered. There are long short stories that run upwards of 40,000 words, and there is at least one famous example of a short story that is exactly six-words long (more about this follows). So, in addition to great variance in genre, short prose includes texts that vary greatly in length.

Given the many differences between these genres, students may be forgiven for feeling a bit of trepidation about reading and analyzing short prose. But, never fear! The purpose of this chapter is to provide you with an overview of the short prose genres that you are most likely to encounter in your college literature class. These include (in fiction) the short story, flash fiction, fairy tales, fables, myth, and legends; and (in nonfiction) the speech, the personal essay, the lyric essay, and the satirical essay. Again, while these genres share much in common with each other and even with longer genres—like, for instance, the novel—each also has its own unique characteristics and history. In this chapter we will examine the characteristics—and some of the historical contexts—of these genres, as a way of preparing you to read, discuss, and analyze the short prose texts that you will encounter in your college literature course.

FICTIONAL SHORT PROSE GENRES

Key Terms

- **short story**
- **narrative**
- **novella**
- *in medias res*
- **unity of impression**
- **specificity of detail**
- **suggestion**
- **epiphany**
- **climax**
- **flash fiction**

- **short-short fiction**
- **postcard fiction**
- **sketch**
- **fairy tale**
- **fable**
- **didactic**
- **myth**
- **mythology**
- **legend**

Short Story

The most common and popular genre of short prose—indeed, the one you're most likely to encounter in your college literature class—is the **short story**. A short story is, simply, a brief fictional **narrative**[1] in prose. Although we can trace the lineage of the short story back thousands of years through ancient Greek fables and Biblical stories like that of Cain and Abel, the modern short story came into existence during the middle of the nineteenth century, in part as a result of the growing popularity of magazines in Europe and America, where short stories were frequently published and often in high demand.

The short story differs from longer works of prose, such as the novel, in terms of both its length and focus, being shorter and more intensely focused on the actions of (usually) one or a few characters, across (often) one or a few unified incidents or events. However, beyond that it's somewhat difficult to discuss short stories in terms of their common or shared features. As many critics have noted, the short story is a very flexible genre. Still, we can generally talk about a few common features of the short story.

---

1 A narrative is a series of connected events presented in such a way as to form a unified whole, either in terms of theme or plot.

Common Features of the Short Story

1. *Length.* There is little consensus about what the term "short" means in describing a short story. Although most critics agree that short stories generally fall somewhere between 1,000 and 10,000 words, there are plenty of exceptions to this rule. For instance, British writer D.H. Lawrence's story "The Fox" (1922) is approximately 30,000 words—some critics characterize it as a **novella**, a long short story, or short novel—while there are also numerous short stories that are fewer than 1,000 words (see the section *Flash Fiction and Sketch*). American writer Ernest Hemingway (1899–1961) is even (apocryphally) credited with having written a story that was only six-words long: "For sale: Baby shoes, never worn." Obviously, then, there is wide variance when it comes to the classification of stories by length. Edgar Allen Poe (1809–1849), who was among the first to propose a theory of the modern short story, suggested usefully that a short story should be readable in a single sitting.

2. *Focus.* Long fictional prose narratives like the novel often depict many characters, complicated plots, and multiple settings. In contrast, the short story usually focuses on a single incident, or a short series of linked incidents, in the life of a single main character or protagonist. To wit, contemporary American author Luke Whisnant (b. 1957) has described the short story as "a brief prose narrative (usually) about a character, in which something (usually) happens." Again, what distinguishes a short story is its specificity of focus, its interest in a single moment of a single character's life.

3. *Brevity of action.* Short stories operate on a principle of focused attention. This means that most short stories don't spend pages and pages building towards a story's climax. Additionally, most short stories open with little or no exposition explaining who the characters are. Frequently, you will find that short stories begin *in medias res*, a literary technique whereby a writer opens her story in the middle of the action. The advantage of this technique is that it brings readers immediately into the story's conflict.

4. *Unity of impression.* Edgar Allen Poe—a famous nineteenth-century poet, but also one of America's earliest and most popular short story writers—helpfully noted that the short story's most prominent characteristics is its "**unity of impression**." What Poe meant by this is that the short story always has as its focus a single, coherent emotional effect, whereas a longer text, like the novel, may contain many different effects, ideas, or themes.

To illustrate this point, we might briefly consider the difference between Mary Shelley's novel *Frankenstein* (1818) and Edgar Allen Poe's short story, "The Tell-Tale Heart" (1843). Both of these texts belong to the tradition of Gothic fiction—narratives that feature elements of horror—and both of these narratives are interested in the horror of madness: in Shelley's novel, the mad scientist Dr. Frankenstein flouts conventional morality when he brings to life his famous creature; in Poe's story, the narrator is driven mad by his neighbor, whom the narrator later murders and dismembers. However, these texts differ drastically in scope. *Frankenstein*, for instance, explores many additional themes (science vs. nature, man vs. God, and good vs. evil), narrative threads, and even narrative points of view (there are, in fact, three different narrators in *Frankenstein*). Conversely, "The Tell-Tale Heart" focuses exclusively on the narrator's crimes and the way these crimes eat at his soul. Put simply, the scope and focus of the storytelling is more limited in Poe's story than in Shelley's novel. The same is generally true when we compare most stories to most novels.

5. *Specificity of detail.* Above, we observed that most novels are more structurally complicated than short stories. What's important to note is that this isn't to say that short stories are any less rich in theme or meaning than longer texts. In fact, some critics have argued that because short story writers work within stricter limits than novelists and dramatists, short stories often operate through suggestion and **specificity of detail**. This means that the text on the page presents specific details that hint at a whole universe of meaning that isn't necessarily or explicitly stated by the narrator. A novelist, for instance, might take several pages to explain the origins of characters—their family's history, their professional life, or their romantic relationships—whereas a short story writer is likely to suggest a character's entire life's history in a single detail or phrase.

Consider the German-language author Franz Kafka's story "The Metamorphosis" (1919), about a lonely traveling salesman who wakes up one morning to discover that he has been transformed into a giant insect. Early in the story, Kafka suggests much about how lonely and alienated this character is. What's interesting is that Kafka doesn't accomplish this by providing a long summary of the salesman's hardships or an account of his difficulties finding a girlfriend. Instead, Kafka describes the only item in the young man's room: a gilt picture frame with a magazine illustration in it, "[depicting] a lady, who decked out in a fur hat and a fur boa, sat upright, raising toward the viewer a heavy fur muff in which her whole forearm was encased" (11). Attentive readers will understand that this detail hasn't been chosen at random, but rather deliberately, as Kafka is using it to suggest several things about the character. Specifically, we learn that the character is lonely (since there is nothing in his room—no keepsakes from his family or friends, no love letters, not even a potted plant—just plain furniture, a few work items, and this photograph); that maybe what he desires is the company of a woman (since there is an implicit suggestion that his interest in this photograph is erotic in nature); that he desires money (since the woman is wearing expensive furs, she may represent wealth); and finally, that perhaps he is *really* lonely (since he has cut the photograph out of a magazine—it's not a picture of somebody he knows or cares about). Again, what's remarkable here is that Kafka is able to suggest a lot about his character, through imagery in a just a few, seemingly simple details. This technique of **suggestion**—using a few details to evoke a large, complex picture—is common to the short story.

6. *Technique of suggestion.* Owing to their brevity, many short stories work from a principle of suggestion, understatement, or implication. To understand what this means, we need only to consider the six-word story mentioned previously as being attributed to Ernest Hemingway: "For sale: Baby shoes, never worn." What makes this very short story so compelling is that it doesn't present the reader with all the details needed to understand the events of the story. It leaves much of the story up to our imagination. What has happened to the baby? Did it die during birth? After? Was it given up for adoption? The truth is that we don't know, and that we can't know. Operating on the principle of suggestion, the story demands that the reader fill in the blanks. It's also worth noting that this six-word story generates its emotional power precisely from its ambiguity. The story packs more emotional wallop because it is delivered in such swift and uncertain terms.

7. *Revelation.* A final common feature of short stories—especially literary short stories that are interested primarily in the nuances of character—is the **epiphany** (or revelation) of the main character. In many cases, short stories depict a crucial moment in a character's life, a moment in which a character is faced with an important, even life-changing, decision. Usually, this moment arrives during, or in the aftermath, of the story's **climax**. A climax is the turning point in a narrative, when the intensity of the story's action has reached its highest point and brought the protagonist to the precipice of change. Often, this is a moment when the character is presented with an opportunity to change that s/he may or may not take.[2] Alternatively, it may be a moment when the character is presented with some new knowledge about him- or herself or the world. In this case, the character hasn't necessarily changed, but has come to an understanding that differs from what s/he knew at the beginning of the story. This sudden, new understanding is an epiphany. This may strike some readers as too subtle a climax; an epiphany isn't as exciting a climax as a shootout

---

2 Questions we should always be asking of the characters in short stories include: *Have the characters been transformed by their experience? Are they different in the aftermath of the story? How have they changed?* See "Character" in the Literary Elements section of this book.

or an exploding helicopter. However, many story writers prefer this kind of introspective resolution and many literary short stories deal in these kinds of small climaxes. (For an example analysis of epiphany, please see the end of this chapter.)

To summarize, a short story is a brief, fictional narrative in prose, often delivered in suggestive rather than explicit ways, in which a character often is presented with a moment of revelation. This, in general, is what we expect when we sit down with a short story. Of course, it's important to remember that there are many examples of short stories that don't meet one or more of these criteria. There are short stories that ignore the conventions of length and focus outlined above presenting us with many storylines and characters. Because most short stories do respect the conventions outlined above, if and when we discover a short story that doesn't meet these expectations, we can assume that the author is making a deliberate decision to ignore them. In fact, recognizing this claim helps us to be better readers of short stories, because it positions us to ask the very basic questions of literary analysis: *How has the author ignored the conventions of her genre? How is the author's story different from our expectations of genre? What might this difference tell us about the story's meaning or the author's approach to the genre?* Asking these questions can provide insight into an author's agenda.

Flash Fiction and Sketch

In the last twenty years or so, the genre of **flash fiction** (sometimes called **short-short stories** or **postcard fiction**) has become increasingly popular. Flash fiction can be described as an *extremely* short story, not surpassing 1,000 words. It's probably easiest to understand flash fiction as a compressed—and therefore more intense—kind of short story. Because it shares many features with short stories—but uses much less space to accomplish them in—flash fiction is an even more economical form in terms of how it approaches character and plot. This economy, in turn, means that when we read a piece of flash fiction we need to be especially attentive to the author's use of language and detail. Since there is so little space for an author to maneuver, every word counts and we can assume that every detail has been carefully chosen by the author for maximum efficiency and effect. In fact, some critics advise us to approach reading flash fiction with the same careful, deliberate attention that we bring to reading a poem.

One example of flash fiction—and of the kind of attention it requires—comes to us courtesy of the American writer Ernest Hemingway. One of Hemingway's early story collections, *In Our Time* (1925), features several *very* short stories. One of these stories, "Chapter VII," is about a terrified WWI soldier who is desperately praying as mortar shells explode above him. The story is only 134 words long:

> While the bombardment was knocking the trench to pieces at Fossalta, he lay very flat and sweated and prayed, "Oh Jesus Christ get me out of here. Dear Jesus, please get me out. Christ, please, please, please, Christ. If you'll only keep me from getting killed I'll do anything you say. I believe in you and I'll tell everybody in the world that you are the only thing that matters. Please, please, dear Jesus." The shelling moved further up the line. We went to work on the trench and in the morning the sun came up and the day was hot and muggy and cheerful and quiet. The next night back at Mestre he did not tell the girl he went upstairs with at the Villa Rossa about Jesus. And he never told anybody. (67)

Although this story is extremely brief, it still delivers many of the elements we might expect from a longer story or even a novel. We have a complex main character, a plot, and even a surprise ending—given that the soldier is spared, we might expect him to keep his promise to spread the word of God. Instead, Hemingway surprises us by revealing that the soldier forgets his promise before the end of the day. Also noteworthy is the way that Hemingway is able to deliver a complex, even nuanced, depiction of the fickleness of the soldier's faith. Consider that the utter desperation of the soldier's prayers (as evidenced by his frantic repetition of the word "please") is abandoned by the story's end, when the soldier's fear disappears and the setting becomes unthreatening and placid. The soldier abandons his promise to God and reveals to us that his faith in God was only ever self-serving. Again, what's remarkable about Hemingway's story craft is that he is able to present such a complicated theme—here, the nature of humanity's fickle relationship to God—in such a brief moment.

Finally, flash fiction should not be confused with another short prose form, the **sketch**. A sketch is a short prose form related to the short story and flash fiction, but different in that it has little interest in plot or story. Instead, a sketch provides impressions of characters or a setting. Often, we say that a sketch is interested in a mood, or an emotional atmosphere or feeling. Again, the key difference between a sketch and flash fiction is that in flash fiction we can expect to find (in a concentrated if limited form) the basic elements of a short story, whereas in a sketch we will likely find characters and setting, but no plot or dramatic arc.

For more information on literary elements such as character, setting, mood, atmosphere, and plot, see the "Literary Elements" section later in this book.

Fairy Tale, Fable, Myth, and Legend

In addition to the short story and flash fiction, you're likely to encounter several other kinds of fictional short prose narratives in your college literature class. These include the fairy tale, the fable, the myth, and the legend. These genres often employ many of the same techniques as the short story, but they also have their own unique characteristics. Let's take a close look at some of these genres' more important features.

1. *Fairy Tale.* A **fairy tale** is a fictional narrative that typically features supernatural or fanciful creatures like witches, goblins, ogres, fairies, sprites, or dragons, and that moreover often features magic, charms, and disguises. In terms of plot, fairy tales usually follow the adventures and misfortunes of heroes and heroines, many of whom are children or adolescents. Many of these stories conclude with a happy ending. Indeed, the most common feature of modern fairy tales as we generally understand them is the happy ending (or "fairy-tale ending").

   In truth, the "happy ending" isn't always a feature of the traditional fairy tale and it only became a convention of the genre in the nineteenth century, when readers began to think of fairy tales as primarily written for children. Early versions of fairy tales might have been considered too scary, gory, sexual, or mature for children. For instance, though we now consider "Little Red Riding Hood" to be appropriate material for children, in early versions of the fairy tale, Red Riding Hood is tricked by the wolf into eating the flesh of her dead grandmother and into taking off her clothes and climbing naked into the bed with him. Other early versions of this tale have Red Riding Hood gorily gobbled up by the wolf. It's not until the Brothers Grimm, two German folklorists of the early nineteenth century who recorded a version of the story in *Children's and Household Tales* (1812), that we see a version of the story in which Red Riding Hood and her grandmother manage to best the wolf.

   This brings us to another important feature of the fairy tale; namely, its variability. The fairy tale comes to us from older, oral forms of folkloric storytelling. What this means is that before writers and historians began recording fairy tales by writing them down, the people that told them could change the details in the stories, such that any given storyteller might have a different, even drastically different, version of a story. In turn, when writers and historians began recording the stories, they often discovered that they had multiple versions of the same story. Recall, again, how different the details are in the versions of "Little Red Riding Hood" described above. Or, consider the fact that Red Riding Hood's riding hood isn't red until Charles Perrault (1628–1703) decides to make it red in his 1697 version of the tale.[3] There are so many different versions of this story! What's wonderful from the point of view of someone interested in analyzing these texts is that we can use these discrepancies and differences in the story versions as a way to begin understanding them. By asking how the versions of the story differ—and then asking *why* they differ—we can see how different writers emphasize different aspects of the stories, and we can see how the writers shape common material to their own thematic and literary purposes.

2. *Fable*. A **fable** is a short prose narrative that is **didactic** in nature, meaning that it presents the reader with a moral or lesson. Unlike fairy tales, which often feature human protagonists, the fable is usually about non-human characters like animals or inanimate objects. Scholars generally agree that the fable originated in ancient Greece, most attributing its invention to the storyteller Aesop (c. 620–564 BC), who wrote several hundred stories that were collected as Aesop's *Fables*. These stories feature animals like grasshoppers, frogs, geese, foxes, and wolves, using the conflicts that arise between these characters to teach lessons about morality and virtue.

For instance, in "The Grasshopper and the Ant," Aesop tells the story of a lazy grasshopper that spends the summer months singing and playing, while an industrious ant gathers food for the coming winter. When the cold winter arrives the starving grasshopper begs food from the ant, who in turn scolds the grasshopper for his laziness. As the narrator explains, the story is about the importance of preparing for the future. (Modern readers sometimes observe that the story also inadvertently criticizes the ant, since the ant callously and uncharitably dismisses the grasshopper's hunger.) Among the most famous of Aesop's fables are "The Boy Who Cried Wolf" and "The Tortoise and the Hare." Finally, it's worth noting that while many fables offer direct or explicit statements of their moral messages, as critical readers we don't necessarily need to take the stories at face value. For instance, the story of "The Tortoise and the Hare" is often interpreted as an illustration of the maxim that "slow and steady wins the race." However, a critical reader might point out that the story could also be interpreted as a warning against wasting an obvious advantage, as the hare does when it decides to take a nap in the middle of the race.

3. *Myth*. A **myth** is a traditional story about heroes or supernatural beings (often gods or deities); specifically, a story that serves an important religious or spiritual purpose in the culture that creates and tells it. Every culture has its own

---

3 Another notable detail in Perrault's version of the story is that Red Riding Hood isn't a girl, as she's often depicted, but an attractive, well-bred young lady.

mythology (group or collection of shared myths) and these myths attempt to explain for members of a culture the spiritual and cosmological conditions of their universe. Put in simplest terms, myths are the stories that cultures use to explain their own origins, the nature of their own gods, and the histories of their own heroes.

For example, consider the myth of Prometheus, an important story in ancient Greek mythology. Prometheus was a deity, a trickster figure, who was condemned and punished by the gods for giving fire to human beings. (Fire, the story goes, was reserved for the privileged gods.) Many readers understand this myth as an explanation of the origins of human culture, since fire is often associated with knowledge, progress, and even warfare. For ancient Greeks, the myth of Prometheus connected their understanding of their civilization to the machinations and dramatic conflicts of their gods. Put another way, this story allowed ancient Greeks to connect their culture with the larger forces of their universe. Thus, some questions we can ask when reading myths are: *What does this story tells us about the culture that produced it? What does myth explain about the universe? What is human society's place in it?*

Of course, oftentimes we don't encounter myths on their own, but as part of some other text, often as allusions [see Meghan McGuire's chapter in the Literary Elements section of this book]. Additionally, many of the myths that you may encounter in your English literature course are not native to English or even American culture. English literature borrows many of its myths from other cultures, notably from Greek, Roman, and Norse cultures. For instance, the Irish writer James Joyce's novel *Ulysses* (1922)—about a day in the life of a middle-aged Irish advertiser in Dublin—relies heavily on the Greco-Roman myth of Odysseus, a Greek warrior who spent 10 years lost after the end of the Trojan War. In his novel, Joyce makes numerous allusions to the myth of Odysseus (whose name, in Latin, is Ulysses) as a way of drawing parallels between the heroic Odysseus and the unheroic protagonist of his novel, Leopold Bloom. Readers who do not recognize or who are unfamiliar with the story of Odysseus will miss an important aspect of Joyce's novel and will fail to understand part of that novel's theme—that Joyce's unheroic everyman is, in his own way, as grand and heroic as the heroes of Greek myth.

4. *Legend.* A **legend** is a hybrid genre that combines elements of fiction and nonfiction. Specifically, we define a legend as a narrative that mixes historical fact and myth to tell a story about an historical (or reputedly historical) person or people. Although it may include elements of the miraculous or supernatural,

we generally expect a legend to be grounded in realism and history. That is, we may expect a legend to be plausible, if not quite believable.[4]

For example, consider the legend of King Arthur—a British king who supposedly lived during the early 6th century and whom legend credits with having defended Britain against a hostile invasion by the Saxons. Although the historical conflict is well-documented, there is scant evidence to support that King Arthur defended Britain against the Saxons or even that he existed. Despite this lack of evidence, King Arthur and his Knights of the Round Table became popular characters in the 12th century in part because of Geoffrey of Monmouth's *Historia Regum Brittonum* (c. 1136). Stranger yet, though the King Arthur legend has its origins in the historical invasion of Britain by the Saxons, many Arthurian stories are fantastical or supernatural. For instance, one of King Arthur's closest allies is the wizard Merlin, who is the offspring of a demon and a virgin. Or, consider that King Arthur attains the throne because he performs the impossible feat of pulling a magical sword out of a stone. Again, what we see in the legends of King Arthur is the ways in which history and myth collide to form a new genre entirely.

In terms of analysis, when we read legends we should remind ourselves that what we are reading is not entirely true, nor is it entirely untrue. Rather, legend is a hybrid form that combines traditional storytelling with historical fact to present significant historical narratives as fantastical tales. What we should always consider when reading a legend is how the fantastical or non-historical elements in the story change or modify the history and what these changes may mean. For instance, the story of the sword in the stone transforms Arthur from an important historical personage into a hero chosen by destiny—a transformation that signals Arthur as being divinely ordained to rule as the King of the Britons. In this way the legend of King Arthur transforms ordinary history into an exciting account of a great and fabled hero.

These are by no means all of the fictional short prose forms, but they provide a good overview of the range and diversity of forms associated with this literary category. They are also the fictional short prose forms you are most likely to encounter in your literature courses. You may, however, also find yourself studying nonfiction short prose works, to which we now turn.

---

4 To understand this distinction, we might consider the legend of Robin Hood. Although there is little evidence of an historical Robin Hood, the legend of the character—a rogue and a heroic outlaw living in Medieval England—could conceivably be true. After all, he's often depicted as living in Sherwood Forest—a very real location.

NONFICTIONAL SHORT PROSE GENRES

Key Terms

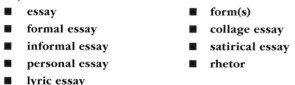

- **essay**
- **formal essay**
- **informal essay**
- **personal essay**
- **lyric essay**
- **form(s)**
- **collage essay**
- **satirical essay**
- **rhetor**

Though we often tend to think of literature as exclusively comprised of fiction, there are many writers who work in nonfiction forms. Like fiction, nonfiction is also home to many diverse genres of short prose, including speeches, essays, letters, and even diary entries. Here, we will examine several genres of nonfiction short prose, including the essay, the personal essay, the lyric essay, and the satirical essay.

The Essay. No doubt you are familiar with a certain kind of scholastic essay—that which asks students to persuade their readers by positing theses and supporting their arguments with evidence in the form of research, data, and facts. Every student in high school and college has at some point in his or her academic career written this kind of essay. What may surprise you to learn is that there are, in fact, many subgenres of the essay. These include the personal essay, the autobiographical essay, the informal essay, and the lyric essay, just to name a few. Most of these essay subgenres have little to do with argumentation and thesis-support—they are much more aligned with the idea of the author expressing who s/he is, than in making some claim about the world. So while we might generally describe the essay as a written, nonfiction composition that requires the writer to prove his or her point through argumentation, logic, and evidence, the truth is that the essay is a much more versatile and flexible genre.

In his introduction to *The Art of the Personal Essay*, essayist and scholar Phillip Lopate (b. 1943) helpfully distinguishes between the **formal essay** and the **informal essay** by noting that while the formal essay can be characterized by its "logical organization" and "seriousness of purpose," the informal essay is characterized by the "personal element" as exemplified by humor, self-revelation, and the non-argumentative quality of the writing (xxiii–xxiv). It is in this latter subgenre of the essay—the informal essay—that we find many nonfiction writers working. The essay subgenres that you are most likely to encounter in your literature course are the personal essay and the lyric essay. In the following sections we will explore these two subgenres of the essay.

The Personal Essay. In general, we can understand the personal essay as being less interested in argument, persuasion, and logic, and more interested in the communication of the essayist's personal experience. The personal essay often involves the essayist writing about an experience, then using this experience to illuminate some aspect of the world. The personal essay is often written in conversational tone, often employs humor, and is characterized by its lack of formality.

Of course, one important distinction to make between the personal essay (or, essay writing in general) and, say, the short story, is that the personal essay is a *nonfiction genre*, while the short story is *fiction*. This means that when we read an essay, as opposed to a short story, we expect a certain amount of fidelity to the truth. In short, we tend to think of essays as "true" and short stories as inventions or fabrications—as, well, literary lies. However, there are a couple of important observations to make here. For one, just because the essay is "true" and the short story is "invented" doesn't mean that the essay isn't necessarily a highly constructed art form. That is, the essay involves a certain amount of invention as well. Any time a writer sits down to write an essay, s/he must decide what form the essay will take, which facts to include, which stories to tell, which specific details to use to clarify and elucidate his/her narrative. When a writer sits down to write an essay, s/he isn't merely reproducing the reality of the world. S/he is, instead, producing a highly structured—even sometimes artificial—version an experience. Therefore, we can think of personal essays as representations of authors' experiences that draw on the truth of their lives, but that are also organized, artful, and therefore, not strictly speaking, "true."

The Lyric Essay. The lyric essay may be considered a form of personal essay, but one that combines elements of the personal essay with aspects of poetry. It's also the newest, most innovative and experimental nonfiction genre, having come to be taken seriously as a literary form only in the last fifteen years or so. Because of its relative newness, it requires a little more explanation than more traditional essay forms.

As described by Deborah Tall and John D'Agata, editors of the literary journal *Seneca Review* (where the term "lyric essay" first appeared in 1997), lyric essays "give primacy to the artfulness over the conveying of information. They forsake narrative line, discursive logic, and the art of persuasion in favor of idiosyncratic meditation" ("The Lyric Essay"). In simple terms, the lyric essay is even less interested in "logical organization" than the personal essay. It is often fragmented, nonlinear, and may be home to strange experiments in style and form. A lyric essay may be written as a list, or as a series of impressionist vignettes. Like some kinds of poetry, it is interested in the associative connections between ideas more so than the logical movement between ideas. This means that the lyric essay will often move quickly between dramatically different ideas without explaining the connection between those ideas, leaving it to the reader to intuit how these ideas illuminate one another.

For example, a short essay by Stephen Dunn entitled "Two" opens with the essayist's complaint that people seem less scrupulous than they did a few years ago. (He observes this because every semester he asks his students if they would "push a button that would kill a nondescript peasant in another land, for which they would receive a million dollars and the guarantee of never being caught" (137–138), and every semester more of his students seem comfortable saying "yes.") Quickly, however, Dunn turns his attention from these complaints to an inquiry into the nature of Sainthood and what it means to sacrifice oneself to a cause. Attentive readers will understand that Dunn is trying to draw our attention to the huge gap that exists between contemporary morality and our ideal version of it. The essay never explicitly states this observation of the discrepancy between ideal and real forms of morality, but in moving quickly between these ideas it draws our attention to it.

When we encounter a lyric essay, there are two important questions that we, as readers, should ask. The first question is: *How do we know that we're looking at a lyric essay?* As noted above, the lyric essay is an experimental genre—one in which you're likely to see the essayist taking risks on how s/he is shaping and structuring the essay. Helpfully, there are a few **forms**—i.e., common structures and shapes—that lyric essayists often employ. The most common of these forms is the collage. As you probably already know, in art a collage is a technique whereby an artist makes something new by combining random materials together. In terms of literary production, a **collage essay** is when a writer brings together many different and (seemingly random ideas). To be sure, the effect of this can often be disorienting, but it also offers the writer an opportunity to build a new impression for the reader. This kind of approach to essay writing forces readers to intuit the connection between different ideas. The reader must consider how the ideas are in conversation with one another in order to construct meaning. Thus, the meaning in a collage essay often comes from the reader's interpretive choices of the author's juxtaposition of ideas.

The second question we should ask when we encounter a lyric essay is: *How should we analyze it?* Given how divergent the lyric essay form can be, coming up with a strategy for analyzing it would seem difficult. The genre thrives on the novelty of experiment and play; no two essays seem much alike and in fact, they're often wildly different. One possible way of solving this problem is by closely examining the essay's form. After all, it's important to remember that writers don't choose the shape or structure of their essays accidentally. Often, the essay's form is as important as its content. (Consider, again, how the collage essay creates meaning through the juxtaposition of content, not merely through content alone.) So, one final way of approaching the lyric essay is to ask: *How does the form of this essay work to support its content?*

The Satirical Essay. The satirical essay employs exaggeration, ridicule, and irony to undermine and attack human vices and political folly. The satirical essayist often exaggerates the characteristics of those holding opposing viewpoints to emphasize their stupidity or silliness, thus inviting the scorn of the reader. Consider Stephen Colbert, a comic who attacks conservative media and political institutions by pretending to be a conservative television pundit. In his performance, Colbert exaggerates and embellishes problematic ideologies upheld by the conservative movement as a way of challenging and undermining them. The same is true of the satirical essayist. Perceptive readers will notice, of course, that unlike the previous essay genres we've examined, the satirical essay is often rhetorical in nature. That is, the satirical essayist aims to make an argument against an idea or principle by embodying and exaggerating the views of the opposition.

One of the most famous examples of the satirical essay is Jonathan Swift's "A Modest Proposal" (1729)[5]. At first glance, the essay appears to be the work of a rational and sympathetic **rhetor**, or writer—a man who wants to solve Ireland's social problems. At the beginning of the essay and under the guise of this unassuming speaker, Swift outlines the plight of the poor Irish. As the speaker sees it, Ireland is suffering because there are too many unwanted babies. These babies make it impossible for their mothers to find work, because all of the mothers' time is spent caring for the babies and begging for money to help care for the babies. Worse yet, when these babies grow up they will inevitably become either criminals or mercenaries, because there won't be enough jobs to go around. As Swift's speaker explains, the surplus of babies in Ireland is causing major social ills.

Though readers may find this explanation for Ireland's problems silly or preposterous, what's important to note is that Swift's speaker's tone is plain and serious, the message delivered without a hint of irony. However, having established his concern and the dire consequences of all of these babies, Swift's speaker proposes a solution: The babies should be eaten. Shockingly, for the rest of the essay Swift's speaker goes on to explain in thorough and certain terms the many benefits of this so-called "modest" proposal. Swift's narrator even proposes recipes for cooking the children. Of course, what's important to remember here is that while seeming to use an unironic tone, Swift *is* employing irony; he doesn't

---

5 This text is included in the Anthology on page 285.

actually want his readers to start eating children! Rather, he's satirizing the rich English elite, who live off the labor of the poor Irish while also proposing simple, patronizing plans to "save" them. Swift's speaker's plan to save the Irish exaggerates England's mistreatment of the poor, turning economic exploitation into infanticide. In this way, Swift attacks English attitudes through satire.

EXAMPLE SHORT PROSE ANALYSIS—EPIPHANY IN JAMES JOYCE'S "ARABY"

Now that we have reviewed a number of fiction and nonfiction forms of short prose, it's helpful to have an understanding of how we might approach reading, interpreting, and analyzing such literary works. The following is an example analysis of James Joyce's story "Araby" (1914). This analysis examines how Joyce uses the literary technique of epiphany (as described previously) to dramatize the narrator's coming-of-age and the sudden disillusionment of his intense romantic feelings for a local girl.

> James Joyce's story "Araby" (1914) is a coming-of-age narrative that ends with a profound moment of disappointment. The story's narrator—a young, nameless boy in Dublin, Ireland—has visited a local bazaar to find a gift for a girl, his friend Mangan's sister, whom he desperately loves. Unfortunately, the boy arrives at the bazaar too late; the merchants are closing up their booths and a lone salesgirl is too busy flirting with a couple of young men to care about the arrival of the narrator. Soon the lights of the bazaar are extinguished and the boy is left standing among the dark, empty stalls; he won't be able to buy a gift for his beloved as he had promised. The story's final sentence sums up the narrator's frustration and dejection: "Gazing up into the darkness I saw myself as a creature driven and derided by vanity; and my eyes burned with anguish and anger" (19). Though we shouldn't be surprised by the narrator's "anguish and anger"—after all, he's failed to find a gift for the girl he's been obsessively thinking about for much of the story— what may surprise some readers is how the narrator's disappointment turns inward. That is, instead of yelling at the salesgirl or blaming his uncle (whose earlier indifference causes the narrator's late arrival at the bazaar), the narrator finds himself looking inward, where he makes a startling realization about the nature of his desire for the girl, which in turn leads to a more bitter disappointment about adulthood. In these ways, the final sentence of the story is an important clue in understanding the transformation of the character, a transformation that is signaled to the reader by the use of epiphany.

Broadly defined, an epiphany is the sudden realization or insight experienced by characters in literary short stories, frequently in the aftermath of the story's climax. Joyce, who is often credited with having introduced the technique of epiphany into literary fiction, uses epiphany in this story to dramatize the narrator's disappointing realization that his love for his friend's sister may in fact be an idealized—and therefore ultimately false—love. Indeed, for much of the story the narrator has been awkwardly and obsessively pining for the girl. The narrator observes, for instance, that "Every morning [he] lay on the floor in the front parlour watching her door" (16) and later, while walking through the market with a handful of parcels, he finds himself daydreaming in terms that suggest he's begun thinking of his love in grand, heroic terms: "I imagined that I bore my chalice safely through a throng of foes" (16). The imagery here, which transforms a crowded market into a "throng of foes" and a parcel into a "chalice" suggests an ideal, courtly vision of love. In short, for much of the story the narrator has been thinking about the girl in the most exalted, impossible terms.

However, as suggested above, the narrator's trip to the bazaar ultimately undercuts these notions of a perfect love and his subsequent epiphany underscores the terrible realization of romantic disappointment. His epiphany replaces his earlier ecstatic vision of love—where the narrator's "body is like a harp and [the girl's] words and gestures were like fingers running upon the wires" (16)—with the sudden realization of his own terrible fate. The narrator sees himself now not as an idealized lover but as "a creature driven and derided by vanity." What Joyce seems to be suggesting is that the narrator has come to see himself not as a romantic hero or a virtuous lover, but as a kind of unthinking beast controlled by desires that won't or can't be satisfied and that will ultimately leave him frustrated, alone and miserable. The narrator has come to understand that the girl won't ever love him back. Moreover, we can understand the narrator's epiphany as suggesting an even larger understanding that the narrator is coming to about desire—how it controls us and disappoints us. Finally, this epiphany suggests to us the narrator's transformation from a naïve, lovesick boy into a disappointed, frustrated adult. Thus, Joyce uses the technique of epiphany as a way of depicting his character's coming of age.

CONCLUSION

As we have seen, short prose is a diverse and dynamic literary category, comprising both fiction and nonfiction forms and serving a variety of functions from entertainment to enlightenment. Despite their shorter length, these texts are often complex and sophisticated, requiring us as readers to pay close attention to every word if we want to avoid missing potentially important clues to their meaning. But, even as we are forced to focus closely on the details, we should be sure to take the time simply to enjoy these literary works in their entirety as well.

Questions to Consider

1. Why might a writer choose to write a narrative in short prose as opposed to a longer form, like the novel? What can be accomplished in short prose forms that can't be in a longer text? Consider examples from your course.

2. Consider a short story from your course. How does it conform to the conventions of the genre? Does it break or challenge the conventions? What might the author's intention be in either breaking or conforming to the conventions of genre?

3. Compare the fiction and nonfiction short prose genres. What common features do you see in, say, the legend and the lyric essay?

4. Consider the genre of myth. What myths are important in American culture? What do these myths tell us about who we believe that we are and how we think we fit in the larger scheme of the universe?

Essay Prompts

1. Consider a short story from your course. Using the concept of *specificity of detail*, analyze how the author's use of specific, economical details produces complex depictions of character. (For an example, see the analysis earlier in the chapter of Kafka's "Metamorphosis.")

2. Consider an essay from your course. Think about how that writer's selection of details produces an accurate or inaccurate representation of the truth. How has the author's selection of detail warped or obscured the truth? What does this approach tell us about the author's attitude toward her subject, herself, or the world?

Works Cited

Dunn, Stephen. "Two." *Short Takes: Brief Encounters with Contemporary Nonfiction.* Ed. Judith Kitchen. New York: Norton, 2005. 137–138. Print.

Hemingway, Ernest. "Chapter VII." *In Our Time.* New York: Scribner, 1996. 67. Print.

Joyce, James. "Araby." *Dubliners.* New York: Dover, 1991. 15–19. Print.

Kafka, Franz. "The Metamorphosis." *The Metamorphosis and Other Stories.* Trans. Stanley Appelbaum. New York: Dover, 1996. 11–52. Print.

Lopate, Phillip. "Introduction." *The Art of the Personal Essay: An Anthology from the Classical Era to the Present.* Ed. Phillip Lopate. New York: Anchor Books, 1995. xxiii–liv. Print.

Poe, Edgar Allen. "The Philosophy of Composition." *Graham's Magazine* 28.4 (1846): 163–167. Print.

Tall, Deborah and John D'Agata. "The Lyric Essay." *Seneca Review.* Hobart and William Smith Colleges, n.d. Web. 16 Feb 2014.

Whisnant, Luke. "The Short Story." Wildacres Writers Workshop. Little Switzerland, North Carolina. July 2011. Lecture.

Long Prose

Crystal Matey

INTRODUCTION

Key Terms
■ **prose**

Prose is often defined as the opposite of verse, in that prose is any form of written or spoken expression that is not written in metered language (Harmon and Holman 418). Literature can be written in prose or verse, but this chapter is concerned with long prose, specifically. Long prose comprises fictional and nonfictional genres, in a variety of forms—the novella, novel, biography, and memoir, to name a few. This chapter begins with some general considerations for reading a work of long prose; then introduces you to some of the many genres of long prose, fiction and nonfiction, that you might encounter in your literature courses; and finally, provides suggestions for how to perform a close reading of a long prose passage.

READING LONG PROSE

Key Term
■ **active reading**

When you are assigned to read a longer piece of prose, such as a novel, how do you approach such a reading? Do you read a novel differently than you would a poem or a short story? Given the change in length and form, it might be helpful to develop strategies for approaching longer texts that can sometimes seem intimidating. One of the biggest mistakes a student can make when approaching a long prose text is to just read the book from cover to cover, never stopping to contemplate or make notations of important characters, symbols, or plot elements. Because it can take a while to finish reading a work of long prose, you may want to follow a few helpful reading tips:

- **Highlight important passages**—Underline or highlight sentences or passages that resonate with you. If you don't like to mark up your book, use Post-it notes or flags.

- **Character trees**—On a separate sheet of paper or on the blank front and back pages of the book, take notes. You can use these notes to keep track of character names and relationships to one another, creating for yourself a family tree, of sorts.

- **React**—In the margins, you might mark your reactions to the text with words like, "Wow!" or "Really?" or "Funny." You might even write down questions to ask in class like: *Why did this character do that?* Or, *what does this mean?*

- **Annotate**—Develop a system of annotation symbols. For example, you might put a star next to moments in the text that you think are important or put a question mark next to parts you do not understand or that you want to research more. Additionally, it can be helpful to circle or highlight repeated images and symbols. Come up with a system that works for you.

- **Develop a system to mark important pages**—One method is to use Post-it tabs for marking significant pages. Write a brief comment on the tab that reminds you what part of that page you think is important. Later, during class discussion, these little notes can help you to find passages quickly and use them to contribute to that discussion. Other people prefer to dog-ear the pages.

- **Review the book**—Before class, go back through the book, doing a quick scan of the annotations you made. Revisit the family tree you created to refresh your memory as to the characters' names and relationships. You might also reread the sections of the text that you previously underlined and starred. This allows you to remember what you considered to be the essential parts of the text, especially if you finish the assigned reading several days before class.

Beyond finding ways such as those listed above to interact with the text— also known as **active reading**—it can be helpful to perform further research. Sometimes discovering a few details about the author's life can shed light on events in the narrative. If you are unfamiliar with the time period in which a book is written, or if the narrative makes reference to a historical event you have not previously encountered, doing a quick search can bring a rich amount of context to your understanding of the narrative. These tips for active reading can be helpful when reading long prose. Furthermore, knowing the difference between fiction and nonfiction, in addition to the various genres that make up each type of long prose, can inform the approach you take to reading.

FICTION

Key Terms
- **fiction**
- **setting**
- **plot**

Fiction is a narrative that comprises imaginative characters and events, as opposed to actual happenings. While a fictional prose narrative can contain information that is true and realistic, it does not have to be based in fact or represent the world in a realistic manner. You can find fiction in verse or prose, but in this chapter we will be focusing on fictional prose.

There are three major genres that fall within the category of prose fiction: the short story (see the chapter on short prose), the novel, and the novella. Like short stories, novels and novellas also focus on characters and events in a particular **setting**, or time and place. Events within the story are narrated from a certain point of view and revolve around **plot**. This section begins with a brief overview of the conventions of novels and novellas, then turns to a consideration of specific genres within these literary forms.

Abigail Lee's chapter in this volume deals in-depth with setting; for more information on plot, see April Williams's chapter.

FICTIONAL GENRES

Key Terms
- **Novel**
- **Chapters**
- **Preface**
- **Epilogue**
- **Novella**
- **Novelette**

The Novel. In some ways, the novel is one of the most indefinable literary genres because it is pliable and can appear in diverse forms. Generally, though, the **novel** is an extended, book-length work of prose narrative. Novels usually contain "abundant characters, varied scenes, and a broader coverage of time than a shorter work provides" (Kennedy, Gioia, and Bauerlein 108). Conventionally, the novel tends to have more intricacies of character, setting, and theme than a short story because its length allows for a more involved plot. Critics interested in narrative tend to praise the form for "its potential to contrast different points of view, to shift from person to person and from objective to subjective, and to experiment with alternative perceptions" (108). Novels can feature one primary or several protagonists and often contain, in general, more characters than do short stories. Furthermore, it is typical for many novels to have a more comprehensive view of the society and culture from which the characters arise, in addition to those characters' feelings and experiences being presented in a more multifaceted manner. Because of the length of the work, the reader will follow the characters through numerous conflicts and changes; there may be multiple subplots or counterplots to the main narrative line, and there can be elements, such as digressions, that take us outside the main story line. Moreover, a novel will usually explore several complex and interrelated themes rather than focusing on a single or main idea throughout the text.

There are several conventions that you might expect to come across when reading a novel, although not all novels will contain the following elements. Typically, a novel is divided into main sections, called **chapters**. Authors often indicate these chapter breaks with numbers or chapter titles. In addition to chapters, authors might divide their book into parts as well, grouping multiple chapters together under a title such as "Part One." Some authors will open their novels with a **preface**, which is a statement at the beginning of the book. In general, a preface is meant to provide the reader with information that the author finds important. You might also come across an **epilogue** at the end of a novel, the purpose of which is to either comment on the novel or to offer the reader a conclusion of sorts.

The Novella. The **novella**, or **novelette**, falls between the novel and the short story, in terms of length and complexity. Sometimes the two terms—novella and novelette—are used as synonyms of one another. However, experts attempt to make a distinction between the two, with the novella classified as the more "serious work of fiction" when compared to the "romantic formula story" of the novelette (Turco 64). A novella is shorter than a novel and longer than a short story, and it is long enough to be published on its own, as opposed to being part of a collection. Generally, a novella will have a more compact plot structure, but compared to a short story, a novella will frequently feature more developed characters and themes. This form of long prose is "an artistic attempt to combine the compression of the short story with the development of the novel" (Harmon and Holman 483). Examples of the novella include Joseph Conrad's *Heart of Darkness* (1899) and Herman Melville's *Billy Budd* (1924).

COMMON LONG PROSE FICTION TYPES

Key Terms

- **bildüngsroman**
- **protagonist**
- **dystopia(n)**
- **speculative fiction**
- **utopia(n)**
- **fantasy**
- **gothic**

- **graphic novel**
- **historical novel**
- **realistic novel**
- **romance**
- **realism**
- **science fiction**
- **hybrid forms**

The allure of the novel lies in its limitless scope, but this also makes it impossible to cover the form in comprehensive fashion in a single chapter. What follows is a brief, introductory presentation of some of the most common types of novels assigned in college literature classes, presented in alphabetical order. There are many other types, and the definitions that follow are intended as introductory remarks, so you may need to perform outside research on genre, should your instructor require it.

Bildüngsroman. This is a novel of growth, sometimes referred to as a coming-of-age novel. Novels such as this will frequently portray a character that undergoes some kind of personal or educational development. Oftentimes, that means the **protagonist** will be a young person that the reader follows from adolescence to maturity. This character, through his or her interaction with society and others, will formulate his or her own worldview or personal philosophies. *The*

Adventures of Huckleberry Finn (1844) by Mark Twain could be considered a *bildüngsroman*.

Dystopia. The term "dystopia" means "bad place." This word is applied to narratives of imaginary societies, usually set in the future. Dystopias take current cultural and societal problems and hypothesize their future ramifications. Like science fiction novels (defined below), dystopias fall under the umbrella of **speculative fiction**—stories that consider "what if" in relation to the development and/or breakdown of human activity such as communication, science, and technology. Science fiction and dystopia may overlap, as in the case of the novel *Brave New World* (1932) by Aldous Huxley; however, a novel can be a dystopia without any reliance on science or technology, while a science fiction novel does not have to represent a dystopian society. A novel is classified as a dystopia when it is set in a world that may appear, on the surface, to be **utopian**, when, in fact, that world is the opposite. *Fahrenheit 451* (1953) by Ray Bradbury is an example of a dystopia.

Fantasy. These are stories that take place in an invented or imagined world, involving incredible characters (Harmon and Holman 213). The fantasy narrative usually portrays events, places, or characters that defy the natural laws of the realistic world. This type of novel "freely pursues the dreamy and nightmarish possibilities of the imagination" (Kennedy, Gioia, and Bauerlein 63). Because science fiction is a form of fantasy, these novels may also rely on scientific principles that have not yet been discovered. Then, what is the difference between fantasy and science fiction? While this is a contentious issue, it may be helpful to consider that many critics see science fiction as rooted in science, and as, therefore, plausible, while what happens in fantasy is not based in reality. J.R.R. Tolkien's *The Lord of the Rings* (1954) trilogy represents the fantasy genre.

Gothic. This is a genre that centers on terror or suspense. Sexuality, passion, and fear are often at the forefront. Typical settings for a gothic narrative include an isolated castle, ancestral mansion, church, or dungeon. The main character usually uncovers secrets, ghostly presences, or has to negotiate with situations that threaten his or her sanity. Sometimes these circumstances end up having rational explanations, but events and people in Gothic texts can also be supernatural. Both *Jane Eyre* (1847) by Charlotte Brontë and *Dracula* (1897) by Bram Stoker are good representations of gothic novels.

Graphic Novel. This type of story is presented in the format of a comic strip, with series of panels employed to develop the plot. Graphic novels are considered long prose due to their length, complex plots, and characters. They differ from a traditional novel because they rely more on visual than textual elements;

the images in a graphic novel, therefore, play an essential role in telling the story. Though this type has been listed as part of long prose fiction, graphic narratives can also be classified as nonfiction. Art Spiegelman's *Maus: A Survivor's Tale* (1986) is an example of a graphic novel.

Historical Novel. As the name might imply, this kind of story is set in another time other than that in which it was written. Essentially this type of novel "reconstructs a past age" (Harmon and Holman 256). The author employs historical figures and situations, often with a nice attention to accuracy, but also inserts fictive characters, actions, and events. *The Scarlet Letter* (1850), by Nathaniel Hawthorne, is an exemplar of historical fiction.

Realistic Novel. This type of novel attempts to "reproduce faithfully the surface appearance of life, especially that of ordinary people in everyday situations" (Kennedy, Gioia, and Bauerlein 128). Essentially, a reader can expect to encounter plausible events, settings, and characters. In a realistic novel, you would not find supernatural plots or characters, nor would you encounter "strange situations and extreme emotional states" (129). Jane Austen's *Pride and Prejudice* (1813) is an example of a realistic novel.

Romance. Historically, and particularly in the medieval era, "romance" simply referred to texts written in vernacular languages rather than Latin. The label "romance" in contemporary and common usage refers to novels set in exotic locales, with fantastic events and idealized characters. For example, in a romance, "heroes are very brave, villains are very villainous [...] and plots incorporate mysterious figures and extraordinary forces" (Kennedy, Gioia, and Bauerlein 134). In a more sophisticated sense the term romance "refers to works relatively free of the more restrictive aspects" associated with **realism** (Harmon and Holman 454). Herman Melville's novel *Moby Dick* (1851) could be considered a romance.

Science Fiction. These novels concern themselves with speculative events, including real and imaginative scientific or medical discoveries. Science fiction is a form of fantasy and can be set in the future or on other planets, and it can involve space or time travel. However, as in the case of Robert Louis Stevenson's *The Strange Case of Dr. Jekyll and Mr. Hyde* (1886), it can also be set within the time period and geographic area in which it was written. Falling under the umbrella of speculative fiction, the author uses scientific discoveries and technologies to rationally and imaginatively estimate the future.

Hybrid Forms. In many ways, the designation of a literary work as belonging to any one genre is arbitrary, and many texts don't perfectly fall into a single category. Authors can mix genres, so you might read a gothic *bildüngsroman* novel, or you could be assigned a dystopian science-fiction narrative. For instance, the novel *Jane Eyre* mixes realism with romance and the Gothic. The epic novels of J.K. Rowling's *Harry Potter* series (1997–2007) could be considered fantasy and *bildüngsoman*. Even the examples that were listed for each of the previous types of novels could also probably have been listed within another category. That is part of what makes the novel so fascinating and experimental.

CLOSE READING LONG PROSE FICTION

Key Terms
- **close reading**
- **diction**
- **syntax**

One of the ways to actively engage with a work of long prose is to perform a **close reading**. A close reading is when a student carefully interprets a passage of literature, paying attention to the **diction**—choices in language use; **syntax**—the arrangement of that language into sentences; and ideas within the passage. Should your instructor request that you perform a close reading of a novel, you do not want to close-read the entire book. Just as you would with a poem, short story, or play, you should select a passage of manageable length—something that is long enough to speak in depth about, but short enough that it can be analyzed within the parameters of your instructor's assignment. When performing a close reading it is important to remember a few key tips. Because your instructor wants to see that you can find the complexities within the language used, after you introduce the text, you should refrain from summarizing, repeating, or paraphrasing the passage or recapping what the whole story is about. Furthermore, your discussion of the passage should interpret the text and not evaluate the author, the story, or the passage. Following are suggestions for some things you will want to consider while performing a close reading of a passage of long prose.

Re-read and Annotate. So, where should you begin? Let the text be your guide. First, choose one passage that you find key to a specific meaning or message of the overall text. Be sure to choose a passage that you think is rich in significance, important to the overall story, and that you understand and can discuss clearly. Read the passage at least once out loud. Then, you should read it, multiple times with a pencil or pen in hand, annotating the text as you go. When you read the passage, try to focus on it both for its own merits and as a part of the overall narrative, and concentrate on all its details. Look for patterns in the elements you have noticed about the text—repetitions, contradictions, and similarities. Then, ask yourself questions about the patterns you've noticed. For instance, how do the author's words and images create meaning and why are they important in the passage?

Identify Diction and Syntax. Once you have read and annotated the passage that you are close reading, pay attention to some of the following attributes within the passage. What do the words mean? Look up any words you don't know or any words that might be used differently than you anticipated. Pay attention to what the words might connote, or in other words, what the diction implies or suggests in the context of the passage. Examine the passage for structure and syntax. How are the words arranged? What about the sentences themselves? Are there remarkable repetitions of sentence structure or parallel structure? Are the sentences short and choppy or filled with an abundance of flowery prose? Once you have identified patterns in diction and syntax, ask yourself how those patterns create meaning in the text. For example, long, flowing sentences might emphasize a character's wandering thoughts or overflowing emotions, while a short, choppy sentence might be used to add emphasis.

List Literary Elements and Figurative Language. Consider literary elements, or **devices**, as well. Is there any irony in the passage? What kind of tone is employed? Are there any interesting metaphors, similes, images, allusions, or symbols? How might this passage both explicitly and implicitly be related to the novel's themes? (For more information on these literary elements, consult the relevant sections in this book.) It should be noted that the point of a close reading is not to answer all these questions. The point of performing a close reading is first to observe, and then to exhibit, your ability to analyze how words create meaning. Therefore, rather than simply pointing out that a passage contains a simile, you need to be able to explain what you think that simile is doing or how that simile is creating meaning. Instead of just indicating that the author repeats a word multiple times, explain the effect that is created for the reader by having that term stressed repeatedly. If you need to refresh your memory or get ideas, take a quick look at the chapters devoted to figurative language in this book. Perhaps rereading will help you make more connections between your ideas, the close reading you have already done, and the literary devices discussed.

SAMPLE CLOSE READING: MARY SHELLEY'S *FRANKENSTEIN*

Key Terms
- **Other**
- **hybrid**

Let's take a look at a passage from Chapter IV of *Frankenstein*. Read it more than once, annotate it as you go, and do your best to formulate a close reading of the following passage:

> I started from my sleep with horror; a cold dew covered my forehead, my teeth chattered, and every limb became convulsed; when by the dim and yellow light of the moon, as it forced its ways through the window-shutters, I beheld the wretch—the miserable monster whom I had created. He held up the curtain of the bed; and his eyes, if eyes they may be called were fixed on me. His jaws opened, and he muttered some inarticulate sounds, while a grin wrinkled his cheeks. He might have spoken, but I did not hear; one hand was stretched out, seemingly to detain me, but I escaped, and rushed down the stairs. I took refuge in the court-yard belonging to the house which I inhabited; where I remained the rest of the night, walking up and down in the greatest agitation, listening attentively, catching and fearing each sound as if it were to announce the approach of the demonical corpse to which I had so miserably given life. (34–5)

Now that you have spent some time practicing how to perform a close reading, read the following sample analysis. Though there is not one way to perform a close reading, nor is there a single interpretation of this passage, it can be helpful to examine an example. After you read it, ask yourself a couple questions. How is the response structured? How does this analysis differ from your own? Through understanding how the sample goes about in its analysis, you may better understand how to craft a future close reading of your own.

Possible Close Reading Analysis

This passage, taken from Chapter IV of Mary Shelley's *Frankenstein*, details a moment shortly after Victor Frankenstein realizes his hopes and dreams of creating life. However, the moment is not the triumph he expected. Shelley employs the use of action-driven diction to emphasize the fear Victor feels— he "started" from his sleep, his teeth "chattered," and his body "convulsed." These words connote the violent movement in Victor's body, which emphasizes his state of panic, while "rushed" and "walking up and down," highlight the urgency with which he responds to the sight of the monster. Interestingly, the creature is much more still. His eyes are "fixed" and his hand "stretched." These juxtaposing descriptions between panic and stillness call into question which of the two men is the most rational. One might expect the doctor to have more control over his behavior, but instead, it is the monster that does, which makes Frankenstein's descriptions of his creation seem that much more cruel and ironic. The images used to describe the monster—"wretch," "monster," and "demonical corpse"—all serve to dehumanize Victor's creation. The word "wretch" can be used to describe animals, birds, or insects, while the term "monster" connotes a creature that is malformed and frightening.

Victor then goes on to assert that his creation is both evil and lifeless. Essentially, Victor is establishing the monster as **"Other,"** and he wavers between referring to his creation as "it" and "him," thereby emphasizing its place as a **hybrid**: both human and non-human. Victor describes the sounds the monster utters as "inarticulate," further aligning the creature as non-human due to his inability to speak. However, by examining the creature's behavior—the sounds it makes and the way in which it reaches for Victor, smiling at him—one could interpret that behavior as infant-like. In such a reading, here is no monster, but a baby, who has happily recognized his father and wants to be with him. Shelley seems in this moment to render the creature as a sympathetic figure, while Victor comes across as irrational and unkind. The juxtaposition of behavior and response in these initial interactions raises questions about Victor's character, leaving the reader to wonder just exactly who the real monster is in this scene.

This short close reading shows how Mary Shelley almost invisibly uses language to support and enhance her characterization and plot, so that the reader is swept along in the story without being aware of how deeply ingrained the language is within this novel's characters and narrative. Only when we pause to really consider the word choice and arrangement do we see the complex and sophisticated nuances of this literary work. If we focused this carefully on every word on every page of a text, it might take us years to read a single novel; however, by doing this work with short passages we can get a sense of the author's craft and artistry, as well as uncover layers of textual and meta-textual meaning created through language. Such close reading can be performed on a passage of any long prose text, whether fiction, as we have seen, or nonfiction, to which we now turn.

NONFICTION

Key Terms

- **nonfiction**
- **creative nonfiction**

Nonfiction is prose based on real facts and information. The author believes his or her story to be factual and tries to represent it as such. Nonfiction narratives are not restricted to prose alone. For instance, the inclusion of photographs, letters, and other memorabilia can aid authors in recreating an accurate story. There are many kinds of nonfiction texts—essays, journals, textbooks, and historical documents, for example. However, this section will focus on those factual texts that fall into the category of long prose. Though informational nonfiction texts, such as technical manuals and blueprints, require clarity and simplicity, many authors of longer prose, such as biography and memoir, incorporate literary devices in constructing their narratives. Sometimes these kinds of works are referred to as **creative nonfiction**, meaning that authors use the techniques of fiction writers in order to present factual occurrences in captivating and dramatic ways. Creative, in the sense of nonfiction, does not mean making up events or characters; instead, it simply allows an author to tell a factual story in a way that might read like fiction. Just as with fiction, there are many types of nonfiction, and below you will find explanations for some of the most common kinds of nonfiction you might be assigned to read for this class.

COMMON NONFICTION TYPES

Key Terms

- **autobiography**
- **biography**
- **memoir**
- **nonfiction novel**

Autobiography. An autobiography is the story of one's own life. Though diaries, journals, and letters are autobiographical, they differ from what is classified as an autobiography because autobiographies are "organized narratives prepared for the public eye" (Harmon and Holman 49). An autobiography places some emphasis on self-examination since it is meant to recount the author's entire life. Benjamin Franklin's *Autobiography* (1791) is an example of this form.

Biography. Biography is the story of the life of someone other than the author of the biographical text. Biography may be defined as "the accurate presentation of the life history from birth to death of an individual, along with an effort to interpret the life so as to offer a unified impression of the subject" (Harmon and Holman 62). Modern biographers focus on objectivity, claiming that they deal in "*fact,* not fiction" (Childs and Fowler 22). James Boswell's *Life of Johnson* (1791) is an exemplar of biography.

Memoir. This is a form written in first person and similar to autobiography. Memoirs usually deal with the "recollections of one who has been a part of or has witnessed significant events" (Harmon and Holman 318). Memoirs differ from an autobiography, in that autobiographies tend to stress the "inner and private life of its subject," while memoir is concerned with personalities and actions outside just the author of the work (Harmon and Holman 318). For example, a memoir might be concerned with a relatively short period of time in the author's life, and the author's recounting of that span of time might be focused on certain themes or circumstances. Unlike an autobiography, which covers an entire life, a memoir centers on important moments or turning points in the author's life. Maya Angelou's *I Know Why the Caged Bird Sings* (1969) is an example of a memoir.

Nonfiction Novel. In a nonfiction novel, readers will find actual events and real people presented in a novel-length narrative, using many of the techniques of fiction, such as flashbacks. This kind of narrative represents the basic facts and characters in an accurate manner, but both are presented stylistically like fiction. For example, the reader might have access to the inner states of mind of the people in the story, something not usually offered in historical writing. A nonfiction novel differs from a historical novel in its attention to accuracy. While the historical novelist might realistically and factually recreate a time period, many of the characters are invented or fictionalized, whereas the nonfiction novel focuses on actual people and what really happened to them. For example, Truman Capote's *In Cold Blood* (1965) was written after Capote spent years researching the Clutter family murders and had spent time interviewing the actual people involved in the event.

CLOSE READING LONG PROSE NONFICTION

Because you are taking an introductory literature course, chances are that if your instructor has you do a close reading of a nonfiction text, s/he wants you to read it for literary elements, as well. That means that your approach to nonfiction close reading will not really differ from the approach you would take to analyzing other long prose. If you need a reminder of what to look for, glance back at the suggestions for close reading on page 72. I have provided here a short sample of a close reading of a passage taken from Maya Angelou's memoir, *I Know Why the Caged Bird Sings* (1969). Notice how both the fiction and nonfiction close readings analyze a passage in similar ways, paying attention to how the words and sentences create a larger meaning within the text.

Sample Passage for Close Reading

Try your hand at close reading this passage before looking to the sample analysis. Read the passage from *I Know Why the Caged Bird Sings* more than once, annotate it as you go, and do your best to formulate a close reading for the excerpt below:

> [Bailey and I] reached the white part of town [...] We were explorers walking without weapons into man-eating animals' territory. In Stamps the segregation was so complete that most Black children didn't really, absolutely know what whites looked like. Other than that they were different, to be dreaded, and in that dread was included the hostility of the powerless against the powerful, the poor against the rich, the worker against the worked for and the ragged against the well-dressed. (25)

Now that you have spent some time practicing how to analyze this passage, read the following sample response. Similar to close reading fictional long prose, there is not just one correct way to interpret Angelou's passage. After you read the sample analysis, compare it to your own. What did you miss? What did you notice that the sample passage missed? Consider how you might conduct future close readings based on these observations—every time you conduct a close reading, you will find that you notice more—and more interesting—details.

Possible Close Reading Analysis

This passage, taken from Chapter Four of Maya Angelou's 1969 memoir *I Know Why the Caged Bird Sings*, describes Maya's and her brother's trip into the area where white people live in Stamps, Arkansas. When Maya notes that she and her brother "reached the white part of town," the reader's attention is drawn to the division created by segregation. It is as though the two siblings have crossed over an imaginary boundary into a foreign land. When Maya refers to herself as an "explorer," she further emphasizes how foreign the white area of town feels. Being an explorer connotes a sense of discovery or investigation into that which is unknown, and yet Maya recounts her and Bailey's complete vulnerability in the face of this exploration. Metaphorically, Maya refers to white people as "man-eating animals," signifying the danger and destruction with which she associates white people. Their behavior does not seem human to her, and though she is not certain what a white person looks like, she knows they are to be feared.

Following this description of her and Bailey's passage into unsafe territory, Maya uses a loose sentence, in that she elaborates on the main idea ("They were different") with several additional modifying clauses. This syntax makes Maya's tone seem more conversational, but it also adds emphasis to the fact that the segregation in Stamps is a division that is larger than just where each race lives. White people are described as "powerful," "rich," "the employer," and "the well-dressed," while black people are described as "powerless," "poor," "worker[s]," and "ragged." By juxtaposing and balancing these terms through parallel structure, Maya is able to give equal weight to both sides of each clause, while also emphasizing the system of oppression that has resulted due to segregation. The dread Maya feels in this moment is grounded in her marginalization; however, it also stems from the "hostility" she associates with the division between black people and white people, for they are "against" one another. Overall, this passage illustrates that segregation is not just physical separation; segregation reinforces the racial separation already in place, leading to a rigid hierarchy within Stamps.

CONCLUSION

While no single chapter can cover everything, hopefully after reading this chapter in conjunction with your professor's instruction you feel more confident going into the study of works of long prose. In this chapter you have learned some strategies for how to approach a work of long prose, some of the major forms and genres associated with this type of literature, and a few ways to conduct a close reading of a passage from long prose. Going forward, you'll want to use this knowledge to engage with the works of long prose assigned in your literature courses in a more active and meaningful way.

Questions to Consider

1. What genre is the most recent long prose you read? How do you know? List the particular characteristics of that genre that you associate with this text. Are

there any characteristics with that genre that are not present in the text? What are they? Does this challenge your idea about the text's genre? Why or why not?

2. Think of a *bildüngsroman*, and select a defining moment in the text that you consider to be an important aspect of the protagonist's growth. Why is that moment so crucial?

3. What literary elements can you find in a nonfiction text? How do those elements enhance or detract from the narrative?

Essay Prompts

1. Choosing a long prose text, or using one you were assigned by your instructor, consider moments in which a character or person has to contend with his or her past. How does the past influence who that character is? How does contending with the past relate to larger themes within the work?

2. Analyze power struggles within a long prose text either chosen by you or assigned by your instructor. Who has power, and who struggles to attain power? How do these power struggles relate to a character's conflicts or development? (You may wish to consult Brian Butler's chapter on Postcolonialism in completing this question.)

Works Cited

Angelou, Maya. *I Know Why the Caged Bird Sings.* New York: Ballantine Books, 1997. Print.

Childs, Peter, and Roger Fowler. *The Routledge Dictionary of Literary Terms.* New York: Routledge, 2006. Print.

Harmon, William and Hugh Holman, eds. *A Handbook to Literature.* Tenth Edition. New Jersey: Pearson Education, Inc., 2006. Print.

Kennedy, X.J., Dana Gioia, and Mark Bauerlein, eds. *Handbook of Literary Terms: Literature, Language, Theory.* Second Edition. New York: Pearson Longman, 2009. Print.

Shelley, Mary. *Frankenstein: The 1818 Text.* New York: W.W. Norton & Company, 1996. Print.

Turco, Lewis. *The Book of Literary Terms: The Genres of Fiction, Drama, Nonfiction, Literary Criticism, and Scholarship.* Hanover: University Press of New England, 1999. Print.

II. Literary Elements

Plot

April Williams

INTRODUCTION

Key Terms

- **story**
- **backstory**
- **plot**
- **conflict**
- **cause-and-effect**
- **narrative arc**

- **exposition**
- **rising action**
- **climax**
- **falling action**
- **denouement**
- **resolution**

When we read a piece of literature for the first time—a novel, short story, narrative poem, play, or memoir, for example—we almost always read first and foremost for plot. In other words, we just try to figure out *what happens* with the story. While it may seem like "plot" and "story" are interchangeable, these terms mean slightly different things to people who write and study literature.

Story is everything that happens to characters, whether we as readers "see" it happening on the page or not. Events from a character's past, a family history, gaps that we have to fill in on our own using our imaginations—these are all parts of the story, or the full sequence of events that affect the lives of the characters. You may, for example, have heard the term **backstory** used to refer to events and situations that occurred prior to the beginning of a work of fiction. Similarly, the story also continues beyond the plot as, for instance, in a fairy tale when "they all lived happily ever after."

Plot, on the other hand, refers to the events that the author chooses to show us. A book composed of every little thing that happens to its characters would be boring (and long!) so the author makes important choices about which scenes s/he will show us and how best to arrange those scenes to achieve a desired effect, whether it is to keep us in suspense, surprise us, make us feel happy or relieved, or something else entirely. To be more specific, **plot**, then, is the deliberate and selective sequence of events that trace a character's struggle with a conflict or problem. The **conflict** of a plot can come in many different forms: one character struggling against another, one character struggling against a group or society, a character battling against nature, or even a character experiencing an internal conflict, a struggle with him- or herself. It is through the interrelated scenes of a plot that we understand how these different kinds of struggles unfold. These scenes or events are connected by **cause-and-effect**—something happens, which leads to something else happening, then something else happens in response, until eventually something happens that changes things in an inalterable way and the conflict is resolved.

We often imagine this common pattern of plot development as a kind of mountain shape or bell curve—called a **narrative arc**—that involves five related stages: exposition, rising action, climax, falling action, and resolution. Occasionally, a plot line might deviate from this pattern; however, the conventional narrative arc is a helpful way to start thinking about plot structure.

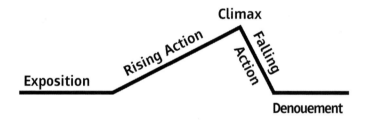

The **exposition** of a plot first introduces the character's problem or conflict to the reader. It lays the groundwork for the rest of the action. The next stage, the **rising action**, usually makes up the majority of the plot. It reveals how the character struggles with the problem. The rising action builds up to the plot's **climax**, which is the turning point in the action. While we often think of the climax as being the most dramatic or exciting part of the plot, a more useful way to think of it is the point when a character makes a decision or takes an action that cannot be reversed and therefore inevitably leads to the conclusion or resolution of the problem. (You can see here how the interrelatedness of the different stages is so important. It is easier to go back and identify the climax once you know the resolution.) The **falling action** is often a shorter stage in the plot. It includes the various events and actions that occur immediately after the climax and that lead up to the **denouement**, or **resolution**, or the point in the plot when the problem is resolved—for better or for worse—and the plot's "loose ends" are tied up. To see how these terms traditionally apply to an actual text, take a look at the table below that briefly outlines the basic plot structure of Shakespeare's play *Romeo and Juliet*.

The Basic Plot of William Shakespeare's *Romeo and Juliet* (1597)		
Exposition	establishes the problem	A street fight in Verona reveals the feud between the Capulet and Montague families.
Rising action	the main part of the story—the character struggles with the problem	Romeo (a Montague) and Juliet (a Capulet) meet, fall in love, and secretly marry. Romeo is banished from Verona for killing a Capulet out of revenge for his friend's death. Juliet drinks a potion to fake her own death so that she and Romeo can run away together. The news of her plan fails to reach Romeo and he thinks that she is dead.
Climax	the turning point in the story—the character makes a decision or takes an action that brings about a resolution to the problem	Grief-stricken, Romeo goes to Juliet's tomb and drinks poison. Juliet wakes up as Romeo dies. Juliet stabs herself with Romeo's dagger.
Falling action	events that follow the climax and lead up to the resolution (i.e., the effects of the climax)	The parents of Romeo and Juliet discover the bodies and learn of their tragic story.
Resolution	solves the problem and ties up the loose ends	The Capulets and Montagues agree to make peace and end their feud.

So, why is it important to think about plot not just as *what happens* but also as the careful arrangement of events that are intricately related and that move a character toward the resolution of a problem? It is important because when we reflect on the plot arrangement of a narrative text, it helps us have a clearer, more integrated understanding of other important elements of the text, things like character, motivation, and theme. In the example of *Romeo and Juliet*, when we consider its plot structure, we come to see that this play is not simply the sad love story of two young people, but also a larger thematic statement about how tragedy and loss inevitably follow our human desire for revenge. Plot, therefore, is not only the first thing we read for, but also one of the most important things, because of its profound influence on every element in the text.

Questions to Consider

1. What is the difference between plot and story? How might understanding this difference affect the reader's experience with a text?

2. Choosing a story or play (or using one that has been selected for you by your instructor), draw a plot line and label it with the parts of the story that you feel correspond to each of the elements of a plot.

3. Using your plot line from question 2, consider how these plot elements relate to one or two other literary elements in the story, such as character and theme. How does understanding the author's choices in plot help you better understand character motivation or the theme of the text?

4. Have you ever read a text that did not seem to follow the traditional narrative arc? What kind of picture (circle, cube, butterfly, or something completely different) would best describe the plot structure? Draw this nontraditional plot line and support your argument by labeling the parts of the story that you feel correspond to each element in the plot.

Essay Prompt

Using your responses from questions 2 and 3 above, and choosing appropriate quotations from the text to support your claims, write a brief essay (2–3 pages) that presents your findings for how plot structure and other literary elements work together to help the reader achieve a deeper understanding of character or theme.

Works Cited

Shakespeare, William. *Romeo and Juliet*. Ed. René Weis. London: Arden, 2012. Print.

Character

Kristine Lee

INTRODUCTION

Characters are the players in a story, play, or poem. The presence of these characters helps to shape the story, and should be considered as we interpret, or work to understand, a text. Character is established not just by the words used to describe actions, mannerisms, gestures, or appearance, but also by interactions with other characters and their choices. Often, character is initially established and is later developed by more details, such as dialogue, actions, or reactions, throughout a work. As readers, our interactions with characters bring us into the action of literature. By examining common character types in literature, the relationships and interactions in the text become more complex, and our analysis and understanding as readers becomes more layered.

CHARACTER TYPES

Key Terms

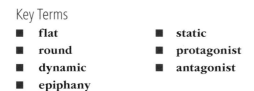

- **flat**
- **round**
- **dynamic**
- **epiphany**
- **static**
- **protagonist**
- **antagonist**

Flat characters may only be identified by a few telling traits, but despite this lack of complexity, a flat character can still influence the action of a story. The motivations and emotions that drive flat characters are largely unknown, and these kinds of characters are typically not the major focus of a work. In F. Scott Fitzgerald's *The Great Gatsby* (1925), Mr. Wolfsheim is characterized by his shady reputation, but his presence in the novel reveals the beginnings of Gatsby's ascension from a lower place in society. As a flat character Wolfsheim remains largely mysterious; Fitzgerald does not provide detailed insights into his inner workings or emotional state. While readers get a glimpse into the relationship between Gatsby and Wolfsheim, which eventually propelled Gatsby into his façade, details about Wolfsheim and even his history with Jay Gatsby remain concealed.

A **round character** can clearly be identified when a text outlines the inner workings of a character, such as her desires, motivations, and emotions. Additionally, round characters are frequently more fully developed through how they are described, the dialogue they use, and their involved responses to a conflict or event in the text. Continuing with characters from *The Great Gatsby*, unlike Mr. Wolfsheim, Nick Carraway is a fully developed, complex character, defined by his patient fascination with Gatsby.

From the beginning of the novel, readers can perceive from the text that Nick is looking for change, adventure, and escape from the dullness of life. For example, when he reflects on his experience at a party with Daisy, Catherine, and Tom, the reader gets an internal view of his thoughts: "I was within and without, simultaneously enchanted and repelled by the inexhaustible variety of life" (Fitzgerald 35). Such access to Nick's internality establishes him as a round character.

Dynamic characters are commonly the essence of a literary work; the major changes they undergo make them dynamic. Often as a result of a conflict, dynamic characters have a significant **epiphany**, or sudden moment of insight or comprehension. This "a-ha!" moment can dramatically alter how these characters perceive themselves or others. In Harper Lee's *To Kill a Mockingbird* (1960), an initially young and inexperienced Scout is dynamic due to her realization by the end of the novel that to truly understand another person, one must empathize with them and be open to their perspective.

By the end of a literary work, **static characters** have either undergone slight changes or have not changed or developed at all. Static characters generally stay in their comfort zones; they tend to revert back to their original mode of being when faced with an opportunity to make significant changes to either their perceptions or actions. Daisy, from F. Scott Fitzgerald's *The Great Gatsby*, is a perfect example of this kind of character. She remains just as shallow and careless at the end of the novel as she was at the beginning, running away with her husband instead of attending Gatsby's funeral.

The main character of a poem, play, novel, or other literary narrative is the **protagonist**. Throughout a text, this character is central to ongoing action, undergoes significant changes, and is frequently associated with a specific idea. For example, Hamlet, the protagonist of Shakespeare's play *Hamlet* (1603), is introspective and skeptical, but he also sometimes acts without forethought. Hamlet's central position throughout the play is evident in the placement of his soliloquies and the conversations other characters have about him.

An **antagonist** is an adversary of the protagonist in a text. While antagonists are also central to the text, they may require additional examination in regard to their motivations. Antagonists generally oppose the protagonist in fundamental ways that create conflict and opposition. In Shakespeare's *Hamlet* (1603), Hamlet's uncle, King Claudius of Denmark, is the antagonist. His desire for power and calculated maneuvers to gain authority contrasts with Hamlet's internality and problematic relationship to power.

While each of these kinds of characters—round, flat, dynamic, static, protagonist, and antagonist—can be found in a text, they may also occasionally overlap. At times, it may prove challenging to place a character in one of these specific categories, due to ambiguities surrounding the character's position. For example, it is evident that Hamlet is a round and dynamic character, since his soliloquies identify his inner motivations and he undergoes major changes throughout the play. The identification of a character therefore largely depends on the evidence provided in the text, and readers should be aware that characters may fit into more than one category.

COMMON CHARACTER ARCHETYPES

Key Terms

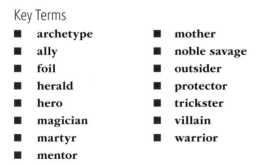

- archetype
- ally
- foil
- herald
- hero
- magician
- martyr
- mentor
- mother
- noble savage
- outsider
- protector
- trickster
- villain
- warrior

As you read, it is useful to identify common character **archetypes**, or specific kinds of characters. Archetypes are universally recognized figures, like a "damsel in distress," and like character types, archetypes may overlap. The following examples are major archetypes you may encounter. Being familiar with these archetypes and how they function in a text will be helpful as you continue to read closely throughout the term.

Allies generally fulfill a support role for the hero, or protagonist, of a text. They often guide the main character and serve as a sounding board or companion as they face obstacles. Athena is depicted as an ally to Odysseus; she offers him guidance and advocates on his behalf throughout *The Odyssey*.

Generally, a **foil** will contrast the qualities of the protagonist of a piece, putting their differences on display to further illuminate some aspect of the protagonist. In Shakespeare's *Hamlet*, King Claudius is the foil to Hamlet, since he is often driven by his desire for power, while Hamlet introspectively ponders his position and the loss of his father.

Heralds often have a relationship to the hero, in that they typically call the hero to action or indicate major changes that will happen in the text. Medon serves as a Herald to Odysseus in Homer's *The Odyssey*, and tries to guide him and defend his actions.

Heroes often endure great challenges to overcome their personal and societal circumstances. Hero figures are destined for greatness, despite the obstacles they face. Odysseus, from Homer's *The Odyssey* (c. 9th century BCE), demonstrates his role as hero with his physical prowess and perseverance against all obstacles, successfully achieving his goal of returning to his family.

The **magician** archetype uses the forces of the physical, and at times, the spiritual world to enact change or resolve conflicts. Prospero, the magician from Shakespeare's *The Tempest* (1611), is a significant example of the magician archetype. He complicates the archetype though, as he uses his sorcery as means of protection and also control.

Martyr: This character is primarily associated with sacrifice, often willingly making a sacrifice for the greater good of the community or the hero of a text. In Harper Lee's *To Kill a Mockingbird* (1960), Atticus Finch sacrifices his reputation and risks his safety in order to defend an innocent man.

A **mentor** is an advisor or teacher that provides guidance to the main character throughout a text. In Harper Lee's *To Kill a Mockingbird* (1960), Atticus Finch is a mentor to his daughter Scout, and his actions and advice eventually lead to major changes for her.

Mother figures provide nurturing, physically, emotionally, and spiritually. They can also be considered teachers or mentors. In Amy Tan's novel *The Joy Luck Club*

(1989), the mother figures nurture and guide their daughters through a variety of life challenges, including growing up.

The **noble savage** in literature is characterized by a lack of corruption from societal forces and intrinsic virtue. Considered to be uncivilized by common standards, these characters can complicate ideas of being "properly civilized." Mowgli, from Rudyard Kipling's *The Jungle Book* (1894), is considered a noble savage figure, coming to live in a human community after having spent much of his life in the jungle.

Outsiders are often marginalized; they operate outside of society within a text. The Creature in Mary Shelley's *Frankenstein* (1818) embodies the outsider archetype, since he is not accepted by anyone in society, including his creator, Victor Frankenstein.

Characters that are perceived as **protectors** support others in some capacity, whether through caregiving or helping others throughout a text. In Fitzgerald's *The Great Gatsby*, Nick Carraway serves as protector for Jay Gatsby, and in some ways, for Daisy, throughout the novel.

Often associated with mischief, a **trickster** goes against the expectations of others and sometimes breaks the rules to create conflict in a text. These kinds of characters also frequently provide a comic tone. Puck, the trickster figure in Shakespeare's *A Midsummer Night's Dream* (1605), complicates the action of the text by subverting and altering Oberon's expectations for him.

Considered representations of evil, **villains** provide contrast to the protagonist of a text. For example, in Washington Irving's "The Legend of Sleepy Hollow" (1820), the Headless Horseman is the villain of the text. Although he is largely ambiguous, his actions prove him to be the villain.

The **warrior** archetype can clearly be seen as defenders of justice and figures of morality. They are characterized by their determination to achieve their goal, despite unfavorable obstacles. Nestor, in *The Odyssey* (1725), serves as a warrior figure, although a more minor one than Odysseus, due to his efforts fighting in the Trojan war, and his subsequent determination to maintain justice and power.

While this may seem like an extensive list of archetypes, there are many more that can be found. As a reader, you have the agency to identify character archetypes, and you can also explore how characters sometimes subvert the expectations placed on them in these specific roles. Identifying archetypes and examining character roles will provide you with a deeper understanding of the motivation behind a character's actions, as well as his relationships to other characters in the text.

Questions to Consider

1. What makes a character dynamic? Think of a character in a recent piece of literature you have read. What major changes has s/he undergone? How has s/he developed or grown throughout the action of the piece?

2. How do flat and round characters differ from one another? How do they serve to complement or contrast one another in a recent work you have read?

3. Either by yourself or with a group, in one or more of the texts you are reading, identify: 1) a character that is round *and* static, and then 2) a character that is round *and* dynamic. Once you have identified these characters, write two paragraphs (one for each character) using evidence—such as actions, dialogue, imagery, or symbols—and analysis to defend your claims.

Essay Prompt

Identify the protagonist and antagonist in a major work assigned in your class. What evidence from the text identifies these characters as the protagonist and the antagonist? How are their traits at odds with one another? What problems are presented by their conflicted roles in the text?

Works Cited

Fitzgerald, F. Scott. *The Great Gatsby*. New York: Scribner, 2004. Print.

Homer. *The Odyssey*. New York: Penguin Classics, 1997. Print.

Lee, Harper. *To Kill a Mockingbird*. New York: HarperCollins, 2002. Print.

Irving, Washington. "The Legend of Sleepy Hollow." *The Legend of Sleepy Hollow and Other Stories*. New York: Dover Publications, 2008. Print.

Kipling, Rudyard. *The Jungle Book*. New York: CreateSpace Independent Publishing Platform, 2014. Print.

Shakespeare, William. "A Midsummer Night's Dream." *The Riverside Shakespeare*. Boston: Houghton Mifflin Company, 1997. 251–283. Print.

Shakespeare, William. "Hamlet." *The Riverside Shakespeare*. Boston: Houghton Mifflin Company, 1997. 1183–1245. Print.

Shakespeare, William. "The Tempest." *The Riverside Shakespeare*. Boston: Houghton Mifflin Company, 1997. 1656–1688. Print.

Shelley, Mary. *Frankenstein*. Boston: Bedford/St. Martin's, 2000. Print.

Tan, Amy. *The Joy Luck Club*. New York: Penguin Books, 1989. Print.

Theme

Kristine Lee

INTRODUCTION

Key Terms

- **interpretations**
- **theme**
- **repeated idea**
- **major theme**
- **motif**
- **minor theme**
- **evidence**

Reading literature is reading life. When we encounter a text, our personal experiences lead us as readers to make connections and **interpretations** that help us relate to and analyze a work. As readers, we interpret a text to find meaning, and one method we can use to discern meaning is to locate a **theme or themes**. Whether in prose, poetry, or drama, a theme is a major idea that is repeated or emphasized throughout a literary text. Interpreting theme requires close reading. Noticing a prominent or **repeated idea** is the first step to locating a textual theme. If the entirety of a work revolves around one central issue, that is a **major theme**, or **motif**. Throughout a text, you may also notice relevant ideas that may only be briefly mentioned, which would constitute **minor themes**.

We have the agency as readers to find themes and recognize *why* they are significant using **evidence** and interpretation. To locate evidence of the presence of a theme in a work of literature, look for details or examples that support the theme you have chosen to explore. Such examples and details can be found in a text's setting, the plot, dialogue, character, and even diction. It is common for readers to use themes as a means of accessing texts and developing arguments about what those texts might mean—in other words, as the basis for an interpretive argument about the ideas that a text is trying to convey.

This chapter first presents a brief examination of some of the most commonly seen themes in literature, and then provides questions geared towards helping you put this knowledge to practical use in reading for your literature course.

COMMON THEMES

Key Terms

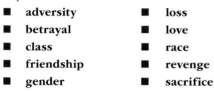

- **adversity**
- **betrayal**
- **class**
- **friendship**
- **gender**
- **loss**
- **love**
- **race**
- **revenge**
- **sacrifice**

As readers, we are usually interested in themes that center on definitive turning points in life and situations that we relate to through our own individual experiences. While there are several major themes that frequently recur across literary genres and in all human cultures, here are a few of the most familiar of those themes, each coupled with an example of how it appears in a canonical text, to get you started thinking about how theme is used in literary works such as those you may be asked to read for class.

Adversity is a universal theme frequently associated with characters that overcome obstacles. Such obstacles can encompass a variety of experiences, including physical triumphs (like completing a marathon), to personal fears (like that of failure), societal barriers (like discrimination and poverty), or personal circumstances (like abuse and immediate environment). Alice Walker's *The Color Purple* (1982) follows a main character, Celie, who proves that adversity can be overcome. After enduring rape, abuse, poverty, and loss, Celie emerges from her circumstances to make a beautiful life for herself on her own terms. By the end of the novel, she has become self-sufficient and independent, feeling younger due to her renewed sense of hope: "We all have to start somewhere if us want to do better, and out of self is what us have to hand" (Walker 12). The message conveyed through Celie's response to adversity is that the determination to live will eventually result in independence, and while this effort may start out small, it will grow.

Betrayal can take a variety of forms as a theme—betrayal that occurs between one character and another, a character and him/herself, or the betrayal of an ideal, such as loyalty or perfection. In Arthur Miller's play *Death of a Salesman* (1949), the main character, Willy Loman, lives in a fantasy world that eventually motivates him to betray his family. As a traveling salesman, Willy has never been happy with his life, and as a result of his own disappointment, he has high expectations that his sons will become successful in the business world, where he could not. When Willy loses his job, he commits suicide in hopes that his son will use the life insurance money for business pursuits. The theme of betrayal is present throughout the play and serves to destroy relationships between the characters. For example, it is evident that Willy's son Biff always tries to live up to his father's dreams for him, and he honestly tries to tell his father that he has failed math. Ironically, when he goes to confess this failure, he discovers his father's affair instead. At this point in the play, betrayal places these two characters in opposition: Biff, who is willing to admit to his failures, and Willy, who cannot admit to his betrayal. Rather, in terms of the affair Willy tells Biff, "You mustn't—you mustn't overemphasize a thing like this" (2.1.1895). As Willy's actions come to light, betrayal, and the detrimental effects it has on his family, prove that he is tragically unfulfilled as an individual. In this example and throughout the play, the theme of betrayal affects every character, resulting in a devastating loss of stability for their relationships.

As a theme, **class** examines the systems of division based on social and economic status or reputation. The context of when a piece is written or published can be a major factor to consider when examining the theme of class. In the Victorian period in England (1837–1901), class divides were a prominent feature of the culture. Stark contrasts between economic groups existed and, as a result, class issues are often a theme in the popular literature of the era. As a leading writer of the time, Charles Dickens revolutionized Victorian literature by including the voices of the working class. While working-class figures are mostly caricatured in his works, his novel *Oliver Twist* (1838) examines the life of the orphan Oliver in a way that brings the plight of the lower class to light. From his birth, Oliver is marked as a figure of the lower class:

> Wrapped in the blanket which had hitherto formed his only covering, he might have been the child of a nobleman or a beggar; it would have been hard for the haughtiest stranger to have assigned him his proper station in society. But now that he was enveloped in the old calico robes which had grown yellow in the same service, he had been badged and ticketed, and fell into his place at once—a parish child—the orphan of a workhouse—the humble half-starved drudge—to be cuffed and buffeted through the world—despised by all, and pitied by none. (Dickens 3)

In this case, Oliver's class is revealed through the very material in which his infant form is wrapped, but Dickens questions such conventional ideas of class labeling by the narrator's statement that Oliver could have just as easily have been wrapped in the clothing of higher classes: "...he might have been the child of a nobleman..." (Dickens 3). Dickens uses Oliver's experiences throughout the novel to challenge Victorian conventions of social mobility. By incorporating the theme of class, Dickens also challenges the reader of his novels to consider how superficial ideas of societal hierarchies can be, sometimes established and upheld simply through one's clothing.

The **friendship** between Nick Carraway and Jay Gatsby provides a strong theme for F. Scott Fitzgerald's *The Great Gatsby* (1925). By the end of the novel, it is clear that while Nick and Gatsby never shared a conventional friendship, Nick feels the need to honor his memory by finding attendants for Gatsby's funeral: "I found myself on Gatsby's side, and alone...I began to have a feeling of defiance, of scornful solidarity between Gatsby and me against them all" (Fitzgerald 164–165). When Gatsby throws his lavish parties, appearances seem to establish that he has an array of friends who come to revel in his celebrations of spectacle, but in the end, only Nick is invested enough in Gatsby personally to look deeper and recognize his loss. The friendship that grows between Nick and Gatsby, while sometimes steeped in tension, is a consistent theme throughout the novel.

Viewed as a literary theme, **gender** generally addresses societal stereotypes, particularly with regard to ideas of femininity and masculinity. Gender factors into the punishment and ostracization of Hester Prynne in Hawthorne's *The Scarlet Letter* (1850). Because of the expectations placed on women's sexuality in the Puritan community of the novel, with her husband lost at sea Hester is considered impure following the birth of her illegitimate daughter. She is forced to wear a scarlet "A" on her dress to let the world know about her sin in committing adultery. Since the expectation for women in this community and time period was sexual purity, a pregnancy occurring while her husband is away results in Hester's experience of public scorn, humiliation, and isolation from the community, even as no one asks the identity of the father or seeks his punishment for participating in the union that led to the child's birth. Hawthorne thus reveals the prejudices of the townsfolk, and also the separated existence Hester endures as a result of their hatred: "It was no great distance...from the prison-door to the market-place. Measured by the prisoner's experience, however, it might be reckoned a journey of some length...as if her heart had been flung into the street for them all to spurn..." (Hawthorne 38). In this community, Hester's gender requires her to become pregnant only while married, but since she has a child out of wedlock, she is literally marked for her "sin" and subsequently shunned. However, while Hester is expected to feel shame for her actions, she reveals herself instead to be strong, resourceful, and dignified as she raises her daughter on her own.

With Hester's experience and the strong opinions of others in consistent contrast, Hawthorne unravels expectations regarding gender.

Loss is a prevalent theme in literature, most often associated with grief following the death of a loved one. Loss serves as a primary theme throughout much of Edgar Allan Poe's work, possibly in response to his own loss of family members and spouses throughout his life. His poem, "Annabel Lee" (1849), captures the loss felt by the speaker following the death of his loved one; he finds comfort in the idea that although they endured criticism for their youth, their love was secure: "But our love it was stronger by far than the love/ Of those who were older than we" (Poe 90). Despite her death and the speaker's overwhelming sense of loss, their love overcomes even the obstacle of death. In this instance, love and loss work together as the primary themes of this poem, and the sense of loss is accentuated by the intense love described.

Love is one of the oldest and most common themes present in literature. Whether it is manifested as love lost, love conquering all, love as healing, unrequited love, or in another capacity, this theme is captivating for readers because of its universality. For example, George Gordon, Lord Byron's familiar poem "She Walks in Beauty" (1814) demonstrates the Romantic conception of love, based on appearance in the form of beauty and temperament: "She walks in Beauty, like the night/ Of cloudless climes and starry skies" (Byron 1345, 1–2). The speaker's love for a mysteriously unnamed "she" is a central theme throughout the poem, and is focused on a damsel whose innocence makes her even more appealing: "Where thoughts serenely sweet express, / How pure, how dear their dwelling place" (Byron 1345, 11–12). Lines from the poem provide evidence that love is a major theme throughout the piece.

Race becomes a literary theme when we focus on differences or disparities between ethnic groups in a text. Racial themes often intersect with issues of justice, inequality, and adversity. Race, and how it affects justice, is pivotal to Harper Lee's *To Kill a Mockingbird* (1960). When Tom Robinson, an African-American man, is accused of rape, popular lawyer Atticus Finch decides to defend him in a court of law. Set in Alabama during the Great Depression, this decision results in dangerous consequences for Atticus and his family. As racial tensions begin to interfere with the trial proceedings, order needs to be restored. As a figure entitled to represent justice, the judge acknowledges the racial prejudices present in the courtroom, but insists that these choices should not be a part of this trial:

> People generally see what they look for, and hear what they listen for, and they have the right to subject their children to it, but I can assure you of one thing: you will receive what you see and hear in silence, or you will leave

this courtroom, but you won't leave it until the whole boiling of you come before me on contempt charges. (Lee 198)

The first part of this statement from the judge echoes the results of the trial—a conviction despite the innocence of the defendant. Atticus Finch's daughter Scout, as the voice of the novel, changes her own ideas in regard to race as a result of this trial, and begins to see the prejudice that surrounds her and her family. She realizes that trying to understand other perspectives is essential: "Atticus was right. One time he said you never really know a man until you stand in his shoes and walk around in them" (Lee 321). Scout discovers that true justice can be achieved with empathy, and this discovery requires that she change her ideas about race. As a result of her experience, Scout learned to consider the humanity of those around her, rather than making a choice to automatically ascribe to the racial prejudices prevalent in her community.

The theme of **revenge** delves into the darker side of human ambition. Mary Shelley's *Frankenstein* (1818) incorporates this theme by revealing how the two main characters, the Creature and Victor, struggle with, and ultimately give in to, the temptation to exact revenge from one another. In this novel, Victor Frankenstein fashions a creature made in the image of man, but then shuns his own creation, which spurns a cycle of revenge. After Victor refuses to create a partner for him, the Creature responds:

Are you to be happy, while I grovel in the intensity of my wretchedness? You can blast my other passions; but revenge remains—revenge, henceforth dearer than light or food! I may die; but first you, my tyrant and tormentor, shall curse the sun that gazes on your misery...Man, you shall repent of the injuries you inflict. (Shelley 176)

While this marks the beginning of the Creature's endeavor to harm Victor, he had already been struggling with the idea of revenge due to his rejection from the human communities he encountered throughout the novel. For his part, Victor desires revenge for the ways in which his own creation is ruining his life. The theme of revenge therefore serves a central role in this novel from the perspective both of the Creature and the creator.

Sacrifice, specifically maternal sacrifice, is a major theme in Amy Tan's *The Joy Luck Club* (1989). In this tale of the relationships between mothers and daughters, the sacrifices of mothers to create the opportunity for a better life for their children are significant. The novel focuses on women who make sacrifices, and how they teach their daughters what sacrifices they should and should not make, based on their own experiences. One character's advice to her daughter demonstrates the prevalence of the theme: "And my mother says, 'You must think for yourself, what you must do. If someone tells you, then you are not trying.' You have to pay attention to what you have lost...You have to undo the expectation" (Tan 130–131). The daughters in the novel learn self-worth from their own experiences and those of their mothers; they learn to sacrifice in ways that aren't harmful to their own identities.

FINAL THOUGHTS

Authors use theme as an organizing principle in literary texts, and theme can be presented in straightforward fashion as a single, unifying idea, as in a short poem or story, or as a complicated web of multiple, interconnected ideas, as in a novel or other long literary work. All literary genres incorporate theme, and while identifying the central, repeating ideas of a text may be challenging at first, practice over time makes this process easier. Ultimately, recognizing and noting themes increases our understanding and appreciation of a work.

Questions to Consider

1. What is your process for locating major themes in a text? How can you locate evidence from the text to back up your claims? What kind(s) of evidence do you look for when you are trying to prove the presence of a particular theme?

2. How can theme be used to make an argument about a text? Using a text you have read recently, identify one or two of the themes and what argument or arguments they might allow you to make about the literary work.

3. What are the major themes in the literary works you enjoy reading? How are they relevant to your interpretation or enjoyment of the texts?

Essay Prompt

Choosing a text, or using one assigned to you by your instructor, identify a major theme and locate several passages in the text in which that theme is clearly present. Using these passages as a starting point, write a brief, 2–3 page essay documenting the presence of the theme and your interpretation of its importance to the text. Be sure to provide evidence from your text in each paragraph to accompany your analysis.

Works Cited

Byron, George Gordon. "She Walks in Beauty." *The Bedford Introduction to Literature*. Ed. Michael Meyer. Boston: Bedford/St. Martins, 2013. 1035. Print.

Dickens, Charles. *Oliver Twist*. Oxford: Oxford University Press, 1999. Print.

Fitzgerald, F. Scott. *The Great Gatsby*. New York: Scribner, 2004. Print.

Hawthorne, Nathaniel. *The Scarlet Letter*. Mineola: Dover, 1994. Print.

Lee, Harper. *To Kill a Mockingbird*. New York: HarperCollins, 2002. Print.

Miller, Arthur. "Death of a Salesman." *The Bedford Introduction to Literature*. Ed. Michael Meyer. Boston: Bedford/St. Martins, 2013. 1401–1466. Print.

Poe, Edgar Allen. *Annabel Lee*. New York: Barnes & Noble, Inc., 2006. Print.

Shelley, Mary. *Frankenstein*. Buffalo: Broadview, 2012. Print.

Tan, Amy. *The Joy Luck Club*. New York: Penguin, 1989. Print.

Walker, Alice. *The Color Purple*. Boston: Mariner Books, 2003. Print.

Point of View

Catherine Hawkins

INTRODUCTION

Key Terms

- **point of view**
- **narrator**

When we are reading fiction, one of the first aspects of the narrative we should consider is the **point of view**, or perspective, from which the story is told. We can determine the perspective of a literary work by first determining its **narrator**—who is telling the story. Sometimes, the narrator is the main character in the story, such as Huck in Mark Twain's *The Adventures of Huckleberry Finn;* however, at other times, the narrator tells the story from a more removed, all-knowing voice, as in many of the *Harry Potter* novels. In other narratives, the author may choose to include several points of view with certain characters narrating different sections of the story, such as in William Faulkner's *As I Lay Dying.* Determining the point of view of the narrative gives us a clearer sense of who is telling the story, and we can begin to ask more complicated questions about the narrator and her/his relationship to the story itself.

Writers often struggle to find the appropriate "point of view" to match the story they want to tell. In fact, it is quite common for a writer to draft the same story from multiple points of view before finally discovering a satisfactory entryway into the story. Why would this happen? In many ways, the point of view of a story is one of the most important structural decisions a writer can make, because the perspective from which the story is told is ultimately what determines the content—and therefore, the meaning—of the story.

IDENTIFYING POINT OF VIEW

Key Terms

- **first-person**
- **second-person**
- **third-person**
- **reliability**
- **limited perspective**

- **reliable narrator**
- **unreliable narrator**
- **third-person limited**
- **third-person omniscient**

At its simplest level, we can discover the point of view of the story by taking a close look at the narrator of the story. The first question we could ask ourselves might be, "*Who is telling this story?*" We can look for clues by paying attention to the author's use of pronouns. In a **first-person** story, the narrator tells the story from her/his perspective, using the pronouns "I" or "we." In a **second-person** story, the narrator speaks directly to the reader, using the pronoun "you." **Third-person** stories use "she," "he," or "they," and the narrator is someone that is more removed from the immediate action in the story.

To begin, let's consider the differences between these three points of view:

- I was willing to work for this relationship.

- You weren't willing to work for this relationship.

- For the first time ever, Jake spoke openly about his feelings, telling Briana over and over again that he was willing to work for the relationship with her.

As you can see, all three sentences are told from different perspectives, or points of view, and therefore, present quite different versions of the same story. The first sentence, told from the first-person, might be a line from Jake's journal or a sentence spoken in dialogue to one of Jake's friends or maybe even to Briana, herself. The second sentence, told from the second-person point of view, is a declarative statement, perhaps directed at Jake, and the third sentence, told from the third-person point of view, indicates a certain level of distance, because the narrator appears to be looking at the scene from afar, rather than directly participating in the scene itself.

All three sentences pose important questions about perspective, **reliability** (whether or not the narrator is trustworthy), and character motivation. In the following pages, let's consider the variety of ways point of view works in fiction. If we are willing to consider the complexities of an author's choice in terms of point of view and the way the point of view pushes the story forward, we will be able to more critically analyze the stories we read and to have a greater sense of the story's thematic and cultural implications.

First-Person. The first-person, "I" narrative point of view is necessarily complicated because of a certain embedded difficulty in sharing one's personal experiences. How can we write about an experience we've had both truthfully and objectively? Often, there are barriers to this form of storytelling. Imagine that your teacher wanted you to write a short personal narrative about your family, but your grandmother has recently gotten sick, and you feel uncomfortable or unprepared to write about her. In such a case, you may choose to take her presence out of your narrative completely, leaving some gaps in your story; or, you may choose to gloss over how much she means to you, telling the story in a more vague fashion. Is this wrong? Not at all, but that doesn't mean that there isn't another story underneath the one you have written on the page: in this case, perhaps, the real story is one about grief or loss.

Good fiction often has a similar layered effect, in which the story written on the page (the beginning, middle, and end) is often revealing a deeper story. In this way, it is important to pay close attention to the variety of ways in which the first person narrator may be biased. The word "bias" often has a negative connotation, but in fiction, we are simply searching for clues that can give us a fuller sense of what the narrator is and isn't telling us. In other words, we are assuming that the first-person narrator (like ourselves, when we write about our own experiences) has a **limited perspective**, simply based on the fact that the narrator is just one person in the world, probably acting out of her/his best interests. For instance, when Jake says, "I am willing to work for this relationship," we might look for clues in the story that could indicate his sincerity. Is he crying? Has he said this multiple times, so we aren't sure we believe him? How are the people around him reacting? What is he noticing about the outside world that may reflect his mood?

What the narrator isn't telling us does not necessarily reflect poorly on the narrator or on the success of the story. Rather, this complicated layering may indicate the great skill of the work of fiction. First-person narrators who speak about their own experiences, both explicitly (what they are telling us) and subconsciously (what they are leaving out), are often the most compelling characters in literature, because these narrators are likely to most truthfully mirror the human psyche, which is invariably full of complication and contradiction.

While some first-person narrators are mostly consistent when they present their story—in other words, **reliable narrators**—more often than not, because of the complexity of the human psyche, authors will create a disconnection between what the narrator tells us and how she/he acts. For instance, if you have read F.

Scott Fitzgerald's *The Great Gatsby*, you may have observed that Nick Carraway, the first-person narrator, is an example of an **unreliable narrator**, because his words often contradict his actions. For example, on the first page of the book, Nick says, "I'm inclined to reserve all judgments, a habit that has opened up many curious natures to me and also made me the victim of not a few veteran bores" (5). However, Nick's idea of himself ends up seeming false by the end of the novel because he spends the next two hundred pages judging the people around him. Ironically, even in that opening sentence, you might argue that Nick is being haughty (a form of judgment) by calling certain people "veteran bores." Yet, it is Nick's unreliability that makes him so human to us, and his judgments that help us more fully understand the characters and the problematic society around him.

Second-Person. The second-person point of view, where the narrator is the "you" in the story, is the one readers encounter least often in fiction. However, Junot Díaz, a contemporary Dominican-American writer born in 1968, frequently uses the second-person point of view. His story, "A Cheater's Guide to Love," written in 2012, opens with this statement: "Your girl catches you cheating. (Well, actually she's your fiancée, but hey, in a bit it so won't matter)."

How do you feel when you read this? In the second person, the reader is invited into the story as an active participant and must imagine herself inside the story. The repetition of "you" can create the sensation that the reader is a character in the story, perhaps even implicating the reader in the narrator's actions. In the Díaz example, you are suddenly a part of a story about infidelity. Sometimes, these stories can feel jarring or affronting, because the reader might not want to be associated with the actions or worldview of the narrator; but at other times, the second-person point of view can effectively ask the reader to consider important socio-cultural questions.

Third-Person. The third-person point of view, which is told from a more removed narrator and often uses the pronouns "she," "he," or "they," prompts the reader to ask questions about the narrator and her/his relationship to the story. For example, in *Harry Potter and the Order of the Phoenix* by J.K Rowling (2003), once Dumbledore says to Harry, "You do care," the narrator adds, "He had not flinched or made a single move to stop Harry demolishing his office. His expression was calm, almost detached" (824). Here, the third-person POV gives the reader the impression that the narrator is looking down at the scene in Dumbledore's office and describing what she/he sees, filling in details to which we otherwise might not have access.

One of the first questions to ask ourselves when we notice a third-person point of view is how closely the narrator reaches inside the heads of her/his characters.

We might ask ourselves: *How well does the narrator seem to know the characters? Does the narrator know what the characters are thinking, or is the narrator simply describing the characters' actions? How many characters does the narrator focus on?* In the case of the *Harry Potter* books, we might remember that the narrator often focuses specifically on the interior life of Harry Potter, the novel's protagonist, but also that the narrator describes the actions of multiple other characters, such as Ron, Hermione, and Dumbledore.

However, when the narrator mainly hones in on just one character (such as Harry, in the *Harry Potter* books), we call the point of view **third-person limited**. In other words, the reader is only privy to what one character is thinking about the world. At other times, the narrator switches in and out of the heads of multiple characters, and we call this point of view **third-person omniscient**. This "God-like" narration may provide the reader with more clues into the society at large. For example, the narrator in the *Prime of Miss Jean Brodie* by Muriel Spark (1961) moves deftly back and forth between multiple characters' heads. Because the novel is focused on a group of six adolescent girls and each of their relationships with their teacher Jean Brodie, the third-person omniscience creates an almost frantic effect on the reader, because the reader isn't sure which girl most accurately understands her relationship to Miss Brodie.

It can help to think of the zoom function on a camera when we consider how the third-person point of view works. Sometimes, the narrator zooms in so closely to one character that the reader only has access to the thoughts and struggles of that specific character (third-person limited). When this happens, the effect can be similar to the first-person point of view, because the reader is forced to consider the biases and limitations of this character's point of view. However, in the next scene the narrator might "zoom out" from one character and "zoom into" another character's head, which might prompt the reader to see the scene from an entirely different perspective and might raise new questions about reliability.

NARRATIVE TONE

Key Terms
- **tone**
- **attitude**

Another important aspect of third-person narration is the narrator's **tone** or **attitude** towards her/his characters. Questions about tone are wrapped up in questions about who the narrator actually is, and it may be helpful at this juncture to think about the narrator as just another character in the story. We may consider asking the same questions of the narrator as we'd ask of the other characters: *What is the narrator's relationship to the other characters? What is her/his gender and racial identity? What is her/his age?* After we've made our best guesses about the narrator, we might then consider her/his attitude towards the characters she writes about. Is the narrator condescending or mocking towards the characters? Or is the narrator compassionate and forgiving of them, even when they make mistakes?

In the earlier example of third-person POV—"For the first time ever, Jake spoke openly about his feelings, telling Briana over and over again that he was will-ing to work for the relationship"—we might look for clues about the narrator's relationship to Jake and Briana. For one, the narrator clearly knows a fair amount about Jake, if s/he is able to say that this is the first time Jake has spoken openly about his feelings. However, the use of the word "ever" might come across as slightly judgmental, because the narrator might be criticizing Jake's inability to open up. As we discussed in the first-person section, finding biases and/or criti-cisms of characters does not necessarily detract from the success of the narrative as a whole. In fact, these biases may create a layered effect that helps the reader more fully understand the story.

To conclude this chapter, here is a chart to help you organize how you think about an author's use of point of view and how it might affect literary analysis and interpretation:

	Pronouns	Example from Texts	Important Considerations
First-Person	I We	F. Scott Fitzgerald's *The Great Gatsby* Mark Twain's *Huckleberry Finn*	Tone Reliability Narrative distance
Second-Person	You	Junot Diaz, "A Cheater's Guide to Love"	Tone Reliability Reader's position in the story
Third-Person	She He It They	J.K Rowling, The Harry Potter series Muriel Spark, *The Prime of Miss Jean Brodie*	Tone Reliability Narrative distance Limited/Omniscient

Questions to Consider

1. How do you determine the point of view of a story?

2. What are the different kinds of point of view an author can choose from? What are some of the advantages and disadvantages of each?

3. Consider the literary works you most like to read. What point of view are they told from? How do you think this affects how you read the story?

Essay Prompt

Choosing a literary text (or using one selected by your instructor), determine the point of view of the narrative, and write an essay explaining how that point of view affects the story, taking into consideration such things as what you might or might not know as a result of the narrator or speaker's knowledge, the reliability of the narrator or speaker, and what the story might look like from someone else's point of view. Use citations from the text to support your claims.

Works Cited

Díaz, Junot. "A Cheater's Guide to Love." *This Is How You Lose Her.* New York: Riverhead, 2012. Print.

Fitzgerald, F. Scott. *The Great Gatsby.* New York: Scribner, 2004. Print.

Rowling, J.K. *Harry Potter and the Order of the Phoenix.* New York: Scholastic Inc., 2003. Print.

Style, Voice, and Tone

Courtney Hartnett

INTRODUCTION

Key Terms

- **style**
- **voice**
- **diction**
- **dialect**
- **tone**
- **mood**

What makes a piece of literature profoundly affecting or memorable? Many of us have read a poem, a piece of prose, or a play that has lingered with us long after we've turned the pages. Good writing is powerful, and in order to develop an understanding of how it works, it's necessary to look at successful pieces of literature on an elemental level. Three especially important—and interconnected—elements of literature are style, voice, and tone.

The Chicago Manual of Style defines **style** as "rules related to capitalization, spelling, hyphenation, and abbreviations; punctuation, including ellipsis points, parentheses, and quotation marks; and the way numbers are treated" (70). While you may take for granted or not assign much value to periods at the ends of sentences, punctuation can impact a piece of literature significantly. In some cases—think of Emily Dickinson's (1830–1886) ubiquitous dashes, or the sparsely punctuated sentences in much of William Faulkner's work—style can become a trademark of sorts for writers. It also can affect the way a piece is perceived: complex, multi-clause sentences will likely bring about a different response than a series of short, simple sentences.

To get a feel for how style affects how we read, let's look at the first stanza of Dickinson's poem "A *Wounded* Deer—leaps highest—" (1890):

A *Wounded* Deer—leaps highest—
I've heard the Hunter tell—
'Tis but the Ecstasy of *death*—
And then the Brake is still!

You might notice the capitalization of "wounded," "deer," "hunter," "ecstasy," and "brake." While these are not typically proper nouns or adjectives, Dickinson's capitalization of them, along with the italicizing of "wounded" and "death," highlights their centrality to the poem. Try reading the lines aloud. How do the dashes and word emphasis affect your reading?

Just as Dickinson's dashes and capitalizations create small pauses in her work, the long, almost stream-of-consciousness sentences of William Faulkner (1897–1962) create fast-flowing pieces that mirror the inner worlds of his characters. In "An Odor of Verbena" (1938), readers are offered a glimpse into the inner monologue of Bayard, the narrator:

By that time, seeing that he was going to finish it, some Northern people sold him a locomotive on credit which he named for Aunt Jenny, with a silver oil can in the cab with her name engraved on it; and last summer the first train ran into Jefferson, the engine decorated with flowers and Father in the cab blowing blast after blast on the whistle when he passed Redmond's house; and there were speeches at the station, with more flowers and a Confederate flag and girls in white dresses and red sashes and a band, and father stood on the pilot of the engine and made a direct and absolutely needless allusion to Mr. Redmond. (2087)

Note how Faulkner's use of punctuation allows for this lengthy collection of words to fit into one grammatically correct sentence.

Style helps shape the voice of a literary work. When speaking with someone, you may notice how he or she enunciates, pauses, or constructs sentences. In literature, "voice" is essentially the written analogue of the spoken voice. **Voice** refers to a literary work's narrative quality, and this can be affected by style and **diction**, or word choice. Authors may choose elevated diction, for example, to signal a level of affluence of the character, or avoid contractions (i.e., "do not" instead of "don't") to create a sense of formality.

Texts written in **dialect**, or the combination of words and pronunciations specific to a region, use a specific kind of diction to influence voice. Consider *Adventures* *of Huckleberry Finn* (1884) by Mark Twain (1835–1910). The opening line of the book establishes Huck's voice with nonstandard English: "You don't know about me, without you have read a book by the name of *The Adventures of Tom Sawyer* but that ain't no matter" (3). Huck's noticeable dialect helps to create an idea of his character and communicates the story to the reader in a way that is distinctly different from communication in non-dialect English.

The element of tone, like that of voice, can be shaped by style and diction. **Tone** refers to the overall **mood** created by a piece of literature. As you read, ask yourself what kind of emotional climate the words suggest. For instance, in the play *The Glass Menagerie* (1944) by Tennessee Williams (1911–1983), Tom Wingfield's opening monologue contributes to the play's elegiac tone by framing it as a memory play. The first few lines establish mood as Tom addresses the audience:

> Yes, I have tricks in my pocket, I have things up my sleeve. But I am the opposite of a stage magician. He gives you illusion that has the appearance of truth. I give you truth in the pleasant disguise of illusion...The play is memory. Being a memory play, it is dimly lighted, it is sentimental, it is not realistic. (Act 1, scene i)

Tom's opening words establish how the play is framed in terms of both its presentation on stage and the mood sustained throughout.

Just as dissection gives medical students a clearer idea of how the parts of the body work in concert to make up the whole, dissecting and analyzing style, voice, and tone within a text will enable you to develop a dynamic understanding of the words that drive great literature. You may even be able to learn something that will be useful in your own writing.

Questions to Consider

1. How would you describe the voice of this chapter in *Lenses*? Is the tone casual, elevated, slang, authoritarian, motivating...or can you think of another way of describing the tone? To help you get started, you may consult the box of tone words below.

elegiac	detached	elevated
casual	authoritarian	slang
disparaging	erudite	impartial

2. How would you describe your speaking voice with friends? With your professor? With a boss at your job? How does voice change in your life, and how does that correspond with the voice in a text you are currently reading?

3. Think of a particularly memorable piece of writing you've read recently—it could be a poem, a piece of fiction, a play, or a nonfiction piece. What do you remember of the piece's voice, tone, and style and how they helped make the piece effective?

4. Rewrite the first paragraph from this chapter using 1) an overly formal academic voice and then 2) a voice in the slang/dialect of where you grew up. Do the changes in diction affect the tone of the paragraph? How? How might your revision compare to another student's?

Essay Prompt

Using a text of your choice, or one that has been assigned to you by your instructor, identify the work's style and consider how the elements of voice and tone are employed by the author to create that particular style. Make sure you include specific quotes to support the argument you are making.

Works Cited

The Chicago Manual of Style. 16th ed. Chicago: U of Chicago, 2010. Print.

Dickinson, Emily. "A *Wounded* Deer— leaps highest—." *Anthology of American Literature.* Gen. ed. George McMichael. 6th ed. Vol. I: *Colonial Through Romantic.* Upper Saddle River, New Jersey: Prentice-Hall, 1997. 2143. Print.

"Emily Dickinson 1830-1886." *Anthology of American Literature.* Gen. ed. George McMichael. 6th ed. Vol. I: *Colonial Through Romantic.* Upper Saddle River, New Jersey: Prentice-Hall, 1997. 2140. Print.

Faulkner, William. "An Odor of Verbena." *Literature of the Western World.* Ed. Brian Wilkie & James Hurt. 3rd ed. Vol. II: *Neoclassicism Through the Modern Period.* New York: Macmillan, 1992. 2087. Print.

Twain, Mark. *Adventures of Huckleberry Finn.* 1884. Ed. Emory Elliott. 1999. New York: Oxford UP, 1999. *WorldCat.* Web. 16 Apr. 2014.

"William Faulkner (1897–1962)." *Literature of the Western World.* Ed. Brian Wilkie & James Hurt. 3rd ed. Vol. II: *Neoclassicism Through the Modern Period.* New York: Macmillan, 1992. 2077–79. Print.

Williams, Tennessee. *The Glass Menagerie*. 1944. BCC.edu. Burlington County College. n.d. Web. 16 Apr. 2014. http://staff.bcc.edu/faculty_websites/jalexand Williams--The_Glass_Menagerie.htm

Setting, Atmosphere, and Mood

Abigail Lee

INTRODUCTION

Key Terms

- **setting**
- **personification**
- **mood**
- **atmosphere**
- **free indirect discourse**

The **setting** of a text is the physical place in which the action of a text takes place (such as a country, city, forest, playground, or the mind, itself) as well as its time frame and cultural context—time of day, season, or historical period and culture, for instance. Without the spatial organization provided by setting, literary characters would move about in a shapeless void, blank and impenetrable. The setting of a narrative text helps us as readers by grounding the story in time and space, and adept authors can use setting to reflect their characters' minds and their novels' themes. Setting connects plot, characters, and themes to a physical time and space, creating a fictional world for us to explore.

Setting is often deployed to straightforward effect, directly reflecting the themes of a piece of writing. Visualize the industrial wasteland between West Egg and New York City, as seen in F. Scott Fitzgerald's *The Great Gatsby* (1925). Consider how Myrtle Wilson lives there among the ashes, junkyards, and the all-seeing eyes of Dr. T. J. Eckleberg. This setting clearly reflects the desperation and fear that lurks at the edges of life for West Egg dwellers. The callousness with which the socialites speed through the ravaged landscape displays their attempts to escape issues of class and their own inner conflicts. The physical setting itself— the burnt-out factories and poverty—directly reflects an inner, emotional truth located in the consciousness of the characters.

Often, through **personification**, the physical landscape will take on almost human qualities, reflecting the rhythms of a character or speaker's consciousness. Take, for example, the opening of T.S. Eliot's poem, "The Love Song of J. Alfred Prufrock" (1920): "Let us go then, you and I,/When the evening is spread out against the sky/Like a patient etherized upon a table" (ll. 1–3).[1] While an evening sunset is often compared to blazes of fire or a gentle blush, T. S. Eliot masterfully turns these usual associations on their head. He uses the setting of an operating room to evoke a strange, dangerous, and unsettling mood without resorting to describing his speaker's thoughts or feelings. From the way that the speaker describes the sunset, not as a beautiful thing, but as a "patient etherized upon the table," readers can infer that the speaker is an unhappy man.

Setting can also help to establish the mood, or atmosphere, of a literary work. Consider the following statements:

> You enter a dark wood and cower before its reaching branches.

> You walk into a bright forest and dance among the waving willow trees.

These two sentences are both located in the same kind of setting, and differ by only a few key words, but the moods evoked by each are very different. The **mood** or **atmosphere** is the emotional tone of a piece of writing created by diction, rhythm, and setting. In the short examples above, the setting of a "dark wood" creates a solemn and shadowy mood. The "bright forest" gives an entirely different feeling of safety and happiness. The word choices made in the two examples—"dance" or "cower," "reaching" or "waving"—serve to cement the mood as either forbidding or joyful. Some literary genres, such as nineteenth-century Gothic fiction, use setting to evoke a dark and foreboding atmosphere.

We cannot ignore the cultural setting of a narrative or poem. The era or time period in which the piece is set can be just as important as the physical landscape. Toni Morrison's *Beloved* (1988) is set in post-Civil War Ohio, right across the border from formerly slave-holding Kentucky. The complex social systems that govern the lives of African-Americans in this time and place are just as much a part of the setting as the tree stump that the Garner family finds Beloved sitting on, appeared out of nowhere. Beloved is a part of the past that continues to haunt the family and without the cultural setting—after the Civil War, right on the edge of freedom—the reader would not understand the ache that Beloved springs from and the rightness of her return. In this novel, the effects of slavery and the ghosts of the past are not easily shaken.

---

1 The full text of this poem is included in the Anthology on pp. 248–251.

Even in a piece of writing that takes place entirely in the mind of a speaker without descriptions of external setting, mood can be powerfully evoked by diction, rhythm, and syntax. In William Blake's "The Tyger," the speaker directly addresses a tiger, musing on the animal's meaning and significance, and ultimately asking what kind of god could have created the tiger's "fearful symmetry." Blake's poem is composed entirely of questions, which sets the mood as inquisitive and unsure, as if the reader is being presented with the speaker's unmediated thoughts. In a climax, the normal grammatical structures break down and the speaker asks, "What the hammer? what the chain?/ In what furnace was thy brain?" (ll. 13–14). The quick rhythm and abbreviated syntax reveal the speaker's desperation and intensity. Blake conveys the speaker's mood solely through rhythms of language that build and intensify, signaling the weight of the issue and the difficulty inherent in expressing such urgent and essential questions.

Gustave Flaubert's long passages of description in *Madame Bovary* are often frustrating to readers who have not yet discerned the power of setting in the novel. For example, the narrator states,

> On the horizon beyond Yonville loom the oaks of the Argueil forest and the escarpments of the bluffs of Saint-Jean, the latter streaked from top to bottom with long irregular lines of red: these are marks left by rain, and their brackish color, standing out so sharply against the gray rock of the hill, comes from the iron content of the many springs just beyond. (67)

This complicated, detailed sentence is much more than simple description. In its detail, it works to convince the reader that the narrator is trustworthy and committed to conveying even the minutest details. The trust this builds between the narrator and the reader is essential when Flaubert's narrator—in a pioneering use of **free indirect discourse**—steps into Emma Bovary's mind and gives us her thoughts. We trust the narrator to relay these thoughts accurately because the narrator's attention to detail in setting has created a mood of exactitude, rigor, and transparency. The long passages of description not only ground the reader in the world of the novel, so we believe the world Flaubert creates, but also give authority and gravitas to the narrator, who is so engaged with both the physical and the mental world of the novel.

Setting, mood, and atmosphere form the field on which all of the other literary elements play. At their best, setting, mood, and atmosphere are subtle and unobtrusive, but when read closely, they reveal volumes about the narrative intentions of the writer and the consciousness of the characters.

Questions to Consider

1. Often readers are frustrated with long descriptions of landscape in a novel; it seems unimportant or boring. Identify a piece of writing with long descriptive passages about the work's setting. Now, thinking about the ways that setting can reflect the themes of a novel, can you see these descriptions of setting differently? Write a short response identifying ways that the setting reflects the themes and characters of the story you have chosen.

2. Using a poem you have read in class or one assigned by your instructor, analyze the diction and syntax of the speaker. What mood is created through the speaker's words? How did the poet create this mood? It may be helpful to imagine all of the stylistic choices (diction, syntax, rhythm, setting, and tone) as blocks that form the "building" of the poem. What kind of "building" is formed? Small, or large and imposing? Ramshackle and broken-down, or perfectly symmetrical? Is it official or personal? Dark or full of light?

3. Using a text you are reading or one suggested by your instructor, look at one scene or moment, and fill out the following setting list with as many aspects as you can:

   a. Time period:

   b. Time of day:

   c. Season:

   d. Physical location (country, city, indoors, outdoors):

   e. Weather:

   f. Objects in the area:

   g. Geographical features:

   h. Characters nearby:

Essay Prompt

Using the list you prepared in question 3 above, write a brief 2–3 page essay discussing how the author of the text uses setting. Does the setting support characterization? Help to establish the mood and atmosphere of the work? Work in conflict against the characters? Make sure you include specific examples from the text to support your claims.

Works Cited

Blake, William. "The Tyger." *The Norton Anthology of Poetry.* Eds. Margaret Ferguson, Mary Jo Salter, Jon Stallworthy. 5th ed. New York: W.W. Norton, 2005. 743–744. Print.

Eliot, T.S. "The Love Song of J. Alfred Prufrock." *Norton Anthology of Modern Poetry.* Eds. Jahan Ramazani, Richard Ellmann, Robert O'Clair. 3rd Edition. New York: W. W. Norton, 2003. 463–466. Print.

Fitzgerald, F. Scott. *The Great Gatsby.* New York: Scribners, 2004.

Flaubert, Gustave. *Madame Bovary.* Trans. Francis Steegmuller. New York: Alfred A. Knopf, 1993.

Morrison, Toni. *Beloved.* New York: Alfred A. Knopf, 1987.

Metaphor, Simile, and Imagery

Corrie Lynn White

Here come real stars to fill the upper skies,
And here on earth come emulating flies,
That though they never equal stars in size,
(And they were never really stars at heart)
Achieve at times a very star-like start.
Only, of course, they can't sustain the part.

—from "Fireflies in the Garden" (1928) by Robert Frost

INTRODUCTION

Key Terms
- **figurative language**
- **figure of speech**
- **trope**

It must be part of the human condition to compare things we cannot touch to the things that we can. The speaker in Robert Frost's poem watches the stars, then the fireflies filling the sky, and by comparing them, realizes both the impulse and the limitation of substituting one for the other. Writers of poetry, fiction, and drama are in the business of making these comparisons and connections using **figurative language**. The examples of figurative language we will explore in this chapter are metaphor, simile, and imagery.

Instances of figurative language can also be called **figures of speech** or **"tropes."** The word "trope" is Greek for "turning" and in literature, that is exactly what a simile, metaphor, or image requires the reader to do: turn from a distant star to an earthbound firefly, or from the pangs of love to the metaphor of a flea (see "The Flea" by John Donne). Figurative language twists our preconceived notions by providing an opportunity to look again or anew at an image that might have become familiar and therefore, lost its ability to relate to the reader. An author's use of figurative language alerts you, the reader, to the mood or emotional atmosphere of the piece, which can help you understand the setting, narrative mode, or historical context. In other words, understanding figurative language provides another lens for understanding the meaning of a poem, story, or play.

IMAGES: "SPEAKING PICTURES"

Key Terms
- **image**
- **imagery**

In his "Defense of Poesy" (1596), Sir Philip Sidney characterizes a poem as a "speaking picture." Images carry with them an emotional currency that Sidney knew to be powerful, to perhaps inspire the audience to live more virtuous lives. In the 20th century, Ezra Pound said, "The image is not an idea. It is a radiant node or cluster; it is a…VORTEX, from which ideas are constantly rushing." In this view, imagery steers a poem or a story away from abstraction and towards particularity. In her poem, "Poetry" (1919), Marianne Moore called poems "imaginary gardens with real toads in them." Here, she explains that while poems are works of the imagination, they must reflect the grit and the authenticity of the human experience. While authors throughout history have debated the moral, social, and aesthetic aims of literature, they have always found opportunity in imagery and images as place-holders for meaning and sensory experience.

But what is an image? While an **image** can occur in a word, phrase, or sentence, **imagery** refers to the collection of images in a story, poem, or play. People often misconceive imagery as language that must depict something visual, but the term actually applies to language that qualifies any sensory experience: visual (sight), auditory (sound), olfactory (smell), tactile (touch), and gustatory (taste). Imagery brings a text to life by engaging the reader's senses. By paying close attention to the imagery in a piece of literature, you may begin to make meaningful observations about the setting, mood, or theme.

If you have ever taken a course in writing, you may have heard your teacher say, "Show. Don't tell." The use of imagery in a poem or story does just this: it presents the reader with sights, sounds, and smells without explicitly connecting them to a certain theme or meaning. As the reader, you have the imaginative agency to notice patterns, make associations, and analyze how the imagery contributes to the development of character, theme, and setting. For example, in William Faulkner's "A Rose for Emily" (1930), the climax of the story occurs after her funeral when the men of the town break down the door of the upstairs room in Emily's house where she had been hiding the corpse of her lover. Imagery is abundant in the scene:

> The violence of breaking down the door seemed to fill this room with pervading dust. A thin, acrid pall as of the tomb seemed to lie everywhere upon this room decked and furnished as for a bridal: upon the valance curtains of faded rose color, upon the rose-shaded lights, upon the dressing table, upon the delicate array of crystal and the man's toilet things backed with tarnished silver, silver so tarnished that the monogram was obscured. Among them lay a collar and a tie, as if they had just been removed, which, lifted, left upon the surface a pale crescent in the dust. Upon a chair hung the suit, carefully folded; beneath it the two mute shoes and the discarded socks. (315)

Here, Faulkner uses images to depict the eerie scene. The faded curtains, the tarnished silver, and the dusty tie show the span of time that has passed since anyone has been in that room. Through this imagery, the reader learns the causes behind Emily's eccentricity—her fear that others will learn her secret—and the passage's attention to detail further highlights the townspeople's insatiable nosiness as they notice every detail upon entering the room. Faulkner chooses the adjective "mute" to describe the shoes, emphasizing how the evidence found in this room harbors a story that, much to the townspeople's chagrin, went into the grave with Emily. Fiction writers use imagery not only to describe setting, but to develop characters, and as Faulkner demonstrates, heighten the story's narrative tension.

Remember the phrase "A picture is worth a thousand words"? While poets, like fiction writers, rely on imagery to establish a mood or characterize a speaker, they have to choose their images very carefully to communicate the driving emotion or thought in a small amount of space. For example, let's look at the short poem, "In a Station of the Metro" (1915) by Modernist poet Ezra Pound:

> The apparition of these faces in the crowd;
> Petals on a wet, black bough.

Ezra Pound wrote this poem in response to an experience he had in a Paris subway station in which he encountered "suddenly a beautiful face, and then another and another." "In a Station of the Metro" was originally thirty lines long, but he cut it down to two, since he believed the images could stand on their own as powerful communicators of emotion.

Pause to Reflect: *Describe the images in Pound's poem in your own words. What do these images and the author's use of diction suggest about the speaker's experience in the metro station?*

METAPHOR

Key Terms

- **metaphor**
- **extended metaphor**
- **conceit**
- **implied metaphor**
- **controlling metaphor**
- **personification**

Metaphors are figurative comparisons that do not contain the words "like" or "as" and often use some variant of the verb *to be*. You've probably heard your mother say, "This room is a pig-sty!" You've called your best friend after taking a midterm and said, "The test was a beast." Like similes, these comparisons are often exaggerative and humorous in nature, and intended to elicit a dramatic response. The English poet and playwright William Shakespeare wrote one of the most recognizable metaphors in literature into his play *As You Like It* (1623): In Act 2, scene 7, one character, speaking to another, compares the world to a stage and life to a play:

> All the world's a stage,
> And all the men and women merely players;
> They have their exits and their entrances;
> And one man in his time plays many parts... (II.vii.139–142)

In the context of the play, this metaphor can be found in a monologue spoken by Jacques, a melancholy man living alongside the exiled Duke Senior in the Forest of Arden. Shakespeare's comparison of the world to a stage, of men and women to "merely players," shines a light on the artifice of the play to momentarily include and challenge the audience to consider their own parts in the ongoing "play of life."

Whether in a play, novel, or poem, metaphors can extend across a large portion of the work and when this occurs, it is called an **extended metaphor** or a **conceit**. In the seventeenth century, metaphysical poets like John Donne used conceits to marry the physical with the abstract world, relying on the element of surprise to keep the reader engaged. In his poem, "Valediction: Forbidding

Mourning" (1633), the speaker convinces his lover that though they will be temporarily separated, they will be like the twin points of a compass: inextricably joined, but able to move independently. Because Donne introduces this conceit in the latter half of the poem, it seems he is using it to solidify the argument that the couple's love is constant even at the "moving of th' earth" (line 9).

When metaphors are not explicitly constructed with the *to be* verb, they are called **implied metaphors**. In "Song of Myself" (1855) by Walt Whitman, the speaker often references or speaks to grass, which becomes an important symbol in the poem. In the final section, the speaker himself becomes the grass, and while Walt Whitman doesn't write "I am the grass," which would make for a more clear-cut metaphor, he implies this transformation and extends it across the final two stanzas:

> I bequeath myself to the dirt to grow from the grass I love,
> If you want me again look for me under your boot-soles.
>
> You will hardly know who I am or what I mean,
> But I shall be good health to you nevertheless,
> And filter and fibre your blood.
>
> Failing to fetch me at first keep encouraged,
> Missing me one place search another,
> I stop somewhere waiting for you. (52.10–17)

Whitman's use of extended and implied metaphor at the end of this poem is powerful, because if you read the entirety of the poem, you'll understand the speaker's transformation as a climax in the developing themes of democracy and transcendentalism. Becoming grass, himself, Whitman's speaker transcends human experience to figuratively take his place in the world as part of the nature. Through the powerful imagery of his transformation from mere flesh and blood into the grass beneath our feet, the speaker conveys at once the humility and beautiful, fleeting quality of human existence. Metaphors have the ability to transform and manipulate meaning in this dramatic way.

Reflection question: *When the speaker of "Song of Myself" becomes the grass through Whitman's use of extended and implied metaphor, what is he suggesting about the nature of life and death?*

When a metaphor dominates and extends across the entire length of a work, it is called a **controlling metaphor**. Perhaps you have read Psalm 23 in the Old Testament, which begins: "The Lord is my shepherd; I shall not want. / He maketh me to lie down in green pastures: he leadeth me / beside the still waters."

Instead of sprinkling the psalm with different metaphors—"The Lord is my shepherd/ The Lord is my bodyguard/The Lord is my bus driver"— the author commits to just one—the shepherd—and develops it over the course of the psalm. This commitment to metaphorical singularity—the employment of a single metaphor in the text—characterizes "the Lord" as a consistent and trustworthy being, which is what the author most likely wished to communicate to his audience.

Application question: *What type of metaphor is Emily Dickinson using in the following poem?*

BECAUSE I COULD NOT STOP FOR DEATH
Emily Dickinson

Because I could not stop for Death—
He kindly stopped for me—
The Carriage held but just Ourselves—
And Immortality.

We slowly drove—He knew no haste
And I had put away
My labor and my leisure too,
For His Civility—

We passed the School, where Children strove
At Recess— in the Ring—
We passed the Fields of Gazing Grain—
We passed the Setting Sun—

Or rather—He passed Us—
The Dews drew quivering and Chill—
For only Gossamer, my Gown—
My Tippet—only Tulle—

We paused before a House that seemed
A Swelling of the Ground—
The Roof was scarcely visible—
The Cornice— in the Ground—

Since then— 'tis Centuries—and yet
Feels shorter than the Day
I first surmised the Horses' Heads
Were toward Eternity— (1862)

If you guessed "controlling metaphor" you would be right! Here, Death is depicted as a kind man who is taking the speaker on an impromptu carriage tour of her town before heading "toward Eternity—". Mortality, or fear of death, is a common theme in literature, and Dickinson's use of controlling metaphor challenges this by giving Death human-like qualities. When a writer gives human qualities to an abstract idea or an inanimate object, it is called **personification**. Rather than leaving Death as a mere abstraction, Dickinson's choice to personify it sets up a human relationship in the poem, which enriches and authenticates the speaker's interaction with Death.

SIMILE

Key Terms
- **simile**
- **analogy**

In literature (and in life), it is common to see love compared to many things: a thorny rose, a deep ocean, skydiving off a cliff, or a consuming fire. While most people can relate to love stories, the word "love" itself can inspire a thousand different associations. To define such a commonly felt emotion or experience in a fresh way, writers use similes and metaphors.

A **simile**, a type of metaphor, is a comparison between two dissimilar things using the words "like" or "as" in its construction. Some examples you might have heard include *"cool as a cucumber," "quiet as a mouse,"* and *"raining like cats and dogs."* Now, our logical selves know that cats and dogs do not fall from the sky, but when fat rain drops are falling loudly on the roof over our heads, our imaginations can easily conjure the image and sound of cats and dogs tumbling down from the sky. Similes are often constructed using exaggeration, humor, and knowledge that the author can assume an audience already has. Similes are usually used in a phrase or sentence, but are not extended into the rest of the story or poem. In the rare case that a simile is extended across an entire work, it is called an **analogy**.

While Faulkner uses imagery to develop the mysterious character of Emily Grierson, Nathaniel Hawthorne in *The Scarlet Letter* (1850)[1] uses simile to show how the characters perceive imagery, and through these perceptions, the reader is able to understand the emotional state and motivations of the characters. This novel is set in Puritan New England and follows the life of Hester Prynne, a

---

1 An excerpt from this novel is included in the Anthology on page 319.

young woman publicly shamed for having a child out of an adulterous affair. In this scene where Hester and her daughter, Pearl, walk through the forest, notice how Hawthorne's use of imagery leads into simile:

> All these giant trees and boulders of granite seemed intent on making a mystery of the course of this small brook; fearing, perhaps, that, with its never-ceasing loquacity, it should whisper tales out of the heart of the old forest whence it flowed, or mirror its revelations on the smooth surface of a pool. Continually, indeed, as it stole onward, the streamlet kept up a babble, kind, quiet, soothing, but melancholy, like the voice of a young child that was spending its infancy without playfulness, and knew not how to be merry among sad acquaintance and events of sombre hue. (Hawthorne, Chapter 16, Paragraph 23)

Here, the narrator describes a stream in a way you may find lovely and familiar, but notice how the mood changes when the narrator compares that stream to "the voice of a young child that was spending its infancy without playfulness." It is not explicit whether this comparison comments on Pearl's character or Hester's guilt, but through this simile, you are instructed to read this scene not merely as a pretty walk in the forest, but as a comment on how the character's emotional state affects the way she sees the world around her. The author, when choosing a simile, has opportunity to externalize the character's thoughts and feelings. Just as when you are happy, you see the world in vibrant colors, the characters see their immediate setting as a reflection of their mental state, so taking a closer look at what is being compared in a simile is one way to better understand a character.

CONCLUDING REMARKS

Remember: writers use figurative language to give you, the reader, a chance to see, hear, touch, taste, and smell without actually doing any of those things. When you are reading, it's important to use these tools to try to experience the scene more fully by envisioning the action unfolding before you in the text. What *do* you see? What *do* you smell? Without your honest responses to these questions and interpretations of literature based upon them, stories, plays, and poems containing figurative language will not accomplish what they set out to do—shake the walls of your heart and your mind. At times, reading literature may feel like solving a riddle or picking a lock, but remember to relax into the process of interpretation. Let the writer's constructions of imagery, metaphor, and simile paint lasting scenes in your imagination.

Questions to Consider

1. Choose a poem or short story in the back of this anthology, or one assigned by your instructor, and describe how the author uses imagery to depict setting, character, and/or mood.

2. Choose a poem or short story in the back of this anthology, or one assigned by your instructor, and describe how the author's usage of metaphor or simile reflects the character's interior thoughts or feelings.

3. Write down the names of three people in your family, or three of your best friends, and pair each of them with an image that you think represents them. Why did you choose those images? Now turn the images into metaphors. For example: Abigail is like a car (simile) or Abigail is a car (metaphor). Does this call to mind a different way of thinking about the person?

Essay Prompt

Using your response to question 2 above, develop an essay in which you document and analyze how the author uses figurative language to support another literary element of the work—for example, the description of setting or characters. Make sure you provide specific examples from the text to support your claims.

Works Cited

Anonymous. "The Twenty-third Psalm." *The Norton Introduction to Literature*. Portable Tenth Edition. Booth and Mays. New York, W.W. Norton & Company Ltd., 2011. 570. Print.

Dickinson, Emily. "Because I could not stop for Death" *Poets.org*. The Academy of American Poets. 1998. Web. 22 April 2014.

Donne, John. "A Valediction: Forbidden Mourning." *Poetry Foundation*. n.d. Web. 22 April 2014.

Faulkner, William. "A Rose for Emily." *The Norton Introduction to Literature*. Portable Tenth Edition. Booth and Mays. New York, W.W. Norton & Company Ltd., 2011. 308–315. Print.

Frost, Robert. "Fireflies in the Garden." *The Norton Introduction to Literature*. Portable Tenth Edition. Booth and Mays. New York, W.W. Norton & Company Ltd., 2011. 583. Print.

Hawthorne, Nathaniel. *The Scarlet Letter.* New York, Bantam Dell, 2003. Print.

"Imagery." *The New Princeton Encyclopedia for Poetry and Poetics.* 3rd ed. 1993. Print.

Pound, Ezra. "In a Station of the Metro." *Poetry Foundation.* Web. 22 April 2014.

Shakespeare, William. *As You Like It.* New York, Simon & Schuster. 2004. Print.

Whitman, Walt. "Song of Myself" (I, II, VI, & LII). *Poets.org.* The Academy of American Poets. n.d. Web. 22 April 2014.

Symbolism

Crystal Matey

INTRODUCTION

Key Terms

- **symbolism**
- **symbol**
- **theme**
- **archetype**
- **irony**

Frequently, there are both literal and metaphorical meanings in the literature you will be reading in this course. One common method through which authors can communicate metaphorical ideas is the use of **symbolism**. **Symbols** are objects, words, actions, events, or characters that represent something beyond what is on the surface meaning of a text. Symbolism may be explicitly present or implied in a literary work, and a symbol's meaning is not fixed or absolute; symbols can mean different things for the author and readers of a text.

You may have studied symbolism primarily in relation to poetry or perhaps more so in relation to novels, but it is present in every literary form and genre. Often, the ability to identify symbols and contemplate their significance adds depth and complexity to your understanding of the text you are reading. Sometimes, symbolism can contribute to the mood of the piece or enhance a **theme**, or main idea, that is present, so keeping your eyes open for symbolism can actually help you understand the greater meaning of a work of literature.

What makes symbolism sometimes tricky is that a symbol can have multiple meanings and associations. There are some symbols, however, that tend to appear on a pretty regular basis in Western literature. Since these symbols have appeared so regularly in so many different texts, they can have similar meanings, even across different texts. Below are some of the most common literary symbols, along with their most basic meanings and examples of their use in various texts. Awareness of common symbols will help you understand and recognize similar patterns of symbolism in literature you read. I do have to caution you, nonetheless. This list is not meant to cover every kind of symbol you might encounter, nor is it meant to limit your interpretation of what a symbol might represent. Instead, it is provided as an introductory guide so that you can begin looking for and contemplating the meaning of symbolism, in whatever text you are assigned to read.

NATURE AS SYMBOLIC: SEASONS, WEATHER, WATER, FAUNA, FLORA

As you read, be on the lookout for repeated images and objects *from* nature. For example, the season during which a story, poem, or play takes place could affect textual interpretation. Does the author make sure to point out that the action takes place during winter, spring, summer, or fall? If so, make note of it! Think, for a moment, about Washington Irving's short story "The Legend of Sleepy Hollow" (1820). Wouldn't it be strange to have the headless horseman galloping through town at the peak of springtime? Irving specifically sets his narrative during the autumn season, but why is that important?

Typically, in literature the seasons represent what we might associate with "life seasons." For example, spring often represents birth, fertility, hope, and new beginnings. In terms of the stages of life, chronologically, spring can also be associated with childhood and youth. Summer, then, is when that child matures and becomes an adult, and summer often can also represent passion and romance, the maturity of spring's youth. Autumn, being the next stage of life, has to do with middle age, and it tends to symbolize fatigue, approaching death, and physical decline, although it can also be a period of harvest and wisdom. Finally, winter represents old age, which comes through death, sleep, or hibernation.

Let's reconsider now "The Legend of Sleepy Hollow." Irving sets his short story during the autumn season, and the townspeople in the story are frightened by talks of ghosts and a headless horseman. Ichabod Crane, the main character, disappears or dies after being attacked by this headless horseman, thereby emphasizing autumn as a season that ushers in destruction and death.

Beyond this example from "The Legend of Sleepy Hollow," a short story, seasons are frequently symbolic in poetry. For example, Edgar Allan Poe's poem "The Raven" (1845) is set in the month of December, or the winter season. The narrator of the poem is mourning for his lost love Lenore, and he fears that he will never get to be with her again. Winter, then, is symbolic of the finality of Lenore's death and the depths of the speaker's depression.

Not only are seasons indicative of the emotional state of the characters or themes, but the weather can also be symbolic. While we might think of rain, snow, sleet, sunshine, and fog as pretty normal occurrences, when they are mentioned in a piece of literature, they may be more than just literal. The streets of London, for instance, are immersed in fog in Robert Louis Stevenson's novella *Strange Case of Dr. Jekyll and Mr. Hyde* (1886). How might the fog be symbolic? Firstly, let's remember that Mr. Hyde remains a mystery through much of the novel and that fog is often present when he is. Fog, literally, is something that is difficult to see through; it can hide objects from our sight. So, the presence of fog comes to stand for the mysterious and sinister aspects of Mr. Hyde's character. To take the matter even further, one could say that the reader sees the story through a kind of fog because much of the action is kept hidden from us. Now, if we think about one of the main themes of Stevenson's novel, that of the duality of human nature (that we have both good and evil within us), perhaps the fog might also represent those hidden aspects within ourselves. In fact, if I were to make a thesis for an essay, I might argue that fog becomes symbolic for 1) mysterious Mr. Hyde, 2) represents sinister aspects of character, 3) mirrors the mystery of the plot itself, and 4) emphasizes the gray area between good and evil as a theme in the novel. See what I mean when I say that a symbol can represent various aspects of a text?

As you read poetry, prose, and drama, be on the lookout for mentions of weather. If it is stormy, that could represent some kind of trouble for the characters. Wind could symbolize change or violent emotions, and beautiful sunny days might indicate hope. Another form of weather is snow, which can be inhospitable, stark, and dangerous. In Act III, Scene i of William Shakespeare's *Romeo and Juliet* (1594?), Shakespeare incorporates weather to emphasize the conflict about to occur. Benvolio worries about the heat, remarking to Mercutio, "I pray thee, good Mercutio, let's retire: / The day is hot, the Capulets abroad, / And, if we meet, we shall not scape a brawl; / For now, these hot days, is the mad blood stirring." In this scene Benvolio associates heat with anger and violence, and in fact, that is exactly what occurs. This is the scene in which Mercutio and Tybalt enter into a fight, a fight in which they both lose their lives. The hot weather predicts, as a symbol, the violent actions of the characters.

Many symbols are multi-faceted in their meanings, and water and rain are common symbols that can have various connotations. Rain can be destructive, but it is also very cleansing. When a character is caught in the rain or rained upon, the author could be using this symbol as a way to represent a metaphorical cleansing. Rain, like fog, can distort vision, making it also a symbol of mystery. But, rain can restore, as well, as it is necessary for life and growth. Water imagery, in general, is something to pay attention to, whether in the form of rain, bathwater, a lake, a river, or an ocean. Once you become aware of it, you might notice that literary characters, for some reason, seem to be getting wet a lot; this often is because a character is symbolically experiencing a kind of rebirth. If someone comes out of the water or rain safely, that often means that his or her old identity has died and s/he has been reborn into a new being. It's a symbolic baptism. In Toni Morrison's *Beloved* (1987), Paul D. escapes from prison during a flood, literally swimming to his freedom, coming out on the other side with a new life (Foster 158). Given the knowledge from this chapter, one could then make the analysis that the flood is a symbolic baptism or rebirth into freedom for the character.

There are many other forms of nature symbolism, from animals to plant life to astronomical bodies. In general, birds often represent freedom, and specific birds tend to be linked to particular traits—such as doves, which represent domestic harmony, peace, or reconciliation; or the nightingale, famed for its beautiful song, which can be symbolic of voice and agency—or times of day, such as the rooster representing daybreak, the lark often representing day, and the owl, a symbol of the night. Samuel Taylor Coleridge incorporates an albatross—a sea bird—in his poem "The Rime of the Ancient Mariner" (1798). This bird appears somewhat miraculously after the Mariner's ship is in need of wind. The ship's crew views the albatross as a good omen, or as something divine, but the Mariner kills it for no reason, after which the crew forces him to carry the dead bird around his neck. The albatross becomes the metaphorical cross that the Mariner is forced to carry. The albatross, then, might be symbolic of the broken connection between nature and man or between God and man. The bird also comes to stand for the sin the Mariner has committed. The albatross's symbolism changes as the poem progresses, which emphasizes how important it is to pay attention to the context in which the symbol is used.

Among other animal forms, lions generally represent nobility or monarchy; foxes often represent slyness or cunning ("the trickster figure"); snakes, evil or temptation; and lambs, innocence, purity, and sacrifice. In Shakespeare's *Hamlet* (1600?), King Hamlet's ghost references the serpent or the snake when relating how he died. He says to Hamlet, "Tis given out that, sleeping in my orchard, / A serpent stung me — so the whole ear of Denmark / Is by a forged process of my death / Rankly abus'd — but know, thou noble youth, / The serpent that did sting thy father's life / Now wears his crown." Hamlet's father has just revealed that his brother, Claudius, was his murderer, and he refers to Claudius as a serpent. This clearly marks Claudius as a rebellious, evil figure.

Flowers are commonly symbolic as well. The rose, for instance, often can mean romantic love or fragility; pansies, as Ophelia tells us in William Shakespeare's tragedy *Hamlet*, are "for thoughts." In fact, there is a whole body of knowledge devoted to the meanings of various flower and tree species.

When authors direct our attention to the heavens, you can trust that the moon, for example, might also be symbolic. The moon changes, so it tends to be associated with femininity, or inconstancy. In fact, Juliet in Shakespeare's *Romeo and Juliet* does not want Romeo to swear his love by the moon, for the moon changes, and she fears that his love will also change. The sun's light and power, on the other hand, is traditionally associated with masculinity. An understanding of the moon and the sun in literature can also be linked to the symbolism of darkness and light. Darkness tends to be related to mystery, ignorance, and danger, for example. Literary characters who are portrayed as being "in the dark" might be feeling lost or hopeless. Moreover, darkness for a character can also represent evil, fear, or the unknown more generally. For the most part light stands for the opposite of darkness, typically signifying hope, knowledge, safety, and truth.

Unfortunately, there is no way to recount all of the nature symbols or all that they can mean in this brief chapter, but if you accustom yourself to actively looking for nature symbolism, you might end up with an interesting insight on the texts you read. Oftentimes authors will repurpose animals, plants, and celestial bodies to fit their own meanings, so you will need to be vigilant in observing the use and occurrence of each possible symbol.

COLOR SYMBOLISM

Colors, just like nature images, have multiple and various connotations. For example, red can symbolize passion and love, but it can also signify blood and violence or power and aggression. Purple can be representative of royalty, and blue might signify religious devotion, as in the Virgin Mary who is often portrayed wearing light blue. Ponder the color yellow for a second. What feelings or ideas do you associate with that color? Well, the sun is yellow, so yellow is often correlated with feelings of happiness or warmth. But cowards are sometimes described as "yellow," and depending on the shade of yellow, the color can be dingy, not bright. The colors black and white have layers of cultural and societal meaning, but if you refer back to our discussion of darkness versus light, black and white also have similar characteristics to those symbols, in that they tend to be portrayed as opposites—black as symbolic of mystery, sadness, and death, while white is often symbolic of innocence, peace, and goodness.

Let's examine the color green for a moment. Both the medieval metrical romance "Sir Gawain and the Green Knight" and the modern novel *The Great Gatsby* extensively employ the color green, but in each text represents the color to stand for something different. This is why it is important to consider the use and context of the symbol when trying to decipher its meaning. In the first tale, the title character—the Green Knight—is wearing green from head to toe. In addition, he carries a holly branch in his hand, which connects the knight to nature; since hollies are evergreens, the color and item he is carrying also suggests the knight as a supernatural, immortal being. Later on in the story, Gawain meets the Green Knight at the Green Chapel, which is located in a natural, wild setting. Taken together, one might conclude that the use of green in this story symbolizes nature, which could lead us to ideas about fertility and youth and the supernatural world of faery, an important element in medieval romance. Therefore, throughout "Sir Gawain and the Green Knight" the color green is symbolic for youth and immortality.

Green in F. Scott Fitzgerald's novel, however, does not mean the same for Jay Gatsby as it did for Sir Gawain. You might recall the repetition of the green light at the end of Daisy's dock; Gatsby is obsessed with staring at it from his own dock, directly across the bay. So what might Fitzgerald want us to associate with green in this context? Well, Gatsby's mind aligns this green light with Daisy, so in that way, the green light could symbolize Gatsby's dream of winning Daisy back. Green, then, represents hope. Hope sounds like a positive emotion, but Gatsby's ambitions are for achieving the American Dream, which in Fitzgerald's novel is associated with materialism and destruction. Therefore, just as Daisy proves unattainable, the green light could also symbolize the impossibility of achieving that American Dream. Green, like most color symbolism, has so many different associations. In this case, green can symbolize nature, youth, wealth, and hope, for instance, as we have seen above.

Taken altogether, it is important to remember that color symbolism, like most symbols, does not have just one right answer or meaning. Pay attention, though, to the use of colors in a text. If you notice that the author mentions a certain color in multiple instances, it probably means something. Make note of it, and ask yourself how the author is referencing the color. What is happening in the story when the color is mentioned? Is it usually associated with a particular character? Is the color brought in at a pivotal moment in the text? Trying to answer some of these questions could lead you to understanding the meaning and importance of that symbol.

SYMBOLIC SETTINGS

Settings are important aspects of a story, and sometimes the setting stands in for more than just the literal location. After all, an author has the whole world and all of time to choose from in deciding where and when a poem, play, or narrative should take place. So why did the author pick that particular place or that particular time in which to set their text? What might it mean that a character is described as dying on a mountaintop, or that a poem is set on a beach?

Let's consider Mark Twain's novel *The Adventures of Huckleberry Finn* (1884). Huck Finn and the escaped slave Jim take a raft down a river. Could it have been any river? Would it make sense to have sent them down the river Thames in London? The fact that Twain sets Huck and Jim on the Mississippi River is purposeful because that landscape runs both north and into the Deep South, with the potential to take them to safety and danger. Slaves were often sold down the river, as well (Foster 165). So, in this case, the setting has historical, political, and economic significance, which means the river works as a symbolic counterpart to the novel's themes.

It's not just physical place that can have a symbolic meaning. *When* a text takes place can be just as important. Sure, the author's choice of timeframe is representative of a historical moment, and therefore, it provides us with cultural context, but it can stand for more than that. The Gothic short story "The Cask of Amontillado" (1846) by Edgar Allan Poe is set during the time of Carnival. The narrator of this short story believes his friend has insulted him, so he decides to enact revenge by murdering this friend. Carnival, which is when the murder takes place, tends to be a time of excess—typical behavior involves eating too much food or drinking too much alcohol. Many people wear costumes during Carnival, as well. Just imagine Mardi Gras in New Orleans, and I think you get the idea. Poe chooses this setting, one that is supposed to be celebratory and reflective of freedom, to detail a dark and sinister act. Carnival, for Poe's characters, becomes symbolic of the suspension of reality, a time in which people can take on another identity, and in this story that leads to harm and allows for the crime to occur. Montresor wears a black mask, by the way (think of the color symbolism discussed previously), which further enhances the symbolism of darkness during what should be a happy celebration. So, in this way, Carnival is symbolic for excess—this time an excess of human depravity.

SYMBOLIC ACTION

You may be noticing a trend by now, in that with literature, you cannot always take the elements of a story at face value. Even a character's actions can be symbolic. You might notice that many characters set off on a trip, and that is not just because they have wanderlust. Oftentimes, a journey or quest in literature is representative of a character's search for truth, in particular self-knowledge (Foster 3). The quest is actually a common archetype in literature (we will get to the meaning of an archetype in just a bit). Flight is another common symbolic action that can be found in literary works. Of course, humans cannot fly, so if a character dreams of flight or actually does fly, make sure to pay attention. Flight usually symbolizes freedom or escape, and sometimes it can emphasize transcendence into the spiritual.

The Crucible (1953) by Arthur Miller contains symbolic action in the form of the witch trials. This play can be read as symbolic of the paranoia about communism during the 1950s in America. The witch trials in the play also represent the "trial" of suspected communists in front of the House Un-American Activities Committee, headed up by Joseph McCarthy. Miller's play is set in Salem, Massachusetts, in 1692, and it is about the witch trials that happened during that time; however, Miller uses that historical time and those characters' actions in putting their neighbors on trial for witchcraft to symbolize narrow-mindedness, extremism, and intolerance in his own time. As you read poetry, prose, or drama, pay attention to the events that happen or actions that characters take. These events and actions might just symbolize something more than their literal meanings.

SYMBOLIC CHARACTERS: ARCHETYPES AND PHYSICAL TRAITS

Not only can objects, settings, and actions be symbolic, but so can characters within the work. When characters are symbolic, they are often classified as **archetypes**. In terms of character, an archetype is a particular figure that occurs frequently in literature, myth, religion, or folklore (there are also archetypal plots and images). For instance, John Steinbeck's novella *Of Mice and Men* (1937) makes use of archetypal, symbolic characters. While the characters in the book can just be read for who they are, they can also be read as representative of certain types of people with particular symbolic associations. For example, you could read Curly's wife as symbolic of biblical Eve, the archetype of a temptress, in that she is presented as a seductress who brings death into the narrative. Slim is symbolic of the archetypal hero, the one character in Steinbeck's novel that is wise, kind, and strong. One of the main characters, George, could be read as an archetypal "everyman," in that he seems to represent the average person—he is neither horrible nor remarkable. The villain, the trickster, the good mother, and the great teacher/mentor are a few other archetypal characters.

Another common archetypal character is the Christ figure. Christ figures display some or all of the characteristics associated with the New Testament representation of Jesus Christ, and they do not necessarily have to be religious or found in religious texts to be Christ-like. Some features that might mark a literary character as a Christ figure are wounds in the hands, feet, side, or head; self-sacrifice either physical or metaphoric in nature; having a forgiving nature; having a humble profession like that of carpenter; being in a wilderness setting and facing temptation; being specifically 33 years old; experiencing change on the third day of a story; offering redemption to others; returning from being dead; having disciples or being good with children; or the author portraying him or her (yes her!) with arms outstretched (Foster 119–20). There can be other symbols associated with a Christ figure, but this list gives you some of the basics.

In Ernest Hemingway's novel *The Old Man and the Sea* (1952), the character of Santiago can be read as a symbolic, archetypal Christ figure. Santiago is a fisherman, which I think we could associate with a modest profession. During his fishing trip, he hooks a large fish that takes him out to sea into a metaphorical wilderness, where he battles great physical suffering. In fact, his hands are ripped, and he's broken something in his side. This whole incident happens over the course of three days. Santiago is triumphant and after he returns to land, he brings with him a kind of hope for the people in his town (Foster 120–21). These specific details are all good indicators that one could identify Santiago, symbolically, as a Christ figure. A Christ figure does not have to meet every criteria of Christ or even be a good character, so don't take the above list too literally. As you read other stories and poems, be on the lookout for this and other common archetypes; such archetypal readings allow us to access deeper cultural implications in the character's actions and interactions throughout the work, rendering it a more universal experience. Additionally, in literature, archetypes can be important because the meaning of a text can be shaped through an archetype's reference to cultural myth.

In addition to reading characters as symbolic, certain physical traits can be read as figurative, as well. If the character is presented as having a physical imperfection, that is usually significant, and oftentimes it represents more than its literal meaning. If a character is described as having a deformity, scar, handicap, or some other physical marking, it might call attention to a theme or to the character's psychology (Foster 200). Therefore, things like blindness, eye patches, missing limbs, a hunched back, illness, and countless other physical limitations are often there for a reason. Let's consider Hemingway's character Jake Barnes in *The Sun Also Rises* (1926). He has returned from World War I with not just mental wounds, but a physical wound, as well. This frequently mentioned war wound, though never described explicitly, has left Jake sexually impotent. This, of course, sets Jake apart from the other men in the novel. Though Jake is the main character, due to this physical limitation, he's also a hero who isn't really a hero. When we try and relate this to war, what might this wound symbolize? Jake is someone who literally cannot reproduce, cannot contribute to the future of society, so perhaps his wound is symbolic of the death caused by war, both the literal loss of life, and also a kind of cultural death.

AUTHORIAL INTENT

At this point, I imagine that you might be starting to feel a little frustrated. You may be thinking, *"Really? Do authors really mean to include these symbols in their work? Aren't we reading too much into it?"* You aren't alone. Many students have expressed this frustration before. A sixteen-year-old high school student named Bruce McAllister was so frustrated by his teachers asking him to look for symbolism that he wrote and mailed a four-question survey to 150 novelists in 1963. One of his questions was, "Do you consciously, intentionally plan and place symbolism in your writing?... If yes, please state your method for doing so. Do you feel you sub-consciously place symbolism in your writing?" The author Isaac Asimov responded, "Consciously? Heavens, no! Unconsciously? How can one avoid it?" Another question that McAllister posed was, "Do readers ever infer that there is symbolism in your writing where you had not intended it to be? If so, what is your feeling about this type of inference? (Humorous? annoying? etc.?)" Novelist Joseph Heller felt, "This happens often, and in every case there is good reason for the inference; in many cases, I have been able to learn something about my own book, for readers have seen much in the book that is there, although I was not aware of it being there." In other words literature, most likely, contains symbolism, even if the author did not consciously insert symbolism into their work. Additionally, readers play an important role in the reception of literature. Finding symbolism in a work of literature can add richness, depth, and complexity to your understanding of the text.

But why can't the snow just be snow, or the flower just a flower, or the river just a river? Well, I suppose we could just take everything a writer presents us with at face value, but that would be a little boring, wouldn't it? If you really stop to think about it, the very nature of our language is symbolic. When I say the word "dog," for instance, that conjures up images in your mind, right? But without mention of a specific breed, you may be picturing a Golden Retriever, while I'm thinking of a Chihuahua. This would mean that ultimately, our personal view of what the word "dog" symbolizes determines how we read the dog in a text. And that is the beauty of literature—it must be interpreted, and each reader brings his or her own interpretation to a text. It might be helpful to remember that works of literature are works of the imagination, and in order to read literature, we must use our imagination, as well. When we look for symbolism in a story, we are engaging with the author and text in a very interesting way. Can we ever really know what an author intended? Probably not. Did the author really mean to use symbolism? I don't know, but maybe. Once a novel, poem, or play has been released to the world, we make our own inferences, given our experiences. A more important question to ask would be, "How does reading the symbol in this-or-that way add to, complicate, or change my thinking about a text?"

DETERMINING A SYMBOL'S MEANING

Whether you choose to look for symbolism or not, there is a good chance that symbolism exists in some form—conscious or unconscious—in the text. How might you go about identifying possible symbols? Here are some basic steps to get you started:

1. **Take notes/annotate the text**—Keep track of images, characters, and ideas.

2. **Look for repetition**—If an author repeats an object or idea, it is probably important.

3. **Look for details**—Pay close attention when an author takes the time to describe a flower, in detail for instance. What color is it? What kind of flower is it? Is there anything unusual in the description, i.e., is the lily black instead of white? Are the roses blue instead of red?

4. **Use your preexisting knowledge**—You don't have to read a lot of literature to know that a character wearing black might be evil.

5. **Research**—It's always okay to look up common meanings for symbols. There are symbolism dictionaries and reference guides to literary symbolism for just that purpose!

6. **List the object's characteristics**—If you are unable to find a meaning for the symbol or can't find a meaning that makes sense with the context provided

in the story or poem, take the time to jot down the typical characteristics of that object. How might some or all of them apply to this situation?

7. **Draw conclusions**—Based on your observations, try to connect the object to theme or plot or to a certain character in the story.

With these guidelines, you can start identifying the patterns of reoccurring symbols that exist throughout the texts that you are reading.

SYMBOLIC IRONY

One final thing to keep in mind with symbolism, though, is **irony**. Remember earlier when we discussed water and rain as symbols for cleansing and rebirth? In Hemingway's novel *A Farewell to Arms* (1929), the main character Frederic walks home in the rain after both his lover and baby have died. That's our last image of Frederic—him, walking home alone in a downpour. How restorative is that? In much of this novel, rain actually represents death. Ironically, rain seems to follow Frederic everywhere, perhaps implying that he cannot escape death (Foster 238–9). It is helpful to remember that authors can play on our expectations of certain symbols, and then use irony, providing us with an unexpected association. For more discussion of irony, see Michael Bedsole's chapter in this book.

I would like to close by referring to Thomas C. Foster's insightful book *How to Read Literature Like a Professor*. In it, he says that students often ask him, "Is that a symbol?" and his response is usually, "Sure, why not?" When students want to know what that symbol means, he turns the question back to them because whatever "*you* think it stands for" is probably what it means, "at least for you" (96). Symbolism is not straightforward. Symbols don't have just one meaning, so pay attention to your instincts, and have some fun with it! Literature is meant to be imaginative, after all.

Questions to Consider

1. In what ways might the setting or geography be symbolic of larger conflicts within a story, poem, or play?

2. In what ways might certain animal figures or human characters in a text seem to stand for something in addition to themselves?

3. Choose a story with at least three symbols. Draw pictures or create some other visual representation of the symbols, and decide what they might stand for. Provide at least one passage from the text for each symbol that could support your interpretations.

Essay Prompt

Focusing on one symbol, write an essay analyzing how that symbol functions in a text and what it reveals about the characters or themes of the work as a whole.

Works Cited

Coleridge, Samuel Taylor. "The Rime of the Ancient Mariner." 1798.

Fitzgerald, F. Scott. *The Great Gatsby*. New York: Scribner, 2004. Print.

Foster, Thomas C. *How to Read Literature Like a Professor*. New York: HarperCollins Publishers, Inc., 2003. Print.

Hemingway, Ernest. *A Farewell to Arms*. New York: Scribner, 2003. Print.

---. *The Old Man and the Sea*. New York: Scribner, 1995. Print.

---. *The Sun Also Rises*. New York: Scribner, 2006. Print.

Irving, Washington. "The Legend of Sleepy Hollow." *Gutenberg.org*. 25 June 2008. Web. 3 Jan 2013.

Poe, Edgar Allan. "The Cask of Amontillado." *PoeStories.com*. Web. 3 Jan 2013.

---. "The Raven." 1845.

Miller, Arthur. *The Crucible*. New York: Penguin Books, 2003. Print.

Morrison, Toni. *Beloved*. New York: Vintage, 2004. Print.

Reilly, Lucas. "Famous Novelists on Symbolism in Their Work and Whether It Was Intentional." *Mental Floss*. 15 June 2012. Web. 10 Jan 2014.

Shakespeare, William. *Hamlet.* New York: Penguin Books, 2001. Print.

---. *Romeo and Juliet.* New York: Penguin Books, 2000. Print.

"Sir Gawain and the Green Knight." *Luminarium: Anthology of English Literature.* 3 June 2010. Web. 3 Jan 2013.

Steinbeck, John. *Of Mice and Men.* New York: Penguin Books, 1993. Print.

Stevenson, Robert Louis. *Strange Case of Dr. Jekyll and Mr. Hyde.* New York: W.W. Norton & Company, 2003. Print.

Twain, Mark. *Adventures of Huckleberry Finn.* New York: W.W. Norton & Company, 1999. Print.

Allusion

Meghan McGuire

INTRODUCTION

Key Terms

- **allusion**
- **intertextuality**
- **parody**

Have you ever used the phrase "we're not in Kansas anymore" to refer to a new and unfamiliar place, or described a personal weakness or vice as your "Achilles' heel"? If so, then you're actually, perhaps unconsciously, engaging in the use of allusion. An **allusion** is an indirect or implied reference to a particular person, place, historical event, work of art, idea, or literary text. Typically, this figure of speech is used in literature as a way to help the reader understand a difficult or abstract concept by referencing something more familiar. It is also a concise way to convey additional levels of meaning and significance in a text without adding a detailed, lengthy explanation. If a reader is familiar with the reference, then s/he can use the allusion to draw comparisons, enhancing her appreciation of the text through an existing understanding of a particular experience or emotion.

For example, if you refer to something as your "Achilles's heel," you are concisely implying that it is not only *a* weakness but your *only* weakness by directly alluding to the classic Greek hero Achilles, who had only one known vulnerability: a spot on his heel that, if struck, would cause his death. An allusion like this is easily understood because the audience is familiar with the myth. Allusions can help the reader gain a deeper level of meaning by broadening the work's context, but they are only effective if the reader recognizes and understands the reference. Therefore, the effectiveness of an allusion is based on an assumption of shared knowledge and experience. That's why many of the allusions in

Western literature refer to the Bible, Greek or Roman mythology, or a work by Shakespeare; these texts are common and familiar within our culture and literary heritage, making them useful shorthand for complex ideas. Although an allusion like "Achilles' heel" is both direct and easily recognized, many literary references are quite subtle, requiring a more analytical and nuanced close reading.

Oftentimes a writer will intentionally allude to concepts, phrases, or forms from another work of literature—a process known as **intertextuality**—in order to expand the meaning of his or her text or to situate the text within or against a particular literary tradition. Intertextuality then becomes a broad term used to describe the relationship that a work of literature has with previously written texts, which can comprise direct textual allusions or an imitation or **parody** of a previous literary work's form or style. Early twentieth-century Modernist writers like T.S. Eliot and James Joyce, for example, are known for their densely intertextual work. Poems like Eliot's "The Love Song of J. Alfred Prufrock" (1917) and *The Waste Land* (1922), or Joyce's experimental novel *Ulysses* (1922), constantly allude to other works of literature as a means of both acknowledging and rebuking tradition. Recognizing and interrogating these complex, and oftentimes subtle, intertextual allusions helps us approach a text with more analytical force. This process, however, requires of the reader a dedication to close reading and critical thinking. First, you must identify the presence of an intertextual allusion in the work of literature that you're reading. Next, you'll need to learn more about the referenced text, so you can begin to analyze potential relationships between the two. If you've read the referenced text before, then you may immediately draw connections between the two literary works. However, if you haven't read the work before, then you may need to research it in order to gain a better understanding of the characters, narrative, or style being referenced. Once you have acquired an understanding of the allusion, then you can begin to look at potential relationships between the texts. For example, does an understanding of the reference change the way you view a character or situation in the text you're reading? Does it impact the tone of the work?

Let's look at T.S. Eliot's well-known poem "The Love Song of J. Alfred Prufrock,"[1] as an example of how understanding an intertextual allusion can enrich our study of a literary work. Towards the end of the poem, Eliot includes a complex allusion to Shakespeare's *Hamlet*. Prufrock—the narrator—declares,

---

1 This text is included in the Anthology on pp. 248–251.

> No! I am not Prince Hamlet, nor was meant to be;
> Am an attendant lord, one that will do
> To swell a progress, start a scene or two,
> Advise the prince; no doubt an easy tool, (111–114)

If the reader is familiar with Shakespeare's *Hamlet* and its title character, Prince Hamlet, then this allusion is helpful because it reveals how Prufrock sees himself and how different this is compared to the way the reader might view him. This allusion suggests that Prufrock sees himself not as a main character in his own life but as a member of the supporting cast, "an easy tool" that can be used and manipulated (114). He also declares that he is nothing like Prince Hamlet, and yet an attentive close reader can conclude that Prufrock is in many ways similar to Prince Hamlet;[2] both characters are indecisive, insecure, and constantly questioning. Through this single allusion, Eliot is able to convey a more complex view of Prufrock's character through an association with a previous literary figure like Hamlet.

Although some allusions can be difficult to identify, most authors include allusions in their work with the expectation that the reader will recognize and utilize the references. W.B. Yeats's 1902 poem "Adam's Curse,"[3] for example, presents numerous allusions that enrich the poem's overall meaning. Beginning with the title, the reader is immediately presented with a link between the poem and the Bible, specifically the book of Genesis and the Fall of Man. The story of Adam and Eve in the Garden of Eden is familiar to most Western readers, who would know that Adam's punishment or "curse" for eating the forbidden fruit is to constantly labor and toil; therefore, when the narrator states

> I said, 'It's certain there is no fine thing
> Since Adam's fall but needs much laboring (21–22)

he is discussing the act of writing, bemoaning the difficulty and labor required to write beautiful poetry and comparing his mental and imaginative work to the physical labor of scrubbing a kitchen floor or breaking stones in the field. At first glance, the allusion is both obvious and helpful to the reader; it connects the narrator of the poem and his personal struggles to the very first man, and by extension to all men. It universalizes his suffering while also emphasizing that mental, creative work is just as difficult and tiresome as manual labor. If we push the allusion a little further, however, we can also see that both men are laboring because of a woman. Adam is cursed because he listened to Eve, and the narrator

---

2 For reference, read Hamlet's speech on page 271 of the Anthology in this book.
3 This poem is included in the Anthology, pp. 259–260.

in the poem is struggling to write beautiful poetry for the woman he loves. The simple allusion in the title of the poem opens the text to multiple interpretations, broadening the reader's understanding of the action of the poem and initiating new, productive questions about this complex intertextual relationship.

Interestingly, Yeats's use of allusion in the poem is not only limited to its content; it is also present in the poem's form and structure. For example, "Adam's Curse" is written in iambic pentameter, using enjambed heroic couplets. This traditional English meter and form is structurally and stylistically reminiscent of John Dryden's (1631–1700) seventeenth-century translations of the epic poetry of Homer and Virgil, and yet the language of the poem is unusually informal and conversational. Similarly, the fourteen-line opening stanza is reminiscent of a traditional sonnet—one of the most popular English poetic forms—which once again connects the poem to an existing English literary tradition. The other stanzas, however, are surprisingly irregular. From the author's use of allusion in both content and form, a reader might conclude that Yeats is asserting his rightful place within the British literary tradition, but also expressing a need to push against convention, to utilize tradition as a means of exploring a new method of poetic expression. Without an understanding of these allusions and Yeats's use of intertextuality, the poem still possesses meaning for the reader. However, by recognizing and interrogating these connections, one can see how a text can begin to open up to new and productive interpretations.

Even though literary allusions may be difficult to recognize at first, the more you read, the more you'll begin to notice connections between texts, and these connections will eventually begin to alter and enrich your understanding of the literature.

Questions to Consider

1. After reading through W.B. Yeats's poem "Adam's Curse" on pages 259–260 of the Anthology in this book, what other allusions do you notice, and how do they impact your understanding of the poem?

2. Why might allusion be a particularly useful literary device for poetry? How might its use in poetry differ from its use in prose?

3. Allusions are not only limited to literary texts. They are frequently used in other mediums like TV and film. Can you identify specific examples of allusions found in TV, film, or other non-literary genres? If so, explain how the allusion impacts your understanding or appreciation of that artistic work.

Essay Prompt

Using a text that you've read in class, or one assigned by your instructor, identify at least one important allusion. Write a brief essay analyzing the author's use of allusion and explaining its impact on your interpretation of the text.

Works Cited

Eliot, T.S. "The Love Song of J. Alfred Prufrock." *The Complete Poems and Plays: 1909–1950.* New York: Harcourt Brace, 1980. 3–7. Print.

---. *The Waste Land. The Complete Poems and Plays: 1909–1950.* New York: Harcourt Brace, 1980. 37–55. Print.

Joyce, James. *Ulysses.* Eds. Hans Walter Gabler, Wolfhard Steppe, and Claus Melchior. New York: Vintage, 1993. Print.

Shakespeare, William. *The Tragedy of Hamlet, Prince of Denmark. The Riverside Shakespeare.* Ed. G. Blakemore Evans and J.J.M. Tobin. Boston: Houghton Mifflin, 1997. 1183–1245. Print.

Yeats, W.B. "Adam's Curse." *The Collected Poems of W.B. Yeats.* Revised 2nd ed. Ed. Richard J. Finneran. New York: Scribner, 1996. 80–81. Print.

Allusion

On Irony

Michael Bedsole

INTRODUCTION

Key Terms

- **irony**
- **verbal irony**
- **situational irony**
- **dramatic irony**
- **tragic irony**
- **cosmic irony**

In *The Anxiety of Influence* (1973), literary critic Harold Bloom argues that irony, in its simplest sense, means "saying one thing while suggesting another" (xix). For Bloom, irony involves the discrepancy between what one says and what one means, and functions as a kind of double-speak, where words and statements can mean the opposite of their literal meaning. As other critics point out, this definition of **irony** is perhaps the oldest, stretching all the way back to Roman and Greek antiquity (Colebrook 1).

Irony involves other modes of discrepancy as well. In addition to describing the difference between what one says and what one means, which we call verbal irony, irony can also refer to the difference between what we expect in a given situation and what actually occurs, which we call situational irony. Irony can also involve the gap between what a character in a text knows about her or his fate and what readers know, a mode of irony we call dramatic irony. We typically understand irony in one of these three ways (i.e., either as verbal, situational, or dramatic). However, in the grandest sense, irony can also refer to what we might call ironies of fate, or cosmic irony. On the following pages, we'll look at each of these four modes of irony in more detail.

VERBAL IRONY

We use irony all the time in our daily conversations. Any time that you make a sarcastic remark, for example, you're employing irony. Let's say it's January and you're walking to class in the rain without an umbrella. Cold and wet, you mumble that you "just *love* the rain." In fact, you mean the opposite of what you've just said. Since very few people actually enjoy being cold and wet, it's clear that you're merely being ironic. Or, imagine that you have to give a presentation in one of your classes, but public presentations terrify you. So, you turn to a friend and mutter that you're "thrilled about standing up in front of the class." Again, it's clear that you mean the opposite of what you've just said. Rather than being "thrilled," you feel anxious and irritated. In other words, you've again made an ironic statement.

As noted above, we call this **verbal irony**, since it involves the discrepancy between what we *say* and what we *mean*. Like you, literary characters use verbal irony all the time. For example, in Shakespeare's *Hamlet* (1603), when Claudius questions Hamlet about the location of Polonius' body, Hamlet remarks that Polonius is "At supper," which in the scene's context is clearly meant ironically. If you have read the text, you will know that Polonius is not "at supper" in the sense that one would normally understand the statement. Instead, as Hamlet goes on rather gruesomely to explain, Polonius has become supper for the worms: "Not where he eats," Hamlet explains, "but where 'a is eaten" (IV.iii 17–19). In this way, Shakespeare uses verbal irony through Hamlet's remark to convey to the audience that Polonius is dead.

Consider, too, Antony's famous funeral oration in Act III, Scene ii of Shakespeare's *Julius Caesar* (1623). The play concerns Caesar's assassination and the tragic conflict between conspirators Cassius and Brutus and Caesar's avengers Antony and Octavius. In Antony's highly ironic but subtle funeral speech he manages not only to generate sympathy for the recently slain Caesar, but also to turn the crowd against Brutus, one of the murderers. At the beginning of his speech, Antony says that he "come[s] to bury Caesar, not to praise him," yet through the course of his oration, he shows in fact that he does come to offer praise for the dead emperor (III.ii 74). It is verbal irony that serves here as his rhetorical tool for achieving this goal. For example, he repeatedly says that "Brutus is an honorable man" (III.ii 82, 94, 99), a statement which grows more and more ironic each time he says it, for it becomes clear with each point that he makes that Antony does not believe that Brutus "is an honorable man." In subtly condemning Brutus in this manner, Antony manages to rouse the crowd against Brutus and to redeem Caesar's tarnished name. These examples from *Hamlet* and *Julius Caesar* help illustrate precisely how verbal irony involves a kind of double-speak, where our words do not mean what they might seem literally to mean, but rather point to an *unspoken* level of meaning.

SITUATIONAL IRONY

Verbal irony is perhaps the most easily identifiable form of irony. However, you'll find **situational irony** just as common, and in many ways much more important when analyzing literary texts, since it involves the situations that constitute the narrative structure of the text itself. As noted earlier, situational irony refers to the discrepancy between what one expects as the outcome of a particular situation, and what one actually experiences. For example, imagine yourself taking a walk next to a well-landscaped swimming pool. The lawn's sprinkler system suddenly turns on and, surprised, you stumble to the side to avoid getting wet (from the sprinklers), only to fall into the pool itself! Since the outcome is the opposite of the one you expected, you have a prime example of situational irony.

For literature, let's look at *Hamlet* again. In the play, Claudius, who desires Hamlet's death, arranges to have Hamlet's friends Rosencrantz and Guildenstern escort Hamlet to England, where they will give to the King of England a letter from Claudius asking the King to immediately execute Hamlet. However, while sailing to England, Hamlet unseals and reads Claudius' letter. Unbeknownst to Rosencrantz and Guildenstern, Hamlet then writes a new letter ordering *their* execution, and then reseals it such that his former friends remain unaware of their impending fate. Thus, Rosencrantz and Guildenstern find themselves in a *situation* whose tragic outcome will not be what either they or Claudius expected.

In O. Henry's short story "Gift of the Magi" (1906), we find another well-known example of situational irony. The story involves a young, poor married couple, who struggle one Christmas to find the money to buy gifts for each other. Though poor, they each possess one prized object. The young wife, Della, takes great joy in her hair, which is so long it reaches down nearly to her knees; while Jim, the young husband, values his gold watch, which had belonged both to his father and his grandfather. In order to purchase a gift for Jim, Della sells her hair, and with the money earned, buys Jim an expensive chain for his watch. Meanwhile, Jim sells his watch in order to buy a set of expensive combs for Della to use in her hair. The irony becomes apparent, of course, when they exchange gifts, for both Della and Jim find themselves in possession of expensive gifts for which

161

they no longer have any use. Thus, they experience a *situation* whose outcome differs greatly from the one they had every reason to expect.

Let's turn to Sophocles' *Oedipus Rex* (429 BCE) for a final example. In that play, we learn that as a young man Oedipus hears from the Oracle at Delphi that he will slay his father and wed his mother, a fate that disgusts him as much as it does us. In order to avoid fulfilling the oracle's prophecy, he leaves Corinth (his native city, or so he believes) only to unknowingly encounter on his journey Laius, King of Thebes, who in fact is Oedipus' actual biological father. In a moment of injudicious rage, and ignorant of his true relationship to Laius, he slays the king, only discovering at the play's end that in slaying Laius he has, in fact, slain his own father. Thus, in fleeing the Oracle's prophecy, Oedipus unintentionally chooses a course of action that leads him to fulfill it. As with Rosencrantz and Guildenstern or Della and Jim, Oedipus finds himself in a situation where the outcome proves profoundly, *ironically* contrary to what he expected—which of course is why we call it situational irony.

DRAMATIC IRONY

In contrast to verbal and situational irony, **dramatic irony** involves the relation between the reader and the text, and refers to those moments when the reader knows more than the characters do about some important element in the narrative. We may know some detail about what the future holds for a particular character, even as the character herself remains ignorant of her fate. Or, a character may behave in a particular way which we know will result in an outcome that runs counter to the character's expectations. In other words, we know more about characters' fates and the effects of their choices and actions than they do themselves. As an aside, we should note that when applied to tragedies, we can also refer to dramatic irony as **tragic irony**.

Horror stories typically feature dramatic irony, especially since the suspense of a scene often depends on readers knowing more about the dangers of a particular situation than a given character does. Bram Stoker's *Dracula* (1897) provides a good example here. The first section of the novel relates Jonathan Harker's journey to the Carpathian Mountains of Eastern Europe in order to discuss with Count Dracula the details regarding a real estate transaction (the Count seeks to purchase property in England). Readers, of course, know that the Count is a vampire, but Harker, at least at first, has no notion of the Count's supernatural identity, or of the danger to which his journey has exposed him. The suspense in these opening chapters derives from the fact that we possess more knowledge of

Harker's situation than does Harker himself, and it is this discrepancy in knowledge which we term dramatic irony.

Another example that might help further clarify this mode of irony comes again from *Oedipus Rex*. Certainly when the play was first produced, viewers knew beforehand the story of Oedipus. It was part of the collective cultural mythology of Ancient Greece. Already familiar with the story, the Greeks knew more about Oedipus' actions and the effects of his choices than he did, himself. They knew that he had slain his father and wed his mother. They knew that in fleeing Corinth in an attempt to evade the Oracle's prophecy, he was in fact working to fulfill the prophecy. They knew, too, that in hunting down Laius' killer, he was hunting himself. Indeed, it is the audience's foreknowledge in each of these instances coupled with Oedipus' own ignorance of the effects of his actions that constitutes the play's dramatic irony.

To make this point clearer, let's look more closely at Oedipus' hunt for Laius' murderer. We know that Oedipus is the killer, although Oedipus remains ignorant of that fact. We know, too, that in seeking to ferret out the killer, Oedipus engages in an act that will eventually undo him. He will discover not only that he has slain his father, but that his wife is in fact his mother. We also know that such knowledge will cost Oedipus not only his eyesight (he blinds himself out of disgust and shame) but his kingship and his home. Our foreknowledge of these events and our awareness of the full consequences of Oedipus' detective work provide us with a view of Oedipus that the text denies him. The text thus constructs an epistemological gap between Oedipus' knowledge (of himself, of his situation) and the audiences' own. Indeed, the play's power resides in this knowledge gap, for the gap helps to generate the play's emotional intensity. We know what's coming, yet Oedipus does not, thus producing in us an anxiety that builds and builds as the play progresses. Seen in this sense, a text's use of dramatic irony can be crucial for that text's effect on an audience.

COSMIC IRONY

Cosmic irony involves a different kind of discrepancy than dramatic irony. Rather than referring to the gap in knowledge that separates readers from characters, cosmic irony involves the discrepancy between individuals' designs for shaping their own lives and the designs of Fate, the gods, or God. Cosmic irony implies that supra-human forces predetermine and undermine individuals' efforts at directing the course of their own fates. Literary critic Claire Colebrook suggests that with cosmic irony, "[i]t is as though . . . the course of human events

163

and intentions, involving our awarding of rankings and expectations . . . exists alongside another order of fate beyond our predictions" (14). As with all forms of irony, cosmic irony implies a kind of "doubleness of sense or meaning" that works to undercut our literal expectations (Colebrook 14). Individuals make plans for their lives only to realize how futile their plans have been, since another order of power has all the while been negating individuals' efforts.

We can see cosmic irony at work in any text that dramatizes individuals trapped in a weave of forces of which they have no comprehension. Thomas Hardy, for example, wrote a number of novels exploring this theme. In *Tess of the D'Urbervilles* (1891), Hardy suggests that his heroine, whom he designates as a "Pure Woman" in the novel's subtitle, suffers an unjust and seemingly inescapable fate. Raped, betrayed, and marginalized, Tess finds herself trapped in a complex web of forces which work to delineate her life and undermine her autonomy. After her execution for killing her rapist, Hardy writes, "'Justice' was done, and the President of the Immortals . . . had ended his sport with Tess" (397). In an instance of verbal irony, Hardy places the term "justice" in quotation marks because, of course, Tess's execution was not an expression of "justice." Rather, Hardy suggests that Tess's fate was the result of a kind of cosmic game, in which she was merely the "sport" of the "Immortal" forces whose designs escape her.

Oedipus Rex provides another good example here. As noted above in our discussion of both situational and dramatic irony, Oedipus sought to flee the fate the Oracle predicted for him. His desire to escape such a fate indicates Oedipus' own essential humanity. Like any of us, he found himself revolted by the Oracle's prophecy, and in order to save himself (as well as his mother and father), he fled Corinth to seek out a different fate. Of course, by seeking to avoid his fate he simply (and ironically) ensured it. Like an insect caught in a spider's web, no matter which direction Oedipus turned, his fate was already predetermined. His sense of autonomy, of free will and free choice, was never more than an illusion. Every step he took was merely a step closer to the fate predicted for him by the Oracle. As in Hardy's *Tess of the D'Urbervilles*, in *Oedipus Rex* Sophocles presents a clear disjunction between human and cosmic designs and intentions. And again, it is this disjunction that we term cosmic irony.

READING FOR IRONY

You'll find as you read that these four primary modes of irony (verbal, situational, dramatic, and cosmic) sometimes overlap. Indeed, as you may have already noticed in the examples throughout this chapter, such a conflation of ironies occurs frequently in *Oedipus Rex*, where situational, dramatic, and cosmic ironies converge at key moments. Oedipus' marriage to his mother provides an instance of situational irony. But it also signals an instance of dramatic irony, since Oedipus remains ignorant of the true nature of his relationship to his wife, while we possess full knowledge of it. Moreover, it seems as if fate itself destined Oedipus' marriage to his mother (the Oracle predicted it—doomed him to it), which as explained above suggests an underlying cosmic irony.

Sarah Cleghorn's short poem "[The golf links lie so near the mill]" (1915) can also help illustrate how different modes of irony oftentimes overlap. Cleghorn wrote this poem after seeing a golf course in the American South placed incongruously next to a textile mill that employed children as laborers. In just four lines, Cleghorn subtly paints a picture not only of abhorrent labor practices, but of the gross inequality of a system that would allow children to work in factories while the affluent—presumably, their employers—enjoyed games of golf:

> The golf links lie so near the mill
> That almost every day
> The laboring children can look out
> And see the men at play

The key word here, of course, is "play." Play is an activity that we associate with children, not necessarily with adults. But by suggesting that children work while adults play, the poem overturns our expectations, and does so in a way calculated to arouse our sense of injustice. By placing a double meaning on the word "play," the poem employs verbal irony, but by dramatizing a situation whose outcome runs counter to our expectations (i.e., we do not expect "laboring children" to "look out" on "men at play"), the poem also makes use of situational irony. Combining the two modes lends added force to each, and helps to amplify the emotional power of Cleghorn's social critique.

As Claire Colebrook argues, in the most basic sense, each of the four modes of irony involves "life's capacity to thwart language and understanding" (22). Every instance of irony involves the disjunction between some supposed literal meaning (whether of a statement or of a situation) and a deeper meaning which undercuts the literal one. In this sense, irony can oftentimes serve as a tool for satire or political subversion (as in Hamlet's jabs at Polonius or in Jonathan Swift's "A Modest Proposal" [1729]). But irony is also important in that it can be used as a tool to reveal the nuances of tone and meaning in a text or in a character's comments. As such, when you read for multiple ironies, you gain a more sophisticated understanding of the meaning(s) at play in a text. Thus, as readers, it is crucial to remain ever-sensitive to the presence and play of irony, in whatever mode(s) in which it is employed in a work of literature.

Questions to Consider

1. What is the difference between situational and dramatic irony? Are they mutually exclusive? What purpose might each of these two forms of irony serve? Define each and provide examples to illustrate your grasp of the terms.

2. Either by yourself or with a team of classmates, write down as many instances of verbal, situational, dramatic, and cosmic irony as you can find in the text you are currently reading for the course, including the page number(s) where that type of irony appears. What type(s) of irony does the author use most frequently? Why do you think the author chooses to employ irony this way in this text?

3. What is it that links together the four main modes of irony? In other words, what is it that the four modes have in common with one another?

Essay Prompt

In a text of your choice, or one that your instructor assigns you, construct a short essay (2–3 pages) in which you trace out the various modes of irony present. Describe how each mode helps contribute to the text's central theme or themes.

Works Cited

Bloom, Harold. *The Anxiety of Influence: A Theory of Poetry*. Oxford UP, 1997. Print.

Cleghorn, Sarah. "[The golf links lie so near the mill]." *The Norton Introduction to Literature*. Ed. Kelly J. Mays. New York: Norton, 2013. 975. Print.

Colebrook, Claire, *Irony*. Routledge: London, 2004. Print.

Hardy, Thomas. *Tess of the D'Urbervilles*. New York: Penguin, 1996. Print.

Henry, O. "The Gift of the Magi." *100 Selected Stories*. London: Wordsworth, 1995. 1–6. Print.

Shakespeare, William. "The Tragedy of Hamlet, Prince of Denmark." *The Riverside Shakespeare*. Ed. G. Blakemore Evans and J.J.M. Tobin. Boston, Houghton Mifflin, 1997. 1183–1245. Print.

Shakespeare, William. "The Tragedy of Julius Caesar." *The Riverside Shakespeare.* Ed. G. Blakemore. Evans and J.J.M. Tobin. Boston, Houghton Mifflin, 1997. 1146–1182. Print.

Sophocles. "Oedipus the King." *The Three Theban Plays: Antigone; Oedipus the King; Oedipus at Colonus.* Trans. Robert Fagles. New York: Penguin, 1984. 155–252. Print

Stoker, Bram. *Dracula.* Oxford: Oxford UP, 2011. Print.

III. Theoretical Lenses for Literary Study

New Historicism

Meghan McGuire

INTRODUCTION: A HISTORICAL OVERVIEW OF NEW HISTORICISM

Key Terms

- **New Historicism**
- **New Criticism**
- **formalist**
- **discourse**
- **Marxist Criticism**

- **Postcolonialism**
- **Feminist Theory**
- **literary canon**
- **interdisciplinary**
- **Cultural Materialism**

New Historicism, as the name implies, is a popular critical approach to literary analysis that situates a literary text within its historical and cultural context, questioning how that context influenced the work as well as how the text shaped, altered, and interrogated the culture in which it was written. This critical approach came into prominence in the United States in the early 1980s as a direct response to the ahistorical practices of **New Criticism**.

New Criticism was a **formalist** approach to literature, prominent in the 1950s and '60s, which upheld the belief that a literary text could and should be studied without attention to the cultural or historical context in which it was produced. New Critics deemphasized the role that an author's life experiences might have had on his or her work, and they esteemed the text for its own intrinsic aesthetic value, emphasizing issues of style and form through the practice of dedicated close-reading. In doing so, New Critics represented works of literature as universal and self-contained entities whose value rested solely on their formal literary merits. New Historicists reject this approach primarily because they feel it ignores vital social and historical influences and because it inaccurately suggests that each work of literature is an example of independent authorial genius. By contrast, New Historicism argues that all literary works are a product of intersecting and overlapping social, political, historical, and cultural influences, including those presented by and in other contemporary texts.

For example, a New Critic studying Shakespeare's *Hamlet* would only focus on the text itself. S/he would concentrate on the structure, style, characters, and tone of the play, without taking into account external factors. New Historicists, however, would argue that a textual analysis of *Hamlet* must include an analysis of its cultural, historical, and literary influences. They would attempt to situate the play within a historical framework, asking questions like *How was this play received by its original audience? How does it engage with or challenge the social and political norms in England during the late sixteenth and early seventeenth centuries? What other dramatic or non-literary texts influenced Shakespeare? How does this play compare to other plays written at the same time, and what do those comparisons reveal about the values and interests of Shakespeare's audience?*

As you can see from these hypothetical questions, New Historicism values and interrogates external influences in order to gain a more well-rounded understanding of a literary work and its culture. In order to accomplish this, New Historicists, much like New Critics, practice methods of close-reading. Unlike New Critics, however, New Historicists apply close-reading practices to both literary and non-literary texts, valuing both forms equally. For example, a New Historicist might use legal documents, personal diaries, letters, or political pamphlets in his or her research, treating these texts with the same scholarly attention given to a poem, a play, or a novel. Through this practice, New Historicists remove the literary work from a position of privilege, recognizing that non-literary documents can also reveal important aspects of history and culture through different types of discourse. (Here, **discourse** refers to multiple ways of representing and writing about reality.)

Part of the reason for valuing extra-literary texts resides in an interest in the discourses of those individuals who lack social or political power. Heavily influenced by **Marxist Criticism**—a critical movement founded on the political thinking of Karl Marx (1818–83), which views literature as a material product that reflects or opposes class-based ideologies—New Historicists recognize that most of the literary texts we study in academia are available and admired partly because they represent a privileged discourse. After all, history is rarely recorded by those who are oppressed. Marxist criticism and New Historicism, however, seek to recognize all discourses and place them in conversation with one another. By studying non-literary texts alongside traditional works of poetry, drama, or fiction, a larger and more complicated cultural narrative is revealed. For New Historicists, it is essential to view each discourse as a valid representation of history and culture.

Because of an interest in structures of power and in the narratives of those who lack power in society, a new historical approach to literature frequently overlaps with other critical lenses like **Postcolonialism** and **Feminist Theory**. Like these other critical approaches, New Historicism has a tendency to challenge the **literary canon**—the traditional set of texts that academia values as important and influential—because its research methods can initiate difficult questions: *What is "Literature"? Which texts deserve scholarly attention?*

Although aspects of this critical approach can be seen as quite radical, New Historicists certainly were not the first to recognize the value of a historical approach to literary criticism. In fact, an older form of Historicism—prominent in the 1920s, '30s, and '40s—also valued the role that authorial biography and historical background could have on the interpretation of a text. This older approach, however, used these contexts primarily as a background for the literature, arguing that literature only mimics or reflects its culture.

Based on this assumption, Historicists frequently described texts as representing the cultural reality or "spirit" of their age. Literature was broken down into clear, definable movements and periods, and the historical and/or biographical background of a text was used only as a way to validate a specific interpretation. For example, a Historicist might acknowledge the importance of biography to the study of W.B. Yeats's nineteenth and early twentieth-century poetry and drama. S/he might recognize that Yeats's unrequited love for the political activist Maud Gonne deeply influenced his writing, even suggesting that certain characters, like the young woman in his 1902 poem "Adam's Curse,"[1] are based on Gonne. While this assessment of Yeats's biography might be accurate, a traditional Historicist would have used this information simply as a way of explaining that Yeats's female characters represent real people, failing to interrogate how those characters function in the poem. In this way, the biography becomes a convenient but problematic substitute for literary analysis.

"New" Historicists find this older historical method problematic for a number of reasons. First of all, it reduces the function of a text to a mere reflection of society at a specific historical moment. Although New Historicists adamantly believe that texts can, and frequently do, reflect qualities of the culture in which they are written, they also contend that literary texts actively shape and influence their culture in equally significant ways. For a New Historicist, history and literature are both dynamic. This is one of the primary differences between New Historicism and earlier historical approaches. New Historicists also find the older historical methods unsound because they imply that history is constant, stable,

1 Please refer to the Anthology section pp. 259–260 to find this poem in full.

and ultimately knowable. For New Historicists, history is not composed of fixed events or a progressive, linear series of causes and effects. Instead, history is subjectively constructed through a variety of narrative discourses and cultural artifacts. According to New Historicists, one discourse is not more valid than another, but looking at as many narratives as possible—those of the privileged and the marginalized, alike—at least provides a more multidimensional representation of a given cultural, historical moment. An awareness of the multiple discourses contemporary to a text can yield a richer understanding of that text's subtleties, creating layers of interpretation rather than a single, fixed purpose or meaning.

In addition to the belief that history is constructed through diverse narratives and influenced by multiple social and cultural factors, New Historicists posit that critics are also influenced by similar factors. Just as a work of literature reflects and shapes its culture, the literary critic is also influenced by his or her own cultural values. The critic's interpretation of a text is formed, therefore, through his and her personal experiences and cultural biases. New Historicists believe that it is important for literary critics to acknowledge the role they play in shaping history through their analysis. In fact, many scholars will call attention to their own bias at the beginning of a critical article. This rhetorical move is not meant to undermine their credibility; instead, it allows the reader to situate the critic's argument both historically and culturally, recognizing that it is only one of many interpretations. According to New Historicists, a single, definitive interpretation of a text is impossible. No one can irrefutably say, "This is what *Hamlet* means, and this is what we know about Renaissance England from reading Shakespeare's play," because history and interpretation are both subjective. Instead, a New Historicist might ask, *What discourses are present in* Hamlet? *Are those discourses representative of people in power or do they come from marginalized members of society? How does the play reflect its culture? How does it challenge or unsettle commonly held cultural practices and beliefs during that time? How does* Hamlet *compare to other Shakespearean plays?* According to a New Historicist, a twenty-first century American reader won't read *Hamlet* the same way as an eighteenth-century British reader. Their personal and cultural biases are obviously different, which will inevitably alter their interpretation of the play.

New Critics and Formalists believe that such a fluid critical approach yields questionable results, preferring tangible, fixed interpretations to dynamic, ever-shifting critical responses to texts. This lack of continuity, however, is not seen by New Historicists as a disadvantage. Instead, it allows for a more diverse and engaging critical conversation to take place. It also emphasizes a more **interdisciplinary** approach to literary criticism, utilizing the methods and research practices of historians, cultural anthropologists, psychologists, sociologists, and economists, just to name a few. Since New Historicists view literature as one important representation of history among a variety of competing narratives, each disciplinary approach helps to uncover another form of discourse—a useful new perspective of the same historical moment.

One of the leading figures and early advocates of New Historicism is Shakespearean scholar Stephen Greenblatt (b. 1943). Although the term "new historicism" appears in some scholarship up to a decade earlier, many credit Greenblatt's use of it in his 1982 publication *The Power of Forms in the English Renaissance* as the founding moment for the movement. Greenblatt adamantly rejected what he saw as the reductive practices of New Criticism and sought to interrogate the complex relationship between literature and history. Greenblatt's influence on the field of literary criticism was, and still is, immense. Because he originally applied this theoretical lens to his work on Shakespeare, New Historicism first gained momentum as a critical practice among Renaissance scholars. Its influence quickly spread to other periods of literature, and today almost all literary critical approaches are at least partially indebted to the practices and assumptions of New Historicism.

Greenblatt and other New Historicists developed these critical methods based largely on the work of two prominent twentieth-century theorists: French historian Michel Foucault (1926–84) and British cultural theorist Raymond Williams (1921–88). From Foucault, New Historicists adopted their belief in nonlinear history and an interest in how power shapes and controls discourse. Much like Foucault, Raymond Williams was interested in systems of power, particularly how literature can challenge and oppose those systems. He was deeply invested in the narratives of the marginalized, predominantly those of the working class, and he helped found a new critical approach in the early 1980s known as **Cultural Materialism**. Many scholars refer to Cultural Materialism as the British counterpart to New Historicism. While both approaches share a number of critical assumptions and priorities, Cultural Materialism is even more invested in literature's engagement with politics. It views culture as a social and historical product that is consumed, and it uses the study of literature not only as a way to understand the past, but as a way to interpret the critic's current political culture. Like New Historicism, Cultural Materialism is also extremely interdisciplinary in nature, utilizing the methods and approaches of other academic fields like sociology, anthropology, and political sciences.

USING NEW HISTORICISM FOR LITERARY INTERPRETATION AND ANALYSIS

Now that you have a basic understanding of the background and practices of New Historicism, let's look at its practical application to a work of literature. Using Charlotte Perkins Gilman's frequently anthologized American short story "The Yellow Wallpaper" (1892) as an example, we can see how a New Historicist reading of the text might enrich our appreciation of the story and our understanding of the culture in which it was produced. The story is told from a first-person perspective through a series of diary entries. The narrator is a young married woman who suffers from a mysterious illness described throughout the text as a "nervous condition." Her husband is a doctor, and at his medical request, she is to rest and recover in isolation. In order to aid her recovery, she is not allowed to write or engage in any mental or physical activity. However, as the narrator becomes more and more isolated, she becomes more and more mentally unstable, eventually experiencing a complete break with reality. A new historical approach to this text might begin by asking a few questions about the author's biography and about the historical and cultural context of the piece: *What was Gilman's social class? What other works of literature influenced her writing? What experiences did Gilman have with mental illness and how might these experiences have influenced her work? How was mental illness viewed by society at this time in history? Is Gilman's text reinforcing a dominant discourse or is it challenging the beliefs of its time?*

In order to discover the answers to some of these questions, a New Historicist would not only look at other literary works that were published at the same time as "The Yellow Wallpaper," but s/he would try to find non-literary texts that might reveal something new about late nineteenth-century American culture. For example, s/he might look at medical records from the 1890s in an effort to understand how patients with nervous conditions were treated. In doing this research, the scholar might learn that almost all of the patients who suffered from this broadly defined "condition" were women. S/he might also learn through research that Gilman was personally affected by this condition and treated for it using a popular technique known as the "rest cure." At this point, a New Historicist scholar would begin to ask another series of questions: *How was this text received by its original audience? What kinds of discourses are present in the text? Is it important that the narrative is told from the perspective of a woman and through the form of diary entries? How might this structure and narrative technique challenge certain medical practices of its time?* Utilizing this type of contextual approach, a scholar would not only begin to see the details of Gilman's story in a new way, but s/he could begin to see how the text is also positioned against certain commonly held social and cultural beliefs.

When conducting this type of research, it's also important to remember that cultural values change, and the language that we use to articulate these values can also change. For example, the familiar term "author" meant something very different in the sixteenth century than it did in the eighteenth century or than it does today. The sixteenth century's understanding of this word isn't a better or more accurate definition, but it is different from ours. Recognizing this difference is imperative in new historical scholarship because it reinforces the belief that history isn't linear or strictly progressive. This awareness keeps us from reading too many of our own cultural values back into a text. For example, as modern readers, we might be tempted to see the husband in "The Yellow Wallpaper" as horribly controlling and condescending, completely oblivious to the fact that his wife is suffering and that her isolation is only perpetuating her mental decline. However, an understanding of the way nervous conditions were typically treated in the 1890s and an understanding of the cultural roles of men and women at the time may alter the way we interpret that particular character.

As you can probably see, many of the assumptions and methods of New Historicism are present, at least in some form, in most contemporary critical practices. Many scholars value this theoretical method because of its versatility and interdisciplinary approach; it balances a formalist close reading of a text with an understanding of that text's cultural context. As you begin to utilize this critical method, always begin your analysis with a close reading of the literature. From there, begin to ask questions about the author's biography, the historical events that shaped and impacted that time period, and the cultural beliefs that society valued. Consider which discourses are present in the text and whether those discourses represent the voices of those in power or those without it. Be conscious of your own cultural biases as you read and remain attentive to the value that non-literary texts can provide. Utilizing a new historical approach can enrich your understanding of the literature you read, allowing you to successfully situate that text within a larger historical, cultural, and literary tradition.

Questions to Consider

1. What are some of the advantages and drawbacks to using a New Historical approach to literary analysis?

2. Using a text that you've read in class or one that was assigned by your instructor, research the historical and political background in which the piece was written. Is the text reflecting and reaffirming the cultural values of its time or challenging a dominant discourse?

3. Find a non-literary text like a letter or a legal document that was written at the same time and in the same location as a literary text that you've read for class. Analyze this document using the same close-reading techniques you use for literature. How does this text compare to the literary text? Are the discourses similar or conflicting? What does this document reveal about the historical, cultural, or political context of both texts?

Essay Prompt

Choosing from the questions presented for the text in this chapter, conduct a New Historical analysis of one or more aspects of "The Yellow Wallpaper" or some other text assigned by your instructor. How does this approach change or alter your original reading of the story?

Works Consulted

Barry, Peter. "New Historicism and Cultural Materialism." *Beginning Theory: An Introduction to Literary and Cultural Theory.* 2nd ed. New York: Manchester UP, 2002. 172–191. Print.

Dobie, Ann B. "Cultural Studies: New Historicism." *Theory into Practice: An Introduction to Literary Criticism.* 3rd ed. Boston: Wadsworth, 2012. 175–199. Print.

Gilman, Charlotte Perkins. *The Yellow Wallpaper.* Ed. Dale M. Bauer. Boston: Bedford/St. Martin's, 1998. Print.

Veeser, H. Aram. "The New Historicist." *The New Historicism Reader.* Ed. H. Aram Veeser. New York: Routledge, 1994. 1–32. Print.

Brian Butler

HISTORICAL BACKGROUND

Key Terms

- **colonialism**
- **settler colony**
- **administered colony**
- **ideology**
- **imperialism**
- **Eurocentrism**
- **cultural colonization**
- **postcolonialism**
- **neocolonialism**

The field of postcolonial studies is still relatively new; therefore, there is an ongoing debate on what exactly constitutes postcolonialism. To begin to define this term, we must first understand what colonialism is. **Colonialism** is the subjection of one population by another through the establishment of colonies. By the early 1800s, Western European powers (Britain, France, Germany, Belgium, Portugal, and Spain) held thirty-five percent of the earth's surface, and by 1878, that proportion increased to sixty-seven percent. By 1914, those powers controlled roughly eighty-five percent of the earth as colonies in one form or another.[1] Since we are focusing on literature written in English, we will concentrate on how the British created their empire through the establishment of colonies.

The British established two types of colonies: settler and administered. **Settler colonies** consisted of emigrants from Britain who took most of the land in the colony and dominated the colony both economically and politically. Examples of this type of colony include those founded in Canada and Australia. **Administered colonies**, whose main goal was economic exploitation, were founded by much smaller groups of British emigrants who still dominated politically and

---

1 Edward Said, *Culture and Imperialism*, (New York: Vintage, 1994) 8.

economically, but only settled a very small portion of the land. Examples of previously administered colonies include those in India, Nigeria, and Kenya. The process of colonization was guided by the ideology of imperialism. For our purposes, we will define **ideology** as a system of ideas that govern a group's—in this case the British—economic and political policies. **Imperialism** is defined as the ideologically motivated and systematic settling and/or domination of regions or territories to establish colonies or to exert significant political and economic authority over those territories that would be both politically and economically beneficial to the empire.

Before we move forward it would be helpful for us to fully flesh out the distinctions between colonialism and imperialism in the context of the British Empire. We are focusing on the British Empire, because our focus is on postcolonial literature written in English. Colonialism as a practice was largely based on trade and economic exploitation. From the mid-1600s to the mid-1800s, the British were largely interested in creating a network of colonies they could trade with and extract resources from. Traditionally, postcolonialists identify the year 1835 as the moment when the British changed how they saw their empire and what the goals of that empire should be, for they determined that the empire and its subjects would be much easier to rule if the colonized were more like them. After 1835, the British sought to dominate their colonies culturally in an effort to "civilize" the indigenous peoples who lived in them. The dictates of this "civilizing mission" are best captured by Lord Macaulay's (1800–1859) "Minute on Indian Education" of 1835, in which he states:

> We must at present do our best to form a class who may be interpreters between us and the millions whom we govern; a class of persons, Indian in blood and colour, but English in taste, in opinions, in morals, and in intellect. To that class we may leave it to refine the vernacular dialects of the country, to enrich those dialects with terms of science borrowed from the Western nomenclature, and to render them by degrees fit vehicles for conveying knowledge to the great mass of the population.[2]

While this speech is specifically focused on India, the ideas captured within it were dispersed throughout the British Empire, becoming an integral part of the ideology of British imperialism. In essence, the British attempted to remake the indigenous people living in their colonies in their own image. They did this through a process of education, Christian missionary work, technical and infrastructural improvements (railroads, bridges, telegraph systems), as well as political and social reforms. Entire generations of people in colonized countries were

---

2 Ashley Jackson, *The British Empire: A Very Short Introduction*, (Oxford: Oxford UP, 2013) 33–4.

impacted by these changes in how their societies were governed and structured. For instance, a young boy growing up in India would learn English history and literature instead of Indian history and literature. Primarily through this education policy, the British were able to create classes of people all throughout their empire who worked for the British and helped them to maintain control of the indigenous populations. As a result, the connections these peoples had with their historical and cultural roots became tenuous. In other words, the colonized were inculcated with **Eurocentrism**, which is the "assumption that European ideals and experiences are the standard by which all other cultures are to be measured and judged inferior."[3] This process is known as **cultural colonization**, the practice of replacing the cultural practices and beliefs of an indigenous people with European values, governance, and laws. From 1835 through the early 20th century, the British systematically tried to improve and implement this doctrine.

By the early 1920s, the British governed one-fifth of the world's population and controlled one-fourth of the world's landmass. In fact, "Of the world's 203 nation states, sixty-three were once ruled by Britain."[4] Despite the immensity of the empire, the British, weakened by World War I and World War II, began to lose control over their empire. Starting in 1947, British decolonization was in full swing, beginning first with South Asia colonies such as Burma, Ceylon (Sri Lanka), India, and Pakistan. By the mid-1950s, the British lost much of their holdings in the Middle East, and by the 1960s, the majority of British-held African colonies gained independence. Over the course of the 1970s and 1980s, the remainder of the colonies gained independence, specifically in the Caribbean and in the white settler colonies of South Africa and Rhodesia (Zimbabwe). Although not a traditional colony, the British maintained a 99-year lease over Hong Kong, which it finally released to the Chinese in 1997.[5] What students using postcolonial theory should take away from this is that the process of decolonization was both uneven and different for each of the former colonies, thus necessitating that a postcolonial analysis of any former colony should be largely informed by and governed by the specific political and cultural idiosyncrasies of that colony.

This brings us back to the debate identified in the beginning of this essay about what exactly constitutes postcolonialism. Initially, **postcolonialism**, as the prefix "post" indicates, focused on the aftermath of colonial rule; however, recent scholarship has expanded this definition to account for our understandings of colonialism and imperialism across periods. But when does this time begin? In India, the postcolonial period begins in 1947; for Nigeria, 1960. Thus, postcolonialism

---

3 Ann Dobie, *Theory into Practice*, (New York: Thomson, 2002) 195.

4 Ashley Jackson, *The British Empire: A Very Short Introduction*, (Oxford: Oxford UP, 2013) 4.

5 Ibid. 95-6.

is not a catch-all definition for every former colony. Each of these colonies was ruled differently, gained independence under different circumstances, and struggled with the aftermath of colonialism in very different ways.

In fact, many former colonies still experience colonialism in completely new forms known as **neocolonialism**, which is the continuation of colonial conditions under more indirect forms of control. For instance, whereas colonialism relied on either settlers or administrative institutions to govern the colonies directly, neocolonialism arises as a result of economic, political, and legal implementations, both by governments and international corporations, which create similar conditions as those in the colonial era. Thus, students using postcolonial theory should always be aware that their reading of a text, and indeed the text itself, is isolated to specific colonial encounters and situations and should in no way be taken to be examples of postcolonialism for all former colonies for all time.

POSTCOLONIAL THEORY

The field of postcolonial theory primarily rests on the ideas of three key thinkers: Edward Said (1935–2003), Homi Bhabha (b. 1949), and Gayatri Spivak (b. 1942). These scholars developed the foundation of postcolonial theory and its basic assumptions, which are that by reading a text in its colonial/postcolonial context we can not only understand that work, but also the various dynamics of the complex colonial relationships and networks in which the text was produced, circulated, read, and interpreted. From here we can begin to understand the attitudes of the colonizers and colonized in both a colonial and postcolonial setting. Some of the questions postcolonial theory helps us to engage with include:

- Does the work support or resist the ideology and practices of imperialism?

- Does the text depict political and cultural domination explicitly or allegorically?

- Does the work champion a new national identity for the formerly colonized? If so, what are the values of that identity? Who is included in that group? Who is left out?

- How does the text address the colonial past? What does the text suggest about the future?

- What does the nation look like in the aftermath of colonialism?

- What are the author's hopes for the future of their country?

There are many more questions the field asks, but for now it might be more helpful to discuss the key concepts of the founders of the field, which are used to construct answers to these questions.

EDWARD SAID: "THE ORIENT," "THE OCCIDENT," AND "THE OTHER"

Key Terms
- **Orientalism**
- **the Orient**
- **the Occident**
- **the Other**
- **colonial discourse**
- **colonial discourse analysis**

Edward Said, in his landmark critical work *Orientalism* (1994), presented the ideas of the Orient, the Occident, and the Other. **Orientalism** is the process by which Europe, through various disciplines such as anthropology and history, constructed an image of the "Orient." **The Orient**, quite simply, is the East—the Middle East and Asia; **the Occident** is Europe. For Said, the practice of Orientalism was a process by which those living in the Occident created entire fields of study of the Other living in the Orient. In other words, Orientalism was used to create exoticized representations of spaces and peoples outside of Europe. **The Other**, generally anyone who is separate from one's self, is characterized by those living in the Occident in a binary relationship of opposition. In other words, I see myself as a Self who is defined in relation to Others. Their differences from me are the source of my identity, which inform how I see myself as well as how I perceive them. In simple terms, the colonizers represent the Occident, the colonized represent the Orient. This process is known as **colonial discourse**.

In popular depictions of the Orient and the Others who lived there, the colonized were depicted as primitive, while European colonizers were depicted as civilized. An example of this kind of discourse is cannibalism, which is the term for the eating of human flesh by other human beings. By painting the colonized as uncivilized, the colonizers were able to distinguish themselves from the colonized as more civilized, which in turn gave them a moral justification for colonization—colonization became a civilizing mission. There are a slew of binary oppositions that originate with colonial discourse, but the most readily useful to the beginning student of postcolonial theory are savage/civilized, black/white, child/adult, ignorant/enlightened, primitive/modern, and masculine/feminine. In each of these examples, the colonizers are usually represented by the latter privileged positions, and the colonized are always represented by the former, which are always cast in derogatory terms. For Said, this process had a lasting effect on both the colonizers and the colonized throughout the colonial era and on through the postcolonial era. His primary means for analyzing this phenomenon is **colonial discourse analysis**. Colonial discourse analysis seeks to identify evidence of this process and its resultant effects in colonial and postcolonial settings. An obvious example of this is Joseph Conrad's *Heart of Darkness* (1899).

In *Heart of Darkness*, Conrad, through his narrator Marlow, paints a portrait of Africa that in many ways exemplifies the tenets of Orientalism. Africans are voiceless over the course of the novella. What we learn about them is filtered by Marlow and other European characters who are given lines of dialogue throughout. No African characters ever speak about their condition or critique the colonizers who have placed them in this position. The narrative itself, through its depictions of a savage and ever-threatening setting—which constantly creates an atmosphere or mood of foreboding and fear throughout the novella—offers little in the way of overt critique of imperialism. Notable postcolonial writers such as Chinua Achebe have critiqued the novella for its dehumanizing portrayal of Africans, going so far as to say that Conrad presents Africa as the exact antithesis of Europe. Thus, a student wishing to perform a colonial discourse analysis of *Heart of Darkness* would identify how the text presents binary oppositions through narrative, dialogue, and characterization, noting what binaries (e.g., savage/civilized) are erected and reinforced over the course of the novella. Such a reading might include the depiction of Africans as backwards or uncivilized and the Europeans as modern and civilized. Students performing this kind of analysis would identify the ways that representation is used as a method for establishing, maintaining, and legitimizing forms of colonial power, including the presentation of colonizers as the knowers and the colonized as the object (rather than subject) of knowledge.

HOMI BHABHA: "AMBIVALENCE," "MIMICRY," AND "HYBRIDITY"

Key Terms
- **ambivalence**
- **mimicry**
- **hybridity**

Homi Bhabha also uses colonial discourse analysis, but his theories go beyond to account also for the psychological impact imperialism had on both the colonized and the colonizer, which is evident in the speech/representations of colonial discourse itself. His primary contributions to the field include the key concepts of ambivalence, mimicry, and hybridity. Bhabha takes the term ambivalence from psychoanalysis and appropriates it for colonial discourse analysis. In its original definition, ambivalence is used to describe a continual fluctuation between wanting one thing and its opposite. In the imperial context in which Bhabha uses it, **ambivalence** captures the phenomenon within colonial discourse itself of the colonized being torn between the will of the colonizers and the resistance of the colonized. If colonial discourse attempts to reshape colonial subjects in the image of the colonized, then ambivalence captures the psychological impact on the colonized, who is both attracted to and repulsed by the colonizer and his values. Thus, the relationship is ambivalent, because the colonized is never completely opposed to the colonizer.

Because of cultural colonization, the colonized in many cases experienced a deep sense of loss, for in many cases their ties to their cultural past were effectively severed as a result of the processes of imperialism and Orientalism. As a consequence of the devaluing of native cultures, the colonized came to see themselves as inferior to the colonizers. Thus, the colonized began to imitate the culture of the colonizer in a practice Bhabha calls **mimicry**, which is the imitation of dress, language, and behaviors. However, mimicry is also impacted by ambivalence, in that the colonizer can never be sure if he is being mimicked or mocked, which in turn may disrupt or subvert the dominance of the colonizer.

Both ambivalence and mimicry interact in a continuous negotiation between colonizer and colonized, creating hybrid subjects. **Hybridity** is the process by which new forms are created as a result of the interaction of colonizer and colonized. Hybridity can emerge in several forms: linguistic, cultural, political, and racial. An example of linguistic hybridity would be pidgin and creole languages, which are common languages shared in colonial spaces where there exist many languages.

A perfect text for this type of analysis would be Jean Rhys' "The Day They Burned the Books" (1960). Set in the Dominican Republic in the early 1900s, the story focuses on a group of kids who are themselves examples of hybridity. These children represent a variety of racial distinctions, many of which are hybrids, from Eddie who is English to the unnamed narrator who is Creole (English, but born in a Caribbean colony) to other children of mixed race. The culture of the community is also hybrid, in that it is a mixture of British, creole, and former slave cultures. The language throughout the story ranges from "proper" English to creole and pidgin. An analysis of the ambivalence that occurs within this story would seek to identify and address how each of the characters are pulled between the cultures of the colonizer and colonized linguistically, culturally, politically, and racially.

GAYATRI SPIVAK: "SUBALTERN" AND "HEGEMONY"

Key Terms
- **subaltern**
- **hegemony**

Probably one of the most debated (and difficult) postcolonial theorists is Gayatri Spivak, who famously asked, "Can the subaltern speak?" Before we can answer her question, we must first determine what a subaltern is. Spivak draws on Marxist critic Antonio Gramsci's uses of the term. According to Gramsci, the **subaltern** is a person of inferior rank who is subject to the hegemony of the ruling classes. In simple terms, **hegemony** is the power of the ruling classes to convince other classes that their interests are the interests of all. Thus, the ruling class is able to rule by consent, rather than by direct force. Subaltern classes may include peasants, workers, and other classes who are not represented by the ruling powers.

Spivak takes these two concepts and expands them to account for the exclusion of peoples based on their class, age, gender, and political orientation. Spivak's work seeks to redress the voicelessness of these groups throughout history into the present. For her, the fields of history, anthropology, and literary studies lack the ability to address the plight of the subaltern. Therefore, the subaltern cannot speak, for there is not adequate existing representation for them. It falls upon the scholar of postcolonial theory to assist in giving voice to the subaltern. The colonized subaltern is always identified by his or her difference from the elite. As a result, this difference is always specific to the individual and there is no single totalizing or essential identity that can be used for everyone who fits the criteria of being a subaltern. Instead, we must continuously seek to identify how discursive notions of race, class, and gender exclude subalterns from political representation.

Students wishing to employ these theoretical concepts would need to identify texts which contain characters that are largely voiceless or those texts which have been "rewritten" by postcolonial authors. Probably the quintessential example of this would be Jean Rhys' *Wide Sargasso Sea* (1966), which is a rewriting of Charlotte Brontë's *Jane Eyre* (1847). In rewriting *Jane Eyre*, Rhys gives voice to the subaltern by placing Antoinette Cosway (Bertha Mason in *Jane Eyre*) as the protagonist of the story. Antoinette was largely invisible in *Jane Eyre*, but she is given a voice in *Wide Sargasso Sea*. The subaltern is thus allowed to speak by shifting the focus from the Victorian home and the turmoil within it—as depicted in *Jane Eyre*—to the issues of slavery and the slave trade that both impacted Antoinette's life growing up in the Caribbean and made the Victorian estate a

186

possibility. Thus, Rhys enacts a form of resistance against the hegemony of the English canon, which privileges novels such as *Jane Eyre*, by illustrating how subalterns like Antoinette suffered invisibly in novels such as *Jane Eyre*. In so doing, Antoinette is not just some obstacle to Rochester and Jane Eyre's happiness, as depicted in *Jane Eyre*, but is instead someone who is suffering deeply because of her isolation and displacement from her homeland, thus highlighting the imperial ideology that overlooks the suffering of subalterns present in many of the great "classics" of literature.

Ultimately, the field of postcolonial studies is challenging both because of the difficulty of the competing theories that comprise it as well as the huge range of texts which qualify to be analyzed by it. Indeed, poetry, drama, and prose fiction written in colonial, postcolonial, and neocolonial settings can all fall under the umbrella of postcolonial literary studies. As a consequence, the student of postcolonial studies has the twofold challenge of identifying texts that constitute postcolonial literature and then selecting from the variety of theories he or she can use to analyze those texts. Oftentimes, one theoretical perspective or concept cannot address all of the multiplicities a student encounters in reading a postcolonial work of literature. However, a firm understanding of the foundations of the field will be invaluable in surmounting these obstacles.

Questions to Consider

1. According to Edward Said's ideas of colonial discourse, the construction of binaries is a central tool in the creation of the colonized/colonizer relationship. The essay lists a number of such binaries—savage/civilized, black/white, child/adult, ignorant/enlightened, primitive/modern, and masculine/feminine. Can you think of other possible binaries?

2. In the section on Homi Bhabha's theories, the author states that hybridity can be found in linguistic, cultural, political, or social forms, and offers an example of linguistic hybridity. What might be an example of cultural, political, or social hybridity?

3. The author provides a definition of the subaltern figure and offers an example of how this figure is largely ignored or invisible in canonical British texts. Can you think of other such figures in works you have read? What does considering the absence of the subaltern's point of view or situation do in terms of allowing us to read more deeply into a narrative?

4. What might a text approached through a postcolonial lens reveal about the operations of cultural difference—the ways in which race, religion, class, gender, sexual orientation, cultural beliefs, and customs combine to form individual identity—in shaping our perceptions of ourselves, others, and the world in which we live?

Essay Prompt

In a unified essay, apply one of the postcolonial key concepts listed in this chapter to one of the texts we have read this semester. Detail how this concept illuminates the text and underlying ideologies that the text either supports or critiques.

Feminist Theory

Carrie Hart

HISTORICAL BACKGROUND

Key Terms

- **first-wave feminism**
- **second-wave feminism**
- **patriarchy**
- **third-wave feminism**
- **power**
- **post-feminist**
- **sex**
- **gender**
- **essentialism**
- **social constructivism**
- **intersectionality**
- **assemblage**
- **positionality**
- **transnational feminism**

Thinking about feminist theory necessarily involves thinking about social movements within and beyond university classrooms. People within these movements have thought of feminism in many ways. For example, liberal feminists promote equality between genders by reforming systems that already exist. One example of liberal feminism is to investigate wage discrepancies between men and women and to propose ways to level out these gaps. Radical feminists, on the other hand, claim that reforming systems is not enough; it is necessary to dismantle inequitable systems rather than attempt to change them from within. Within each approach, feminist theory has been a way to think about social injustices and inequities that are connected to sex and gender.

One way that scholars frequently describe the history of feminist movements in the United States is in terms of waves. Though there has been debate about whether or not this framing is overly simplistic, it is helpful to have a basic understanding of what people mean when they reference each wave. In the **first wave** of feminism, the struggle for suffrage played a large role. From the late 18th century through the beginning of the 20th century, feminists advocated for the recognition of women's legal status and the right to vote. Often present within these efforts was an emphasis on the rights of white women over the rights of women of color—a set of tensions that carried forward into what many characterize as the **second wave** of feminist movements. The time frame of this wave coincides with the women's rights movements of the 1960s and 1970s. On one hand, the main concern of the second wave emerged as opposition to **patriarchy**, a system of male domination that oppresses women and is evident within a range of social phenomena—the disproportionate rate of male-to-female violence in interpersonal relationships, the overrepresentation of men in positions of power (e.g., political offices and business executives), and legal restrictions on women's reproductive rights. At the same time that some within feminism's second wave spoke out against these issues, others critiqued the framework of the movement for prioritizing the rights of white, middle-class, heterosexual women over women of color, poor and working-class women, and lesbians. During this time, women of color feminists drew attention to the ways in which gendered oppression is not separable from oppression on the basis of race and class. They insisted that for white, middle-class women to isolate gendered oppression as the primary form of power imbalances is to participate in the same systems they claimed to oppose.

These tensions gave rise to what many describe as the contemporary **third wave** of the feminist movement. Keeping in mind that second-wave feminist movements had been fraught with tensions over who had the right to claim feminism, many within the third wave sought to widen the scope and potential of feminist thinking to include all groups marginalized by diverse forms of patriarchy. As such, the role of women of color, lesbian and queer women, and working-class women has become a less contentious and more visible part of feminist social movements. In the shift from second to third wave, a critique of patriarchy came to be framed in relation to broader concerns with many systems of **power**, the ways in which people control and influence the actions and agency of others. In focusing on systems of power, feminist theory can be used to consider how patterns in economic and political activity, understandings of identity, and the production of cultural texts such as literature and film may all be influenced by who is able to make decisions that impact a broad range of people. During this period of time (the 1970s forward), feminist theory has also become a more common feature of analysis in college classrooms. Often, the most overt courses that incorporate feminist theory are housed within Women's and Gender Studies programs, but many scholars across various fields within the humanities and social sciences make use of the ideas of identity, agency, control, and authority that feminist theory has to offer. Students using feminist theory to analyze a text can do so in order to think about how the politics of sex and gender are present in the narrative, as well as how these politics influence related issues such as race and socioeconomic class.

There are other ways to think about feminism beyond these often-referenced "waves." Historically and contemporarily, people have interpreted the idea of feminism in diverse ways. For example, those who claim that we now live in a **post-feminist** world—implying that feminist movements have been so success-ful in generating gender equality that they are no longer necessary—are often referencing a narrow form of feminism focused on equal rights between men and women. A possible counter argument for this perspective could point to gendered forms of discrimination that also take race and class into consideration. When thinking about the various ways in which feminism is understood, it is helpful to look back through historical examples to consider how various groups have used the ideas of feminism to challenge the status quo. Since feminist the-ory involves asking questions about who gets to narrate history—those with the power usually determine what the historical record says about a given time and place—it is also important to apply this thinking to histories of feminism. This brings us back to the reason why the use of the three waves to explain the history of feminism can be contested. To frame all feminist thinking in the U.S. during the 19th and early 20th centuries as involving the predominantly white suffrage movement is to ignore the ways in which people may also have been employing feminism in race and labor organizing at the same time. As this example dem-onstrates, it is important to be aware of power dynamics at work even in uses and representations of feminist thinking, and to be aware of the ways in which one's own relationship to power may inform one's perspectives on the meanings, histories, and potential uses of feminism as a cultural lens.

FEMINIST THEORY

Though there is not necessarily a single historical origin for feminist theory, ex-amples from a few scholars can provide a good starting point for understanding the field. One of the main undertakings of feminist theorists has been to explore the question: "What is a woman?" Monique Wittig (1935–2003) explores this ques-tion in terms of the idea of "woman" as being both produced and devalued by social systems. Judith Butler's ideas of sexuality and gender are also often used in feminist discourse (see Queer Theory). A major contribution that Wittig and other scholars such as Butler have made to feminist theory has been to think about the relationship between **sex** (genitalia, chromosomes, and other biological mat-ters) and **gender** (dress, behavior, and performance). Distinguishing these ideas helps to understand that there is not necessarily a "natural" link between sex and gender, and it also helps students to inquire about the role that socialization plays in creating the world they know.

There are two main schools of thought in regard to the idea of socialization in relation to sex and gender: **essentialism**, which maintains that femininity and masculinity are biologically rooted expressions, and **social constructivism**, which understands ideas about sex and gender to be created through various cultural rules and expectations. In other words, essentialism rests on the traditional idea that sex and gender are linked and biologically determined conditions, while social constructivism revises this view to consider that while sex is biologically determined it can be changed, and gender can be the result of choice, convention, or performance. A social constructionist understanding allows students to look to the social world for both the production of sexed and gendered norms and the potential to challenge, subvert, and change them.

This exploration of gender as a social construction leads to a consideration of the features of power involved in producing and maintaining gendered norms, as well as the role of feminism in addressing inequities that systems of power produce. Though people have defined feminism in diverse ways, bell hooks (b. 1952) summarizes the version of feminism we are using in this chapter as a way of addressing these broad systems of oppression. She states, "Feminism is a movement to end sexism, sexist exploitation, and oppression."[1] Towards these ends, it is important to think about the various ways that sexism manifests and how these ways relate to and are involved in other modes of oppression. Kimberlé Crenshaw (b. 1959) developed the term **intersectionality** to refer to the ways that different kinds of social categories and oppressions are present within each other. The Combahee River Collective, an organization of black feminist socialist lesbians, provides a clear example of intersectional analysis in a 1977 statement in which they describe "racial, sexual, heterosexual and class oppression" as "interlocking."[2] For members of the Collective and other women of color, intersectionality became an important way of addressing race-based oppression within white feminist movements. A notable example lies in Audre Lorde's (1934–1992) statement that since "the master's tools will never dismantle the master's house," it is necessary for feminists to consider differences among them in order to adequately address all forms of oppression.[3] More recently, the idea of an **assemblage**, a collection of ideas and objects with situational, but not necessarily permanent or inherent relationships to one another, has become an

---

1 bell hooks, *Feminism Is For Everybody: Passionate Politics* (Cambridge: South End Press, 2000), 1.

2 Combahee River Collective, "A Black Feminist Statement." *Words of Fire: An Anthology of African-American Feminist Thought.* Ed. Beverly Guy-Sheftall. (New York: The New Press, 1995), 232.

3 Audre Lorde, *Sister Outsider* (Freedom: The Crossing Press, 1984), 99.

additional way of thinking about both personal and group relationships as being fluid and contextual, rather than fixed and universal.[4]

APPLYING FEMINIST THEORY TO LITERARY ANALYSIS

In general, as a student applying feminist theory to analysis of texts, you should think about power dynamics as they emerge in identity categories and the politics that surround them. This may involve thinking about how these categories are created, as well as what access people have to power based on them. Additionally, it is important to consider your own **positionality**, or personal relationship to power and oppression, and how it informs your reading of the text.

For example, in analyzing Zora Neale Hurston's 1937 novel *Their Eyes Were Watching God*, feminist theory can help to consider how the social terrain that protagonist Janie navigates is rife with rules regarding how she should behave and what consequences will befall her should she fail to do so. A feminist analysis could look into the production of these rules, the ways that Janie resists them, and what Janie's experiences have to do with systems of oppression like racism, sexism, and classism. In thinking about the role of power in the novel, you might note how Janie responds to expectations about who she should marry, the judgments of the townspeople, and forms of violence within her interpersonal relationships. Additionally, feminist theory could help to ask questions about Hurston's choice to represent language in the way that she does and how her choice relates to and challenges dominant understandings of English. In thinking further about Hurston's authorship, you could use feminist theory to consider how the narrative and its original reception relates to the political context of the 1930s in which Hurston was writing. How might the novel have functioned as a political statement at this time, and how does it function today?

AN INTERDISCIPLINARY FRAMEWORK

In approaching this and other texts, it is important to remember that feminist theory does not operate in isolation from other ways of thinking. As a framework that involves asking complex questions about power and oppression, it is often necessarily interdisciplinary, emerging in analysis of literature, media, history, science, and politics, for example. Also, as is hopefully evident by this point, the scope of feminist theory is much broader than simply "women's issues." As a way

4 Jasbir K. Puar, *Terrorist Assemblages: Homonationalism in Queer Times* (Durham: Duke University Press, 2009), 211.

to understand and challenge social injustice on a wide scale, it has the capacity to address issues connected to femininity, masculinity, and other gendered constructions, as well as the ways that these constructions are inflected with other elements, such as race, class, ability, and sexuality, as mentioned above.

An example of the capacity of feminist theory to address a range of issues is the development of **transnational feminism**, in which scholars ask questions about the role of power in relation to the production of nation-states and feminist movements within and across them. Transnational feminists such as Chandra Mohanty (b. 1955) and Gloria Anzaldúa (1942–2004) have looked into the role that the production of political borders plays within understandings of identity, distribution of resources, and even feminist thinking, itself. Transnational feminist readings of literature look for the treatment of national identities and the relationship that these identities have to other political formations and claims. Students could use transnational feminism to consider the construction of the United States in Willa Cather's *My Ántonia* (1918). Questions within this line of thought could include:

- How do the characters in the novel relate to their setting both in terms of land and nationality?

- How is the protagonist's gender identity and presentation related to her role in white settlement?

- What mention, if any, is present of the political process of settlement and the implications for indigenous people?

- How does Cather's treatment of time relate to the way you understand the history of the United States?

- Does the extension of the United States to the western shore appear as inevitable, or as a process that involves active decision-making and oppressive treatment toward indigenous people who were already living on the land that the U.S. government claimed as new territory?

In this novel as well as others that deal with the ways that nations form, the lens of transnational feminism can help to ask questions about how politics of gender play into the process of settlement. Additionally, transnational feminism gives readers a way to read "against the grain" by noting if, when, and how indigenous people appear in the narrative. If representations are superficial, negative, or otherwise lacking, it is valuable to consider how these choices relate to the author's intended audience, as well as how readers receive them.

GENDER, POWER, AND ACTION

At this point, it may be unclear what feminist theory has to do with "women" anymore. If this is the case, it is helpful to understand that a central task of feminist theory is to understand power, which includes the ways that gender comes to make sense as a way to categorize people and also to justify imbalances in power. As such, this kind of analysis involves thinking about how ideas about gender and other kinds of categorization, such as race, nationality, and class status, are a part of how people understand and experience these imbalances. One way to think about this is on a personal level. For example, when you think about yourself as a person, you can probably identify a gender category you belong to. Feminist theory helps to think about where this idea comes from, how it is connected to the way other people think, and how it is connected to your experiences with power (or lack thereof). Likewise, feminist theory can be helpful in considering how these kinds of power dynamics emerge within literary texts—for example, in the way that authors chose to represent characters, readers are able to relate to the narrative, and the relationship that the text has to lived political experiences.

Before concluding, it is important to note and respond to the idea that like most theories, feminist theory is "only talk," and inasmuch, is less important than "action." In responding to this idea, feminist theorists have posited that, as ideas are a large part of actions, there is indeed no real separation between theory and practice—that since ideas are an inseparable part of actions and vice versa, theory is always present within and as action. In thinking about how this critique applies to the use of feminist theory as an analytical tool, it is helpful to consider analysis as a form of action, and to think about the relationship between thinking and other forms of action. In using a feminist framework to analyze literary texts, it is helpful to consider the ways in which reading, interpreting, and writing are all actions that have significance regarding the way that writers and readers understand the world around them.

Questions to Consider

1. Audre Lorde's idea that "the master's tools will never dismantle the master's house" provides a way to think about oppressive social systems, who builds them, and possible ways to change them. What social systems can you think of? What and who is responsible for building those systems, and how and why might they be changed?

2. The idea of positionality helps us to consider our own social position and reflect on how it influences the way we, as social beings, relate to the world around us. What are parts of your identities and experiences that inform your positionality? How do you think this might influence your reading?

3. One of the main tasks of feminist theory has been to respond to the idea of oppression. Feminist theorists have described oppression broadly, in terms of sexism, racism, and classism, and also specifically, in terms of the concrete ways that beliefs in these systems emerge in everyday life, such as street harassment, the limited focus on people of color in high school curricula, and the assumption that people are only poor if they are also lazy. Can you think of other examples of oppression?

Essay Prompts

1. In a clear argument, apply one of the main concepts above to a text you have read for class. Explain what the concept allows you to notice about the story and the way the author has told it.

2. A feminist slogan that emerged in the 1970s was that "the personal is political." Consider what this idea means in the context of a text you've read this semester, and use a feminist theoretical lens to discuss your findings.

Queer Theory

Carrie Hart

HISTORICAL BACKGROUND

Key Terms

- **GLBT/LGBT**
- **deconstruction**
- **discourse**
- **subject**
- **performativity**
- **disidentification**
- **heteronormativity**
- **homonormativity**
- **interpellation**

Since queer theory is a relatively recent academic field, it is helpful to understand its relationship to the intellectual and social movements of the 1960s and '70s that influenced its development. Similar to feminist theory, queer theory came about in response to challenges that scholars and activists were making to the ways that people understand gender and sexuality. Whereas "queer" has negative connotations in some contexts, queer theorists understand the term to be associated with thinking critically about oppressive systems and emphasizing the fluidity of human experience.

In particular, queer theory has a close, though not synonymous, relationship with movements for **GLBT** (gay, lesbian, bisexual, and transgender/transsexual; also known as **LGBT**) liberation. One event that historians frequently cite as important to these movements is the 1969 Stonewall Riots, in which patrons of the predominantly gay and transgender Stonewall Inn bar in New York City actively resisted a violent police raid. In doing so, the Stonewall patrons demonstrated the possibility of counteracting oppression through collective efforts. Another historical moment that is significant to queer theory, though it predates the naming of the field, is the 1970 organization of the Lavender Menace, a group of radical lesbian feminists who protested the National Organization of Women's characterization of lesbians as a threat to the feminist movement. Both the Stonewall protesters and the women involved in the Lavender Menace engaged in queer politics, in that they were antagonistic towards groups and ideas that they saw as justifying exclusionary, oppressive politics in order to maintain the status quo.

During the 1980s and 1990s, a strand of radical politics emerged within the broader movement for gay and lesbian rights. Activist groups such as Queer Nation and ACT UP used the idea of queerness to separate their approaches and demands from those of the mainstream gay and lesbian movements that were calling for assimilation into and greater acceptance by dominant society. Those who ascribed to radical gay stances rejected the goal of assimilation and sought to think about the possibilities that might emerge in not claiming that their identities were similar to those within the group in control. A specific example of this political stance is available in the 1987 formation of ACT UP (AIDS Coalition to Unleash Power), which AIDS activists formed in response to what they perceived as the shortcomings of the Gay Men's Health Crisis (GMHC), an organization that provided services for those with HIV/AIDS but did not address some of the governmental policies that made it difficult to do so. Unlike the GMHC, ACT UP favored strategies of direct political action, such as public protests and acts of civil disobedience, to demand affordable treatment for the HIV virus.

It is important to note that in all of these examples, queer politics are not necessarily the same as lesbian and gay politics; though they are often simultaneous and complementary, they frequently embody meaningful differences in thinking and strategy about how to approach the issues at stake. A contemporary example is available in approaches to the issue of marriage. While gay and lesbian organizing often advocates for equal access for gay and lesbian couples to the institution of marriage, queer approaches call for an assessment of why access to marriage seems necessary, as well as how granting gay and lesbian couples the right to marry does not address systemic oppression on a broader scale.

Just as has been the case with feminist theory, racial and class dynamics have played a part in the way that people have articulated their work and goals in queer social movements and scholarship. As is evident in the work of Cherríe Moraga (b. 1952), Audre Lorde (1934–1992), and Gloria Anzaldúa (1942–2004), women of color feminists have been actively resisting the "whitewashing"—an overwhelming emphasis on the work of white theorists over the work of theorists of color—of queer theory for a long time. Anzaldúa, for example, introduced the idea of "mestiza consciousness" as a way to think about how gendered, sexual, racial, and national identities can seem "mixed" when dominant ways of thinking place them in between recognized categories (such as male/female gender categories or U.S./Mexican nationalities). Anzaldúa used the idea of the mestiza both to call attention to the dominant modes and also to reclaim and affirm these "in-between" identities as valid.[1] Her idea of the mestiza offers a way to think about how "mixed" status can involve not only marginalization by but also connectedness to multiple cultural groups. For example, she explains that although her lesbian identity may be linked to marginalization, or alienation, within her own racial group, it also connects her to queer people from all racial groups. These ideas are particularly important to keep in mind when thinking about how race and class are always a part of gendered and sexual identities and experiences.

ACADEMIC APPROACHES

Queer theory became more visible in academic studies during the 1990s, when scholars began to pay more direct attention to the idea of "queerness" as both a descriptor for radical gay politics and also an active way to read texts against the grain. As an academic discipline, "queer theory" is not the same as "lesbian and gay studies," since one of the main tasks of queer theory is to question the role that identities play in understanding the social world. In addition to GLBT social movements, poststructuralist theory has played an important role in informing the work of the field. The poststructuralist idea of **deconstruction**, or critical analysis of the way that ideas come to make sense within a particular context, is helpful to queer theory in that it provides a way to think about how gender and sexuality come to seem innate and fixed. Additionally, deconstruction enables scholars to call attention to the beliefs and practices in a given culture that instill certain norms centered around gender and sexuality that privilege certain expressions and practices over others. For example, deconstruction helps us to consider what is involved in making claims that heterosexuality is more ethical or natural than homosexuality instead of the other way around, or that one's moral character is even tied to sexuality, as well as what is at stake in understanding the two to be opposite identities. Since queer theory provides a way to think about broad social patterns, it is useful in more than one academic discipline. In addition to literary studies, queer theory can be found in other areas of the humanities, such as Media Studies and Art, as well as interdisciplinary programs such as American Studies and Women's and Gender Studies.

Though "queer" as a descriptor of identity exists as a derogatory term that various people and groups have reclaimed as an umbrella term for GLBT identity, the idea of queerness that is available within queer theory is, in some ways, also an anti-identity that calls attention to the limits of employing identity as a tool

---

1 Gloria Anzaldúa, *Borderlands / La Frontera: The New Mestiza* (San Francisco: Aunt Lute Books, 1987).

for generating political change. Rather than seeing the world as a series of binaries—male/female or gay/straight—people make use of queer theory to expand our understanding of such categories as much more **multivalent**. Additionally, queerness is a way of thinking about what establishes socio-cultural norms and how to challenge the systems of oppression involved in maintaining them. At this point, scholars often use the word "queer" as a verb to describe such acts of challenge. For example, it would be possible to describe the strategies that ACT UP used as a means of "queering the political landscape" regarding public health and HIV/AIDS. For the purpose of literary analysis, it is possible to "queer" a text by intentionally reading it in a way that challenges the status quo.

QUEER THEORY

Discourse: Michel Foucault

There are several scholars who are helpful to know when working with queer theory. Most people using queer theory will be familiar with the work of Michel Foucault (1926–1984), a French philosopher who wrote throughout the 1960s, 1970s and 1980s about a range of ideas—among them, the invention of the terms "heterosexual" and "homosexual" within the medical field in 1869. Foucault explained that these ideas are not "natural" in and of themselves, but rather, that they are a way of understanding sexuality that is specific to a contemporary time and place. This analysis is helpful for understanding how sexual acts have not always been understood in the form of personal identity; in fact, the association of sexual acts or preferences with the idea of who someone "is" is less than two centuries old. Understanding sexual identity as a contemporary phenomenon defined by the medical field is connected to the ways in which the ideas of homosexuality and heterosexuality depend on the other's existing in order to make any sense; in other words, without "homosexuality," there would be no "heterosexuality." This example enables students to think about how identity categories based on sexual behavior are not timeless; rather, they have a specific history, and while they may be politically useful, their uses may also have limits.

It is important to note how Foucault's ideas here are much broader than sexuality. They can be helpful in understanding the role of power in many social interactions and ideas—for example, how it is that people reflect power in **discourse**, or the ways that they articulate in language ideas about gender, sexuality, and identity. The invention of specific medical terms for referring to sexual orientation is but one example of how power works through discourse. In a more expansive sense, discourse can also help to think about how people come to make sense of themselves as **subjects**—as beings whose thoughts and beliefs about themselves and others come from the social world in which they exist.

Performativity: Judith Butler

Another important queer theorist is Judith Butler (b. 1956), who has called attention to the distinction that many people draw between the idea of the construction of sex (as biological) and gender (as social). Butler's claim that both sex and gender are products of social understandings is helpful for considering how queer theory can help to trouble common assumptions about "normal" bodies and behaviors. Butler is also well known for developing the idea of **performativity**, which describes how gender is a result of repeated actions, rather than an expression of a "true" self. This concept helps us to recognize that our expressions and understandings of gender are highly connected to historical and social contexts.

A very important point here is that gender is unstable rather than natural and fixed. One way to understand this idea is according to the ways that people attempt to police gender expressions through the threat of violence. For example, if a person understood to be "male" wears a skirt, paints his nails, or presents himself in ways otherwise typically coded as "female," people may respond with physical or verbal violence (e.g., calling that person a "sissy" or a "faggot"). Such acts of violence represent the available means with which people maintain specific gender norms, as well as the extent to which people will sometimes go to enforce those norms. For Butler and other queer theorists, these acts of maintenance represent precisely the ways in which gender is performed through repeated actions, rather than being a natural occurrence, because if specific gender norms were "natural," they would require no maintenance at all.

Students can use this concept of performativity to think about the relationship of gendered and sexual expressions to power. Butler asserts that the ability to claim that some gendered expressions or sexual relations are more natural or original than others is connected to power, rather than truth. For this reason, certain expressions of gender and sexuality do not experience marginalization because they are inherently strange or inferior, but rather because people marginalize them through the persistent articulation of social norms. An example of how to apply this idea is to consider how heterosexuality comes to seem more "normal" than other expressions of sexuality, as well as what is involved in the efforts that are necessary to render and maintain those norms.

Disidentification: José Esteban Muñoz

Many other scholars have contributed to the main ideas and approaches associated with queer theory. José Esteban Muñoz (1967–2013), for example, posited the term **disidentification** to describe the way that queer people of color have purposefully misused, or disidentified, with popular representations that do not explicitly include them. For example, it is possible to read for queer desire between the lines of a text, in the places where, even if an author might not include explicit description of marginalized identity or expressions, there might exist an opening for interpretation. Muñoz explained this act of recoding as both a critique of widespread exclusions of queer people of color from mainstream media and also as a form of resistance and survival.[2]

Compulsory Heterosexuality: Adrienne Rich and Homonormativity: Lisa Duggan

Though much of her work predates the formal beginning of queer theory, Adrienne Rich's (1929–2012) work is widely cited for the ways in which her idea of "compulsory heterosexuality"—an understanding of heterosexual relationships as being a product of social and economic coercion rather than "natural" desire (particularly for women)—laid the foundation for the development of the idea of **heteronormativity**, or the construction of heterosexual relationships as not only the most valuable, but also the only most legitimate option for intimate relationships.[3] Notably, Rich traced this pattern back to gendered and socioeconomic dynamics.

More recently, Lisa Duggan (b. 1954) developed the idea of **homonormativity** to describe trends in which lesbian and gay people come to adopt, rather than critique, values and practices of mainstream culture, such as in my earlier description of movements for gay and lesbian couples to have access to the institution of marriage.[4]

Interpellation: Louis Althusser

In thinking back to the elements of poststructuralist theory that inform queer theory, the idea of **interpellation**, or the dynamics that situate a subject within already existing ways of thinking, is helpful in understanding the way that each

---

2 José Esteban Muñoz, *Disidentifications: Queers of Color and the Performance of Politics* (Minneapolis: University of Minnesota Press, 1999).

3 Adrienne Rich, "Compulsory Heterosexuality and Lesbian Existence." *The Lesbian and Gay Studies Reader.* Eds. Henry Abelove et al. (New York: Routledge, 1993) 227–54.

4 Lisa Duggan, *The Twilight of Equality?: Neoliberalism, Cultural Politics, and the Attack On Democracy* (Boston, MA: Beacon Press, 2003).

of these theorists has navigated the role of social dominance in relation to normative identifications and behaviors. Louis Althusser (1918–1990) used the idea of interpellation to describe the process in which people come to make sense of themselves by answering the call, or "hail," of dominant ways of naming. For example, people are only able to understand their desires and actions as "heterosexual" when that identity category pre-exists them. What is important about this concept is the idea that even when people believe their identities to be true descriptors of themselves, they do not create these identities of their own free will; rather, their identities are made possible by cultural understandings. In one sense, the work of Muñoz, Rich, and Duggan all relates to the ways that people resist, subvert, or become aligned with oppressive ideologies as a result of interpellation.

Since the field of queer theory is much vaster than the work of scholars I have named here, it is valuable to look beyond this brief introduction for a better understanding of the kinds of inquiry that queer theory can produce. Perhaps more than in other areas of thought, scholars in queer theory have been particularly resistant to claiming a singular, coherent meaning to or use of the field.

USING QUEER THEORY IN LITERARY ANALYSIS

When thinking about ways to apply queer theory to a text, it is helpful to understand that queer theory can be useful for thinking about how to locate queerness within a text, and it can also be productive in "queering" a text. For example, in using queer theory to analyze Alice Walker's *The Color Purple* (1982), students could look into the relationships that exist within the book that challenge the dominance of heterosexual desire, such as the relationship between Shug and Celie. From there, students could use queer theory to consider how and why this relationship is non-normative within the context of the text. This kind of analysis might include a reading of the way that Walker is offering an alternative about the process of resistance and survival for Celie, whose sexual pleasure with Shug is significant not only because it is the first she ever experiences, but also because it plays a role in her healing from abuse. While it may be easy to read Celie and Shug's relationship as a lesbian one and leave it at that, queer theory can assist in analyzing how Shug's desires disrupt such a simple categorization through her relationships with people of many genders. This kind of interpretation is important because it enables an understanding of human experiences that is diverse and fluid in a way that strict categorization according to specific identities such as "lesbian" is not.

In considering these examples, however, it is important to know that queer theory is useful not only in thinking about gender and sexuality, but also when thinking about expansive structures that relate to power and social norms. For example, one could read Mary Shelley's *Frankenstein* (1823) through the lens of queer theory, even though, on the surface, this book is not overtly related to themes of gender and sexuality. A queer theoretical approach to Shelley's text could yield such questions as: What features make Frankenstein's Creature different from "normal" people, and what do these features reveal about the construction of normalcy? What role does Frankenstein's desire for knowledge play in his creation of the Creature? How does science play a part in creating new ways to understand normative and non-normative bodies in the text? What social norms from the early 1800s might Shelley have been queering when she was writing the novel? In what ways are the relationships between women significant in the novel, even though the primary characters are men? How might it be possible to disidentify with the narrative?

FOR FURTHER THOUGHT

I hope it is clear by this point that queer theory has diverse meanings and uses. Like feminist theory, it is a helpful tool for destabilizing binary understandings of the world, as well as for questioning the construction and meaning of social identities. Beyond that, queer theory offers active ways to approach texts in searching for both dominant meanings and representations as well as alternatives to them. In this way, queer theory is both a critical and a creative endeavor.

Questions to Consider

1. One of the main ideas in queer theory has been to question what makes something seem "natural." What is an example of something that seems natural to you, and how might social processes also contribute to your understanding of that thing? What do people think, write, or say about it that reflects that people also play a part in shaping your understanding?

2. Michel Foucault claimed that power works through discourse, or the ways we name and reference things. Can you think of an example in which power works through language?

3. In queer theory, "queer" can be used as a noun, an adjective, and a verb. When used as a verb, "to queer" means to question, challenge, or intentionally use something differently than intended. When is a time that you have queered something? What was the outcome of your actions?

4. Choosing a text, or using one that has been assigned to you, reflect on what approaching the text using queer theory might reveal about the social norms present within the narrative. Consider the author's use of language, characterization, and descriptions of social interactions to make a clear argument about what messages the text sends about what is and should be "normal."

Essay Prompt

Consider a text you have read for class. What is the role of gender and sexuality within it, and how might you use one of the main concepts of queer theory described above to help you understand those elements more deeply? Choose specific examples to illustrate your application of the concept.

Queer Theory

IV. Writing about Literature

Writing Essays for College Literature Classes: A General Introduction

Melissa Ridley Elmes

Although college classes vary widely in terms of workload, in college literature courses your major assignments will almost always include a midterm, a final examination, and one or more essays. While in high school the essay constitutes one of a number of formal assessment practices, at the college level essays are often the primary means of assessing how students think about and respond to literature. The essays you write for your college literature courses will likely be worth a much larger percentage of your final grade than your high school essays were, and because of this, you should expect to spend much more time and effort on these assignments than you perhaps are used to expending on a single assignment for a class.

While every professor has his and her own purposes and guidelines for assignments in association with the student learning outcomes for a class, in general the essays that you will be asked to write in introductory literature courses will be interpretive and analytical in nature. They will require you to have read carefully the text(s) you intend to write about, to have come up with and developed a thesis you intend to prove, to quote, cite, and/or paraphrase from primary and often secondary texts using MLA or some other formal citation style, and to have paid attention to the organization and arrangement of your argument, as well as the mechanics of writing such as grammar, style, and syntax.

This chapter provides a brief general overview of the nuts and bolts of writing a college-level essay, explanatory descriptions of the major essay types most often assigned in introductory college literature courses, and a basic summary of the MLA citation style most often favored by literature professors. While the information in this chapter is a good place to start in terms of thinking about writing essays for your literature course, it is not intended to substitute for instructions issued by your professor; you should always read carefully and attentively any assignment sheets or other information provided to you by your instructor when s/he assigns an essay.

I. Writing a College Literature Essay: Some General Guidelines

It is impossible in the space of a single chapter to convey everything you need to know about writing a successful essay at the college level; whole books and websites are devoted to the subject. There are, however, general guidelines that can help you avoid some of the most common problems associated with writing essays in general, and with writing essays about literature more specifically. It goes without saying that you should follow any and all formatting requests your professor makes of you; this includes things like which fonts to use, the size of your essay's margins, whether or not you need a cover sheet, which citation style to use (MLA, APA, Chicago, or similar), and how many and what kind of sources to use in making your argument. Beyond such formatting considerations, you'll want to make sure that you:

1. Know what you want to say.

By the time you sit down to draft an essay, you should already have a good idea as to the argument or point(s) you intend to make. Maybe you have done a prewriting activity, such as brainstorming, diagramming, or outlining your ideas; at the very least, you should already have read the primary text(s) you are writing about, taking notes and making special note of the specific passages and lines you want to use as evidence to support your claims. Having a strong idea of what you want to say before you sit down to write your essays saves you time. Instead of just sitting in front of a blank Word document wondering what you are going to write about, you can spend your time trying to figure out how to express the thinking you have already done. The four questions that can help you get started fastest are:

1. What is my professor asking me to do in this essay?

2. What do I want to say about this [idea, character, plot point, symbol, *etc.*]?

3. What proof did I see in the literary work(s) to support my claims?

4. In what order should I place these examples in order to best present my point?

If you can answer these four questions before you actually turn to drafting your essay, then you are well on your way to a solid first draft. If not, you want to take the time to answer them prior to beginning, so you can focus your attention on the actual writing, rather than on trying to come up with what to write about in your essay. If you are having trouble organizing your thoughts, try free-writing on the topics that interest you, or explaining what you want to say in your essay to a roommate or friend, or making an appointment to talk with your professor about your ideas. Many of the end-of-chapter questions in this book are specifically designed to elicit responses that could potentially be used as the basis for an essay, and answering them can start you towards a first draft as well. A little advance organization prior to sitting down to compose a formal literary essay can make what seems like a difficult task much easier.

2. Provide the basic information about each text you are writing on in your essay.

Early on in your essay—preferably in the introductory paragraph—you should be sure to include the author, title, genre, and era or specific date, when available, of each of the primary texts you are using to make your argument. Because you are writing for your literature professor, it's easy to forget to be thorough in the presentation of your primary sources; after all, the professor knows what literary works s/he has assigned. But a quality essay should be detailed and specific, and that includes making sure that you provide all of the important identifying information for the literary work(s) about which you are writing—not "Shelley's *Frankenstein*," but **Mary** Shelley's **nineteenth-century gothic novel** *Frankenstein*; not "Yeats's Adam's Curse poem" but **William Butler** Yeats's **modern** poem, "Adam's Curse"—or, better yet, **William Butler** Yeats's **1903** poem "Adam's Curse." Providing this kind of specific information for every primary source near the beginning of your essay conveys to your professor a depth of knowledge: the genre, the publication date, the author's full name; these details, in turn, demonstrate that you understand how to write clearly, concisely, and precisely about literary texts.

3. Identify and define any terms or theoretical lenses you are using in your essay.

If you are writing an analytical or interpretive essay that is based on a word or set of words, or that makes use of a theoretical frame such as postcolonialism, new historicism, feminist, or queer theory, you'll need to set the parameters of your argument early on in your essay, so that your reader knows precisely how you are defining that term or using that theoretical frame. Ideally, you'll provide this information in its own short paragraph directly following the introduction and before the textual examples you are using to support your claims. If as a reader of your essay the professor doesn't know what you mean when you write, "courage," then it is difficult for him or her to know whether you have successfully proven that a character is behaving courageously. If you write, "I'm using feminist theory" without telling which theorist's ideas you are using—or worse, just use the theory with no explanation at all that this is going on—it makes your essay harder for you to write, and much more difficult for your reader to understand. Take the time to provide the contextual information on which your argument depends.

Providing the definition of key terms and/or explaining how you plan to make use of a theoretical lens doesn't have to entail a long, drawn-out explanation; it really can be done in just a sentence or two. But if, for instance, you are basing your entire essay on the idea of "courtly love," then you need to let your reader know how you are defining and understanding that term. Even though you might assume that your essay's readers have the same definition as you do, a short explanation can help bridge the gap between your knowledge and theirs. Again, the more precise you can be, the better you are supporting your overall argument; not "courtly love was an important idea in the Middle Ages" but, "for the purposes of this argument, I define 'courtly love' as the twelfth-century cultural movement begun by the troubadours at the court of Eleanor II and focusing on interpersonal relationships that followed a strict set of guidelines." Generally, you want to use a good quality dictionary to define your term (most scholars use the *Oxford English Dictionary*, or *OED*, which is accessible online through the Jackson Library databases). When you are using theory, you will want to explain to your reader which specific point(s) of a theoretical model you are using; not "I'm taking a new historical approach to this analysis of politics in *The Great Gatsby*," but, "focusing on cultural materialism permits me to critique F. Scott Fitzgerald's presentation of 1920s politics in *The Great Gatsby*." You can find the main ideas of major theorists in the theory section of this book, or do a little more research to locate a particular idea you want to focus on.

Giving the specific parameters of your argument, including defining key terms and explicitly mentioning what theoretical model(s) you are using, not only helps to keep you more clearly focused on what you are trying to write about; it also provides your reader with the information necessary to determine whether or not your argument is successfully made.

4. Don't just summarize; you need to include specific quotes from the primary sources to support your argument.

A common error students make when they are writing about literature is summarizing the text, rather than specifically quoting examples to support their claims. Don't spend a paragraph or more telling the whole plot of a short story or novel, or describing a poem or the scene of a play. At most, you should limit any summary work you undertake in an essay to one or two sentences that provide your reader with the context necessary to understand the quote you are using (for example, "In Act 1, scene iii of William Shakespeare's *Hamlet*, Ophelia is speaking with her brother Laertes concerning her relationship with Hamlet, when they are interrupted by their father, Polonius") and then move on to the meat of your argument.

More importantly, every main point you make should be supported by a specific quote or set of quotes from the text. You should introduce the quote by providing the name of the speaker(s) and the situation in which it is being said (if it is dialogue or monologue) or a short description of the scene or setting of the quote, followed directly by the quote, itself, in quotation marks. After the quote, you MUST provide the citation's location in the text; either page number(s)—in the case of a story or work of long prose—line numbers, in the case of poetry, or by act, scene, and line numbers, in the case of a play. You also must document all of the sources that you discuss or quote in your essay on a Works Cited page (discussed in more detail later in this chapter). Each quote should be followed by an interpretation of what is happening in the quote, and an explanation of why the quote is important to your own argument.

In the University Writing Center, this is referred to as a MEAL plan for writing an essay: you first state your **M**ain point in a paragraph, followed by an **E**xample from the text, supported by your **A**nalysis of that example, which you then **L**ink back to your main argument, or thesis. In simplest terms, an essay consists of several shorter MEAL segments that work together to prove your point.

5. You need to give yourself time to work on the essay.

Many students have grown accustomed to sitting down one or two nights before an essay is due and writing what is essentially a draft, then turning this in as a final version of the essay. This approach to writing an essay rarely results in a quality product. Furthermore, most students who made successful use of this tactic in high school find that it no longer results in a high grade at the college level. Ideally, you will give yourself at least a week to work on a formal essay, preferably two or more. You shouldn't try to write a whole 3–5 page essay in a single sitting; when you write for sustained periods of time—as in the traditional "all-nighter" to write an essay due the next day—you can grow fatigued and end up losing track of what you intended to say ("going off on a tangent") or missing errors that you would ordinarily catch when you are more alert. Break the work up into chunks: maybe one day you draft the central argument you are making and list the examples you want to use, while on another day you write those examples out and analyze them, then on a third day you write the introduction and conclusion, using the next few days to revise, proofread, and make sure your Works Cited page is correct.

Giving yourself extra time allows you to think more about your essay; you may find yourself coming up with more evidence or even a better argument as you reconsider your essay each time you sit down to work on it. You should also consider visiting the Writing Center with your draft-in-progress, the assignment sheet, and a copy of each literary work you are using; a consultant will go over what you have with you and give you an unbiased reader's response to your essay that can help you identify what needs to be added, left out, or changed in order to best meet the essay guidelines. At the very least, always run Spellcheck and Grammar Check on your essays, and make certain your citations are correctly done. Most literature professors assign a relatively large percentage of your final grade to the essays you write for their classes, so you want to give yourself the time you need to create a quality product.

II. Common Types of Essays Assigned in Literature Courses

In general, you can expect the essays you write for college literature courses to be analytical, interpretive, or comparative in nature. Each type of essay requires a slightly different kind of thinking and a different approach to identifying and using textual evidence in support of that thinking. The most commonly assigned essay types are the thematic or character analysis, analysis of a literary element, a poetic analysis, a close reading, a problem paper, or a compare/contrast essay (you may also be assigned a multi-genre or multimodal essay, which is covered in Brenta Blevins's chapter in this section of *Lenses*). Any of these essays may or may not require a research component, and if you do need to conduct research, you'll want to read Jenny Dale's chapter on that subject. What follows here are brief descriptions of and suggestions for how you might approach the most common literary essay assignments in introductory literature courses at UNCG.

Thematic analysis. A thematic analysis examines the presence of one abstract idea in multiple instances throughout the course of a literary work. In general, you should choose any one theme—loyalty, courage, strength, honor, cowardice, guilt, betrayal, love, friendship, community, isolation, exile, prophecy, and similar—and focus specifically on two or three instances in the text where that theme seems to be important, in order to give yourself room to analyze. Generally, to write a thematic analysis you will want first to define the term as you are using it, and then to explain how this theme helps to create meaning, develop a character, further the plot, or performs some other function in the narrative. Come up with an overall argument about the theme's role in the story based on your evidence, and use this statement as your essay's thesis. Looking through Kristine Lee's theme section in this book will provide you with ideas and strategies for locating and writing about themes in a literary work.

Character analysis. For a character analysis, choose any one character, explain briefly who s/he is in relation to the narrative, and then discuss how s/he is presented both directly and indirectly in the text. Some questions you might ask in starting out on a character analysis include: *What does this character do or say? What do others in the text do or say about him or her? What is his or her function in the story?* Come up with an overall argument about this character based on your evidence, and use this statement as your essay's thesis. Looking through Kristine Lee's character section in this book will help you come up with ideas and strategies for locating and writing about themes in a literary work.

Poetic analysis. A poetic analysis, or explication, is the close reading of a poem for its literary elements. By studying closely the poem's use of symbolism, figurative language, and sound imagery, we can often uncover layers of meaning that lead to interpreting and understanding it beyond the surface presentation of the poem's subject. Fausto Barrionuevo's chapter on poetry in this book includes some excellent advice for how to get started on a poetic explication, and the Poetic Forms section (Appendix) provided by Shawn Delgado can help guide you to thinking more deeply about form.

Close reading. A close reading may focus on several lines, a stanza or more, or the entirety of a poem (in which case it is a poetic analysis or explication, as seen above); or, it may center on several lines of dialogue, a monologue, or a scene in a drama text; or, you may choose a few lines, a paragraph, or a few pages of a work of prose fiction or nonfiction. Whatever type of literary work is involved, your role in a close reading is to read the text you are working with several times, noting everything you possibly can about how the author put that text together. Some questions you might ask in beginning a close reading are:

- What is happening in the literary work before this passage?

- What happens in the passage, itself?

- What are the specific images, characters, actions, or ideas in this passage?

- Does the writer use any literary elements, such as figurative language, sound imagery, or symbolism?

- What point of view is the passage coming from, and how does that reveal or conceal information from me as a reader?

■ Do the speaker's, narrator's, or characters' actions or words reveal anything about them, or about the ideas in this work?

Considering these questions will permit you to uncover any particular meaning or relevance this passage may have for the overall text. Crystal Matey provides more advice for performing a close reading of a text in the long prose section of this book.

Problem paper. In simplest terms, a problem paper first sets forth a problem you noticed while you were reading a literary work, and then offers up one or more possible solutions or responses to that problem based in textual evidence and, in some cases, secondary research. You can begin a problem paper by simply considering the questions you had while you were reading a text.

For example, let's say hypothetically you were reading Mary Shelley's *Frankenstein* for a class, and you really wanted to write about that novel. You would begin by asking yourself, WHY do you want to write about *Frankenstein*? WHAT SPECIFICALLY are you interested in? What problem(s) do you see in the story? Your answers might be, "Because it's cool"; "that Victor Frankenstein is supposed to be the good guy, but he's kind of a self-centered jerk with a genius complex"; and "that the main character is someone I don't like, and I like the Creature he hates better." You are therefore interested in Shelley's characterization in the novel. This, in turn, might lead you to wonder about the problem: *"Is Victor Frankenstein a sympathetic character, or does he actually deserve what he gets?"* You would then identify specific passages in the text where Victor seems especially unsympathetic, and try to ascertain why you think so. You could also research what others have written about Frankenstein and his creature to find evidence to support your thinking.

Or, let's say (again, hypothetically) that you were reading *The Geste of Robin Hood*. You might wonder, *"Why is it that we always think about Robin Hood and Maid Marian as this major romantic thing, but she barely appears in the actual legend?"* Your interest lies in questions of gender and audience. You could focus on the lack of textual space devoted to the female characters and why that might be so, and you might set forth the problem: *"Why is Robin Hood more focused on male characters?"* Research might include historical inquiry into the other kinds of stories that were popular when this one came out, and the society in which it was written, to determine what was valued and found to be interesting in that culture.

To write the problem paper, you'll want to follow these guidelines:

1. Set forth your problem, restated as a thesis with your answer(s);

2. Define any terms necessary for understanding your argument; and

3. Present the answers you have come up with to the problem by documenting the examples and research you used to arrive at these answers. You should include relevant quotes from your primary text(s) that support your answers to the problems, and quote the major points in your research, if you have done research for this paper.

Compare/contrast essay. The compare/contrast essay is frequently misinterpreted as being simply an essay that compares similarities and differences between two works. Students often forget that as much so as in any other essay, with the compare/contrast essay they should have an argument they are trying to make. It's not enough simply to compare two works and discuss how they are alike and different; you also want to use those similarities and differences to make a claim about the literary works, themselves. In other words, you *begin* a compare/contrast essay by noting the similarities and differences between the texts, but then you use that comparative work to support a "bigger picture" argument you are seeking to make about those texts.

It's a good idea to approach the compare/contrast essay in stages. Start by simply noting the similarities and differences you observe as you are reading. You may want to map these out visually using an advanced organizer technique, such as the Venn diagram, or a simple list of "similarities" and "differences." Think beyond just the story and the characters when you are comparing and contrasting two texts; consider, for instance, some of the other literary elements discussed throughout this book, such as theme, symbolism, figurative language, irony, and allusion. Don't try to compare and contrast *everything* about the texts; depending on the length requirement for the essay, the goal is to come across three or four good points at which the texts either converge (compare) or diverge (contrast).

Once you have enough listed that you notice clearly how the works are alike and different in several ways, you can begin to formulate an argument. The argument should extend the comparisons and contrasts you have located to say something more meaningful about the texts than, "they are alike in these ways, and not alike in those ways." For instance, let's say you were comparing and contrasting Bram Stoker's *Dracula* with Mary Shelley's *Frankenstein*. Obvious areas of comparison include the novels' antagonists—Count Dracula, a vampire, and Victor's Creature, are both monstrous figures—and the narrative structure: both works are epistolary—novels told through letters written by several characters. You might also notice that both protagonists, Jonathan Harker and Victor Frankenstein, are engaged to young women who are victimized by the monstrous antagonists as an act of revenge. But these comparisons happen at the surface level of the text, focusing on narrative structure and characterization. Considering other literary elements provides other, potentially more interesting lenses for comparison and contrast; in terms of symbolism, for instance, in *Dracula* the main symbol is blood, which is red, while in *Frankenstein* the color yellow represents evil; therefore, while both texts make use of color symbolism, they do so in different ways. Both novels explore, in different ways, individual themes such as the sublime, individual transformation, and the effects of industrialization and technology on society, as well as thematic dualities, such as community and isolation, innocence and corruption, and good and evil. *Dracula* makes allusions to Christianity and the historical East European figure Vlad the Impaler, while *Frankenstein* makes allusions to Christianity and John Milton's *Paradise Lost*, an expressly English literary text; we might then consider how the works treat the theme of England and Englishness. The mood and atmosphere in both texts is gothic horror, and this is reinforced by the ways in which the authors employ setting and weather; this might permit us to make arguments such as that the weather serves as an extension of the antagonist or protagonist in each story by mirroring his emotions, or can lead to an eco-critical study of how the novels characterize and explore the English landscape and weather.

Once you start looking more closely at literary elements beyond narrative structure, plot, and character, you begin to see much more complex and interesting ways of comparing literary texts; those comparisons, in turn, lead to important arguments about the function and meaning of the books you are examining.

III. MLA Citation Style

With few exceptions, the essays you write for college literature classes are going to require that you provide textual evidence, or quotes, to support the arguments you make. When you quote from a source, it is important to cite it properly in order to develop your own credibility as a scholar writing about literature. There are many different citation styles used in academic writing; some of the more well-known and commonly used ones include Chicago, APA (American Psychological Association), and Turabian. The citation style preferred for most essays written for English classes is that of the MLA (Modern Language Association). This section provides a brief, introductory explanation of what MLA citation is and how to perform it in an essay.

MLA citation in a student essay consists of in-text, or parenthetical, documentation in the essay itself, which corresponds to a full citation in the Works Cited page at the end of an essay. Any time you summarize, paraphrase (put into your own words), or directly quote information from a source in your essay, you must use a parenthetical citation to mark that these words are not your own, original thinking, but rather that of another person. You have seen this form of documentation used throughout this book whenever our authors have quoted the work of other writers. It looks like this:

"When you quote from a source, it is important to cite it properly" (Ridley Elmes 218).

If you mention an author's name at the beginning of the statement you are quoting, then you just need to put the page or line number(s) into the parenthetical citation. It then looks like this:

According to Melissa Ridley Elmes, the MLA citation style includes "in-text, or parenthetical, documentation in the essay itself, which corresponds to a full citation in the Works Cited page at the end of an essay" (218).

If you are quoting from a source with no known author, you use a shortened version of the title of the source you are using in the parentheses, in place of the author's last name and page number. If, for instance, you were quoting from it but this essay did not have a known author, you might call it ("MLA Citation Style") for the purposes of parenthetical documentation.

If you are quoting from a poem, you would cite it parenthetically by line numbers, rather than by page numbers, since many poems are shorter than a page in length; you see examples of this method of citation in the poetry chapter of this book. Likewise, if you are citing from a drama text, your parenthetical documentation would include the act, scene, and line numbers, as you see in the Drama chapter of this book.

These parenthetical citations serve as a notice to your essay's readers that the full textual citation for the source you have quoted can be found on the Works Cited page at the end of the essay. The Works Cited page is the full list of sources you used in writing your essay. Anything you use—books, journal or magazine articles, Web sources, videos, music lyrics, photographs, artworks, and so forth—must be documented on the Works Cited page. MLA documentation style is actually very straightforward; you always begin with the same basic information, and then either add to, or take away from, that basic citation format as needed for a given source. The basic MLA format for a single-authored book is:

Author's last name, first name. *Title of Book in Italics.* City: Publisher, Copyright Date. Print.

For other sources, you simply modify this basic citation to include the relevant information that is not already there. For instance, if you were citing the "Drama" section of this book, you would be citing a work by one author, located in a specific range of pages in a book now in its second edition, with two editors. When you account for all of this information, it looks like this:

> Carter, Matt. "Drama." *Lenses: Perspectives on Literature.* Second Edition. Abigail Browning and Melissa Ridley Elmes, eds. Plymouth: Hayden-McNeil Publishing, 2015. 33–49. Print.

Most journal articles follow a similar format to this one; rather than the title of the book, you would include the title of the journal in which the article appears, and rather than simply giving the copyright date, you would need to give the journal's volume, issue, and date of publication. Everything else remains the same:

> Author's last name, first name. "Title of the Article in Quotation Marks." *Title of Journal in Italics.* Volume. Issue (Year): Pp. Print.

Any time a source that you quote comes from the Internet, you replace "Print" with "Web." Many of the articles you use for your literature classes are likely to come from one of the library's databases, such as JSTOR. Here's how you would cite those:

> Author's last name, first name. "Title of the Article in Quotation Marks." *Title of Journal in Italics.* Volume. Issue (Year): Pp. *JSTOR.* Web. Day Month Year.

The final "Day Month Year" at the end of the citation is the date you accessed the article online. Notice that the only real difference between citing a print journal and one you locate on a database like JSTOR, is that you now include the name of the database you used and the date when you retrieved the article.

This is a very basic introduction to the MLA citation method. You should be certain to consult the most recent edition of the *MLA Handbook,* or an online citation resource center such as Owl Purdue, or our own University Writing Center or the UNCG Library webpage, to make sure you have correctly cited any sources you use when you are writing essays. If you are ever in doubt about whether or not to cite something, you should always check with your professor; it's better to be safe than sorry. Neglecting to properly document the sources you use in an essay, or not citing the sources you have used at all—even if you only forget or neglect to cite one of the sources you have used—is not only unprofessional and unscholarly, but it is considered an act of plagiarism, the theft of someone else's intellectual property. Plagiarism is a violation of the Academic Integrity Policy of UNCG, and if you are found guilty of plagiarism the consequences run from failing the assignment, to failing the course, to facing a disciplinary hearing before the Academic Honor Council. It is therefore best to learn and use appropriate citation methods early on in your college career.

CONCLUSION

When you have carefully read the text or texts about which you intend to write, the hardest part of writing an essay on literature is deciding what you want to say and how you want to say it. These decisions are largely determined by the kind of essay you are being asked to write. Knowing the different kinds of essays you may be asked to write, and what kinds of approaches and strategies you might use to begin writing them, should make you feel more confident about your ability to write a good essay. And always, *always*: **remember to cite your sources!**

IV. WRITING ABOUT LITERATURE

Multimodal and Multigenre Assignments in Literature Classes

Brenta Blevins

Key Terms

- **multimodal**
- **multigenre**

In a literature class, you might expect an essay assignment requiring you to compare and contrast themes, characters, or other literary elements appearing in different pieces of literature. Or perhaps you might expect to make a claim based on your research into the historical and geographic context in which an author produced a literary work. In some literature classes, you might also receive assignments for creating compositions referred to as "multimodal" or "multigenre." While these two types of assignments might be new to you, they require similar techniques that you are already familiar with from writing essays, such as analysis, interpretation, and synthesis. Just as with traditional written assignments, multimodal and multigenre assignments require careful reading, research, and making an argument.

MULTIMODAL ASSIGNMENTS

Multimodal texts are compositions that combine multiple communication modes, such as text, image, speech, sound, and body language. Thus, a multimodal assignment asks students to compose in multiple forms of communication. Examples of multimodal compositions include slide presentations such as those made with Powerpoint or Prezi, Web pages, blogs, videos, podcasts, posters, brochures, and collages. Each of these compositions calls for the creation of more than plain text to effectively convey a message—they ask you to also make use of images, audio, color, movement, and arrangement to support your composition's point.

To fulfill a multimodal assignment, you begin as you would with a traditional text essay. You read and reread the text(s) you are analyzing, perform any required research, and then determine what point you want to make about the text(s). Just as you cite textual evidence in an essay, you will likewise incorporate textual evidence in your multimodal assignment. In addition to quotes, however, multimodal assignments enable you to incorporate evidence in the form of images, video and audio clips, and so forth.

The decisions you make about which visuals to include, what audio to incorporate, what color backgrounds and text to use, and even what font you use should support the overall point you want to make about the text. For example, consider the difference expressed by different font choices, such as this one:

What's in a name? that which we call a rose
By any other name would smell as sweet.
(Romeo and Juliet II, ii, 1-2)

In comparison with this one:

What's in a name? that which we call a rose
By any other name would smell as sweet.
(Romeo and Juliet II, ii, 1–2)

This is part of a famous soliloquy delivered by Juliet Capulet in William Shakespeare's Romeo and Juliet; in this scene, the lovelorn Juliet wonders why they must stay apart simply because of their families' ongoing feud, and suggests that this should not be a hindrance to their love. These lines in particular address the idea that Romeo's last name doesn't define who he is for Juliet; she loves him. In the sample multimodal approach above, each font choice conveys a different interpretation of the text. For instance, in the first example, the color "red" is reminiscent of a rose, while the font used, Brush Script MT, seems "romantic," thereby underscoring the sentimental nature of Juliet's remark. In the second example, on the other hand, the size and plainness of the font (called Frutiger Condensed) isolates the word "rose" calling extra attention to it as the object of the remark. Such deliberate choices bring out different valences in the lines you are considering. In addition to making certain that every design decision supports the point you are making about the text, you will also want to make sure that your composition selections are clear and understandable to your audience, just as you would ensure that an essay contains comprehensible writing.

Examples of multimodal projects you might receive could include creating a presentation that you deliver in class. Presentations can include visual images or short videos and audio clips. Or, you might also be asked to create a video about an author or a text. If you are creating a contextual project about how the Jazz Age influenced F. Scott Fitzgerald's *The Great Gatsby* (1925), you might choose jazz music clips that align with your interpretation of the novel. For any of these projects, every selection is a decision. For example, in selecting a photo of an author to incorporate into your project, consider which you should choose: a photo at the end of the author's life or a photo of the author at or near the time the author wrote the literary piece? If you want to select an image of the literary work's setting or the landscape in which the author was writing, consider which image better reflects the atmosphere or mood of the piece you are examining. Every choice you make about what materials to include in your multimodal project can support your analysis of literary work as a form of textual evidence.

MULTIGENRE ASSIGNMENTS

Another type of project you might work on in a literature class is a "multigenre assignment." This project requires students to work with more than one genre. Genre is often thought of in literary terms, such as poems, short stories, plays, novels, and even essays; however, genre also describes other, more common forms of texts, such as letters, journals, newspaper articles, maps, manuals, advertisements, and photo essays. Thus, a **multigenre** assignment requires a composition made up of more than one genre. Individual multigenre assignments will have different specifications that you will also need to consider.

When you get a multigenre assignment, you might wonder how this type of assignment involves analysis. One type of multigenre assignment requires you to convert a literary text into a different genre than its current form. In doing so, you will first have to determine what your analysis of a literary text reveals, then you will have to make composition decisions that demonstrate your analysis. For example, you might create an interpretation of the story as if it were taking place today. If *Romeo and Juliet* were set in a modern context, how might the two teenagers communicate—using Facebook, through text messages, or on Instagram? Before you can make such decisions, you need to analyze how the two communicate within Shakespeare's original text. You need to examine not just the language they use, but other parameters affecting their communication, including how the setting affects them and which characters and what plot events prevent them from communicating. Then, you need to determine how those effects would transfer to the modern era to accurately represent your analysis.

Another multigenre assignment might ask you to create multiple documents from the points of view of multiple characters in a literary work. In doing so, you need to analyze character voice, diction, and language—for example, whether characters use similes, metaphors, or irony, and how all of those work to support the themes or conflicts you see in the original text.

You can also apply techniques for multimodal assignments to your multigenre work. For example, you might create an advertisement that announces an event that takes place within your literary work, or perhaps you would create a scrapbook or Pinterest page for a literary character. You would then select and create material, keeping in mind the guidelines for creating multimodal works that support your overall point.

REVISING AND COMPLETING THE MULTIMODAL OR MULTIGENRE ASSIGNMENT

As this chapter has discussed, both multimodal and multigenre assignments require you to analyze texts using techniques similar to those for traditional written essays, albeit with the addition of more than written text. As with other kinds of analyses, you need in multimodal and multigenre assignments to support your interpretation with textual evidence. As with an essay assignment, you should develop a list of Works Cited, which includes traditional research as well as listing the sources for any materials (video, audio, image, and so forth) that you incorporate into your project. Throughout the entire composition process for multimodal and multigenre assignments, you will make a number of thoughtful decisions about textual evidence and inclusion, logical and spatial arrangement, and style, to demonstrate your critical engagement with a text. Once you have completed a draft of a multimodal or multigenre text, you will want to review that draft to ensure that your use of additional communication modes or multiple genres maintains good focus, consistently supports your argument, and demonstrates your critical thinking about literature. In so doing, you will find that you are talking about literature in multiple ways.

Literary Research

Jenny Dale

INTRODUCTION

Key Terms

- **sources**
- **primary texts**

In literature classes, students are expected to write essays providing their own unique analysis of a text—symbolism in F. Scott Fitzgerald's *The Great Gatsby*, for instance, or the role of social class in *Pride and Prejudice* by Jane Austen. When your focus is on textual analysis, you typically need two **sources** of information: the **primary text** and your own ideas. You might find, however, that you need or want to bring in additional sources—other textual analyses, for instance, or other scholarship dealing with your primary text(s). That is where literature research comes in. Other sources might help you go beyond your own ideas or help you support your argument. Effectively integrating additional sources often adds richness and depth to your writing, and given the right sources, also builds your credibility as an author by proving that your argument is supported by existing research. This chapter will provide a brief introduction to literature research, the process of finding, accessing, and using outside sources to build and support an effective argument.

TYPES OF SOURCES

Key Terms

- **primary sources**
- **secondary sources**
- **book review**

- **literary criticism**
- **popular sources**
- **scholarly sources**

Before you begin conducting literature research, it is useful to be aware of the types of sources that you are likely to come across. This section will briefly introduce the different types of sources you can expect to find in the process of literature research, and how you can identify them.

Primary and Secondary Sources. You may have heard "sources" referred to as either primary or secondary when you have done research in the past. The University of Maryland provides the following definition of **primary sources**:

> Primary sources are original materials. They are from the time period involved and have not been filtered through interpretation or evaluation. Primary sources are original materials on which other research is based. They are usually the first formal appearance of results in physical, print or electronic format. They present original thinking, report a discovery, or share new information. (University of Maryland Libraries)

While this definition is clear and succinct, you might notice that it does not provide any specific examples of primary sources but focuses instead on general guidelines. This is because what constitutes a primary source varies widely depending on the context or academic discipline. In history courses, a primary source might be a letter that provides a firsthand account of an experience, or a newspaper article that reports on an event that just happened. In psychology, a primary source might be an original research article that reports on an experiment. All of these examples "present original thinking, report a discovery, or share new information." However, when we are working with literature, that "new information" is often a literary text: a novel, short story, poem, play, or even a song or film.

Secondary sources, on the other hand, are removed in some way from primary sources. Considering the examples in the last paragraph, a secondary source in history might be a book on World War I that relies on numerous primary sources like letters and newspaper articles to provide context. In psychology, secondary sources might be review articles that summarize and evaluate original research articles. In literature, secondary sources come in many forms; book reviews and scholarly articles or books that analyze one or more primary texts are the types you are most likely to come across.

Book Reviews vs. Literary Criticism. Speaking of book reviews, it is useful to be able to distinguish reviews from what is often called "literary criticism." The primary purpose of a **book review** is to provide readers with a short overview of a book along with the reviewer's opinion of it so the reader can decide if he or she wants to read or buy it. Book reviews tend to be relatively short and less detailed because the assumption is that, if you are reading the review, you have not yet read the book. Typically, this means that there are no spoilers, but it also means that there are many aspects of the book that are not fully discussed. Many of the library resources that will be introduced later in this chapter will help you locate book reviews. Some common publications that publish book reviews are *Booklist, Library Journal, New York Times, New York Review of Books,* and *Publisher's Weekly.*

Literary criticism, on the other hand, generally refers to longer works that go into more depth on the primary text(s). They are less likely to provide a plot summary because, if you are consulting them, the author assumes that the reader has read the primary work(s) that are being analyzed. Works of literary criticism vary widely in terms of length and scope, but their primary purpose is to provide a more in-depth look at a text or a specific aspect of that text. These are more likely to be written by literature scholars and to be found in scholarly journals as opposed to the popular sources like the *New York Times, Booklist,* and *Publisher's Weekly.*

Popular vs. Scholarly Sources. When you are doing literature research, you are likely to find a mix of popular sources, like the book reviews mentioned earlier, and scholarly sources. The following chart from UNCG Libraries provides a quick overview of the differences between popular sources (often magazines and newspapers) and scholarly journals:

	Popular	**Scholarly**
Who writes the articles?	Professional journalists	Researchers or scholars in a field
Who is the primary audience?	The general public	Other researchers and scholars
Do the authors cite their sources?	Maybe in passing, but you usually won't find formal references	Always – look for a reference list or footnotes/ endnotes
Are there ads?	Always	Rarely
Are current events covered?	Yes	No – the peer review process is long

Figure 1

Notice in the right column that scholarly sources (also called academic, peer-reviewed, or refereed) are written both *by* and *for* scholars. They are often written by professors or graduate students of literature or related fields and are read by those same professors and graduate students as well as other students of literature, like you.

It is important to note that scholarly sources are not "better" than popular sources; the two serve different purposes. Scholarly sources are typically going to provide more in-depth analysis of one or more primary texts. They will cite not only those primary texts, but also secondary sources, including other scholarly sources. Popular sources tend to be shorter, written for a more general audience, and rarely cite sources. However, if you are studying an author who is currently publishing or a text that was published within the last five years, popular sources like book reviews may be your best bet; scholarly sources take significant time to research and write, and then go through a review by other scholars before finally being published, so the timeline to publication is much longer.

FINDING AND ASSESSING SOURCES

Key Terms

- **authority**
- **accuracy**
- **bias**
- **currency**

Now that you know what you are looking for, you are ready to start searching for those sources. There is a great deal of information available on the web about literature, including specific authors and texts. Many of us start any search for information in Google or similar search engines. A quick Google search for Charles Dickens, for instance, brings back 17.2 million results in .4 seconds (at the time of writing this chapter). Of course, many of these will not be sources that could be cited in an academic paper, like Wikipedia, but there are likely to be quite a few useful sites among those 17.2 million.

Using the web for research is convenient and is second nature to many of us, but since most of what is available on the web has not been edited or reviewed, it is particularly important to carefully evaluate the sources before deciding to use them. There are many tests that you can use to evaluate sources—a Google search for evaluating web sources brings back more than 2 million results—but librarians at UNCG tend to use the ABCs.

A has a double meaning: **authority** and **accuracy**. Determining authority requires you to assess the person, people, or organization responsible for the website. Look for "about" or "contact" links at the top or bottom of the webpage if the author is not immediately clear. Think about your context: a website on Dickens written by someone with a master's degree in literature probably has more authority than a site written by a professor of biology. In any case, it is critical to be able to identify the person, people, or organizations responsible for a website. When authors cannot be identified, authority is *significantly compromised*. That is one major issue with sources like Wikipedia. Instead of improving your essay, using a source without a credible author may, in fact, negatively affect your analysis. **A**ccuracy can be difficult to determine if you are new to a topic, but look for clues like citations and for information that you can easily fact-check.

Bias can be tricky to identify, but it relies heavily on establishing authority. Do the people or organizations responsible for the site have any clear **biases**, or emotionally-fueled ideas, about the content? This can be very nuanced—it is often not as easy as finding a site entitled "Charles Dickens: Racist and Bad Writer" (the bias there is fairly clear). Bias is also a sticky issue because, when we are dealing with literature, opinions are often important to consider. You can help mitigate bias by seeking out multiple perspectives on a topic so that you have a fuller picture of the information available.

Currency, the last element of the ABC test, is relative. If we stay with our Charles Dickens search, a source from five or ten years ago might be acceptable, because Dickens has been dead for quite some time now. If, on the other hand, we want to research James McBride, winner of the 2013 National Book Award, we would want our search to include sources that are more current. **Currency**, too, may depend on the needs of your research. You might be writing in response to contemporary interpretation of Dickens. In that case, a search limited to the last five years would be more appropriate.

When evaluating web sources in particular, it is important to consider the full picture that you get from these ABCs—authority, accuracy, bias, and currency. When doing research on a contemporary author, for instance, that author's website is a great place to start. Using the ABC test, that author is most likely to be the foremost authority on themselves and on their work. They are also likely to provide you with accurate information because they want you to be able to find and read their work. Bias, however, can become a big issue. An author is not likely to include bad reviews, scandals, or information about why you should not buy their work on their own website. They are, however, likely to provide current information about where to find their work, what events they have coming up, and more. Just because the site will have a clear bias does not mean that you should discard it as a source, but rather that you should seek out additional sources that are more neutral.

IV. WRITING ABOUT LITERATURE

USING LIBRARY RESOURCES

Key Term
- **Ask Us!**

One way to ensure that you are getting the highest quality information available is to use the resources provided by UNCG Libraries. The libraries have millions of books and articles that are at your disposal as a UNCG student. This section will provide a brief overview of a few of those sources, but there are dozens of resources relevant to literature research that are available through the Libraries' website at http://library.uncg.edu. If you need help with literature research, you can always contact the English librarian at UNCG or use the **Ask Us!** button on the Libraries' homepage.

As you use library resources, be aware that our search engines do not speak Google. In general, you cannot type in a question or a long phrase and expect to get useful results. The best strategy is to do some brainstorming before you start searching to help you consider the main terms you want to use. If you are looking for secondary sources on symbolism in *The Great Gatsby*, for instance, you should make note of the critical terms related to your topic: *The Great Gatsby* is an obvious one, as is symbolism, but you might also want to consider F. Scott Fitzgerald (the author), Gatsby and Daisy (two of the characters), the green light (one of the major symbols in the novel), and other possible search terms based on your close reading. When you have identified a handful of useful terms, you can use those to search for relevant sources in the library catalog or databases. To make your search as effective as possible, use connectors like AND and OR to help target your search. A search for *The Great Gatsby* AND symbolism will bring back results that deal with both of these topics, which helps you narrow down your results to those that are likely to be relevant. A search for Gatsby OR Daisy will bring back any results that deal with either of those characters, so that broadens your results.

LIBRARY CATALOG

Key Term
- **truncation symbol**

The library catalog is your gateway to the millions of books mentioned earlier. You can access the catalog anytime and from anywhere that you have internet access. Visit http://library.uncg.edu and click on the "Catalog" tab in the large red box. This will search for items that we own, including print and electronic books, DVDs, CDs, and more.

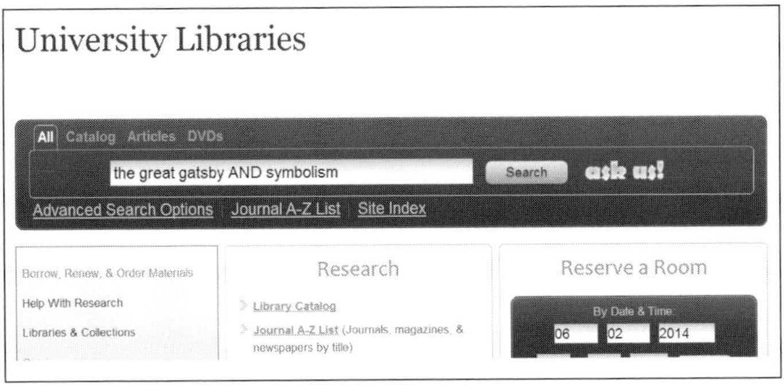

Figure 2: UNCG Libraries Catalog Search.

The search depicted in Figure 2 brings back five results from UNCG Libraries, including primary sources (copies of *The Great Gatsby* itself) and secondary sources (books about *The Great Gatsby* or books with chapters about it). These five sources may be sufficient, or you may want to make some changes to your search. A search for F. Scott Fitzgerald AND symbolism more than doubles the results. A search for *The Great Gatsby* AND symbol* brings back 20 results. The * symbol after a root word brings back anything that starts with that root and is referred to as a **truncation symbol**. In this case, symbol* will search for symbol, symbols, symbolism, symbolic, etc. This trick works well when your root word could have many endings, but be sure that you do not shorten your term too soon—a search for bio* would also look for biography and biographical, but also bioforms, biomass, and the like.

To get more information about one of your search results, you can simply click on the title. One result that came back for all three of the above searches related to symbolism in *The Great Gatsby* was *The Gun and the Pen: Hemingway, Fitzgerald, Faulkner, and the Fiction of Mobilization*. Clicking on the title leads to a page with more information about that book, including basic publication information, a summary, and location information within UNCG Libraries (see Figure 3).

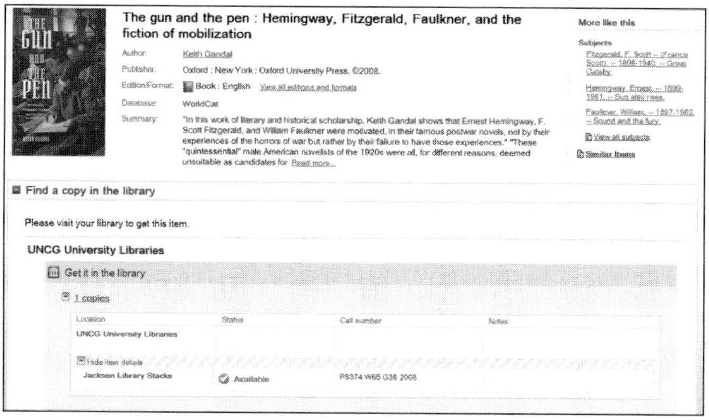

Figure 3: Catalog page for *The Gun and the Pen.*

Scrolling a bit further down the page, you can see that, while this entire book is not relevant to the topic I searched, it has at least one chapter on *The Great Gatsby* (see Figure 4). In order to use a book as a source, you do not need to have read the entire work—focusing on the chapter or chapters that are most useful to you is your best bet.

Notes:	**UNCG University Libraries notes:** Pt. I. Introduction -- 1. Rethinking Post-World War I Classics: Recovering the Historical Context of the Mobilization -- 2. Methodology and the Study of Modernist Fiction -- Pt. II. Fitzgerald, Hemingway, Faulkner, and the 1920s -- 3. The Great Gatsby and the Great War Army: Ethnic Egalitarianism, Intelligence Testing, the New Man, and the Charity Girl -- 4. The Sun Also Rises and "Mobilization Wounds": Emasculation, Joke Fronts, Military School Wannabes, and Postwar Jewish Quotas -- 5. The Sound and the Fury and Military Rejects: The Feebleminded and the Postmobilization Erotic Triangle -- 6. Postmobilization Romance: Transforming Military Rejection into Modernist Tragedy and Symbolism -- Pt. III. The 1930s and After -- 7. Postmobilization Kinkiness: Barnes, West, Miller, and the Military's Frankness about Sex and Venereal Disease -- 8. The Sound and the Fury Redux and the End of the World War I Mobilization Novel -- Afterword: Here We Go Again: World War II Mobilization Blues in William Burroughs's Junky.
Description:	xii, 271 p. : ill. ; 25 cm.
Contents:	Rethinking post-World War I classics: recovering the historical context of the mobilization -- Methodology and the study of modernist fiction -- The Great Gatsby and the great war army: ethnic egalitarianism, intelligence testing, the new man, and the charity girl -- The Sun also rises and "mobilization wounds": emasculation, joke fronts, military school wannabes, and postwar Jewish quotas -- The sound and the fury and military rejects: the feebleminded and the postmobilization erotic triangle --

Figure 4: Notes and contents for *The Gun and the Pen.*

LIBRARY DATABASES

Key Terms
- **library databases**
- **Literary Resource Center**
- **Literary Reference Center**
- **MLA International Bibliography**

You may have used **library databases**—searchable online collections of re-sources—before, perhaps in other classes at UNCG or in high school. Some of the databases that we have are very general, like Academic Search Complete, which searches for articles in nearly every subject area. Many, however, are specific to certain disciplines. The UNCG Libraries provide access to hundreds of these databases, and most of the content included is content that cannot be found on the free web. Each database is unique, but they all work on the same basic principles. Three of the most popular literature-related databases at UNCG are Literature Resource Center, Literary Reference Center, and the MLA (Modern Language Association) International Bibliography. You can access all of these resources through the UNCG Libraries website by clicking "Databases" on the homepage and navigating to the alphabetical listing. You can also find recommended databases by subject by clicking on "Research Guides by Subject" and navigating to the appropriate subject area.

Literature Resource Center provides access to a huge amount of full-text content, including literature criticism, book reviews, author biographies, interviews, audio and video clips, and more. A quick keyword search for the author Maya Angelou brings back hundreds of results in a variety of categories (see Figure 5).

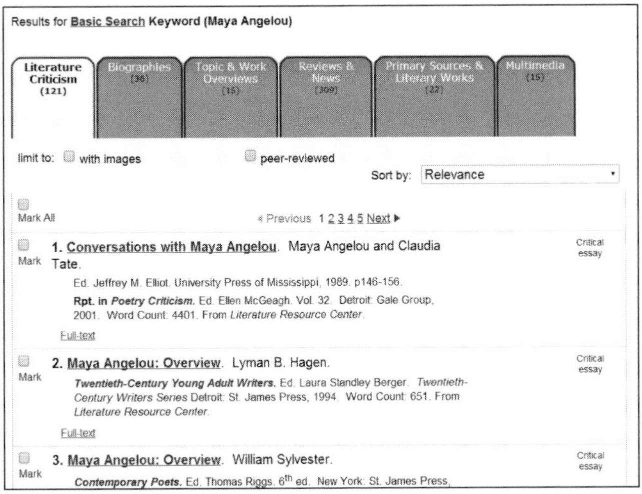

Figure 5: Partial Literature Resource Center results.

Note that you can limit to peer-reviewed sources. You can also refine your search by adding new search terms. Maya Angelou AND feminism brings back a much smaller set of search results. To access a source so that you can determine how useful it might be for you, simply click on the title. You can then read the source in its entirety and access a variety of other options, including citation help and the ability to email the source to yourself so that you can read or refer to it later (see Figure 6). Emailing yourself the sources you are considering using for a paper is an easy way to keep up with them so that you can easily find them later to use and cite.

Figure 6: Literature Resource Center article page.

Literary Reference Center is similar to Literature Resource Center, but the interface looks different. This database also provides full-text access to a variety of source types, including biographies, bibliographies, plot summaries, literary criticism, and reviews. Though these two resources are similar, it is a good idea to search both because they pull from different sources.

The **MLA International Bibliography** is the primary article database used for scholarly literature research. Unlike Literature Resource Center and Literary Reference Center, it does not include background information like author biographies or plot summaries. Its focus is primarily on literature criticism, and it searches for scholarly articles, books, book chapters, dissertations, conference papers, and more. When using a database with such a large amount of content, it is particularly important to use good search strategies. Putting "Maya Angelou feminism" all in one search box brings back only one result, and it does not appear to be particularly relevant. Breaking apart search terms is more effective: putting Maya Angelou in the first search box and putting feminism in the box below (which is automatically connected to the first search box with the connector "AND") brings back three results, and using the truncation symbol * for feminism (feminis*) brings back nine. Chances are that your very first search will not bring back exactly what you need, so it is important to be willing to try different terms and different strategies. While many sources that you find in the MLA International Bibliography have full-text available, you will most likely have to click on a full-text icon or use the "Check for full-text" option to access that text (see Figure 7). This can get tricky if the source is actually a book or book chapter rather than an online article. If you have any questions about accessing sources from this database, you can contact your English Librarian or use the Ask Us! service.

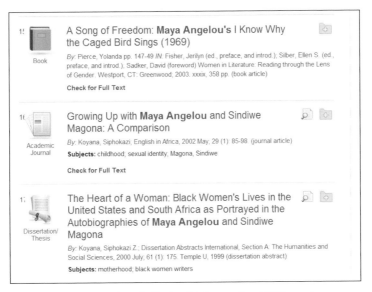

Figure 7: Partial results list in MLA International Bibliography.

CITING SOURCES AND AVOIDING PLAGIARISM

Key Terms

- **citation**
- **plagiarism**

Ideally, you will be collecting potential sources throughout your writing process, from brainstorming through your drafts. Keeping track of those sources in your email or with a citation management tool like Zotero is an important step in the research process, and it also makes it much easier to find those sources for the purposes of citation. In literature research, as with any research process, it is critical to cite any sources that you consult. **Citation** serves multiple purposes: it builds your credibility as an author by showing that you consulted additional sources, it provides your reader with a clear sense of where you found your information, and it helps you avoid plagiarism. Plagiarism is a serious offense at UNCG, and is a direct violation of the Academic Integrity Policy (http://sa.uncg.edu/dean/academic-integrity/). The Academic Integrity Policy defines **plagiarism** as *"Representing the words of another, as one's own in any academic exercise"* (Dean of Students, "Plagiarism"). Failing to cite your sources is one of the major types of plagiarism violations at UNCG, according to the Dean of Students Office ("Plagiarism").

In the last paragraph, I avoided plagiarism by citing both a direct quote and my own paraphrase. Citing your sources is required for direct quotes, paraphrasing and summarizing, and describing any ideas that are not your own. Citing your sources is not required when you are writing exclusively about your own opinions, or in cases where the information can be considered common knowledge. In a paper about candy bars, I would not need to cite the fact that Snickers is a candy bar, or that I think Snickers is the best candy bar, but I would need to cite statistics about the number of Snickers bars sold in a given year. There are many excellent resources on the web to help you avoid plagiarism. See, for instance, the Online Writing Lab (OWL) at Purdue University, which provides guidance on avoiding plagiarism and on using major citation styles (https://owl.english.purdue.edu/owl/).

In literature classes at UNCG, you are likely to be asked to use MLA style for citation and formatting. Melissa Ridley Elmes's essay in this book provides a summary overview of MLA citation practices.

GETTING HELP

If you need help with any part of the literature research process, from brain-storming search terms to selecting the appropriate library resource to citing your sources, you can always contact the UNCG Libraries. You can contact the Reference Desk in Jackson Library for help in person, by phone, by text, or by chatting with us. Click the Ask Us! button on the library homepage for more de-tails. The Libraries also have subject librarians for each academic department at UNCG, including English. You can find information about library resources for literature research, including contact information for the English Librarian, on the English research guide at http://uncg.libguides.com/eng.

Questions to Consider

1. What are the differences between primary and secondary texts? For a literature essay, give examples of two types of secondary texts.

2. How, using the ABCs, can you determine if a source (such as a website or article) is credible?

3. If you have questions about searching for, accessing, or citing sources, what are two ways you can get help from the UNCG Libraries?

4. Which of the following statements would need a citation within a paper?

    a. Charles Dickens published *Great Expectations* in 1860 and 1861.

    b. *Great Expectations* is my favorite of Dickens' novels.

    c. *Great Expectations* was well received in its time, and the magazine in which it was published sold 100,000 copies a week.

5. Use the MLA resources discussed in this chapter to identify and correct prob-lems with the following citations:

    a. G.H Metz. *Shakespeare's Earliest Tragedy: Studies in Titus Andronicus.* Madison: Fairleigh Dickinson University Press, 1996. Book.

    b. Green, Douglas E. "Interpreting 'Her Martyr'd Signs': Gender and Tragedy in *Titus Andronicus*." "Shakespeare Quarterly" 40.3 (1989): 317–326. Print.

    c. DiPietro, Cary, and Grady, Hugh. Presentism, anachronism, and the case of *Titus Andronicus. Shakespeare* 8.1 (2012): 44–73. Print.

Works Cited

Dean of Students. "Academic Integrity Process." *Dean of Students Office*. University of North Carolina at Greensboro, n.d. Web. 11 Jan. 2014.

Dean of Students. "Plagiarism." *Dean of Students Office*. University of North Carolina at Greensboro, n.d. Web. 11 Jan. 2014.

Eliot, T. S. "The Waste Land." *Waste Land* (1922): 1–16. *Literary Reference Center Plus*. Web. 11 Jan. 2014.

Russell, Tony, Allen Brizee, Elizabeth Angeli, Russell Keck, and Joshua M. Paiz. "MLA Formatting Quotations." *The Purdue OWL*. Purdue U Writing Lab, 6 Apr. 2013. Web. 11 Jan. 2014.

University of Maryland Libraries. "Primary, Secondary, and Tertiary Sources." *University Libraries*. University of Maryland, 30 Oct. 2013. Web. 11 Jan. 2014.

V. Anthology

My Last Duchess

Robert Browning

FERRARA

That's my last Duchess painted on the wall,
Looking as if she were alive. I call
That piece a wonder, now; Frá Pandolf's hands
Worked busily a day, and there she stands.
Will't please you sit and look at her? I said
"Frá Pandolf" by design, for never read
Strangers like you that pictured countenance,
The depth and passion of its earnest glance,
But to myself they turned (since none puts by
The curtain I have drawn for you, but I)
And seemed as they would ask me, if they durst,
How such a glance came there; so, not the first
Are you to turn and ask thus. Sir, 'twas not
Her husband's presence only, called that spot
Of joy into the Duchess' cheek; perhaps
Frá Pandolf chanced to say, "Her mantle laps
Over my lady's wrist too much," or "Paint
Must never hope to reproduce the faint
Half-flush that dies along her throat." Such stuff
Was courtesy, she thought, and cause enough
For calling up that spot of joy. She had
A heart—how shall I say?— too soon made glad,

Too easily impressed; she liked whate'er
She looked on, and her looks went everywhere.
Sir, 'twas all one! My favour at her breast,
The dropping of the daylight in the West,
The bough of cherries some officious fool
Broke in the orchard for her, the white mule
She rode with round the terrace—all and each
Would draw from her alike the approving speech,
Or blush, at least. She thanked men—good! but thanked
Somehow—I know not how—as if she ranked
My gift of a nine-hundred-years-old name
With anybody's gift. Who'd stoop to blame
This sort of trifling? Even had you skill
In speech—which I have not—to make your will
Quite clear to such an one, and say, "Just this
Or that in you disgusts me; here you miss,
Or there exceed the mark"—and if she let
Herself be lessoned so, nor plainly set
Her wits to yours, forsooth, and made excuse—
E'en then would be some stooping; and I choose
Never to stoop. Oh, sir, she smiled, no doubt,
Whene'er I passed her; but who passed without
Much the same smile? This grew; I gave commands;
Then all smiles stopped together. There she stands
As if alive. Will't please you rise? We'll meet
The company below, then. I repeat,
The Count your master's known munificence
Is ample warrant that no just pretense
Of mine for dowry will be disallowed;
Though his fair daughter's self, as I avowed
At starting, is my object. Nay, we'll go
Together down, sir. Notice Neptune, though,
Taming a sea-horse, thought a rarity,
Which Claus of Innsbruck cast in bronze for me!

In Town

H. Austin Dobson

'The blue fly sung in the pane.'—Tennyson

Toiling in Town now is 'horrid,'
  (There is that woman again!)—
June in the zenith is torrid,
    Thought gets dry in the brain.

There is that woman again:
  'Strawberries! fourpence a pottle!'
Thought gets dry in the brain;
    Ink gets dry in the bottle.

'Strawberries! fourpence a pottle!'
  Oh for the green of a lane!—
Ink gets dry in the bottle;
    'Buzz' goes a fly in the pane!

Oh for the green of a lane,
  Where one might lie and be lazy!
'Buzz goes a fly in the pane;
    Bluebottles drive me crazy!

Where one might lie and be lazy,
  Careless of Town and all in it!—
Bluebottles drive me crazy:
    I shall go mad in a minute!

Careless of Town and all in it,
  With some one to soothe and to still you;—
I shall go mad in a minute;
    Bluebottle, then I shall kill you!

With some one to soothe and to still you,
  As only one's feminine kin do,—
Bluebottle, then I shall kill you:
    There now! I've broken the window!

245

As only one's feminine kin do,—
   Some muslin-clad Mabel or May!—
There now! I've broken the window!
   Bluebottle's off and away!

Some muslin-clad Mabel or May,
   To dash one with eau de Cologne;—
Bluebottle's off and away;
   And why should I stay here alone!

To dash one with eau de Cologne,
   All over one's eminent forehead;—
And why should I stay here alone!
   Toiling in Town now is 'horrid.'

Villanelle of His Lady's Treasures

Ernest Dowson

I took her dainty eyes, as well
   As silken tendrils of her hair:
And so I made a Villanelle!

I took her voice, a silver bell,
   As clear as song, as soft as prayer;
I took her dainty eyes as well.

It may be, said I, who can tell,
   These things shall be my less despair?
And so I made a Villanelle!

I took her whiteness virginal
   And from her cheek two roses rare:
I took her dainty eyes as well.

I said: "It may be possible
   Her image from my heart to tear!"
And so I made a Villanelle.

I stole her laugh, most musical:
  I wrought it in with artful care;
I took her dainty eyes as well;
And so I made a Villanelle.

We Wear the Mask

Paul Laurence Dunbar

We wear the mask that grins and lies,
It hides our cheeks and shades our eyes,—
This debt we pay to human guile;
With torn and bleeding hearts we smile,
And mouth with myriad subtleties.

Why should the world be over-wise,
In counting all our tears and sighs?
Nay, let them only see us, while
    We wear the mask.

We smile, but, O great Christ, our cries
To thee from tortured souls arise.
We sing, but oh the clay is vile
Beneath our feet, and long the mile;
But let the world dream otherwise,
    We wear the mask!

Hysteria

T.S. Eliot

As she laughed I was aware of becoming involved in her laughter and being part of it, until her teeth were only accidental stars with a talent for squad-drill. I was drawn in by short gasps, inhaled at each momentary recovery, lost finally in the dark caverns of her throat, bruised by the ripple of unseen muscles. An elderly waiter with trembling hands was hurriedly spreading a pink and white checked cloth over the rusty green iron table, saying: "If the lady and gentleman wish to take their tea in the garden, if the lady and gentleman wish to take their tea in the garden…" I decided that if the shaking of her breasts could be stopped, some of the fragments of the afternoon might be collected, and I concentrated my attention with careful subtlety to this end.

The Love Song of J. Alfred Prufrock

T.S. Eliot

S'io credesse che mia risposta fosse
A persona che mai tornasse al mondo,
Questa fiamma staria senza piu scosse.
Ma percioche giammai di questo fondo
Non torno vivo alcun, s'i'odo il vero,
Senza tema d'infamia ti rispondo.

Let us go then, you and I,
When the evening is spread out against the sky
Like a patient etherized upon a table;
Let us go, through certain half-deserted streets,
The muttering retreats
Of restless nights in one-night cheap hotels
And sawdust restaurants with oyster-shells:
Streets that follow like a tedious argument
Of insidious intent
To lead you to an overwhelming question ...
Oh, do not ask, "What is it?"

Let us go and make our visit.
In the room the women come and go
Talking of Michelangelo.

The yellow fog that rubs its back upon the window-panes,
The yellow smoke that rubs its muzzle on the window-panes,
Licked its tongue into the corners of the evening,
Lingered upon the pools that stand in drains,
Let fall upon its back the soot that falls from chimneys,
Slipped by the terrace, made a sudden leap,
And seeing that it was a soft October night,
Curled once about the house, and fell asleep.

And indeed there will be time
For the yellow smoke that slides along the street,
Rubbing its back upon the window-panes;
There will be time, there will be time
To prepare a face to meet the faces that you meet;

There will be time to murder and create,
And time for all the works and days of hands
That lift and drop a question on your plate;
Time for you and time for me,
And time yet for a hundred indecisions,
And for a hundred visions and revisions,
Before the taking of a toast and tea.

In the room the women come and go
Talking of Michelangelo.

And indeed there will be time
To wonder, "Do I dare?" and, "Do I dare?"
Time to turn back and descend the stair,
With a bald spot in the middle of my hair —
(They will say: "How his hair is growing thin!")
My morning coat, my collar mounting firmly to the chin,
My necktie rich and modest, but asserted by a simple pin —
(They will say: "But how his arms and legs are thin!")
Do I dare
Disturb the universe?
In a minute there is time
For decisions and revisions which a minute will reverse.

For I have known them all already, known them all:
Have known the evenings, mornings, afternoons,
I have measured out my life with coffee spoons;
I know the voices dying with a dying fall
Beneath the music from a farther room.
                So how should I presume?

And I have known the eyes already, known them all—
The eyes that fix you in a formulated phrase,
And when I am formulated, sprawling on a pin,
When I am pinned and wriggling on the wall,
Then how should I begin
To spit out all the butt-ends of my days and ways?
                And how should I presume?

And I have known the arms already, known them all—
Arms that are braceleted and white and bare
(But in the lamplight, downed with light brown hair!)
Is it perfume from a dress
That makes me so digress?
Arms that lie along a table, or wrap about a shawl.
        And should I then presume?
        And how should I begin?

Shall I say, I have gone at dusk through narrow streets
And watched the smoke that rises from the pipes
Of lonely men in shirt-sleeves, leaning out of windows? ...

I should have been a pair of ragged claws
Scuttling across the floors of silent seas.

And the afternoon, the evening, sleeps so peacefully!
Smoothed by long fingers,
Asleep ... tired ... or it malingers,
Stretched on the floor, here beside you and me.
Should I, after tea and cakes and ices,
Have the strength to force the moment to its crisis?
But though I have wept and fasted, wept and prayed,
Though I have seen my head (grown slightly bald) brought in upon a platter,
I am no prophet — and here's no great matter;
I have seen the moment of my greatness flicker,
And I have seen the eternal Footman hold my coat, and snicker,
And in short, I was afraid.

And would it have been worth it, after all,
After the cups, the marmalade, the tea,
Among the porcelain, among some talk of you and me,
Would it have been worth while,
To have bitten off the matter with a smile,
To have squeezed the universe into a ball
To roll it towards some overwhelming question,
To say: "I am Lazarus, come from the dead,
Come back to tell you all, I shall tell you all"—
If one, settling a pillow by her head
        Should say: "That is not what I meant at all;
        That is not it, at all."

And would it have been worth it, after all,
Would it have been worth while,
After the sunsets and the dooryards and the sprinkled streets,
After the novels, after the teacups, after the skirts that trail along the floor—
And this, and so much more?—
It is impossible to say just what I mean!
But as if a magic lantern threw the nerves in patterns on a screen:
Would it have been worth while
If one, settling a pillow or throwing off a shawl,
And turning toward the window, should say:
   "That is not it at all,
   That is not what I meant, at all."

No! I am not Prince Hamlet, nor was meant to be;
Am an attendant lord, one that will do
To swell a progress, start a scene or two,
Advise the prince; no doubt, an easy tool,
Deferential, glad to be of use,
Politic, cautious, and meticulous;
Full of high sentence, but a bit obtuse;
At times, indeed, almost ridiculous—
Almost, at times, the Fool.

I grow old … I grow old …
I shall wear the bottoms of my trousers rolled.

Shall I part my hair behind? Do I dare to eat a peach?
I shall wear white flannel trousers, and walk upon the beach.
I have heard the mermaids singing, each to each.

I do not think that they will sing to me.

I have seen them riding seaward on the waves
Combing the white hair of the waves blown back
When the wind blows the water white and black.
We have lingered in the chambers of the sea
By sea-girls wreathed with seaweed red and brown
Till human voices wake us, and we drown.

To Autumn

John Keats

Season of mists and mellow fruitfulness,
   Close bosom-friend of the maturing sun;
Conspiring with him how to load and bless
   With fruit the vines that round the thatch-eves run;
To bend with apples the moss'd cottage-trees,
   And fill all fruit with ripeness to the core;
     To swell the gourd, and plump the hazel shells
   With a sweet kernel; to set budding more,
And still more, later flowers for the bees,
Until they think warm days will never cease,
     For summer has o'er-brimm'd their clammy cells.

Who hath not seen thee oft amid thy store?
   Sometimes whoever seeks abroad may find
Thee sitting careless on a granary floor,
   Thy hair soft-lifted by the winnowing wind;
Or on a half-reap'd furrow sound asleep,
   Drows'd with the fume of poppies, while thy hook
     Spares the next swath and all its twined flowers:
And sometimes like a gleaner thou dost keep
   Steady thy laden head across a brook;
   Or by a cyder-press, with patient look,
     Thou watchest the last oozings hours by hours.

Where are the songs of spring? Ay, Where are they?
   Think not of them, thou hast thy music too,—
While barred clouds bloom the soft-dying day,
   And touch the stubble-plains with rosy hue;
Then in a wailful choir the small gnats mourn
   Among the river sallows, borne aloft
     Or sinking as the light wind lives or dies;
And full-grown lambs loud bleat from hilly bourn;
   Hedge-crickets sing; and now with treble soft
   The red-breast whistles from a garden-croft;
     And gathering swallows twitter in the skies.

Sestina of the Tramp-Royal

Rudyard Kipling

Speakin' in general, I 'ave tried 'em all—
The 'appy roads that take you o'er the world.
Speakin' in general, I 'ave found them good
For such as cannot use one bed too long,
But must get 'ence, the same as I 'ave done,
An' go observin' matters till they die.

What do it matter where or 'ow we die,
So long as we've our 'ealth to watch it all—
The different ways that different things are done,
An' men an' women lovin' in this world;
Takin' our chances as they come along,
An' when they ain't, pretendin' they are good?

In cash or credit—no, it aren't no good;
You 'ave to 'ave the 'abit or you'd die,
Unless you lived your life but one day long,
Nor didn't prophesy nor fret at all,
But drew your tucker some'ow from the world,
An' never bothered what you might ha' done.

But, Gawd, what things are they I 'aven't done?
I've turned my 'and to most, an' turned it good,
In various situations round the world—
For 'im that doth not work must surely die;
But that's no reason man should labour all
'Is life on one same shift—life's none so long.

Therefore, from job to job I've moved along.
Pay couldn't 'old me when my time was done,
For something in my 'ead upset it all,
Till I 'ad dropped whatever 'twas for good,
An', out at sea, be'eld the dock-lights die,
An' met my mate—the wind that tramps the world!

It's like a book, I think, this bloomin' world,
Which you can read and care for just so long,
But presently you feel that you will die
Unless you get the page you're readin' done,
An' turn another—likely not so good;
But what you're after is to turn 'em all.

Gawd bless this world! Whatever she 'ath done—
Excep' when awful long I've found it good.
So write, before I die, "E liked it all!'

The Passionate Shepherd to His Love
Christopher Marlowe

Come live with me and be my love,
And we will all the pleasures prove,
That Valleys, groves, hills, and fields,
Woods, or steepy mountain yields.

And we will sit upon the Rocks,
Seeing the Shepherds feed their flocks,
By shallow Rivers to whose falls
Melodious birds sing Madrigals.

And I will make thee beds of Roses
And a thousand fragrant posies,
A cap of flowers, and a kirtle
Embroidered all with leaves of Myrtle;

A gown made of the finest wool
Which from our pretty Lambs we pull;
Fair lined slippers for the cold,
With buckles of the purest gold;

A belt of straw and Ivy buds,
With Coral clasps and Amber studs:
And if these pleasures may thee move,
Come live with me, and be my love.

The Shepherds' Swains shall dance and sing
For thy delight each May-morning:
If these delights thy mind may move,
Then live with me, and be my love.

If I should learn, in some quite casual way

Edna St. Vincent Millay

If I should learn, in some quite casual way,
 That you were gone, not to return again—
Read from the back-page of a paper, say,
 Held by a neighbor in a subway train,
How at the corner of this avenue
 And such a street (so are the papers filled)
A hurrying man—who happened to be you—
 At noon to-day had happened to be killed,
I should not cry aloud—I could not cry
 Aloud, or wring my hands in such a place—
I should but watch the station lights rush by
 With a more careful interest on my face,
Or raise my eyes and read with greater care
Where to store furs and how to treat the hair.

The Emperor of Ice-Cream

Wallace Stevens

Call the roller of big cigars,
The muscular one, and bid him whip
In kitchen cups concupiscent curds.
Let the wenches dawdle in such dress
As they are used to wear, and let the boys
Bring flowers in last month's newspapers.
Let be be finale of seem.
The only emperor is the emperor of ice-cream.

Take from the dresser of deal,
Lacking the three glass knobs, that sheet
On which she embroidered fantails once
And spread it so as to cover her face.
If her horny feet protrude, they come
To show how cold she is, and dumb.
Let the lamp affix its beam.
The only emperor is the emperor of ice-cream.

Ulysses

Alfred, Lord Tennyson

It little profits that an idle king,
By this still hearth, among these barren crags,
Match'd with an aged wife, I mete and dole
Unequal laws unto a savage race,
That hoard, and sleep, and feed, and know not me.
I cannot rest from travel: I will drink
Life to the lees: All times I have enjoy'd
Greatly, have suffer'd greatly, both with those
That loved me, and alone, on shore, and when
Thro' scudding drifts the rainy Hyades
Vext the dim sea: I am become a name;
For always roaming with a hungry heart
Much have I seen and known; cities of men
And manners, climates, councils, governments,
Myself not least, but honour'd of them all;
And drunk delight of battle with my peers,
Far on the ringing plains of windy Troy.
I am a part of all that I have met;
Yet all experience is an arch wherethro'
Gleams that untravell'd world whose margin fades
For ever and forever when I move.
How dull it is to pause, to make an end,
To rust unburnish'd, not to shine in use!
As tho' to breathe were life! Life piled on life
Were all too little, and of one to me
Little remains: but every hour is saved
From that eternal silence, something more,

A bringer of new things; and vile it were
For some three suns to store and hoard myself,
And this gray spirit yearning in desire
To follow knowledge like a sinking star,
Beyond the utmost bound of human thought.

This is my son, mine own Telemachus,
To whom I leave the sceptre and the isle,—
Well-loved of me, discerning to fulfil
This labour, by slow prudence to make mild
A rugged people, and thro' soft degrees
Subdue them to the useful and the good.
Most blameless is he, centred in the sphere
Of common duties, decent not to fail
In offices of tenderness, and pay
Meet adoration to my household gods,
When I am gone. He works his work, I mine.

There lies the port; the vessel puffs her sail:
There gloom the dark, broad seas. My mariners,
Souls that have toil'd, and wrought, and thought with me—
That ever with a frolic welcome took
The thunder and the sunshine, and opposed
Free hearts, free foreheads—you and I are old;
Old age hath yet his honour and his toil;
Death closes all: but something ere the end,
Some work of noble note, may yet be done,
Not unbecoming men that strove with Gods.
The lights begin to twinkle from the rocks:
The long day wanes: the slow moon climbs: the deep
Moans round with many voices. Come, my friends,
'T is not too late to seek a newer world.
Push off, and sitting well in order smite
The sounding furrows; for my purpose holds
To sail beyond the sunset, and the baths
Of all the western stars, until I die.
It may be that the gulfs will wash us down:
It may be we shall touch the Happy Isles,
And see the great Achilles, whom we knew.
Tho' much is taken, much abides; and tho'

We are not now that strength which in old days
Moved earth and heaven, that which we are, we are;
One equal temper of heroic hearts,
Made weak by time and fate, but strong in will
To strive, to seek, to find, and not to yield.

O Captain! My Captain!
Walt Whitman

O Captain! my Captain! our fearful trip is done,
The ship has weather'd every rack, the prize we sought is won,
The port is near, the bells I hear, the people all exulting,
While follow eyes the steady keel, the vessel grim and daring;
        But O heart! heart! heart!
        O the bleeding drops of red,
          Where on the deck my Captain lies,
          Fallen cold and dead.

O Captain! my Captain! rise up and hear the bells;
Rise up—for you the flag is flung—for you the bugle trills,
For you bouquets and ribbon'd wreaths—for you the shores a-crowding,
For you they call, the swaying mass, their eager faces turning;
        Here Captain! dear father!
        The arm beneath your head!
          It is some dream that on the deck,
          You've fallen cold and dead.

My Captain does not answer, his lips are pale and still,
My father does not feel my arm, he has no pulse nor will,
The ship is anchor'd safe and sound, its voyage closed and done,
From fearful trip the victor ship comes in with object won;
        Exult O shores, and ring O bells!
        But I with mournful tread,
          Walk the deck my Captain lies,
          Fallen cold and dead.

Adam's Curse

W.B. Yeats

We sat together at one summer's end,
That beautiful mild woman, your close friend,
And you and I, and talked of poetry.
I said, 'A line will take us hours maybe;
Yet if it does not seem a moment's thought,
Our stitching and unstitching has been naught.
Better go down upon your marrow-bones
And scrub a kitchen pavement, or break stones
Like an old pauper, in all kinds of weather;
For to articulate sweet sounds together
Is to work harder than all these, and yet
Be thought an idler by the noisy set
Of bankers, schoolmasters, and clergymen
The martyrs call the world.'
                  And thereupon
That beautiful mild woman for whose sake
There's many a one shall find out all heartache
On finding that her voice is sweet and low
Replied, 'To be born woman is to know—
Although they do not talk of it at school—
That we must labour to be beautiful.'
I said, 'It's certain there is no fine thing
Since Adam's fall but needs much labouring.
There have been lovers who thought love should be
So much compounded of high courtesy
That they would sigh and quote with learned looks
Precedents out of beautiful old books;
Yet now it seems an idle trade enough.'
We sat grown quiet at the name of love;
We saw the last embers of daylight die,
And in the trembling blue-green of the sky
A moon, worn as if it had been a shell
Washed by time's waters as they rose and fell
About the stars and broke in days and years.

I had a thought for no one's but your ears:
That you were beautiful, and that I strove
To love you in the old high way of love;
That it had all seemed happy, and yet we'd grown
As weary-hearted as that hollow moon.

The Final Scene of *A Spanish Tragedie:* Act IV, Scene iii

Excerpted from Thomas Kyd's play, A Spanish Tragedie *(1587)*

ACT IV, SCENE III

[The DUKE's castle.]

Enter HIERONIMO; he knocks up the curtaine.
Enter the DUKE OF CASTILE.

CAS. How now, Hieronimo? wheres your fellows,
That you take all this paine?
HIERO. O sir, it is for the authors credit
To look that all things may goe well.
But, good my lord, let me intreat your Grace
To giue the king the coppie of the plaie:
This is the argument of what we shew.
CAS. I will, Hieronimo.
HIERO. One more thing, my good lord.
CAS.   Whats that?
HIERO. Let me intreat your Grace
That, when the traine are past into the gallerie,
You would vouchsafe to throwe me downe the key.
CAS. I will Hieronimo.

Exit CAS[TILE].

HIERO. What, are you ready, Balthazar?
 Bring a chaire and a cushion for the king.

   Enter BALTHAZAR with a chaire.

 Well doon, Balthazar; hang vp the title:
 Our scene is Rhodes.   What, is your beard on?
BAL. Halfe on, the other is in my hand.
HIERO. Dispatch, for shame! are you so long?

   Exit BALTHAZAR.

 Bethink thy-selfe, Hieronimo,
 Recall thy wits, recompt thy former wrongs
 Thou hast receiued by murder of thy sonne,
 And lastly, [but] not least, how Isabell,
 Once his mother and [my] deerest wife,
 All woe-begone for him, hath slaine her-selfe.
 Behoues thee then, Hieronimo, to be
 Reueng'd! The plot is laide of dire reuenge:
 On then, Hieronimo; persue reuenge,
 For nothing wants but acting of reuenge!

   Exit HIERONIMO.

   Enter SPANISH KING, VICE-ROY, the DUKE
   OF CASTILE, and their traine, [to the
   gallery].

KING. Now, viceroy, shall we see the tragedie
 Of Soliman, the Turkish emperour,
 Performde by pleasure by yor sonne the prince,
 My nephew Don Lorenzo, and my neece.
VICE. Who? Bel-imperia?
KING. I; and Hieronimo our marshall,
 At whose request they deine to doo't themselues.
 These be our pastimes in the court of Spaine.
 Heere, brother, you shall be the booke-keeper:
 This is the argument of that they shew.

He giueth him a booke.

[Gentlemen, this play of Hieronimo in sundrie languages was thought good to be set downe in English more largely, for the easier vnderstanding to euery publique reader.]

> Enter BALTHAZAR, BEL-IMPERIA, and
> HIERONIMO.

BALTHAZAR. [acting] Bashaw, that Rhodes is ours yeeld Heauens the honor
  And holy Mahhomet, our sacred prophet!
  And be thou grac't with euery excelence
  That Soliman can giue or thou desire!
  But thy desert in conquering Rhodes is lesse
  Then in reseruing this faire Christian nimph,
  Perseda, blisfull lamp of excellence,
  Whose eies compell, like powerfull adamant,
  The warlike heart of Soliman to wait.
KING. See, vice-roy, that is Balthazar your sonne,
  That represents the Emperour Solyman:
  How well he acts his amorous passion!
VICE. I; Bel-imperia hath taught him that.
CASTILE: That's because his mind runnes al on Bel-imperia.
HIERO. [acting] What-euer ioy earth yeelds betide your Maiestie!
BALT. [acting] Earth yeelds no ioy without Persedaes loue.
HIERO. [acting] Let then Peerseda on your Grace attend.
BALT. [acting] She shall not wait on me, but I on her!
  Drawne by the influence of her lights, I yeeld.
  But let my friend, the Rhodian knight, come foorth,—
  Erasto, dearer then my life to me,—
  That he may see Perseda, my beloued.

> Enter ERASTO [LORENZO].

KING. Heere comes Lorenzo: looke vpon the plot
  And tell me, brother, what part plaies he.
BEL. [acting] Ah, my Erasto! Welcome to Perseda!
LO. [acting] Thrice happie is Erasto that thou liuest!
  Rhodes losse is nothing to Erastoes ioy;
  Sith his Perseda liues, his life suruiues.
BALT. [acting] Ah, bashaw, heere is loue betweene Erasto
  And faire Perseda, soueraigne of my soule!

HIERO. [acting] Remooue Erasto, mighty Solyman,
  And then Perseda will be quickly wonne.
BALT. [acting] Erasto is my friend; and, while he liues,
  Perseda neuer will remooue her loue.
HIERO. [acting] Let not Erasto liue to greeue great Soliman!
BALT. [acting] Deare is Erasto in our princely eye.
HIERO. [acting] But, if he be your riuall, let him die!
BALT. [acting] Why, let him die! so loue commaundeth me.
  Yet I greeve I that Erasto should so die.
HIERO. [acting] Erasto, Soliman saluteth thee,
  And lets thee wit by me his Highnes will,
  Which is, thou shouldst be thus imploid.

    Stab him.

BEL. [acting] Ay, me, Erasto! See, Solyman, Erastoes slaine!
BALT. [acting] Yet liueth Solyman to comfort thee.
  Faire queene of beautie, let not fauour die,
  Both with gratious eye behlde his griefe,
  That with Persedaes beautie is encreast,
  If by Perseda griefe be not releast.
BEL. [acting] Tyrant, desist soliciting vaine sutes;
  Relentles are mine eares to thy laments
  As thy butcher is pittilesse and base
  Which seazd on my Erasto, harmelesse knight.
  Yet by thy power thou thinkest to commaund,
  And to thy power Perseda doth obey;
  But, were she able, thus she would reuenge
  Thy treacheries on thee, ignoble prince;

    Stab him.

And on herselfe she would be thus reuengd.

    Stab herselfe.

KING. Well said, old marshall! this was brauely done!
HIERO. But Bel-imperia plauies Perseda well.
VICE. Were this in earnest, Bel-imperia,
  You would be better to my sonne then so.

KING. But now what followes for Hieronimo?
HIERO. Marrie, this followes for Hieronimo!
　　Heere breake we off our sundrie languages,
　　And thus conclude I in our vulgare tung:
　　Happely you think—but bootles are your thoughts—
　　That this is fabulously counterfeit,
　　And that we doo as all trageians doo,—
　　To die to-day, for fashioning our scene,
　　The death of Aiax, or some Romaine peer,
　　And, in a minute starting vp againe,
　　Reuiue to please tomorrows audience.
　　No, princes; know I am Hieronimo,
　　The hopeles father of a haples sonne,
　　Whose tung is tun'd to tell his latest tale,
　　Not to excuse grosse errors in the play.
　　I see your lookes vrge instance of these words:
　　Beholde the reason vrging me to this!

　　　　Showes his dead sonne.

　　See heere my shew; look on this spectacle!
　　Heere lay my hope, and heere my hope hath end;
　　Heere lay my hart, and heere my hart was slaine;
　　Heere lay my treasure, heere my treasure lost;
　　Heere lay my blisse, and heere my blisse bereft.
　　But hope, hart, treasure, ioy and blisse,—
　　All fled, faild, died, yea, all decaide with this.
　　From froth these wounds came breath that gaue me life;
　　They murdred me that made these fatall markes.
　　The cause was loue whence grew this mortall hate:
　　The hate, Lorenzo and yong Balthazar;
　　The loue, my sonne to Bel-imperia.
　　But night, the couerer of accursed crimes,
　　With pitchie silence husht these traitors harmes,
　　And lent them leaue—for they had sorted leasure—
　　To take aduantage in my garden plot
　　Vpon my sonne, my deere Horatio.
　　There mercilesse they butcherd vp my boy,
　　In black, darke night, to pale, dim, cruell death!
　　He shrikes; I heard—and yet, me thinks, I heare—

His dismall out-cry eccho in the aire;
With soonest speed I hasted to the noise,
Where, hanging on a tree, I found my sonne
Through-girt with wounds and slaughtred, as you see.
And greeued I, think you, at this spectacle?
Speak, Portuguise, whose losse resembles mine!
If thou canst weep vpon thy Balthazar,
Tis like I wailde for my Horatio.
And you, my l[ord], whose reconciled sonne
Marcht in a net and thought himself vnseene,
And rated me for a brainsicke lunacie,
With "God amend that mad Hieronimo!"—
How can you brook our plaies catastrophe?
And heere beholde this bloudie hand-kercher,
Which at Horatios death weeping dipt
Within the riuer of his bleeding wounds!
It as propitious, see, I haue reserued,
And neuer hath it left my bloody hart,
Soliciting remembrance of my vow
With these, O these accursed murderers!
Which now perform'd, my hart is satisfied.
And to this end the bashaw I became,
That might reuenge me on Lorenzos life,
Who therefore was appointed to the part
And was to represent the knight of Rhodes,
That I might kill him more conueniently.
So, vice-roy, was this Balthazar thy sonne—
That Soliman which Bel-imperia
In person of Perseda murdered,—
So[le]lie appointed to that tragicke part,
That she might slay him that offended her.
Poore Bel-imperia mist her part in this:
For, though the story saith she should haue died,
Yet I, of kindenes and care for her,
Did otherwise determine of her end.
But loue of him whome they did hate too much
Did vrge her resolution to be such.
And princes, now beholde Hieronimo,
Author and actor in this tragedie,
Bearing his latest fortune in his fist;

And will as resolute conclude his parte
As any of the actors gone before.
And, gentles, thus I end my play!
Vrge no more words, I haue no more to say.

He runs to hang himselfe.

KING. O hearken, vice-roy; holde Hieronimo!
　　Brother, my newphew and they sonne are slaine!
VICE. We are betraide! my Balthazar is slaine!
　　Breake ope the doores; runne saue Hieronimo!
　　Hieronimo, doe but enforme the king of these euents;
　　Vpon mine honour, thou shalt haue no harme!
HIERO. Vice-roy, I will not trust thee with my life,
　　Which I this day haue offered to my sonne:
　　Accursed wretch, why staiest thou him that was resolued to die?
KING. Speak, traitor! damned, bloudy murderer, speak!—
　　For, now I haue thee, I wil make thee speak!
　　Why hast thou done this vndeseruing deed?
VICE. Why hast thou murdered my Balthazar?
CAS. Why hast thou butchered both my children thus?
HIERO. O good words! As deare to me was Horatio
　　As yours, or yours, my l[ord], to you.
　　My guitles sonne was by Lorenzo slaine;
　　And by Lorenzo and that Balthazar
　　Am I at last reuenged thorowly,—
　　Vpon whole soules may Heauens be yet auenged
　　With far greater far then these afflictions!
CAS. But who were thy confederates in this?
VICE. That was thy daughter Bel-imperia;
　　For by her hand my Balthazar was slaine,—
　　I saw her stab him.
KING.　　Why speakest thou not?
HIERO. What lesser libertie can kings affoord
　　Then harmles silence? That afford it me!
　　Sufficeth I may not nor I will not tell thee.

KING. Fetch forth the tortures! Traitor as thou art, Ile make thee tell!

HIERO.   Indeed?
  Thou maiest torment me as his wretched sonne
  Hath done in murdring my Horatio;
  But neuer shalt thou force me to reueale
  The thing which I haue vowed inviolate.
  And therefore, in despight of all thy threats,
  Pleasde with their deaths, and easde with their reuenge,
  First take my tung, and afterwards my hart!

        He bites out his tongue.

KING. O monstrous resolution of a wretch!
  See, Vice-Roy, he hath bitten foorth his tung
  Rather than reueale what we requirde.
CAS. Yet can he write.
KING. And if in this he satisfie vs not,
  We will deuise the 'xtreamest kinde of death
  That euer was inuented for a wretch.

        Then he makes signes for a knife to mend his pen.

CAS. O, he would haue a knife to mend his pen.
VICE. Here; and aduise thee that thou write the troth,—
  Look to my brother! saue Hieronimo!

        He with a knife stabs the DUKE and himself.

KING. What age hath euer heard such monstrous deeds?
  My brother and the whole succeeding hope
  That Spaine expected after my dicease.
  Go beare his body hence, that we may mourne
  The losse of our beloued brothers death,
  That he may be entom'd, what-ere befall.
  I am the next, the neerest, last of all.

VICE. And thou, Don Pedro, do the like for vs:
  Take vp our haples sonne vntimely slaine;
  Set me vp with him, and he with wofull me,
  Vpon the maine-mast of a ship vnmand,
  And let the winde and tide [hale] me along

To Sillas barking and vntamed gulfe
Or to the lothsome poole of Archeron,
To weepe my want for my sweet Balthazar.
Spaine hath no refuge for a Portingale!

> The trumpets sound a dead march, the KING OF SPAINE
> mourning after his brothers body, and the KING OF
> PORTINGALE bearing the body of his sonne.

[CHORUS.]

> Enter GHOAST and REUENGE.

GHOAST. I; now my hopes haue end in their effects,
When blood and sorrow finnish my desires:
Horatio murdered in his Fathers bower,
Vilde Serberine by Pedrigano slaine,
False Pedrigano hang'd by quaint deuice,
Faire Isabella by her-selfe misdone,
Prince Balthazar by Bel-imepria stabd,
The Duke of Castile an his wicked sonne
Both done to death by olde Hieronimo,
My Bel-imperia falne as Dido fell,
And good Hieronimo slaine by himselfe!
I, these were spectacles to please my soule.
Now will I beg at louely Proserpine
That, by the vertue of her princely doome,
I may consort my freends in pleasing sort,
And on my foes work iust and sharpe reuenge.
Ile lead my freend Horatio through those feeldes
Where neuer-dying warres are still inurde;
Ile lead faire Isabella to that traine
Where pittie weepes but neuer feeleth paine;
Ile lead my Bel-imperia to those ioyes
That vestal virgins and faire queenes possess;
Ile lead Hieronimo where Orpheus plaies,
Adding sweet pleasure to eternall daies.
But say, Reuenge,—for thou must helpe or none,—
Against the rest how shall my hate be showne?
REUENGE. This hand shall hale them down to deepest hell,
Where none but furies, bugs and tortures dwell.
GHOAST. Then, sweet Reuenge, doo this at my request:

269

Let me iudge and doome them to vnrest;
Let loose poore Titius from the vultures gripe,
And let Don Ciprian supply his roome;
Place Don Lorenzo on Ixions wheele,
And let the louers endles paines surcease,
Iuno forget olde wrath and graunt him ease;
Hang Balthazar about Chimeras neck,
And let him there bewaile his bloudy loue,
Repining at our ioyes that are aboue;
Let Serberine goe roule the fatall stone
And take from Siciphus his endles mone;
False Pedringano, for his trecherie,
Let him be dragde through boyling Acheron,
And there liue dying still in endles flames,
Blaspheming gods and all their holy names.
REUENGE. Then haste we downe to meet thy freends and foes;
To place thy freends in ease, the rest in woes.
For heere though death [doth] end their miserie,
Ile there begin their endles tragedie.

Exeunt.
FINIS.

Hamlet's "To be, or not to be" Speech

Excerpted from William Shakespeare's play, Hamlet *(1604), Act III, Scene i*

HAMLET. To be, or not to be— that is the question:
Whether 'tis nobler in the mind to suffer
The slings and arrows of outrageous fortune
Or to take arms against a sea of troubles,
And by opposing end them. To die— to sleep—
No more; and by a sleep to say we end
The heartache, and the thousand natural shocks
That flesh is heir to. 'Tis a consummation
Devoutly to be wish'd. To die— to sleep.
To sleep— perchance to dream: ay, there's the rub!
For in that sleep of death what dreams may come
When we have shuffled off this mortal coil,
Must give us pause. There's the respect
That makes calamity of so long life.
For who would bear the whips and scorns of time,
Th' oppressor's wrong, the proud man's contumely,
The pangs of despis'd love, the law's delay,
The insolence of office, and the spurns
That patient merit of th' unworthy takes,
When he himself might his quietus make
With a bare bodkin? Who would these fardels bear,
To grunt and sweat under a weary life,
But that the dread of something after death—
The undiscover'd country, from whose bourn
No traveller returns— puzzles the will,
And makes us rather bear those ills we have
Than fly to others that we know not of?
Thus conscience does make cowards of us all,
And thus the native hue of resolution
Is sicklied o'er with the pale cast of thought,
And enterprises of great pith and moment
With this regard their currents turn awry
And lose the name of action.— Soft you now!
The fair Ophelia!— Nymph, in thy orisons
Be all my sins rememb'red.

Othello and Desdemona's Final Kiss: The Opening of Act V, Scene ii: 1–95

Excerpted from William Shakespeare's play, Othello *(1565)*

SCENE II. A bedchamber in the castle: DESDEMONA in bed asleep; a light burning.

Enter OTHELLO

OTHELLO. It is the cause, it is the cause, my soul,—
Let me not name it to you, you chaste stars!—
It is the cause. Yet I'll not shed her blood;
Nor scar that whiter skin of hers than snow,
And smooth as monumental alabaster.
Yet she must die, else she'll betray more men.
Put out the light, and then put out the light:
If I quench thee, thou flaming minister,
I can again thy former light restore,
Should I repent me: but once put out thy light,
Thou cunning'st pattern of excelling nature,
I know not where is that Promethean heat
That can thy light relume. When I have pluck'd the rose,
I cannot give it vital growth again.
It must needs wither: I'll smell it on the tree.

Kissing her

Ah balmy breath, that dost almost persuade
Justice to break her sword! One more, one more.
Be thus when thou art dead, and I will kill thee,
And love thee after. One more, and this the last:
So sweet was ne'er so fatal. I must weep,
But they are cruel tears: this sorrow's heavenly;
It strikes where it doth love. She wakes.
DESDEMONA. Who's there? Othello?
OTHELLO. Ay. Desdemona.
DESDEMONA. Will you come to bed, my lord?
OTHELLO. Have you pray'd to-night, Desdemona?
DESDEMONA. Ay, my lord.
OTHELLO. If you bethink yourself of any crime
Unreconciled as yet to heaven and grace,
Solicit for it straight.

DESDEMONA. Alas, my lord, what do you mean by that?

OTHELLO. Well, do it, and be brief; I will walk by:

I would not kill thy unprepared spirit;

No; heaven forfend! I would not kill thy soul.

DESDEMONA. Talk you of killing?

OTHELLO. Ay, I do.

DESDEMONA. Then heaven

Have mercy on me!

OTHELLO. Amen, with all my heart!

DESDEMONA.   If you say so, I hope you will not kill me.

OTHELLO. Hum!

DESDEMONA. And yet I fear you; for you are fatal then

When your eyes roll so: why I should fear I know not,

Since guiltiness I know not; but yet I feel I fear.

OTHELLO. Think on thy sins.

DESDEMONA. They are loves I bear to you.

OTHELLO. Ay, and for that thou diest.

DESDEMONA. That death's unnatural that kills for loving.

Alas, why gnaw you so your nether lip?

Some bloody passion shakes your very frame:

These are portents; but yet I hope, I hope,

They do not point on me.

OTHELLO. Peace, and be still!

DESDEMONA. I will so. What's the matter?

OTHELLO. That handkerchief which I so loved and gave thee

Thou gavest to Cassio.

DESDEMONA. No, by my life and soul!

Send for the man, and ask him.

OTHELLO. Sweet soul, take heed,

Take heed of perjury; thou art on thy deathbed.

DESDEMONA. Ay, but not yet to die.

OTHELLO. Yes, presently:

Therefore confess thee freely of thy sin;

For to deny each article with oath

Cannot remove nor choke the strong conception

That I do groan withal. Thou art to die.

DESDEMONA. Then Lord have mercy on me!

OTHELLO. I say, amen.

DESDEMONA. And have you mercy too! I never did

Offend you in my life; never loved Cassio

But with such general warranty of heaven
As I might love: I never gave him token.

OTHELLO. By heaven, I saw my handkerchief in's hand.
O perjured woman! thou dost stone my heart,
And makest me call what I intend to do
A murder, which I thought a sacrifice:
I saw the handkerchief.

DESDEMONA. He found it then;
I never gave it him: send for him hither;
Let him confess a truth.

OTHELLO. He hath confess'd.

DESDEMONA. What, my lord?

OTHELLO. That he hath used thee.

DESDEMONA. How? unlawfully?

OTHELLO. Ay.

DESDEMONA. He will not say so.

OTHELLO. No, his mouth is stopp'd;
Honest Iago hath ta'en order for't.

DESDEMONA. O! my fear interprets: what, is he dead?

OTHELLO. Had all his hairs been lives, my great revenge
Had stomach for them all.

DESDEMONA. Alas! he is betray'd and I undone.

OTHELLO. Out, strumpet! weep'st thou for him to my face?

DESDEMONA. O, banish me, my lord, but kill me not!

OTHELLO. Down, strumpet!

DESDEMONA. Kill me to-morrow: let me live to-night!

OTHELLO. Nay, if you strive—

DESDEMONA. But half an hour!

OTHELLO. Being done, there is no pause.

DESDEMONA. But while I say one prayer!

OTHELLO. It is too late.

He stifles her

Flamineo's "Had women navigable rivers in their eyes" Speech

Excerpted from John Webster's play, The White Devil *(1612), Act V, Scene iii*

FLAM[INEO]. Oh, yes, yes;
  Had women navigable rivers in their eyes,
  They would dispend them all. Surely, I wonder
  Why we should wish more rivers to the city,
  When they sell water so good cheap. I'll tell thee
  These are but Moorish shades of griefs or fears;
  There's nothing sooner dry than women's tears.
  Why, here's an end of all my harvest; he has given me nothing.
  Court promises! Let wise men count them curs'd;
  For while you live, he that scores best, pays worst.

The Alchemist

H. P. Lovecraft

High up, crowning the grassy summit of a swelling mount whose sides are wooded near the base with the gnarled trees of the primeval forest stands the old chateau of my ancestors. For centuries its lofty battlements have frowned down upon the wild and rugged countryside about, serving as a home and stronghold for the proud house whose honored line is older even than the moss-grown castle walls. These ancient turrets, stained by the storms of generations and crumbling under the slow yet mighty pressure of time, formed in the ages of feudalism one of the most dreaded and formidable fortresses in all France. From its machicolated parapets and mounted battlements Barons, Counts, and even Kings had been defied, yet never had its spacious halls resounded to the footsteps of the invader.

But since those glorious years, all is changed. A poverty but little above the level of dire want, together with a pride of name that forbids its alleviation by the pursuits of commercial life, have prevented the scions of our line from maintaining their estates in pristine splendour; and the falling stones of the walls, the overgrown vegetation in the parks, the dry and dusty moat, the ill-paved courtyards, and toppling towers without, as well as the sagging floors, the worm-eaten wainscots, and the faded tapestries within, all tell a gloomy tale of fallen grandeur. As the ages passed, first one, then another of the four great turrets were left to ruin, until at last but a single tower housed the sadly reduced descendants of the once mighty lords of the estate.

It was in one of the vast and gloomy chambers of this remaining tower that I, Antoine, last of the unhappy and accursed Counts de C-, first saw the light of day, ninety long years ago. Within these walls and amongst the dark and shadowy forests, the wild ravines and grottos of the hillside below, were spent the first years of my troubled life. My parents I never knew. My father had been killed at the age of thirty–two, a month before I was born, by the fall of a stone somehow dislodged from one of the deserted parapets of the castle. And my mother having died at my birth, my care and education devolved solely upon one remaining servitor, an old and trusted man of considerable intelligence, whose name I remember as Pierre. I was an only child and the lack of companionship which this fact entailed upon me was augmented by the strange care exercised by my aged guardian, in excluding me from the society of the peasant children whose abodes were scattered here and there upon the plains that surround the base of the hill. At that time, Pierre said that this restriction was imposed upon me because my noble birth placed me above association with such plebeian company. Now I know that its real object was to keep from my ears the idle tales of the dread curse upon our line that were nightly told and magnified by the simple tenantry as they conversed in hushed accents in the glow of their cottage hearths.

Thus isolated, and thrown upon my own resources, I spent the hours of my childhood in poring over the ancient tomes that filled the shadow-haunted library of the chateau, and in roaming without aim or purpose through the perpetual dust of the spectral wood that clothes the side of the hill near its foot. It was perhaps an effect of such surroundings that my mind early acquired a shade of melancholy. Those studies and pursuits which partake of the dark and occult in nature most strongly claimed my attention.

Of my own race I was permitted to learn singularly little, yet what small knowledge of it I was able to gain seemed to depress me much. Perhaps it was at first only the manifest reluctance of my old preceptor to discuss with me my paternal ancestry that gave rise to the terror which I ever felt at the mention of my great house, yet as I grew out of childhood, I was able to piece together disconnected fragments of discourse, let slip from the unwilling tongue which had begun to falter in approaching senility, that had a sort of relation to a certain circumstance which I had always deemed strange, but which now became dimly terrible. The circumstance to which I allude is the early age at which all the Counts of my line had met their end. Whilst I had hitherto considered this but a natural attribute of a family of short-lived men, I afterward pondered long upon these premature deaths, and began to connect them with the wanderings of the old man, who often spoke of a curse which for centuries had prevented the lives of the holders of my title from much exceeding the span of thirty-two years. Upon my twenty-first birthday, the aged Pierre gave to me a family document which he said had for many generations been handed down from father to son, and continued by each possessor. Its contents were of the most startling nature, and its perusal confirmed the gravest of my apprehensions. At this time, my belief in the supernatural was firm and deep-seated, else I should have dismissed with scorn the incredible narrative unfolded before my eyes.

The paper carried me back to the days of the thirteenth century, when the old castle in which I sat had been a feared and impregnable fortress. It told of a certain ancient man who had once dwelled on our estates, a person of no small accomplishments, though little above the rank of peasant, by name, Michel, usually designated by the surname of Mauvais, the Evil, on account of his sinister reputation. He had studied beyond the custom of his kind, seeking such things as the Philosopher's Stone or the Elixir of Eternal Life, and was reputed wise in the terrible secrets of Black Magic and Alchemy. Michel Mauvais had one son, named Charles, a youth as proficient as himself in the hidden arts, who had therefore been called Le Sorcier, or the Wizard. This pair, shunned by all honest folk, were suspected of the most hideous practices. Old Michel was said to have burnt his wife alive as a sacrifice to the Devil, and the unaccountable disappearance of many small peasant children was laid at the dreaded door of these two. Yet through the dark natures of the father and son ran one redeeming ray of humanity; the evil old man loved his offspring with fierce intensity, whilst the youth had for his parent a more than filial affection.

One night the castle on the hill was thrown into the wildest confusion by the vanishment of young Godfrey, son to Henri, the Count. A searching party, headed by the frantic father, invaded the cottage of the sorcerers and there came upon old Michel Mauvais, busy over a huge and violently boiling cauldron. Without certain cause, in the ungoverned madness of fury and despair, the Count laid hands on the aged wizard, and ere he released his murderous hold, his victim was no more. Meanwhile, joyful servants were proclaiming the finding of young Godfrey in a distant and unused chamber of the great edifice, telling too late that poor Michel had been killed in vain. As the Count and his associates turned away from the lowly abode of the alchemist, the form of Charles Le Sorcier appeared through the trees. The excited chatter of the menials standing about told him what had occurred, yet he seemed at first unmoved at his father's fate. Then, slowly advancing to meet the Count, he pronounced in dull yet terrible accents the curse that ever afterward haunted the house of C-.

'May ne'er a noble of thy murd'rous line Survive to reach a greater age than thine!'

spake he, when, suddenly leaping backwards into the black woods, he drew from his tunic a phial of colourless liquid which he threw into the face of his father's slayer as he disappeared behind the inky curtain of the night. The Count died without utterance, and was buried the next day, but little more than two and thirty years from the hour of his birth. No trace of the assassin could be found, though relentless bands of peasants scoured the neighboring woods and the meadowland around the hill.

Thus time and the want of a reminder dulled the memory of the curse in the minds of the late Count's family, so that when Godfrey, innocent cause of the whole tragedy and now bearing the title, was killed by an arrow whilst hunting at the age of thirty-two, there were no thoughts save those of grief at his demise. But when, years afterward, the next young Count, Robert by name, was found dead in a nearby field of no apparent cause, the peasants told in whispers that their seigneur had but lately passed his thirty-second birthday when surprised by early death. Louis, son to Robert, was found drowned in the moat at the same fateful age, and thus down through the centuries ran the ominous chronicle: Henris, Roberts, Antoines, and Armands snatched from happy and virtuous lives when little below the age of their unfortunate ancestor at his murder.

That I had left at most but eleven years of further existence was made certain to me by the words which I had read. My life, previously held at small value, now became dearer to me each day, as I delved deeper and deeper into the mysteries of the hidden world of black magic. Isolated as I was, modern science had produced no impression upon me, and I laboured as in the Middle Ages, as wrapt as had been old Michel and young Charles themselves in the acquisition of demonological and alchemical learning. Yet read as I might, in no manner could I account for the strange curse upon my line. In unusually rational moments I would even go so far as to seek a natural explanation, attributing the early deaths of my ancestors to the sinister Charles Le Sorcier and his heirs; yet, having found upon careful inquiry that there were no known descendants of the alchemist, I would fall back to occult studies, and once more endeavor to find a spell, that would release my house from its terrible burden. Upon one thing I was absolutely resolved. I should never wed, for, since no other branch of my family was in existence, I might thus end the curse with myself.

As I drew near the age of thirty, old Pierre was called to the land beyond. Alone I buried him beneath the stones of the courtyard about which he had loved to wander in life. Thus was I left to ponder on myself as the only human creature within the great fortress, and in my utter solitude my mind began to cease its vain protest against the impending doom, to become almost reconciled to the fate which so many of my ancestors had met. Much of my time was now occupied in the exploration of the ruined and abandoned halls and towers of the old chateau, which in youth fear had caused me to shun, and some of which old Pierre had once told me had not been trodden by human foot for over four centuries. Strange and awesome were many of the objects I encountered. Furniture, covered by the dust of ages and crumbling with the rot of long dampness, met my eyes. Cobwebs in a profusion never before seen by me were spun everywhere, and huge bats flapped their bony and uncanny wings on all sides of the otherwise untenanted gloom.

Of my exact age, even down to days and hours, I kept a most careful record, for each movement of the pendulum of the massive clock in the library told off so much of my doomed existence. At length I approached that time which I had so long viewed with apprehension. Since most of my ancestors had been seized some little while before they reached the exact age of Count Henri at his end, I was every moment on the watch for the coming of the unknown death. In what strange form the curse should overtake me, I knew not; but I was resolved at least that it should not find me a cowardly or a passive victim. With new vigour I applied myself to my examination of the old chateau and its contents.

It was upon one of the longest of all my excursions of discovery in the deserted portion of the castle, less than a week before that fatal hour which I felt must mark the utmost limit of my stay on earth, beyond which I could have not even the slightest hope of continuing to draw breath that I came upon the culminating event of my whole life. I had spent the better part of the morning in climbing up and down half ruined staircases in one of the most dilapidated of the ancient turrets. As the afternoon progressed, I sought the lower levels, descending into what appeared to be either a mediaeval place of confinement, or a more recently excavated storehouse for gunpowder. As I slowly traversed the nitre-encrusted passageway at the foot of the last staircase, the paving became very damp, and soon I saw by the light of my flickering torch that a blank, water-stained wall impeded my journey. Turning to retrace my steps, my eye fell upon a small trap-door with a ring, which lay directly beneath my foot. Pausing, I succeeded with difficulty in raising it, whereupon there was revealed a black aperture, exhaling noxious fumes which caused my torch to sputter, and disclosing in the unsteady glare the top of a flight of stone steps.

As soon as the torch which I lowered into the repellent depths burned freely and steadily, I commenced my descent. The steps were many, and led to a narrow stone-flagged passage which I knew must be far underground. This passage proved of great length, and terminated in a massive oaken door, dripping with the moisture of the place, and stoutly resisting all my attempts to open it. Ceasing after a time my efforts in this direction, I had proceeded back some distance toward the steps when there suddenly fell to my experience one of the most profound and maddening shocks capable of reception by the human mind. Without warning, I heard the heavy door behind me creak slowly open upon its rusted hinges. My immediate sensations were incapable of analysis. To be confronted in a place as thoroughly deserted as I had deemed the old castle with evidence of the presence of man or spirit produced in my brain a horror of the most acute description. When at last I turned and faced the seat of the sound, my eyes must have started from their orbits at the sight that they beheld.

There in the ancient Gothic doorway stood a human figure. It was that of a man clad in a skull-cap and long mediaeval tunic of dark colour. His long hair and flowing beard were of a terrible and intense black hue, and of incredible profusion. His forehead, high beyond the usual dimensions; his cheeks, deep-sunken and heavily lined with wrinkles; and his hands, long, claw-like, and gnarled, were of such a deadly marble-like whiteness as I have never elsewhere seen in man. His figure, lean to the proportions of a skeleton, was strangely bent and almost lost within the voluminous folds of his peculiar garment. But strangest of all were his eyes, twin caves of abysmal blackness, profound in expression of understanding, yet inhuman in degree of wickedness. These were now fixed upon me, piercing my soul with their hatred, and rooting me to the spot whereon I stood.

At last the figure spoke in a rumbling voice that chilled me through with its dull hollowness and latent malevolence. The language in which the discourse was clothed was that debased form of Latin in use amongst the more learned men of the Middle Ages, and made familiar to me by my prolonged researches into the works of the old alchemists and demonologists. The apparition spoke of the curse which had hovered over my house, told me of my coming end, dwelt on the wrong perpetrated by my ancestor against old Michel Mauvais, and gloated over the revenge of Charles Le Sorcier. He told how young Charles has escaped into the night, returning in after years to kill Godfrey the heir with an arrow just as he approached the age which had been his father's at his assassination; how he had secretly returned to the estate and established himself, unknown, in the even then deserted subterranean chamber whose doorway now framed the hideous narrator, how he had seized Robert, son of Godfrey, in a field, forced poison down his throat, and left him to die at the age of thirty-two, thus maintaining the foul provisions of his vengeful curse. At this point I was left to imagine the solution of the greatest mystery of all, how the curse had been fulfilled since that time when Charles Le Sorcier must in the course of nature have died, for the man digressed into an account of the deep alchemical studies of the two wizards, father and son, speaking most particularly of the researches of Charles Le Sorcier concerning the elixir which should grant to him who partook of it eternal life and youth.

His enthusiasm had seemed for the moment to remove from his terrible eyes the black malevolence that had first so haunted me, but suddenly the fiendish glare returned and, with a shocking sound like the hissing of a serpent, the stranger raised a glass phial with the evident intent of ending my life as had Charles Le Sorcier, six hundred years before, ended that of my ancestor. Prompted by some preserving instinct of self-defense, I broke through the spell that had hitherto held me immovable, and flung my now dying torch at the creature who menaced my existence. I heard the phial break harmlessly against the stones of the passage as the tunic of the strange man caught fire and lit the horrid scene with a ghastly radiance. The shriek of fright and impotent malice emitted by the would-be assassin proved too much for my already shaken nerves, and I fell prone upon the slimy floor in a total faint.

When at last my senses returned, all was frightfully dark, and my mind, remembering what had occurred, shrank from the idea of beholding any more; yet curiosity over-mastered all. Who, I asked myself, was this man of evil, and how came he within the castle walls? Why should he seek to avenge the death of Michel Mauvais, and how had the curse been carried on through all the long centuries since the time of Charles Le Sorcier? The dread of years was lifted from my shoulder, for I knew that he whom I had felled was the source of all my danger from the curse; and now that I was free, I burned with the desire to learn more of the sinister thing which had haunted my line for centuries, and made of my own youth one long-continued nightmare. Determined upon further exploration, I felt in my pockets for flint and steel, and lit the unused torch which I had with me.

First of all, new light revealed the distorted and blackened form of the mysterious stranger. The hideous eyes were now closed. Disliking the sight, I turned away and entered the chamber beyond the Gothic door. Here I found what seemed much like an alchemist's laboratory. In one corner was an immense pile of shining yellow metal that sparkled gorgeously in the light of the torch. It may have been gold, but I did not pause to examine it, for I was strangely affected by that which I had undergone. At the farther end of the apartment was an opening leading out into one of the many wild ravines of the dark hillside forest. Filled with wonder, yet now realizing how the man had obtained access to the chateau, I proceeded to return. I had intended to pass by the remains of the stranger with averted face but, as I approached the body, I seemed to hear emanating from it a faint sound, as though life were not yet wholly extinct. Aghast, I turned to examine the charred and shrivelled figure on the floor.

Then all at once the horrible eyes, blacker even than the seared face in which they were set, opened wide with an expression which I was unable to interpret. The cracked lips tried to frame words which I could not well understand. Once I caught the name of Charles Le Sorcier, and again I fancied that the words 'years' and 'curse' issued from the twisted mouth. Still I was at a loss to gather the purport of his disconnected speech. At my evident ignorance of his meaning, the pitchy eyes once more flashed malevolently at me, until, helpless as I saw my opponent to be, I trembled as I watched him.

Suddenly the wretch, animated with his last burst of strength, raised his piteous head from the damp and sunken pavement. Then, as I remained, paralyzed with fear, he found his voice and in his dying breath screamed forth those words which have ever afterward haunted my days and nights. 'Fool!' he shrieked, 'Can you not guess my secret? Have you no brain whereby you may recognize the will which has through six long centuries fulfilled the dreadful curse upon the house? Have I not told you of the great elixir of eternal life? Know you not how the secret of Alchemy was solved? I tell you, it is I! I! I! that have lived for six hundred years to maintain my revenge, for I am Charles Le Sorcier!'

A Modest Proposal
Dr. Jonathan Swift

For preventing the children of poor people in Ireland,
from being a burden on their parents or country,
and for making them beneficial to the publick.

It is a melancholy object to those, who walk through this great town, or travel in the country, when they see the streets, the roads and cabbin-doors crowded with beggars of the female sex, followed by three, four, or six children, all in rags, and importuning every passenger for an alms. These mothers instead of being able to work for their honest livelihood, are forced to employ all their time in stroling to beg sustenance for their helpless infants who, as they grow up, either turn thieves for want of work, or leave their dear native country, to fight for the Pretender in Spain, or sell themselves to the Barbadoes.

I think it is agreed by all parties, that this prodigious number of children in the arms, or on the backs, or at the heels of their mothers, and frequently of their fathers, is in the present deplorable state of the kingdom, a very great additional grievance; and therefore whoever could find out a fair, cheap and easy method of making these children sound and useful members of the common-wealth, would deserve so well of the publick, as to have his statue set up for a preserver of the nation.

But my intention is very far from being confined to provide only for the children of professed beggars: it is of a much greater extent, and shall take in the whole number of infants at a certain age, who are born of parents in effect as little able to support them, as those who demand our charity in the streets.

As to my own part, having turned my thoughts for many years, upon this important subject, and maturely weighed the several schemes of our projectors, I have always found them grossly mistaken in their computation. It is true, a child just dropt from its dam, may be supported by her milk, for a solar year, with little other nourishment: at most not above the value of two shillings, which the mother may certainly get, or the value in scraps, by her lawful occupation of begging; and it is exactly at one year old that I propose to provide for them in such a manner, as, instead of being a charge upon their parents, or the parish, or wanting food and raiment for the rest of their lives, they shall, on the contrary, contribute to the feeding, and partly to the cloathing of many thousands.

There is likewise another great advantage in my scheme, that it will prevent those voluntary abortions, and that horrid practice of women murdering their bastard children, alas! too frequent among us, sacrificing the poor innocent babes, I doubt, more to avoid the expence than the shame, which would move tears and pity in the most savage and inhuman breast.

The number of souls in this kingdom being usually reckoned one million and a half, of these I calculate there may be about two hundred thousand couple whose wives are breeders; from which number I subtract thirty thousand couple, who are able to maintain their own children, (although I apprehend there cannot be so many, under the present distresses of the kingdom) but this being granted, there will remain an hundred and seventy thousand breeders. I again subtract fifty thousand, for those women who miscarry, or whose children die by accident or disease within the year. There only remain an hundred and twenty thousand children of poor parents annually born. The question therefore is, How this number shall be reared, and provided for? which, as I have already said, under the present situation of affairs, is utterly impossible by all the methods hitherto proposed. For we can neither employ them in handicraft or agriculture; we neither build houses, (I mean in the country) nor cultivate land: they can very seldom pick up a livelihood by stealing till they arrive at six years old; except where they are of towardly parts, although I confess they learn the rudiments much earlier; during which time they can however be properly looked upon only as probationers: As I have been informed by a principal gentleman in the county of Cavan, who protested to me, that he never knew above one or two instances under the age of six, even in a part of the kingdom so renowned for the quickest proficiency in that art.

I am assured by our merchants, that a boy or a girl before twelve years old, is no saleable commodity, and even when they come to this age, they will not yield above three pounds, or three pounds and half a crown at most, on the exchange; which cannot turn to account either to the parents or kingdom, the charge of nutriments and rags having been at least four times that value.

I shall now therefore humbly propose my own thoughts, which I hope will not be liable to the least objection.

I have been assured by a very knowing American of my acquaintance in London, that a young healthy child well nursed, is, at a year old, a most delicious nourishing and wholesome food, whether stewed, roasted, baked, or boiled; and I make no doubt that it will equally serve in a fricasie, or a ragoust.

I do therefore humbly offer it to publick consideration, that of the hundred and twenty thousand children, already computed, twenty thousand may be reserved for breed, whereof only one fourth part to be males; which is more than we allow to sheep, black cattle, or swine, and my reason is, that these children are seldom the fruits of marriage, a circumstance not much regarded by our savages, therefore, one male will be sufficient to serve four females. That the remaining hundred thousand may, at a year old, be offered in sale to the persons of quality and fortune, through the kingdom, always advising the mother to let them suck plentifully in the last month, so as to render them plump, and fat for a good table. A child will make two dishes at an entertainment for friends, and when the family dines alone, the fore or hind quarter will make a reasonable dish, and seasoned with a little pepper or salt, will be very good boiled on the fourth day, especially in winter.

I have reckoned upon a medium, that a child just born will weigh 12 pounds, and in a solar year, if tolerably nursed, encreaseth to 28 pounds.

I grant this food will be somewhat dear, and therefore very proper for landlords, who, as they have already devoured most of the parents, seem to have the best title to the children.

Infant's flesh will be in season throughout the year, but more plentiful in March, and a little before and after; for we are told by a grave author, an eminent French physician, that fish being a prolifick dyet, there are more children born in Roman Catholick countries about nine months after Lent, the markets will be more glutted than usual, because the number of Popish infants, is at least three to one in this kingdom, and therefore it will have one other collateral advantage, by lessening the number of Papists among us.

I have already computed the charge of nursing a beggar's child (in which list I reckon all cottagers, labourers, and four-fifths of the farmers) to be about two shillings per annum, rags included; and I believe no gentleman would repine to give ten shillings for the carcass of a good fat child, which, as I have said, will make four dishes of excellent nutritive meat, when he hath only some particular friend, or his own family to dine with him. Thus the squire will learn to be a good landlord, and grow popular among his tenants, the mother will have eight shillings neat profit, and be fit for work till she produces another child.

Those who are more thrifty (as I must confess the times require) may flea the carcass; the skin of which, artificially dressed, will make admirable gloves for ladies, and summer boots for fine gentlemen.

As to our City of Dublin, shambles may be appointed for this purpose, in the most convenient parts of it, and butchers we may be assured will not be wanting; although I rather recommend buying the children alive, and dressing them hot from the knife, as we do roasting pigs.

A very worthy person, a true lover of his country, and whose virtues I highly esteem, was lately pleased, in discoursing on this matter, to offer a refinement upon my scheme. He said, that many gentlemen of this kingdom, having of late destroyed their deer, he conceived that the want of venison might be well supply'd by the bodies of young lads and maidens, not exceeding fourteen years of age, nor under twelve; so great a number of both sexes in every country being now ready to starve for want of work and service: And these to be disposed of by their parents if alive, or otherwise by their nearest relations. But with due deference to so excellent a friend, and so deserving a patriot, I cannot be altogether in his sentiments; for as to the males, my American acquaintance assured me from frequent experience, that their flesh was generally tough and lean, like that of our school-boys, by continual exercise, and their taste disagreeable, and to fatten them would not answer the charge. Then as to the females, it would, I think, with humble submission, be a loss to the publick, because they soon would become breeders themselves: And besides, it is not improbable that some scrupulous people might be apt to censure such a practice, (although indeed very unjustly) as a little bordering upon cruelty, which, I confess, hath always been with me the strongest objection against any project, how well soever intended.

But in order to justify my friend, he confessed, that this expedient was put into his head by the famous Salmanaazor, a native of the island Formosa, who came from thence to London, above twenty years ago, and in conversation told my friend, that in his country, when any young person happened to be put to death, the executioner sold the carcass to persons of quality, as a prime dainty; and that, in his time, the body of a plump girl of fifteen, who was crucified for an attempt to poison the Emperor, was sold to his imperial majesty's prime minister of state, and other great mandarins of the court in joints from the gibbet, at four hundred crowns. Neither indeed can I deny, that if the same use were made of several plump young girls in this town, who without one single groat to their fortunes, cannot stir abroad without a chair, and appear at a play-house and assemblies in foreign fineries which they never will pay for; the kingdom would not be the worse.

Some persons of a desponding spirit are in great concern about that vast number of poor people, who are aged, diseased, or maimed; and I have been desired to employ my thoughts what course may be taken, to ease the nation of so grievous an incumbrance. But I am not in the least pain upon that matter, because it is very well known, that they are every day dying, and rotting, by cold and famine, and filth, and vermin, as fast as can be reasonably expected. And as to the young labourers, they are now in almost as hopeful a condition. They cannot get work, and consequently pine away from want of nourishment, to a degree, that if at any time they are accidentally hired to common labour, they have not strength to perform it, and thus the country and themselves are happily delivered from the evils to come.

I have too long digressed, and therefore shall return to my subject. I think the advantages by the proposal which I have made are obvious and many, as well as of the highest importance.

For first, as I have already observed, it would greatly lessen the number of Papists, with whom we are yearly over-run, being the principal breeders of the nation, as well as our most dangerous enemies, and who stay at home on purpose with a design to deliver the kingdom to the Pretender, hoping to take their advantage by the absence of so many good Protestants, who have chosen rather to leave their country, than stay at home and pay tithes against their conscience to an episcopal curate.

Secondly, The poorer tenants will have something valuable of their own, which by law may be made liable to a distress, and help to pay their landlord's rent, their corn and cattle being already seized, and money a thing unknown.

Thirdly, Whereas the maintainance of an hundred thousand children, from two years old, and upwards, cannot be computed at less than ten shillings a piece per annum, the nation's stock will be thereby encreased fifty thousand pounds per annum, besides the profit of a new dish, introduced to the tables of all gentlemen of fortune in the kingdom, who have any refinement in taste. And the money will circulate among our selves, the goods being entirely of our own growth and manufacture.

Fourthly, The constant breeders, besides the gain of eight shillings sterling per annum by the sale of their children, will be rid of the charge of maintaining them after the first year.

Fifthly, This food would likewise bring great custom to taverns, where the vintners will certainly be so prudent as to procure the best receipts for dressing it to perfection; and consequently have their houses frequented by all the fine gentlemen, who justly value themselves upon their knowledge in good eating; and a skilful cook, who understands how to oblige his guests, will contrive to make it as expensive as they please.

Sixthly, This would be a great inducement to marriage, which all wise nations have either encouraged by rewards, or enforced by laws and penalties. It would encrease the care and tenderness of mothers towards their children, when they were sure of a settlement for life to the poor babes, provided in some sort by the publick, to their annual profit instead of expence. We should soon see an honest emulation among the married women, which of them could bring the fattest child to the market. Men would become as fond of their wives, during the time of their pregnancy, as they are now of their mares in foal, their cows in calf, or sow when they are ready to farrow; nor offer to beat or kick them (as is too frequent a practice) for fear of a miscarriage.

Many other advantages might be enumerated. For instance, the addition of some thousand carcasses in our exportation of barrel'd beef: the propagation of swine's flesh, and improvement in the art of making good bacon, so much wanted among us by the great destruction of pigs, too frequent at our tables; which are no way comparable in taste or magnificence to a well grown, fat yearly child, which roasted whole will make a considerable figure at a Lord Mayor's feast, or any other publick entertainment. But this, and many others, I omit, being studious of brevity.

Supposing that one thousand families in this city, would be constant customers for infants flesh, besides others who might have it at merry meetings, particularly at weddings and christenings, I compute that Dublin would take off annually about twenty thousand carcasses; and the rest of the kingdom (where probably they will be sold somewhat cheaper) the remaining eighty thousand.

I can think of no one objection, that will possibly be raised against this proposal, unless it should be urged, that the number of people will be thereby much lessened in the kingdom. This I freely own, and 'twas indeed one principal design in offering it to the world. I desire the reader will observe, that I calculate my remedy for this one individual Kingdom of Ireland, and for no other that ever was, is, or, I think, ever can be upon Earth. Therefore let no man talk to me of other expedients: Of taxing our absentees at five shillings a pound: Of using neither cloaths, nor houshold furniture, except what is of our own growth and manufacture: Of utterly rejecting the materials and instruments that promote foreign luxury: Of curing the expensiveness of pride, vanity, idleness, and gaming in our women: Of introducing a vein of parsimony, prudence and temperance: Of learning to love our country, wherein we differ even from Laplanders, and the inhabitants of Topinamboo: Of quitting our animosities and factions, nor acting any longer like the Jews, who were murdering one another at the very moment their city was taken: Of being a little cautious not to sell our country and consciences for nothing: Of teaching landlords to have at least one degree of mercy towards their tenants. Lastly, of putting a spirit of honesty, industry, and skill into our shop-keepers, who, if a resolution could now be taken to buy only our native goods, would immediately unite to cheat and exact upon us in the price, the measure, and the goodness, nor could ever yet be brought to make one fair proposal of just dealing, though often and earnestly invited to it.

Therefore I repeat, let no man talk to me of these and the like expedients, 'till he hath at least some glympse of hope, that there will ever be some hearty and sincere attempt to put them into practice.

But, as to my self, having been wearied out for many years with offering vain, idle, visionary thoughts, and at length utterly despairing of success, I fortunately fell upon this proposal, which, as it is wholly new, so it hath something solid and real, of no expence and little trouble, full in our own power, and whereby we can incur no danger in disobliging England. For this kind of commodity will not bear exportation, and flesh being of too tender a consistence, to admit a long continuance in salt, although perhaps I could name a country, which would be glad to eat up our whole nation without it.

After all, I am not so violently bent upon my own opinion, as to reject any offer, proposed by wise men, which shall be found equally innocent, cheap, easy, and effectual. But before something of that kind shall be advanced in contradiction to my scheme, and offering a better, I desire the author or authors will be pleased maturely to consider two points. First, As things now stand, how they will be able to find food and raiment for a hundred thousand useless mouths and backs. And secondly, There being a round million of creatures in humane figure throughout this kingdom, whose whole subsistence put into a common stock, would leave them in debt two million of pounds sterling, adding those who are beggars by profession, to the bulk of farmers, cottagers and labourers, with their wives and children, who are beggars in effect; I desire those politicians who dislike my overture, and may perhaps be so bold to attempt an answer, that they will first ask the parents of these mortals, whether they would not at this day think it a great happiness to have been sold for food at a year old, in the manner I prescribe, and thereby have avoided such a perpetual scene of misfortunes, as they have since gone through, by the oppression of landlords, the impossibility of paying rent without money or trade, the want of common sustenance, with neither house nor cloaths to cover them from the inclemencies of the weather, and the most inevitable prospect of intailing the like, or greater miseries, upon their breed for ever.

I profess, in the sincerity of my heart, that I have not the least personal interest in endeavouring to promote this necessary work, having no other motive than the publick good of my country, by advancing our trade, providing for infants, relieving the poor, and giving some pleasure to the rich. I have no children, by which I can propose to get a single penny; the youngest being nine years old, and my wife past child-bearing.

The Hunt

by Mahasweta Devi, Translated by Gayatri Spivak

I

The place is on the Gomo-Daltonganj line. Trains stopped at this station once upon a time. The expense of having trains stop was perhaps too much. Now one sees a stray cow or a goat in the station room, in the residential quarters and the porters' shanties. The board says "Kuruda Outstation, Abandoned." Arrived here the train slows. It gasps as it climbs. It climbs Kuruda Hill bit by bit right from here. It is a low hill. After a while the train enters a ravine. On both sides of the half-mile ravine there are blasted stones. There's a bamboo thicket on the hill, and occasionally the bamboo bends in the wind and hits the train. Then the train descends and it gathers speed. Now the station is Tohri. The busiest station in this area. The junction of many bus routes. Tohri is also a coal halt. The train picks up coal. There are surface collieries all around. In these parts lowgrade coal is to be found almost above ground. But Tohri's real benefactors are the timber brokers. It is a Sal-growing area. Sal-logs arrive night and day by truck. They are split in timberyards and sent in every direction. Tohri's bustle is an experience after the silence of Kuruda.

It is an experience to watch the train move on the hilltop from distant villages. The villagers see this every day, yet their amazement never ends. The train goes on, the engine gasps; now the ravine swallows the train. If you run you can see where it will spit it out. There were some elephants seen one day at the top of the hill. The elephants stopped as they ate the bamboo. From a distance they looked like toy elephants. After the train passed on they ran off trumpeting, trunks raised.

The village of Kuruda is a good way behind the station. There are two hills, one beyond the wide meadow. If it had been a bit closer the villagers might have started living in the abandoned brickbuilt house.

For people who live in the villages like Kuruda, life holds few breaks other than annual feastdays. So their eyes are charmed by the scenes on top of Kuruda Hill.

When Mary Oraon comes up, she looks at the train, as the passengers look at her if they see her. Eighteen years old, tall, flat-featured, light copper skin. Usually she wears a print sari. As she looks at the train, so the passengers look at her if she catches their eye. At a distance she looks most seductive, but up close you see a strong message of rejection in her glance.

You wouldn't call her a tribal at first sight. Yet she is a tribal. Once upon a time whites had timber plantations in Kuruda. They left gradually after Independence. Mary's mother looked after the Dixons' bungalow and household. Dixon's son came back in 1959 and sold the house, the forest, everything else. He put Mary in Bhikni's womb before he left. He went to Australia. The padre at the local church christened her Mary. Bhikni was still a Christian. But when Prasadji from Ranchi came to live in the Dixon bungalow and refused to employ Bhikni, she gave up Christianity. Mary pastures the Prasads' cattle. She is a most capable cowherd. She also sells custard apple and guava from the Prasad's orchards, driving terrifically hard bargains with the Kunjaras, the wholesale fruit buyers. She takes the train to Tohri with vegetables from the field.

Everyone says Prasadji is most fortunate. He pays Bhikni a wage. With Mary the agreement is for board and lodging, clothing and sundries. The Dixon bungalow was built as a residence for whites. Bhikni says the whites kept twelve ayahs-servants-sweepers. Under Prasadji Mary alone keeps the huge bungalow clean.

Mary has countless admirers at Tohri market. She gets down at the station like a queen. She sits in her own rightful place at the market. She gets smokes from the other marketeers, drinks tea and chews betel leaf at their expense, but encourages no one. Jalim, the leader of the marketeers and a sharp lad, is her lover. They will marry when either's savings reach a hundred rupees.

She has let Jalim approach her on the promise of marriage. Daughter of an Oraon mother, she looks different, and she is also exceptionally tall. So she couldn't find a boy of her own kind. The color of Mary's skin is a resistant barrier to young Oraon men. Mrs. Prasad had looked for a match. Their gardener's son. She had said, you can stay on the compound.

Bhikni was ecstatic. Mary said, "No. Mistress Mother has said it to keep her worker captive."

—She will give shelter.

—A shack.

—He's a good boy.

—No. Living in a shack, eating mush, the man drinking, no soap or oil, no clean clothes. I don't want such a life.

Mary was unwilling. She is accepted in the village society. The women are her friends, she is the best dancer at the feasts. But that doesn't mean she wants to live their life.

Many men had wanted to be her lover. Mary had lifted her machete. They are outsiders. Who can tell that they wouldn't leave her, like Bhikni with a baby in her belly?

There was a fight over her once in Tohri market. Ratan Singh, the driver of a timber truck, had got drunk and tried to carry her off. It was then that Jalim had cut in and hit Ratan Singh. It was after that that Mary was seen selling vegetables or peanuts or corn sitting beside Jalim. She has never been to his room. No, marriage first. Jalim respects this greatly. Yes, there is something true in Mary, the power of Australian blood.

There is distrust in Mary somewhere. She doesn't trust even Jalim fully. Even the marketeers of Tohri know that they'll marry as soon as there is a hundred rupees. Jalim's version is that he himself will save those hundred rupees. It will be good if Mary brings something herself. So she has left to Jalim the responsibility of saving money. It's not easy for Jalim. He has his parents, brothers, and sisters in the village. Here he'll have to rent a place, buy pots and pans. He won't be able to carry all the expenses. And he wants to give Mary clothes, the odd cake of soap.

Mary gave him the first present. A colored cotton vest.

—Your gift?

Jalim is delighted.

—No. Your wife sent it.

After that Jalim gave her presents now and then. Mary doesn't wear those clothes. She'll wear them after the wedding.

Mary understands that Jalim is taking many pains to save money. Even so she says nothing, for she has saved ninety-two if not a hundred rupees.

She has earned that money. At the Prasad establishment. By government regulation, if there are mahua trees on anyone's land in the forest areas, the right to the fruit goes to the picker. Mahua is a cash fruit. You get liquor from mahua, the oil of the black seed of the mahua fruit goes to make a blackish washing soap. It is Mary who picks the fruit of the four mahua trees at the Prasad property. No villager has been able to touch the fruit even in jest. Mary has instantly raised her machete. This is hers by right. This is why she works so hard for no wages at the Prasad house.

Mrs. Prasad doesn't like it much, but Lachhman Prasad says, "Take no notice. Who will clean so well, pasture the cows so well? Sell fruit and vegetable and nuts at a profit at Tohri?"

Mary works like a dog but does not tolerate familiarity from Prasadji.

—So Mary, how much did you make on your sale of mahua?

—What's it to you?

—Open a moneylending business.

—Yes, I will.

—It's good of me to let you pick the mahua. It is government property. I could hire people and have the fruit picked and I don't do it.

—Let the hired people come and see. I have my machete.

Mary's voice is harsh and grim.

Prasadji says, "It figures. White blood."

Mrs. Prasad has Mary give her an oil rubdown. Out of her lardy body she looks at Mary's hard perfect frame. She says, "So, what about your marriage? What does Jalim say?"

—What do you want with poor folks' talk? Will you organize my marriage?

—God be praised! With a Muslim? I run such a marriage?

—Why not? The Muslim says he'll marry. Your brother wanted only to keep me.

This mistress swallows the slap and says nothing. You have to take words from a girl who works like an animal, carries a forty pound bag on her back and boards the train, cleans the whole house in half an hour.

Everyone is afraid of Mary. Mary cleans house, and pastures cattle, with her inviolate constitution, her infinite energy, and her razor sharp mind. On the field she lunches on fried corn. She stands and picks fruit and oversees picking. She weighs the stuff herself for the buyers. She puts the fruit bitten by bats and birds into a sack, and feeds it to her mother's chickens. When the rains come she re-plants the seedlings carefully. She watches out for everything. She buys rice, oil, butter, and spices for the Prasads at Tohri market. She says herself, "The money I save you, and the money I make for you, how much do you put together out of it yearly, Mistress Mother? Why should I take a cheap sari? I'll dress well, use soap and oil, give me everything."

Mrs. Prasad is obliged to dress her well. Sometimes Mary goes to the village to gossip. When she can. Then she puts her sari around her belly and becomes Mrs. Prasad, limps and becomes Prasadji, makes everyone laugh. There she is easy. When the young men say, "Hey Mussulman's chick, why here?"

—Would any of you marry me?

—Would you?

—Why aren't you tall and white like me?

—You are a white man's daughter. "Big white chief! Puts a child in a woman's belly and runs like a rat. My mother is bad news. When you see a white daughter, you kill her right away. Then there are no problems!"

—What about you if she'd killed?

—I wouldn't have been.

—Stop that talk. Be a Mussulman if you like. Before that for us . . .

—What?

—Rice-chicken-mutton and booze?

—Sure. I'll throw a fan-tas-tic feast. When have I not fed you? Tell me?

—Yes, true, you do give.

The same Mary who pulls hundreds of pounds, fights the Kunjaras over fruit, doesn't hand out a single peanut to keep Prasadji's profits intact, also steals peanut oil, flour, molasses from the house. Salt and spices.

She sits at any Oraon house in the village, fries wheatcakes on a clay stove, eats with everyone. Just as she knows she'll marry Jalim, she also knows that if she had resembled any Oraon girl—if her father had been Somra or Budhra or Mangla Oraon—the Oraons would not have let this marriage happen.

Because she is the illegitimate daughter of a white father the Oraons don't think of her as their blood and do not place the harsh injunctions of their own society upon her. She would have rebelled if they had. She is unhappy that they don't. In her inmost heart there is somewhere a longing to be part of the Oraons. She would have been very glad if, when she was thirteen or fourteen some brave Oraon lad had pulled her into marriage. Mary has seen two or three Hindi films in Tohri. At harvest time itinerant film people come to Tohri. They show moving pictures in the open field. Not only the girls, but even the boys of Kuruda village have hardly ever been to the movies. They haven't been to the movies, haven't worn good clothes, haven't eaten a full meal. Mary has a certain sympathy for them as well.

So goes Mary's life. Suddenly one day, stopping the train, Collector Singh descends with Prasadji's son, and Mary's life is troubled, a storm gathers in Kuruda's quiet and impoverished existence.

II

Seventy five acres or two hundred and twenty five bighas of land are attached to Prasadji's bungalow. Nobody around here obeys the land ceiling laws. All the far-flung bungalows of the old timber planters have large tracts of attached land. Mr. Dixon had planted Sal on fifty acres. Not the dwarf Sal of the area but giant Sal. In time they've grown immense and ready for felling. Prasadji used to lament about all that he could have done with this land if there had been no Sal. Now that he knows the price of Sal, his one goal is to sell the trees at the highest price. Lalchand and Mulniji, the two other forest proprietors of the area, are also happy at this news. Prasad's son Banwari takes the initiative and starts looking around in Daltonganj and Chhipador. The fruit of his labors is Collector Singh.

The first thing Collector Singh looks at is the trees to be felled. Then they start negotiating prices. Prasad says, "Such Sal wood! How can I sell at such a price?"

—Why sell? You'll sell where you can make a profit.

—Name a proper price.

—Prasadji! Banwari is a real friend. He does service in Chhipador, and I'm a broker. Why tell a lie, the trees are mature, and the wood solid.

—The whites planted the stuff.

—Yes. But here I'll have them cut, in pieces! Trucks won't come here. This is not the white man's rule when I could have brought elephants from the Forest

Department and pulled the timber to Tohri. I'll have to take it to Murhai. Flat tires on the dirt roads. I'll have to cut the trees before that, think of the expense!

—But you'll make a profit!

—Sure. Who works without profit? Still your profit is higher. Bought the bungalow dirt cheap, got a ready-made Sal forest! Whatever you get is your profit. Because you had no investment for it. Not corn that buffaloes pulled the plough, and fieldhands reaped. Not custard apple or guava that you chased birds and bats. Forest area, Sal area, have trees, sell straight off.

Lalchand and Mulni also said, "Don't make so much trouble brother. What do we do if he leaves? Do you want to watch the flowers of a tree that bears no fruit? He wants to buy, we'll sell."

The broker wants the same thing. What trees the whites had planted! The tops break the sky, the trunks are as big as railway engines. Why buy only Prasadji's trees? He'll buy all the trees of the area.

—Every five years or so some trees will be ready and I'll buy. One two three. This is still a virgin area, and I'll do the monopoly on tree felling.

That was the decision. Prasadji realized later that the argument about the expense of carrying the trees was not altogether correct. For the trucks came past Murhai, close to Kuruda. That side is flat and stony. No problem with the arrival of trucks. The broker pitched his tent there. Two experts came to fell trees.

The broker started planning the deployment of manpower. Oraon and Munda men and women came from six villages—Kuruda, Murhai, Seeho, Thapari, Dhuma, Chinaboha. Unbelievable. Money at home. Others will fell the trees, twelve annas daily for men, eight annas for women for trimming branches and carrying the pieced timber to the trucks. And a tiffin of cornmeal in the afternoon. Unbelievable! Salt and cayenne with the meal. The village priest and elders will bring the men and women. A sack of salt weekly for each village. The elders said, "How about the women's honor if they work?"

The broker said, "They are everybody's mothers and sisters! Whoever forgets will be sacked."…

Mary is a regular contact and bridge between the outside world of Tohri and Kuruda. At night when she brought Prasadji warm water for his medicine she said, "The bastard tricked you. He took all the profit. Everyone from Tohri to Chhipador is laughing."

Prasadji took off his false teeth and put them in a bowl of water. Then he took his medicine. In a while he said, "What to do Mary? With no road, have I the power to sell at profit to anyone? This happens if you live in the forest. Banwari brought him. Banwari is pig-headed and takes after his mother. I first said 'no,' then Lalchand and Mulni got angry. There were many objections at home."

—Banwari's taken his cut.

—You know this?

—I am aware of it.

—What a shame.

Prasadji sighed and gave her a rupee. He gives her like this from time to time. "You take such trouble so I don't get tricked over a piece of fruit, a grain of corn," he said. "My own son understands nothing. What shall I do? Don't I know that he'll sell everything and take off when I die?"

—When you sell trees later, there will be a road, don't give it to him. Go yourself to Chhipador. Talk to the big companies and do your business. Don't be soft then.

—You're right.

Mary told the Kuruda elders as well, "Twelve annas and eight annas! No porter carries gentlemen's cases for this price."

The elders said, "What to do Mary? If I said 'no' the villagers would go wild. They would say, 'Who gives us this kind of money?'"

Mary said, "He's greedy now. He'll come again in five years. Then he'll bargain for three or two rupees. And he'll have to give. Otherwise how will he get an outsider here?"

—No road, no jobs, you know how it is.

Mary thought, in return for the broker's glance she had shrewdly revealed the man's true nature to everyone. But Collector Singh didn't forget her. A few days later, when Mary was running on a water buffalo's back herding other cattle, the Collector came up to her. "How pretty," he said. "You look like Hema Malini."

—What?

—You look like Hema Malini.

—You look like a monkey.

Collector Singh felt much encouraged by such a remark and came up close. Mary didn't stop her water buffalo. As she moved on she took out a sharp machete and said in a lazy voice, "Brokers like you, with tight pants and dark glasses, are ten a rupee on the streets of Tohri, and to them I show them this machete. Go ask if you don't believe me." The Collector found her way of speaking most beguiling. Banwari said at the evening meal, "Mary has insulted my friend." He was speaking to his father, but it was Mary who replied, "How did I insult your friend?"

—You spoke to him rudely.

—This time I let him go with words. If he comes to fuck with me again I'll cut off his nose.

Banwari was scared as well. He said, "What, did he do something crazy?"

—It's crazy talk to me. It may be good talk to you.

Prasadji said, "Ask him not to. These problems don't go with buying trees."

—And Mary shouldn't talk about selling Sal Trees at Tohri market.

—It is illegal to sell Sal trees if they are on your own land. The Sal belongs to the government.

—Ah keep your laws. Who keeps land legally here, who doesn't sell Sal in these parts?

Mary said straight to Banwari, "Have I spoken about your tree sale in Tohri market?"

—Have I said you said? I just asked you not to.

—Don't try to set me straight.

Mary left. Prasadji said, "This is not correct. Tell your friend. Lives in house, like a daughter, I am insulted if she's accosted."

Banwari said to Collector, "She's a real bitch, a rude girl, doesn't give a damn for anyone."

—Who wants a damn?

—Besides, her marriage is fixed.

—Where?

—A Muslim's house.

—Dear God! No man in her tribe?

—Her taste.

Collector didn't believe that a Mary Oraon from a wild village like Kuruda could blow him away. He stuck to Mary through marking and felling the trees, cutting and transporting them. That Mary wouldn't look at him and would rather marry a Muslim increased his anger.

Then he brings a nylon sari for Mary from Daltonganj, sweets for Prasadji. He says to Prasadji, "I come and go, she feeds me tea, I give her a sari." Prasadji didn't accept it, but Collector insisted. Mary had gone to Tohri. She heard about the sari when she got back. First she gave Prasadji the accounts for Tohri market. Then she had tea and toast in the kitchen. Then she went out with the sari.

Collector was sitting in the tent paying the men and women. Lots of people. Mary enters and throws the sari at him. She says, "You think I'm a city whore? You want to grab me with a sari? If you bother me again, I'll cut off your nose." She goes off proudly swinging her arms.

Collector loses face in everyone's eyes. He wants to say, "I gave something in good faith..."

The elders say, "Don't give again."

—What?

—Don't give again.

—Is she a good character? Would a good one marry a Muslim?

—It's too much.

Suddenly Collector understands, he and his men are in a minority, the others are greater in number. Everyone has a spear or a machete. He shuts up.

The driver knows Collector has a wife and children. He knows that Collector still lusts after women. Mary is indeed an eyeful, but it would be stupid to provoke the tribals and create a police case on her account. If Mary was willing, there would have been no problem. Mary is unwilling. Collector must accept that.

Now Prasadji gets serious as well. It is Bhikni who brings tea these days. Collector stops going to the house. But he doesn't give up chasing Mary.

When Mary returns from pasturing cattle, returns from Tohri, or goes the three miles to Murhai station to go to Tohri, or goes marketing to Dhuma, Collector keeps his distance and follows her.

The girls say, "Mary, that broker loves you."

—Because he can't catch me. If he does his love will vanish. The white man also loved my mother.

—He'll marry you.

—He has a wife.

—So what?

—Let it go.

The felling goes on. Slowly the weather warms. There are miles and miles of poppy fields around here. New buds appear. Then the gong sounds one day in the priest's house. It is revealed that the ritual of the hunt that the tribes celebrate at the Spring festival is for the women to perform this year. For twelve years men run the hunt. Then comes the women's turn. Like the men they too go out with bow and arrow. They run in forest and hill. They kill hedgehogs, rabbits, birds, whatever they can get. Then they picnic together, drink liquor, sing, and return home at evening. They do exactly what the men do. Once in twelve years. Then they light the fire of the Spring festival and start talking. Budhni tells them stories. "That time we killed a leopard. I was young then."

The old women listen, the aging women cook, the young women sing.

They don't know why they hunt. The men know. They have been playing the hunt for a thousand million moons on this day.

Once there were animals in the forest, life was wild, the hunt game had meaning. Now the forest is empty, life wasted and drained, the hunt game meaningless. Only the day's joy is real.

Mary was getting tired of the Collector's tireless singleminded pursuit. Jalim might get to know. He'd be wild if she let him know. He might go to kill Collector if he got the chance. Collector has a lot of money, a lot of men. A city bastard. He can destroy Jalim by setting up a larceny case against him.

Collector too was losing patience. The felling would soon be over, they would have to pull up stakes and then what?

Collector caught Mary's hand one day.

The timing was good. No hunt for the men this year. The men will drink and make up new songs for the Spring festival, dress up as clowns and go out to sing for money. Collector has promised them liquor for the festival.

Returning from the felling there is singing every day. In a droning monotone. Mary was listening. On the way back from market. Dusk fell as she listened. She started home.

Collector knew she would come. Collector caught her hand. He said, "I won't let you go today."

At first Mary was scared. Struggling she lost her machete. With great effort, after a good deal of struggling, Mary was able to spring out of his grasp. Both of them stood up. Collector did not have his dark glasses on. Long sideburns, long hair, polyester trousers, pointed shoes, a dark red shirt on his back. Against the background of the Spring songs Mary thought he was an animal. A-ni-mal. The syllables beat on her mind. Suddenly Mary smiled.

—Mary!

—Stop, stop right there. Don't move up.

—What are you looking at?

—You.

—I, you—

—You want me a lot, no?

—A lot.

—Good.

—What's good?

—To see what you really want.

—Really want. I've never seen a woman like you. You are worth a million. How will that marketeer know your worth? That Muslim?

—Will you?

—Sure. I'll give you clothes, jewels—

—Really?

—Everything. Mary took a deep breath. Then said, "Not today. Today I'm unclean."

—When Mary, when?

Mary's eye and face softened. She said, "On the day of the feast. Stay near that rock. The women will go far to play the hunt. I will come to you. You know which rock! You look for me from behind that stone."

—All right.

—Then that's our pact?

—Yes Mary.

—But don't tell anyone! A man can do no wrong, but a woman is soiled. As it is I am illegitimate, and then I was going to marry a Muslim.

—Tell me you won't. Why any more?

—Have a bit of patience. Don't follow me around like that.

—I took so much trouble over you...

—I'll make up for everything. On the day of the Spring festival.

Mary patted his cheek. She said, "You are nice, dear! I didn't see at first." She took off sinuously. She knew Collector wouldn't clasp her from behind a second time.

III

The fire burned last night and tonight as well. Last night the Spring festival fire burned very high and reddened the sky for quite some time. Today from first light the men are wild with drink and songs and color. The very old women are looking after the children. The women are all in the forest. Each woman had stood excited in front of her own door armed with spears and the men's bows and arrows. As soon as the priest struck the gong they burst the sky with sharp halloos and ran forward. Bhikni is running in Prasadji's shirt and Mrs. Prasad's petticoat. Budhni, Mungri, Somari, Sanichari—their running days are over. They have gone to the abandoned Bomfield bungalow with bottles of liquor, food for cooking, pots, snacks, fried corn, onion-chili. There is water in the well there. The men too cook and eat there after the hunt. Budhni had said to the women, "In our time we never returned without something, a hedgehog, a hare, a partridge. Let's see what you do. How you hunt." Mary is wearing a new sari today. Jalim's gift. There are beads around her neck. Dancing she clasps Budhni and says, "I'll marry you after I play the hunt. Then I am the husband, you the wife."

—Good.

—I'll make you dance.

—I'll dance.

Mary is running over with joy today. She has put ten rupees into her mother's hands and bought four of her mother's chickens. The chickens are now in Sanichari's hands. Mary has also contributed two bottles of liquor. This is over and above. The women have already asked and received liquor from Collector. Collector has given the men a goat plus the liquor. He has promised to demonstrate the twist dance of the city in the evening. He will drink bottle after bottle. His tree-felling is done, just small pieces are left. Many bits. With great generosity he has given them to the people of Kuruda as firewood. He has said, "I'll come again, I'll hire only you to fell trees. I'll keep you pickled in liquor then."

Joking with Budhni's group Mary also ran along. Sanichari said, "Look how Mary is looking today. As if she's Mulniji's daughter-in-law."

Budhni said, "When she leaves after marriage Kuruda will lose an eye."

303

Mungri said, "She has never come to the village empty-handed. You see her now, you've forgotten how pretty Bhikni was as a young woman?"

Somri was half-asleep as she walked. Suddenly she sang out with eyes almost closed:

Fire in the Spring	Fire at the feast
Look and come home	Please don't forget.

The others took up the refrain. Four elderly decrepit women long past their youth singing songs of love, the sun warming, the mood thickening, and the sound of gong and horn in the distance.

Mary ran on. The women are all going up Kuruda Hill entering the forest, going to the side of the Cut. Mary is laughing. They won't find a kill. Like all games the hunt game has its rules. Why kill hedgehogs or hares or partridges? You get the big beast with bait.

In her colored sari and red blouse Mary is now like the flamboyant flower in motion. As if a bunch of flowers from the flamboyant tree is running in the wind. Red flowers on all sides. Everything is red. A hare ran past. Mary laughed. She knows where the hare lives. Go back! No fear! Mary said laughing. In her drunken abandon. A great thirst dances in her blood. Collector, Collector. I'm almost there. Collector wants her a lot. Now Jalim is nothing to her. With how much violence can Collector want her? How many degrees Fahrenheit? Is his blood as wild as Mary's? As much daring?

A hedgehog. Go, go away! If it hadn't been today Mary would have killed it, eaten the flesh. Today a small thing cannot please her. She wants to hunt the big beast! A man, Collector. She sees the rock from the distance. Straight, steep stone. Stone jutting out from the top like a ledge. Gitginda vines have come down in a dense mat. On it the yellow flower of the gitginda. Behind the creeper is concealment. Mary's blood burst up at the thought. Forward behind the creeper is the ravine, loose stones on its sides. No one knows how deep the ravine is. No one has gone all the way down. If one could go down into that bottomless cold darkness? She and Collector! She noticed Collector's red shirt.

—Imported liquor, cigarettes, Collector.

—Come inside dear.

—Where is inside? Inside you?

—Yes dear, yes.

—By the ravine. Behind the creeper.

—First have a drink?

—Why just a drink? Give me a cigarette.

—How does it taste?

—Great.

—Not so fast.

—I want to get drunk.

—How drunk?

—I want to get very very drunk.

More booze. She's getting drunk. Stars are strobing in her head. Ah, the stuff is putting spangles in front of her eyes. Shining spangles. Behind them is Collector's face. More liquor. The bottle rolls off. Into the depths of the ravine. Not even a sound. How deep is the ravine? Yes, the face is beginning to look like the hunted animals.

Mary caresses Collector's face, gives him love bites on the lips. There's fire in Collector's eyes, his mouth is open, his lips wet with spittle, his teeth glistening. Mary is watching, watching, the face changes and changes into? Now? Yes, becomes an animal.

—Now take me?

Mary laughed and held him, laid him on the ground. Collector is laughing, Mary lifts the machete, lowers it, hits, lowers.

A few million moons pass. Mary stands up. Blood? On her clothes? She'll wash in the Cut. With great deftness she takes the wallet from Collector's pocket. A lot of money. A lot of money. She undoes the fold in the cloth at her waist and puts the money with her own savings.

Then first she throws Collector in the ravine, his wallet, cigarettes, his handkerchief. Stone after stone. Hyenas and leopards will come at night, smelling blood. Or they won't.

Mary comes out. Walks naked to the Cut. Bathing naked in the Cut her face fills with deep satisfaction. As if she has been infinitely satisfied in a sexual embrace.

In the women's gathering Mary drank the most wine, sang, danced, ate the meat and rice with the greatest relish. At first everyone mocked her for not having made a kill. Then Budhni said, "Look how she's eating? As if she has made the biggest kill."

Mary kissed Budhni with her unwashed mouth. Then she started dancing, beating two empty bottles together. The night air is cool. Sanichari lights the fire.

Drink and song, drink and dance. When everyone is dancing around the fire and singing

Ooh Haramdeo our god

Let there be a Spring feast like this every year—

Let us hunt this way every year—

We'll give you wine We'll give you wine—

Then Mary moves back as she dances. Backing in the dark they are dancing, dancing hard. Mary runs fast in the dark. She knows the way by heart. She will walk seven miles tonight by way of Kuruda Hill and reach Tohri. She will awaken

Jalim. From Tohri there are buses, trucks. They will go away somewhere. Ranchi, Hazaribagh, Gomo, Patna. Now, after the big kill, she wants Jalim.

The Spring festival fires are scattered in the distance. Mary is not afraid, she fears no animal as she walks, watching the railway line in the dark, by starlight. Today all the mundane blood-conditioned fears of the wild quadruped are gone because she has killed the biggest beast.

Long Prose: Chapter Excerpts from Novels

Jane Eyre
Charlotte Brontë

Chapter I

There was no possibility of taking a walk that day. We had been wandering, indeed, in the leafless shrubbery an hour in the morning; but since dinner (Mrs. Reed, when there was no company, dined early) the cold winter wind had brought with it clouds so sombre, and a rain so penetrating, that further out-door exercise was now out of the question.

I was glad of it: I never liked long walks, especially on chilly afternoons: dreadful to me was the coming home in the raw twilight, with nipped fingers and toes, and a heart saddened by the chidings of Bessie, the nurse, and humbled by the consciousness of my physical inferiority to Eliza, John, and Georgiana Reed.

The said Eliza, John, and Georgiana were now clustered round their mama in the drawing-room: she lay reclined on a sofa by the fireside, and with her darlings about her (for the time neither quarrelling nor crying) looked perfectly happy. Me, she had dispensed from joining the group; saying, "She regretted to be under the necessity of keeping me at a distance; but that until she heard from Bessie, and could discover by her own observation, that I was endeavouring in good earnest to acquire a more sociable and childlike disposition, a more attractive and sprightly manner—something lighter, franker, more natural, as it were—she really must exclude me from privileges intended only for contented, happy, little children."

"What does Bessie say I have done?" I asked.

"Jane, I don't like cavillers or questioners; besides, there is something truly forbidding in a child taking up her elders in that manner. Be seated somewhere; and until you can speak pleasantly, remain silent."

A breakfast-room adjoined the drawing-room, I slipped in there. It contained a bookcase: I soon possessed myself of a volume, taking care that it should be one stored with pictures. I mounted into the window-seat: gathering up my feet, I sat cross-legged, like a Turk; and, having drawn the red moreen curtain nearly close, I was shrined in double retirement.

Folds of scarlet drapery shut in my view to the right hand; to the left were the clear panes of glass, protecting, but not separating me from the drear November day. At intervals, while turning over the leaves of my book, I studied the aspect of that winter afternoon. Afar, it offered a pale blank of mist and cloud; near a scene of wet lawn and storm-beat shrub, with ceaseless rain sweeping away wildly before a long and lamentable blast.

I returned to my book—Bewick's History of British Birds: the letterpress thereof I cared little for, generally speaking; and yet there were certain introductory pages that, child as I was, I could not pass quite as a blank. They were those which treat of the haunts of sea-fowl; of "the solitary rocks and promontories" by them only inhabited; of the coast of Norway, studded with isles from its southern extremity, the Lindeness, or Naze, to the North Cape—

> "Where the Northern Ocean, in vast whirls,
> Boils round the naked, melancholy isles
> Of farthest Thule; and the Atlantic surge
> Pours in among the stormy Hebrides."

Nor could I pass unnoticed the suggestion of the bleak shores of Lapland, Siberia, Spitzbergen, Nova Zembla, Iceland, Greenland, with "the vast sweep of the Arctic Zone, and those forlorn regions of dreary space,—that reservoir of frost and snow, where firm fields of ice, the accumulation of centuries of winters, glazed in Alpine heights above heights, surround the pole, and concentre the multiplied rigours of extreme cold." Of these death-white realms I formed an idea of my own: shadowy, like all the half-comprehended notions that float dim through children's brains, but strangely impressive. The words in these introductory pages connected themselves with the succeeding vignettes, and gave significance to the rock standing up alone in a sea of billow and spray; to the broken boat stranded on a desolate coast; to the cold and ghastly moon glancing through bars of cloud at a wreck just sinking.

I cannot tell what sentiment haunted the quite solitary churchyard, with its inscribed headstone; its gate, its two trees, its low horizon, girdled by a broken wall, and its newly-risen crescent, attesting the hour of eventide.

The two ships becalmed on a torpid sea, I believed to be marine phantoms.

The fiend pinning down the thief's pack behind him, I passed over quickly: it was an object of terror.

So was the black horned thing seated aloof on a rock, surveying a distant crowd surrounding a gallows.

Each picture told a story; mysterious often to my undeveloped understanding and imperfect feelings, yet ever profoundly interesting: as interesting as the tales Bessie sometimes narrated on winter evenings, when she chanced to be in good humour; and when, having brought her ironing-table to the nursery hearth, she allowed us to sit about it, and while she got up Mrs. Reed's lace frills, and crimped her nightcap borders, fed our eager attention with passages of love and adventure taken from old fairy tales and other ballads; or (as at a later period I discovered) from the pages of Pamela, and Henry, Earl of Moreland.

With Bewick on my knee, I was then happy: happy at least in my way. I feared nothing but interruption, and that came too soon. The breakfast-room door opened.

"Boh! Madam Mope!" cried the voice of John Reed; then he paused: he found the room apparently empty.

"Where the dickens is she!" he continued. "Lizzy! Georgy! (calling to his sisters) Joan is not here: tell mama she is run out into the rain—bad animal!"

"It is well I drew the curtain," thought I; and I wished fervently he might not discover my hiding-place: nor would John Reed have found it out himself; he was not quick either of vision or conception; but Eliza just put her head in at the door, and said at once—

"She is in the window-seat, to be sure, Jack."

And I came out immediately, for I trembled at the idea of being dragged forth by the said Jack.

"What do you want?" I asked, with awkward diffidence.

"Say, 'What do you want, Master Reed?'" was the answer. "I want you to come here;" and seating himself in an arm-chair, he intimated by a gesture that I was to approach and stand before him.

John Reed was a schoolboy of fourteen years old; four years older than I, for I was but ten: large and stout for his age, with a dingy and unwholesome skin; thick lineaments in a spacious visage, heavy limbs and large extremities. He gorged himself habitually at table, which made him bilious, and gave him a dim and bleared eye and flabby cheeks. He ought now to have been at school; but his mama had taken him home for a month or two, "on account of his delicate health." Mr. Miles, the master, affirmed that he would do very well if he had fewer cakes and sweetmeats sent him from home; but the mother's heart turned from an opinion so harsh, and inclined rather to the more refined idea that John's sallowness was owing to over-application and, perhaps, to pining after home.

John had not much affection for his mother and sisters, and an antipathy to me. He bullied and punished me; not two or three times in the week, nor once or twice in the day, but continually: every nerve I had feared him, and every morsel of flesh in my bones shrank when he came near. There were moments when I was bewildered by the terror he inspired, because I had no appeal whatever against either his menaces or his inflictions; the servants did not like to offend their young master by taking my part against him, and Mrs. Reed was blind and deaf on the subject: she never saw him strike or heard him abuse me, though he did both now and then in her very presence, more frequently, however, behind her back.

Habitually obedient to John, I came up to his chair: he spent some three minutes in thrusting out his tongue at me as far as he could without damaging the roots: I knew he would soon strike, and while dreading the blow, I mused on the disgusting and ugly appearance of him who would presently deal it. I wonder if he read that notion in my face; for, all at once, without speaking, he struck suddenly and strongly. I tottered, and on regaining my equilibrium retired back a step or two from his chair.

"That is for your impudence in answering mama awhile since," said he, "and for your sneaking way of getting behind curtains, and for the look you had in your eyes two minutes since, you rat!"

Accustomed to John Reed's abuse, I never had an idea of replying to it; my care was how to endure the blow which would certainly follow the insult.

"What were you doing behind the curtain?" he asked.

"I was reading."

"Show the book."

I returned to the window and fetched it thence.

"You have no business to take our books; you are a dependent, mama says; you have no money; your father left you none; you ought to beg, and not to live here with gentlemen's children like us, and eat the same meals we do, and wear clothes at our mama's expense. Now, I'll teach you to rummage my bookshelves: for they are mine; all the house belongs to me, or will do in a few years. Go and stand by the door, out of the way of the mirror and the windows."

I did so, not at first aware what was his intention; but when I saw him lift and poise the book and stand in act to hurl it, I instinctively started aside with a cry of alarm: not soon enough, however; the volume was flung, it hit me, and I fell, striking my head against the door and cutting it. The cut bled, the pain was sharp: my terror had passed its climax; other feelings succeeded.

"Wicked and cruel boy!" I said. "You are like a murderer—you are like a slave-driver—you are like the Roman emperors!"

I had read Goldsmith's History of Rome, and had formed my opinion of Nero, Caligula, etc. Also I had drawn parallels in silence, which I never thought thus to have declared aloud.

"What! what!" he cried. "Did she say that to me? Did you hear her, Eliza and Georgiana? Won't I tell mama? but first—"

He ran headlong at me: I felt him grasp my hair and my shoulder: he had closed with a desperate thing. I really saw in him a tyrant, a murderer. I felt a drop or two of blood from my head trickle down my neck, and was sensible of somewhat pungent suffering: these sensations for the time predominated over fear, and I received him in frantic sort. I don't very well know what I did with my hands, but he called me "Rat! Rat!" and bellowed out aloud. Aid was near him: Eliza and Georgiana had run for Mrs. Reed, who was gone upstairs: she now came upon the scene, followed by Bessie and her maid Abbot. We were parted: I heard the words—

"Dear! dear! What a fury to fly at Master John!"

"Did ever anybody see such a picture of passion!"

Then Mrs. Reed subjoined—

"Take her away to the red-room, and lock her in there." Four hands were immediately laid upon me, and I was borne upstairs.

Chapter II

I resisted all the way: a new thing for me, and a circumstance which greatly strengthened the bad opinion Bessie and Miss Abbot were disposed to entertain of me. The fact is, I was a trifle beside myself; or rather out of myself, as the French would say: I was conscious that a moment's mutiny had already rendered me liable to strange penalties, and, like any other rebel slave, I felt resolved, in my desperation, to go all lengths.

"Hold her arms, Miss Abbot: she's like a mad cat."

"For shame! for shame!" cried the lady's-maid. "What shocking conduct, Miss Eyre, to strike a young gentleman, your benefactress's son! Your young master."

"Master! How is he my master? Am I a servant?"

"No; you are less than a servant, for you do nothing for your keep. There, sit down, and think over your wickedness."

They had got me by this time into the apartment indicated by Mrs. Reed, and had thrust me upon a stool: my impulse was to rise from it like a spring; their two pair of hands arrested me instantly.

"If you don't sit still, you must be tied down," said Bessie. "Miss Abbot, lend me your garters; she would break mine directly."

Miss Abbot turned to divest a stout leg of the necessary ligature. This preparation for bonds, and the additional ignominy it inferred, took a little of the excitement out of me.

"Don't take them off," I cried; "I will not stir."

In guarantee whereof, I attached myself to my seat by my hands.

"Mind you don't," said Bessie; and when she had ascertained that I was really subsiding, she loosened her hold of me; then she and Miss Abbot stood with folded arms, looking darkly and doubtfully on my face, as incredulous of my sanity.

"She never did so before," at last said Bessie, turning to the Abigail.

"But it was always in her," was the reply. "I've told Missis often my opinion about the child, and Missis agreed with me. She's an underhand little thing: I never saw a girl of her age with so much cover."

Bessie answered not; but ere long, addressing me, she said—"You ought to be aware, Miss, that you are under obligations to Mrs. Reed: she keeps you: if she were to turn you off, you would have to go to the poorhouse."

I had nothing to say to these words: they were not new to me: my very first recollections of existence included hints of the same kind. This reproach of my dependence had become a vague sing-song in my ear: very painful and crushing, but only half intelligible. Miss Abbot joined in—

"And you ought not to think yourself on an equality with the Misses Reed and Master Reed, because Missis kindly allows you to be brought up with them. They will have a great deal of money, and you will have none: it is your place to be humble, and to try to make yourself agreeable to them."

"What we tell you is for your good," added Bessie, in no harsh voice, "you should try to be useful and pleasant, then, perhaps, you would have a home here; but if you become passionate and rude, Missis will send you away, I am sure."

"Besides," said Miss Abbot, "God will punish her: He might strike her dead in the midst of her tantrums, and then where would she go? Come, Bessie, we will leave her: I wouldn't have her heart for anything. Say your prayers, Miss Eyre, when you are by yourself; for if you don't repent, something bad might be permitted to come down the chimney and fetch you away."

They went, shutting the door, and locking it behind them.

The red-room was a square chamber, very seldom slept in, I might say never, indeed, unless when a chance influx of visitors at Gateshead Hall rendered it necessary to turn to account all the accommodation it contained: yet it was one of the largest and stateliest chambers in the mansion. A bed supported on massive pillars of mahogany, hung with curtains of deep red damask, stood out like a tabernacle in the centre; the two large windows, with their blinds always drawn down, were half shrouded in festoons and falls of similar drapery; the carpet was red; the table at the foot of the bed was covered with a crimson cloth; the walls were a soft fawn colour with a blush of pink in it; the wardrobe, the toilet-table, the chairs were of darkly polished old mahogany. Out of these deep surrounding shades rose high, and glared white, the piled-up mattresses and pillows of the bed, spread with a snowy Marseilles counterpane. Scarcely less prominent was an ample cushioned easy-chair near the head of the bed, also white, with a footstool before it; and looking, as I thought, like a pale throne.

This room was chill, because it seldom had a fire; it was silent, because remote from the nursery and kitchen; solemn, because it was known to be so seldom entered. The house-maid alone came here on Saturdays, to wipe from the mirrors and the furniture a week's quiet dust: and Mrs. Reed herself, at far intervals, visited it to review the contents of a certain secret drawer in the wardrobe, where were stored divers parchments, her jewel-casket, and a miniature of her deceased husband; and in those last words lies the secret of the red-room—the spell which kept it so lonely in spite of its grandeur.

Mr. Reed had been dead nine years: it was in this chamber he breathed his last; here he lay in state; hence his coffin was borne by the undertaker's men; and, since that day, a sense of dreary consecration had guarded it from frequent intrusion.

My seat, to which Bessie and the bitter Miss Abbot had left me riveted, was a low ottoman near the marble chimney-piece; the bed rose before me; to my right hand there was the high, dark wardrobe, with subdued, broken reflections varying the gloss of its panels; to my left were the muffled windows; a great looking-glass between them repeated the vacant majesty of the bed and room. I was not quite sure whether they had locked the door; and when I dared move, I got up and went to see. Alas! yes: no jail was ever more secure. Returning, I had to cross before the looking-glass; my fascinated glance involuntarily explored the depth it revealed. All looked colder and darker in that visionary hollow than in reality: and the strange little figure there gazing at me, with a white face and arms specking the gloom, and glittering eyes of fear moving where all else was still, had the effect of a real spirit: I thought it like one of the tiny phantoms, half fairy, half imp, Bessie's evening stories represented as coming out of lone, ferny dells in moors, and appearing before the eyes of belated travellers. I returned to my stool.

Superstition was with me at that moment; but it was not yet her hour for complete victory: my blood was still warm; the mood of the revolted slave was still bracing me with its bitter vigour; I had to stem a rapid rush of retrospective thought before I quailed to the dismal present.

All John Reed's violent tyrannies, all his sisters' proud indifference, all his mother's aversion, all the servants' partiality, turned up in my disturbed mind like a dark deposit in a turbid well. Why was I always suffering, always browbeaten, always accused, for ever condemned? Why could I never please? Why was it useless to try to win any one's favour? Eliza, who was headstrong and selfish, was respected. Georgiana, who had a spoiled temper, a very acrid spite, a captious and insolent carriage, was universally indulged. Her beauty, her pink cheeks and golden curls, seemed to give delight to all who looked at her, and to purchase indemnity for every fault. John no one thwarted, much less punished; though he twisted the necks of the pigeons, killed the little pea-chicks, set the dogs at the sheep, stripped the hothouse vines of their fruit, and broke the buds off the choicest plants in the conservatory: he called his mother "old girl," too; sometimes reviled her for her dark skin, similar to his own; bluntly disregarded her wishes; not unfrequently tore and spoiled her silk attire; and he was still "her own darling." I dared commit no fault: I strove to fulfil every duty; and I was termed naughty and tiresome, sullen and sneaking, from morning to noon, and from noon to night.

My head still ached and bled with the blow and fall I had received: no one had reproved John for wantonly striking me; and because I had turned against him to avert farther irrational violence, I was loaded with general opprobrium.

"Unjust!—unjust!" said my reason, forced by the agonising stimulus into preco-cious though transitory power: and Resolve, equally wrought up, instigated some strange expedient to achieve escape from insupportable oppression—as running away, or, if that could not be effected, never eating or drinking more, and letting myself die.

What a consternation of soul was mine that dreary afternoon! How all my brain was in tumult, and all my heart in insurrection! Yet in what darkness, what dense ignorance, was the mental battle fought! I could not answer the ceaseless inward question—why I thus suffered; now, at the distance of—I will not say how many years, I see it clearly.

I was a discord in Gateshead Hall: I was like nobody there; I had nothing in harmony with Mrs. Reed or her children, or her chosen vassalage. If they did not love me, in fact, as little did I love them. They were not bound to regard with affection a thing that could not sympathise with one amongst them; a hetero-geneous thing, opposed to them in temperament, in capacity, in propensities; a useless thing, incapable of serving their interest, or adding to their pleasure; a noxious thing, cherishing the germs of indignation at their treatment, of contempt of their judgment. I know that had I been a sanguine, brilliant, careless, exacting, handsome, romping child—though equally dependent and friendless—Mrs. Reed would have endured my presence more complacently; her children would have entertained for me more of the cordiality of fellow-feeling; the servants would have been less prone to make me the scapegoat of the nursery.

Daylight began to forsake the red-room; it was past four o'clock, and the becloud-ed afternoon was tending to drear twilight. I heard the rain still beating continu-ously on the staircase window, and the wind howling in the grove behind the hall; I grew by degrees cold as a stone, and then my courage sank. My habitual mood of humiliation, self-doubt, forlorn depression, fell damp on the embers of my decaying ire. All said I was wicked, and perhaps I might be so; what thought had I been but just conceiving of starving myself to death? That certainly was a crime: and was I fit to die? Or was the vault under the chancel of Gateshead Church an inviting bourne? In such vault I had been told did Mr. Reed lie buried; and led by this thought to recall his idea, I dwelt on it with gathering dread. I could not remember him; but I knew that he was my own uncle—my mother's brother—that he had taken me when a parentless infant to his house; and that in his last moments he had required a promise of Mrs. Reed that she would rear and maintain me as one of her own children. Mrs. Reed probably considered she had kept this promise; and so she had, I dare say, as well as her nature would permit her; but how could she really like an interloper not of her race, and unconnected with her, after her husband's death, by any tie? It must have been most irksome to find herself bound by a hard-wrung pledge to stand in the stead of a parent to a strange child she could not love, and to see an uncongenial alien permanently intruded on her own family group.

A singular notion dawned upon me. I doubted not—never doubted—that if Mr. Reed had been alive he would have treated me kindly; and now, as I sat looking at the white bed and overshadowed walls—occasionally also turning a fascinated eye towards the dimly gleaning mirror—I began to recall what I had heard of dead men, troubled in their graves by the violation of their last wishes, revisiting the earth to punish the perjured and avenge the oppressed; and I thought Mr. Reed's spirit, harassed by the wrongs of his sister's child, might quit its abode— whether in the church vault or in the unknown world of the departed—and rise before me in this chamber. I wiped my tears and hushed my sobs, fearful lest any sign of violent grief might waken a preternatural voice to comfort me, or elicit from the gloom some haloed face, bending over me with strange pity. This idea, consolatory in theory, I felt would be terrible if realised: with all my might I endeavoured to stifle it—I endeavoured to be firm. Shaking my hair from my eyes, I lifted my head and tried to look boldly round the dark room; at this mo- ment a light gleamed on the wall. Was it, I asked myself, a ray from the moon penetrating some aperture in the blind? No; moonlight was still, and this stirred; while I gazed, it glided up to the ceiling and quivered over my head. I can now conjecture readily that this streak of light was, in all likelihood, a gleam from a lantern carried by some one across the lawn: but then, prepared as my mind was for horror, shaken as my nerves were by agitation, I thought the swift darting beam was a herald of some coming vision from another world. My heart beat thick, my head grew hot; a sound filled my ears, which I deemed the rushing of wings; something seemed near me; I was oppressed, suffocated: endurance broke down; I rushed to the door and shook the lock in desperate effort. Steps came running along the outer passage; the key turned, Bessie and Abbot entered.

"Miss Eyre, are you ill?" said Bessie.

"What a dreadful noise! it went quite through me!" exclaimed Abbot.

"Take me out! Let me go into the nursery!" was my cry.

"What for? Are you hurt? Have you seen something?" again demanded Bessie.

"Oh! I saw a light, and I thought a ghost would come." I had now got hold of Bessie's hand, and she did not snatch it from me.

"She has screamed out on purpose," declared Abbot, in some disgust. "And what a scream! If she had been in great pain one would have excused it, but she only wanted to bring us all here: I know her naughty tricks."

"What is all this?" demanded another voice peremptorily; and Mrs. Reed came along the corridor, her cap flying wide, her gown rustling stormily. "Abbot and Bessie, I believe I gave orders that Jane Eyre should be left in the red-room till I came to her myself."

"Miss Jane screamed so loud, ma'am," pleaded Bessie.

"Let her go," was the only answer. "Loose Bessie's hand, child: you cannot suc- ceed in getting out by these means, be assured. I abhor artifice, particularly in children; it is my duty to show you that tricks will not answer: you will now stay here an hour longer, and it is only on condition of perfect submission and still- ness that I shall liberate you then."

"O aunt! have pity! Forgive me! I cannot endure it—let me be punished some other way! I shall be killed if—"

"Silence! This violence is all most repulsive:" and so, no doubt, she felt it. I was a precocious actress in her eyes; she sincerely looked on me as a compound of virulent passions, mean spirit, and dangerous duplicity.

Bessie and Abbot having retreated, Mrs. Reed, impatient of my now frantic an- guish and wild sobs, abruptly thrust me back and locked me in, without farther parley. I heard her sweeping away; and soon after she was gone, I suppose I had a species of fit: unconsciousness closed the scene.

The Scarlet Letter

Nathaniel Hawthorne

Chapter II: The Market-Place

The grass-plot before the jail, in Prison Lane, on a certain summer morning, not less than two centuries ago, was occupied by a pretty large number of the inhabitants of Boston, all with their eyes intently fastened on the iron-clamped oaken door. Amongst any other population, or at a later period in the history of New England, the grim rigidity that petrified the bearded physiognomies of these good people would have augured some awful business in hand. It could have betokened nothing short of the anticipated execution of some noted culprit, on whom the sentence of a legal tribunal had but confirmed the verdict of public sentiment. But, in that early severity of the Puritan character, an inference of this kind could not so indubitably be drawn. It might be that a sluggish bond-servant, or an undutiful child, whom his parents had given over to the civil authority, was to be corrected at the whipping-post. It might be that an Antinomian, a Quaker, or other heterodox religionist, was to be scourged out of the town, or an idle or vagrant Indian, whom the white man's firewater had made riotous about the streets, was to be driven with stripes into the shadow of the forest. It might be, too, that a witch, like old Mistress Hibbins, the bitter-tempered widow of the magistrate, was to die upon the gallows. In either case, there was very much the same solemnity of demeanour on the part of the spectators, as befitted a people among whom religion and law were almost identical, and in whose character both were so thoroughly interfused, that the mildest and severest acts of public discipline were alike made venerable and awful. Meagre, indeed, and cold, was the sympathy that a transgressor might look for, from such bystanders, at the scaffold. On the other hand, a penalty which, in our days, would infer a degree of mocking infamy and ridicule, might then be invested with almost as stern a dignity as the punishment of death itself.

It was a circumstance to be noted on the summer morning when our story begins its course, that the women, of whom there were several in the crowd, appeared to take a peculiar interest in whatever penal infliction might be expected to ensue. The age had not so much refinement, that any sense of impropriety restrained the wearers of petticoat and farthingale from stepping forth into the public ways, and wedging their not unsubstantial persons, if occasion were, into the throng nearest to the scaffold at an execution. Morally, as well as materially, there was a coarser fibre in those wives and maidens of old English birth and breeding than in their fair descendants, separated from them by a series of six or seven generations; for, throughout that chain of ancestry, every successive mother had transmitted to her child a fainter bloom, a more delicate and briefer beauty, and a slighter physical frame, if not character of less force and solidity than her own. The women who were now standing about the prison-door stood within less than half a century of the period when the man-like Elizabeth had been the not altogether unsuitable representative of the sex. They were her countrywomen: and the beef and ale of their native land, with a moral diet not a whit more refined, entered largely into their composition. The bright morning sun, therefore, shone on broad shoulders and well-developed busts, and on round and ruddy cheeks, that had ripened in the far-off island, and had hardly yet grown paler or thinner in the atmosphere of New England. There was, moreover, a boldness and rotundity of speech among these matrons, as most of them seemed to be, that would startle us at the present day, whether in respect to its purport or its volume of tone.

"Goodwives," said a hard-featured dame of fifty, "I'll tell ye a piece of my mind. It would be greatly for the public behoof if we women, being of mature age and church-members in good repute, should have the handling of such malefactresses as this Hester Prynne. What think ye, gossips? If the hussy stood up for judgment before us five, that are now here in a knot together, would she come off with such a sentence as the worshipful magistrates have awarded? Marry, I trow not."

"People say," said another, "that the Reverend Master Dimmesdale, her godly pastor, takes it very grievously to heart that such a scandal should have come upon his congregation."

"The magistrates are God-fearing gentlemen, but merciful overmuch—that is a truth," added a third autumnal matron. "At the very least, they should have put the brand of a hot iron on Hester Prynne's forehead. Madame Hester would have winced at that, I warrant me. But she—the naughty baggage—little will she care what they put upon the bodice of her gown! Why, look you, she may cover it with a brooch, or such like heathenish adornment, and so walk the streets as brave as ever!"

"Ah, but," interposed, more softly, a young wife, holding a child by the hand, "let her cover the mark as she will, the pang of it will be always in her heart."

"What do we talk of marks and brands, whether on the bodice of her gown or the flesh of her forehead?" cried another female, the ugliest as well as the most pitiless of these self-constituted judges. "This woman has brought shame upon us all, and ought to die; is there not law for it? Truly there is, both in the Scripture and the statute-book. Then let the magistrates, who have made it of no effect, thank themselves if their own wives and daughters go astray."

"Mercy on us, goodwife!" exclaimed a man in the crowd, "is there no virtue in woman, save what springs from a wholesome fear of the gallows? That is the hardest word yet! Hush now, gossips for the lock is turning in the prison-door, and here comes Mistress Prynne herself."

The door of the jail being flung open from within there appeared, in the first place, like a black shadow emerging into sunshine, the grim and gristly presence of the town-beadle, with a sword by his side, and his staff of office in his hand. This personage prefigured and represented in his aspect the whole dismal severity of the Puritanic code of law, which it was his business to administer in its final and closest application to the offender. Stretching forth the official staff in his left hand, he laid his right upon the shoulder of a young woman, whom he thus drew forward, until, on the threshold of the prison-door, she repelled him, by an action marked with natural dignity and force of character, and stepped into the open air as if by her own free will. She bore in her arms a child, a baby of some three months old, who winked and turned aside its little face from the too vivid light of day; because its existence, heretofore, had brought it acquaintance only with the grey twilight of a dungeon, or other darksome apartment of the prison.

When the young woman—the mother of this child—stood fully revealed before the crowd, it seemed to be her first impulse to clasp the infant closely to her bosom; not so much by an impulse of motherly affection, as that she might thereby conceal a certain token, which was wrought or fastened into her dress. In a moment, however, wisely judging that one token of her shame would but poorly serve to hide another, she took the baby on her arm, and with a burning blush, and yet a haughty smile, and a glance that would not be abashed, looked around at her townspeople and neighbours. On the breast of her gown, in fine red cloth, surrounded with an elaborate embroidery and fantastic flourishes of gold thread, appeared the letter A. It was so artistically done, and with so much fertility and gorgeous luxuriance of fancy, that it had all the effect of a last and fitting decoration to the apparel which she wore, and which was of a splendour in accordance with the taste of the age, but greatly beyond what was allowed by the sumptuary regulations of the colony.

The young woman was tall, with a figure of perfect elegance on a large scale. She had dark and abundant hair, so glossy that it threw off the sunshine with a gleam; and a face which, besides being beautiful from regularity of feature and richness of complexion, had the impressiveness belonging to a marked brow and deep black eyes. She was ladylike, too, after the manner of the feminine gentility of those days; characterised by a certain state and dignity, rather than by the delicate, evanescent, and indescribable grace which is now recognised as its indication. And never had Hester Prynne appeared more ladylike, in the antique interpretation of the term, than as she issued from the prison. Those who had before known her, and had expected to behold her dimmed and obscured by a disastrous cloud, were astonished, and even startled, to perceive how her beauty shone out, and made a halo of the misfortune and ignominy in which she was enveloped. It may be true that, to a sensitive observer, there was some thing exquisitely painful in it. Her attire, which indeed, she had wrought for the occasion in prison, and had modelled much after her own fancy, seemed to express the attitude of her spirit, the desperate recklessness of her mood, by its wild and picturesque peculiarity. But the point which drew all eyes, and, as it were, transfigured the wearer—so that both men and women who had been familiarly acquainted with Hester Prynne were now impressed as if they beheld her for the first time—was that SCARLET LETTER, so fantastically embroidered and illuminated upon her bosom. It had the effect of a spell, taking her out of the ordinary relations with humanity, and enclosing her in a sphere by herself.

"She hath good skill at her needle, that's certain," remarked one of her female spectators; "but did ever a woman, before this brazen hussy, contrive such a way of showing it? Why, gossips, what is it but to laugh in the faces of our godly magistrates, and make a pride out of what they, worthy gentlemen, meant for a punishment?"

"It were well," muttered the most iron-visaged of the old dames, "if we stripped Madame Hester's rich gown off her dainty shoulders; and as for the red letter which she hath stitched so curiously, I'll bestow a rag of mine own rheumatic flannel to make a fitter one!"

"Oh, peace, neighbours—peace!" whispered their youngest companion; "do not let her hear you! Not a stitch in that embroidered letter but she has felt it in her heart."

The grim beadle now made a gesture with his staff. "Make way, good people—make way, in the King's name!" cried he. "Open a passage; and I promise ye, Mistress Prynne shall be set where man, woman, and child may have a fair sight of her brave apparel from this time till an hour past meridian. A blessing on the righteous colony of the Massachusetts, where iniquity is dragged out into the sunshine! Come along, Madame Hester, and show your scarlet letter in the market-place!"

A lane was forthwith opened through the crowd of spectators. Preceded by the beadle, and attended by an irregular procession of stern-browed men and un-kindly visaged women, Hester Prynne set forth towards the place appointed for her punishment. A crowd of eager and curious schoolboys, understanding little of the matter in hand, except that it gave them a half-holiday, ran before her progress, turning their heads continually to stare into her face and at the winking baby in her arms, and at the ignominious letter on her breast. It was no great dis-tance, in those days, from the prison door to the market-place. Measured by the prisoner's experience, however, it might be reckoned a journey of some length; for haughty as her demeanour was, she perchance underwent an agony from every footstep of those that thronged to see her, as if her heart had been flung into the street for them all to spurn and trample upon. In our nature, however, there is a provision, alike marvellous and merciful, that the sufferer should never know the intensity of what he endures by its present torture, but chiefly by the pang that rankles after it. With almost a serene deportment, therefore, Hester Prynne passed through this portion of her ordeal, and came to a sort of scaffold, at the western extremity of the market-place. It stood nearly beneath the eaves of Boston's earliest church, and appeared to be a fixture there.

In fact, this scaffold constituted a portion of a penal machine, which now, for two or three generations past, has been merely historical and traditionary among us, but was held, in the old time, to be as effectual an agent, in the promotion of good citizenship, as ever was the guillotine among the terrorists of France. It was, in short, the platform of the pillory; and above it rose the framework of that instrument of discipline, so fashioned as to confine the human head in its tight grasp, and thus hold it up to the public gaze. The very ideal of ignominy was em-bodied and made manifest in this contrivance of wood and iron. There can be no outrage, methinks, against our common nature—whatever be the delinquencies of the individual—no outrage more flagrant than to forbid the culprit to hide his face for shame; as it was the essence of this punishment to do. In Hester Prynne's instance, however, as not unfrequently in other cases, her sentence bore that she should stand a certain time upon the platform, but without undergoing that gripe about the neck and confinement of the head, the proneness to which was the most devilish characteristic of this ugly engine. Knowing well her part, she ascended a flight of wooden steps, and was thus displayed to the surrounding multitude, at about the height of a man's shoulders above the street.

Had there been a Papist among the crowd of Puritans, he might have seen in this beautiful woman, so picturesque in her attire and mien, and with the infant at her bosom, an object to remind him of the image of Divine Maternity, which so many illustrious painters have vied with one another to represent; something which should remind him, indeed, but only by contrast, of that sacred image of sinless motherhood, whose infant was to redeem the world. Here, there was the taint of deepest sin in the most sacred quality of human life, working such effect, that the world was only the darker for this woman's beauty, and the more lost for the infant that she had borne.

The scene was not without a mixture of awe, such as must always invest the spectacle of guilt and shame in a fellow-creature, before society shall have grown corrupt enough to smile, instead of shuddering at it. The witnesses of Hester Prynne's disgrace had not yet passed beyond their simplicity. They were stern enough to look upon her death, had that been the sentence, without a murmur at its severity, but had none of the heartlessness of another social state, which would find only a theme for jest in an exhibition like the present. Even had there been a disposition to turn the matter into ridicule, it must have been repressed and overpowered by the solemn presence of men no less dignified than the governor, and several of his counsellors, a judge, a general, and the ministers of the town, all of whom sat or stood in a balcony of the meeting-house, looking down upon the platform. When such personages could constitute a part of the spectacle, without risking the majesty, or reverence of rank and office, it was safely to be inferred that the infliction of a legal sentence would have an earnest and effectual meaning. Accordingly, the crowd was sombre and grave. The unhappy culprit sustained herself as best a woman might, under the heavy weight of a thousand unrelenting eyes, all fastened upon her, and concentrated at her bosom. It was almost intolerable to be borne. Of an impulsive and passionate nature, she had fortified herself to encounter the stings and venomous stabs of public contumely, wreaking itself in every variety of insult; but there was a quality so much more terrible in the solemn mood of the popular mind, that she longed rather to behold all those rigid countenances contorted with scornful merriment, and herself the object. Had a roar of laughter burst from the multitude—each man, each woman, each little shrill-voiced child, contributing their individual parts—Hester Prynne might have repaid them all with a bitter and disdainful smile. But, under the leaden infliction which it was her doom to endure, she felt, at moments, as if she must needs shriek out with the full power of her lungs, and cast herself from the scaffold down upon the ground, or else go mad at once.

Yet there were intervals when the whole scene, in which she was the most conspicuous object, seemed to vanish from her eyes, or, at least, glimmered indistinctly before them, like a mass of imperfectly shaped and spectral images. Her mind, and especially her memory, was preternaturally active, and kept bringing up other scenes than this roughly hewn street of a little town, on the edge of the western wilderness: other faces than were lowering upon her from beneath the brims of those steeple-crowned hats. Reminiscences, the most trifling and immaterial, passages of infancy and school-days, sports, childish quarrels, and the little domestic traits of her maiden years, came swarming back upon her, intermingled with recollections of whatever was gravest in her subsequent life; one picture precisely as vivid as another; as if all were of similar importance, or all alike a play. Possibly, it was an instinctive device of her spirit to relieve itself by the exhibition of these phantasmagoric forms, from the cruel weight and hardness of the reality.

Be that as it might, the scaffold of the pillory was a point of view that revealed to Hester Prynne the entire track along which she had been treading, since her happy infancy. Standing on that miserable eminence, she saw again her native village, in Old England, and her paternal home: a decayed house of grey stone, with a poverty-stricken aspect, but retaining a half obliterated shield of arms over the portal, in token of antique gentility. She saw her father's face, with its bold brow, and reverend white beard that flowed over the old-fashioned Elizabethan ruff; her mother's, too, with the look of heedful and anxious love which it always wore in her remembrance, and which, even since her death, had so often laid the impediment of a gentle remonstrance in her daughter's pathway. She saw her own face, glowing with girlish beauty, and illuminating all the interior of the dusky mirror in which she had been wont to gaze at it. There she beheld another countenance, of a man well stricken in years, a pale, thin, scholar-like visage, with eyes dim and bleared by the lamp-light that had served them to pore over many ponderous books. Yet those same bleared optics had a strange, penetrating power, when it was their owner's purpose to read the human soul. This figure of the study and the cloister, as Hester Prynne's womanly fancy failed not to recall, was slightly deformed, with the left shoulder a trifle higher than the right. Next rose before her in memory's picture-gallery, the intricate and narrow thoroughfares, the tall, grey houses, the huge cathedrals, and the public edifices, ancient in date and quaint in architecture, of a continental city; where new life had awaited her, still in connexion with the misshapen scholar: a new life, but feeding itself on time-worn materials, like a tuft of green moss on a crumbling wall. Lastly, in lieu of these shifting scenes, came back the rude market-place of the Puritan, settlement, with all the townspeople assembled, and levelling their stern regards at Hester Prynne—yes, at herself—who stood on the scaffold of the pillory, an infant on her arm, and the letter A, in scarlet, fantastically embroidered with gold thread, upon her bosom.

Could it be true? She clutched the child so fiercely to her breast that it sent forth a cry; she turned her eyes downward at the scarlet letter, and even touched it with her finger, to assure herself that the infant and the shame were real. Yes these were her realities—all else had vanished!

Anthology Works Cited

Brontë, Charlotte. *Jane Eyre: An Autobiography.* London: Service & Paton, 1897. *Project Gutenberg.* Web. 23 April 2014.

Browning, Robert. "My Last Duchess." *Poetry Foundation.* Poetry Foundation, 2014. Web. 23 April 2014.

Devi, Mahasweta. "The Hunt." *Women & Performance: A Journal of Feminist Theory* 5.1 (1990): 61–79.

Dobson, H. Austin. "In Town." *The Complete Poetical Works of Austin Dobson.* Ed. Alban Dobson. New York: Oxford University Press, 1923. 290–291. Print.

Dowson, Ernest. "Villanelle of His Lady's Treasures." *The Poems of Ernest Dowson: Verses, the Pierrot of the Minute, Decorations in Verse and Prose* Ed. Arthur Symons. Portland, ME: Thomas B Mosher, 1902. 46. Print.

Dunbar, Paul Laurence. "We Wear the Mask." *Poetry Foundation.* Poetry Foundation, 2014. Web. 23 April 2014.

Eliot, T.S. "Hysteria." Poetry Foundation. *Poetry Foundation,* 2014. Web. 23 April 2014.

Eliot, T.S. "The Love Song of J. Alfred Prufrock." *Poetry Foundation.* Poetry Foundation, 2014. Web. 23 April 2014.

Hawthorne, Nathaniel. *The Scarlet Letter.* Boston: Ticknor, Reed & Fields. 1850. *Project Gutenberg.* Web. 23 April 2014.

Keats, John. "To Autumn." *Poetry Foundation.* Poetry Foundation, 2014. Web. 23 April 2014.

Kipling, Rudyard. "Sestina of the Tramp Royal." *Poetry Foundation.* Poetry Foundation. 2014. Web. 23 April 2014.

Kyd, Thomas. *The Spanish Tragedie.* London: Edward Allde, ca. 1592. *Project Gutenberg.* Web. 24 Apr. 2014.

Lovecraft, H. P. "The Alchemist." *Writings in the United Amateur, 1915–1922.* Volume 41, Number 4. November 1916. Project Gutenberg. Web. 23 April 2014.

Millay, Edna St. Vincent. "If I Should Learn, in Some Quite Casual Way." *Renascence and Other Poems*. New York: Harper, 1917. Bartleby.com. Web. 24 Apr. 2014.

Marlowe, Christopher. "The Passionate Shepherd to His Love." *Poetry Foundation*. Poetry Foundation, 2014. Web. 23 April 2014.

Stevens, Wallace. "The Emperor of Ice-Cream." *Poetry Foundation*. Poetry Foundation, 2014. Web. 23 April 2014.

Swift, Jonathan. "A Modest Proposal." Dublin: S. Harding. 1795. *Project Gutenberg*. 2013. Web. 23 April 2014.

Shakespeare, William. *Hamlet*. n.p., n.d. *Project Gutenberg*. Web. 24 Apr. 2014.

Shakespeare, William. *Othello*. n.p., n.d. *The Complete Works of William Shakespeare*. Massachusetts Institute of Technology. Web. 24 Apr. 2014.

Lord Tennyson, Alfred. "Ulysses." *Poetry Foundation*. Poetry Foundation, 2014. Web. 23 April 2014.

Webster, John. *The White Devil*. n.p., n.d. *Project Gutenberg*. Web. 24 Apr. 2014.

Whitman, Walt. "O Captain! My Captain!" *Poetry Foundation*. Poetry Foundation, 2014. Web. 23 April 2014.

Yeats, William Butler. "Adam's Curse." *Poetry Foundation*. Poetry Foundation, 2014. Web. 23 April 2014.

V. ANTHOLOGY

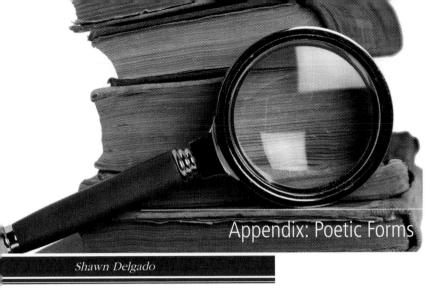

Appendix: Poetic Forms

Shawn Delgado

Traditional poetic forms attempt to harness specific patterns in order to enhance the ideas that the poet is attempting to express. Just as you might select different-shaped boxes for different items (a ring might be in a small box, whereas a refrigerator would need a much larger box), poets select a form that, in some way, "fits" the content of the poem they are writing. In addition to adhering to form, some poets deliberately select forms that are at odds with the content or ideas of the poem (like placing the ring inside a refrigerator box), to challenge the role of the form or to encourage inquiry about the relationship between form and function.

In this Appendix, we briefly examine several of the most common forms in the English language. It is important to note that poetic forms are continually evolving; some gain popularity or disappear from common use—they diverge, develop, and are repurposed over time. We hope you will use this section as an entry point for learning about form, and conduct further research to better understand the complexities of poetic form. We also encourage you to take a moment to look up some of the listed examples of each poetic form (selected poems can be found either in the Anthology section or within the chapters of this book, as denoted in **bold**).

NARRATIVE FORMS: BALLAD, HEROIC COUPLET, AND BLANK VERSE

The following forms are typically used in poetry that tells a story. While many lyric poems begin with a story, but then diverge into a meditation or entirely different subject, narrative poems focus on unfolding a plot (rather than the story being used as an associative trigger which simply serves as a way into the poem).

Ballad. The ballad began as a popular type of song that was often shared orally, so many of the authors of these popular tales are now forgotten, even as the poems endure. These folk tales frequently contained supernatural elements, fatal relationships, and other sensational or tragic topics with major attention to the building of suspense until the climax of the story. While early ballads were narrated with omniscience, rather than from personal accounts, the characters within the ballad were frequently allowed to speak, so that dialogue became an important dramatic force within the genre.

Structurally, the ballad is comprised of quatrains which alternate between iambic tetrameter and iambic trimester in an ABCB rhyme scheme. There is no prede-termined length for the ballad, and with the oral tradition of the ballad in mind, the meter and rhyme served as useful mnemonic devices, so these poems could be more easily memorized and performed.

Examples of this form include Samuel Taylor Coleridge's "Rime of the Ancient Mariner" (1798), "Lord Randall," an anonymous folk ballad first published by Sir Walter Scott in 1803, **"Because I could not stop for Death—" by Emily Dickinson (1863)**—which is included in Corrie White's "Metaphor, Simile, and Imagery" chapter of this book—and "The Ballad of Birmingham" by Dudley Randall (1969).

Heroic Couplet. The heroic couplet was adapted from French verse in the 14th century by Geoffrey Chaucer, and comprises poetry written in rhymed couplets, typically in iambic pentameter, although it may also be written in iambic tetram-eter. During the period of transition in English verse from the tetrameter line to the new standard of the pentameter line, poets would incorporate a caesura near the center of the line, a remnant of Old English alliterative verse which was writ-ten in tetrameter with a pause after two feet. The heroic couplet form typically was used to write about an elevated subject matter and was often utilized when translating epic poetry from Latin or Greek, although many poets have taken advantage of the very obvious rhyme and rhythm for epigrams or satirical work.

Examples of this form include "To S.M., a Young African Painter, on Seeing His Works" by Phillis Wheatley (1773), **"My Last Duchess" by Robert Browning (1842)**—included in the Anthology of this book—and "The J Car" by Thom Gunn (1992).

Blank Verse. Blank verse can be described as any poem written in unrhymed iambic pentameter. Initially taken from Italian literature in the 16th century, this form can be described—with the exception of free verse—as the form most resembling our natural speech patterns. The iambic meter mimics the English cadence of accentuation, and the length of the line approximately simulates the standard length of our phrases based on the natural pause of breath. Unlike other metrical forms, it is remarkably flexible, and it is a frequent component of dramatic poetry.

Examples of this form include "Paradise Lost" by John Milton (1667), "Change" by Letitia Elizabeth Landon (approx. 1832–1837), **"Ulysses" by Lord Alfred Tennyson (1842)**—included in the Anthology section of this book—and "Home Burial" by Robert Frost (1915).

OPEN FORMS: FREE VERSE AND PROSE POETRY

Open forms, rather than being defined by a prescribed arrangement, theme, occasion, or mode of operation (such as narrative, lyric, or dramatic), challenge traditional definitions of poetry by letting the poet develop a system of his or her own rules which govern an individual poem. The prose poem even goes so far as to defy the basic premise that poetry be written as lineated verse.

Free Verse. Free verse poetry, originating in 19th-century France as *vers libre*, became hugely popular with the advent of Modernism, wherein poets began to discard the traditional conventions of highly metrical and regularly rhymed poetry. Instead, these poets opted for a sense of freedom and control of the structures and variations within their work, often placing additional emphasis on imagery and figurative language to provide a lyric aspect for their work.

While there is a certain amount of comfortable predictability in traditional verse, this new form allowed authors to acknowledge the irregularity and complexities of the world for a sense of surprise. This is not, however, simply a move toward chaos. In free verse poems, rather than following a predetermined line length, rhythm, or rhyme scheme, authors have the opportunity to play with these poetic elements, personalizing them to the poem's own voice, idiosyncrasies, or experiences. Because the author is making all decisions about the poem's form, rather than filling the container of a traditional form, the poet does not have the benefit of utilizing the expectations and tropes involved with a traditional form. Instead, the reader of free verse is expected to approach each poem with relatively few expectations and an open mind, so each line break, each rhyme (internal or end rhyme), and each phrasing has importance to the overall experience of the poem.

Examples of this form include **"The Emperor of Ice-Cream" by Wallace Stevens (1923)**—included in the Anthology of this book, "Danse Russe" by William Carlos Williams (1938), "Cinderella" by Anne Sexton (1971), "Diving into the Wreck" by Adrienne Rich (1972), and "What Women Want" by Kim Addonizio (2000).

Prose Poetry. At its core, a prose poem is a poem written without line breaks, so that it has a paragraphic appearance on the page. These poems were first popularized by 19th-century French poets, most prominently Charles Baudelaire in the collections *Les Fleurs du Mal* (1857) and *Paris Spleen* (1869). Despite the appearance of being purely prose, these poems do exhibit the careful attention to language seen in verse poetry, and frequently employ the same strategies and poetic devices while straddling the middle-ground between poetry and prose fiction.

Prose poems are frequently narrative, often employ humor, and, at times, may be an attempt to minimize the inherent artifice within the structure of verse. Even when these poems are narrative, they also have much less of a burden to conclude the story than typical prose fiction and will often leave off at a seemingly critical plot point without providing resolution.

Examples of prose poetry include the poems collected in *Tender Buttons* by Gertrude Stein (1914), **"Hysteria" by T.S. Eliot (1920)**—included in the Anthology of this book, "For My People" by Margaret Walker (1937), "The Colonel" by Carolyn Forché (1981), and "A Story about the Body" by Robert Hass (1990).

REPEATING FORMS: VILLANELLE, PANTOUM, AND SESTINA

The following poetic forms all employ regularly repeating lines or end words in a predictable, set pattern. Because of the emphasis on repetition, the content within the poem is often more recursive in nature, and has a meditative or obsessive quality.

Villanelle. The villanelle is a French form which poet Jean Passerat adapted from an Italian folk song during the late 16th century. Originally, the word "villain" did not refer to a criminal, but rather a simple country servant. With this in mind, the first villanelles were about love of country living, although more recent iterations have taken on the somber subjects of death and loss.

Structurally, the villanelle is a 19-line, rhyming poem written in six stanzas—5 tercets with a concluding quatrain. The poem also establishes two refrains with the first and third line of the first stanza. These lines are repeated, alternating, at the ends of the following 4 tercets, before both are used to conclude the poem in the final quatrain, a common location for the volta. The simple rhyme scheme is *aba aba aba aba aba abaa*. If we label the refrain lines established in the first stanza A_1 and A_2, the repetition can be observed: $A_1bA_2\ abA_1\ abA_2\ abA_1\ abA_2abA_1A_2$.

Examples of the villanelle include **"Villanelle of His Lady's Treasures" by Ernest Dowson (1893)**—included in the Anthology of this book, "Do not go gentle into that good night" by Dylan Thomas (1951), and "One Art" by Elizabeth Bishop (1976).

Pantoum. The word "pantoum" is the English adaptation of the Malayan form named "pantun" which arose in published verse during the 15th century, although it existed orally before that period. The pantoum establishes its structure through the repetition of lines across a series of quatrains. In each quatrain, the second and fourth lines are repeated as the first and third lines, respectively, of the next stanza. At the end of the poem, the final stanza's second and fourth lines are the same as the first and third lines of the first stanza, which gives the entire form a sense of circular motion, like an ocean's tides. As a result, each line in the poem is used exactly twice.

There is a common, optional variation to this pattern at the end of the poem. Rather than having the second and fourth lines of the final stanza reiterate the first and third lines of the poem, sometimes they're switched, so that the third line of the first stanza is the second line in the final stanza, allowing the first and last lines in the poem to be the same. This gives a bookend effect to the poem and allows for the cycle to be even more apparent. Rhyming in a pantoum is optional, and there is no standard meter or line length. Additionally, rather than repeating lines exactly, some authors use variations of those initial lines.

Examples of the pantoum include **"In Town" by H. Austin Dobson (1873)**—included in the Anthology of this book, "Iva's Pantoum" by Marilyn Hacker (1969), "Another Lullaby for Insomniacs" by A.E. Stallings (2004), and "Stillbirth" by Laure-Anne Bosselaar (2007).

Sestina. The sestina is a 39-line poem made up of 6 sextets followed by a final tercet. Each of the sextets uses the same 6 words to end its lines, but a mathematical algorithm rearranges their order, so that each word inhabits a different line in each sextet. The final tercet, known as the "envoi," contains all 6 of these key words, 2 in each line. The pattern for these key words at the end of the lines is as follows: Stanza 1—*ABCDEF*; Stanza 2—*FABEDC*; Stanza 3—*CFDAEB*; Stanza 4—*BCEFAD*; Stanza 5—*DBACFE*; Stanza 6—*EDFBCA*; Stanza 7 (envoi; two words per line)—*AB|CD|EF*. If you look closely, you'll see that each stanza rearranges the end words of the previous stanza in the order of 615243, so that by the end of the poem, each repeated word has taken every position possible within the stanza as the terminal word of a line. Because of this formula, it's extremely rare to find a rhyming sestina, although they can be written in meter. While this form may seem a bit arbitrary at first, it often will let the author discover the many possibilities of a small grouping of words, sometimes utilizing homonyms or homophones, since an accomplished sestina can reuse these words in such a way as to not become repetitive or dull. The repetition of these end words can also be useful in establishing tone or a system of imagery.

Examples of the sestina include **"Sestina of the Tramp-Royal" by Rudyard Kipling (1896)**—included in the Anthology of this book, "Sestina" by Elizabeth Bishop (1965), and "Like" by A.E. Stallings (2013).

SHAPING FORMS: ELEGY, ODE, PASTORAL, AND DRAMATIC MONOLOGUE

The following forms are defined, especially in a contemporary context, by their content more than their structures, so themes and subject matter are the defining features of their classification.

Elegy. Dating back to ancient Greece, the elegy is one of the oldest forms of Western poetry and deals with one of the most common human tragedies: death. In fact, the word "elegy" comes from the Greek word "elegeia" which literally means "song of mourning." While elegies may take a variety of tones ranging from bitter grief to nostalgia to adoration of the person(s) who have passed, they all deal with the central ideas of death and loss. While not a requirement of the form, many poets elect to use regular meter and rhyme to indicate the formality and somberness of the occasion.

Examples of this form include "On the Death of Anne Brontë" by Charlotte Brontë (approx. 1850), **"O Captain! My Captain!" by Walt Whitman (1865)**—included in the Anthology section of this book, "Funeral Blues" by W.H. Auden (1940), and "Elegy for Jane" by Theodore Roethke (1950).

Ode. The ode, like the elegy, is another of the oldest recorded forms of poetry in the Western world. Its creation is attributed to the 5th century BCE Greek poet Pindar, whose odes were often accompanied by music and dancing. The ode is also commonly associated with the 1st century CE Roman poet Horace, who brought a highly philosophical quality to the form.

Traditionally, the ode maintained a serious tone, an elevated level of diction, and tended to be rather long and elaborately constructed. Often, these poems were performed publically at important official ceremonies such as coronations or funerals. Today, the ode is viewed as a poem of praise or celebration, without the requirement to use elevated diction or address a serious subject. Many love poems—a common theme in poetry—can be considered odes as well.

Examples of this form include "Ode to a Nightingale" by John Keats (1819), "Ode on the Whole Duty of Parents" by Francis Cornford" (1934), **"To Autumn" by John Keats (1820)**—included in the Anthology of this book, "Ode to My Socks" by Pablo Neruda (1956), and "For My Daughter, Who Loves Animals" by Dorianne Laux (1994).

Pastoral. Pastoral poetry imitates, often celebrating or praising, nature and the natural world. In fact, the Latin word *pastor* means "shepherd," so these poems often depict a calm or idealized rural life. Traditionally, lyric pastorals tended to be short poems wherein a speaker from the city admires or longs for rural life, while more dramatic poems tended to have a speaker or multiple speakers from the country who engage in either a monologue or conversation about their daily lives. Today, the term is used more loosely to describe "nature poetry" while some poets even play with the traditional emphasis of setting within the pastoral while adapting it to city life, creating urban and suburban pastorals.

Examples of the pastoral include **"The Passionate Shepherd to His Love" by Christopher Marlowe (1599)**—included in the Anthology of this book, "I Wandered Lonely as a Cloud" by William Wordsworth (1807), "To Autumn" by John Keats (1820), "Pastoral" by Lilian Bowes Lyon (1932), "A Blessing" by James Wright (1963), and "Turtle" by Kay Ryan (1994).

Dramatic Monologue. A dramatic monologue is a poem that employs a single speaker addressing the reader or audience at length. This form is born out of the theatrical convention of the soliloquy, wherein an actor breaks the fourth wall by speaking directly to the audience, often at a pivotal moment of personal crisis. This allows the audience to see the thoughts and preoccupations of the character from that character's own perspective. Since these poems involve characters, we can consider them persona poems, and while we should expect to learn information known by the speaker, most dramatic monologues also reveal feelings, thoughts, or characteristics about the speaker which he or she might be unaware of. While not a requirement, many dramatic monologues are written in blank verse.

Examples of the dramatic monologue include "The Author to Her Book" by Anne Bradstreet (1678), "Soliloquy of the Spanish Cloister" by Robert Browning (1842), **"The Love Song of J. Alfred Prufrock" by T.S. Eliot (1917)**—included in the Anthology of this book, and "Half-Hanged Mary" by Margaret Atwood (1995).

THE SONNET

The **sonnet** was an Italian form and originates from the word *sonnetto*, meaning "a little song." The sonnet consists of 14 lines and a pattern of end rhyme; the difference in the pattern of rhyme (or **rhyme scheme**) marks the most notable difference between each of the main sonnet types: Italian (or Petrarchan) sonnets, and English sonnets. This rhyme scheme changes pattern at a set point within the poem to audibly represent a shift known as the "volta" or "turn." This shift either marks a change in the speaker's point of focus, tone, or can comment on the ideas and language of the preceding lines. This turn may or may not be visually represented with a stanza break. In both English and Italian, the standard sonnet is written in iambic pentameter, although in French the line has an extra foot, being written in iambic hexameter.

Although as the most commonly employed tradition English poetic form the sonnet is used for a wide variety of subjects, it is particularly popular for love poetry. It is also noteworthy, that while we will discuss a few of the most common arrangements of the sonnet, there are dozens of variations on these patterns which experiment with different rhyme schemes, line lengths, or metrical patterns which ultimately demonstrate the flexibility of this form.

Italian Sonnets: Petrarchan. The Italian, or Petrarchan, sonnet was first attributed to Francesco Petrarcha (commonly translated to "Petrarch") and is the oldest and most popular form of the sonnet, dating back to the 14th century. It is a 14-line poem in iambic pentameter which is divided into an octave and a sestet. This division is marked in the rhyme scheme (octave: *abbaabba*; sestet: *cdecde* or *cdcdcd* or some similar variation) as well as the poem's turn.

Examples of the Italian sonnet include **"How do I love thee? Let me count the ways" by Elizabeth Barrett Browning (1850)**—included in the Fausto Barrionuevo's "Poetry" chapter of this book, "The New Colossus" by Emma Lazarus (1883), "[What lips my lips have kissed and where and why]" by Edna St. Vincent Millay (1923), and "Design" by Robert Frost (1936).

English Sonnets: Shakespearean and Spenserian. The English sonnet, like the Italian sonnet, is composed in 14-lines of iambic pentameter, but it differs from the Italian sonnet in its usage of rhyme. The English sonnet features three rhyming quatrains followed by a rhymed couplet. The major turn of the poem also comes with those final two lines, challenging the poet to make a fairly quick or witty turn in just two lines. While many consider the Shakespearian Sonnet to be the "true" English sonnet, we've included both the Shakespearian and Spenserian forms below.

The **Shakespearian sonnet**, created by William Shakespeare, was a 16th-century adaptation of the Italian sonnet and is divided into three quatrains and a couplet. These grouped lines are displayed through the rhyme scheme of *abab cdcd efef gg*. It is notable that each "stanza" of the poem (these may not be represented with physical stanza breaks) adopts new rhyming sounds, so the author is only required to find 2 words that sound alike, rather than 3 or 4. Theoretically, this was to help adapt the form for the English language which, when compared to a romance language such as Italian, is relatively rhyme-poor.

Examples of the Shakespearian sonnet include "Let me not to the marriage of true minds" by William Shakespeare (1609), "My mistress' eyes are nothing like the sun" by William Shakespeare (1609), "Outcast" by Claude McKay (1921), **"If I Should Learn, in Some Quite Casual Way" by Edna St. Vincent Millay (1916)**—included in the Anthology of this book, "First Poem for You" by Kim Addonizio (1994), and "Eurydice is Wed" by Chelsea Rathburn (2005).

The **Spenserian sonnet**, while less popular than the Shakespearean sonnet, is another attempt to adapt the sonnet form to the English language. It was developed by Edmund Spenser in the 16th century. This variation is rather similar to the Shakespearean form, being composed of three rhyming quatrains and a couplet. However, instead of establishing a new pair of rhyming sounds in each quatrain, the quatrains are linked through one of the rhyming pairs so that the rhyme scheme can be described by the pattern *abab bcbc cdcd ee*. It is also important to note that the "Spenserian stanza" is not a part of the Spencerian sonnet; instead, it refers to a specific 9-line stanzaic form used in Spencer's poem "The Faerie Queene."

The most famous examples of the Spenserian sonnet come from Edmund Spenser's sonnet sequence *Amoretti* (1595), notably "Happy ye leaves! when as those lily hands," "The sovereign beauty which I do admire," and "One day I wrote her name upon the strand."

FINAL THOUGHTS ON FORM

As poets write, their structural choices are informed by and in conversation with the historical evolution of poetic forms. Having a solid foundation in basic forms can give you, the reader, a shorthand into a poem's main ideas.

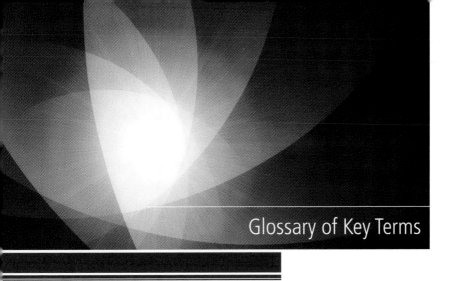

Glossary of Key Terms

ABCs of Citations: a means for evaluating web sources based on authority, accuracy, bias, and currency

accentual meter: poetic rhythm based on how the pronunciation of words and their stresses affect the cadence of the line

accentual-syllabic meter: poetic rhythm in which lines in a poem follow patterns both in syllables and in stresses

accuracy: a term that relates to the viability of the content of a source; necessary criteria for selecting good research

active reading: critically thinking while reading a text; often characterized by highlighting important passages, making character trees, reacting to the text, annotating, and reviewing a text

administered colonies: were founded for the purposes of economic exploitation by small groups of British emigrants who dominated the colonized country politically and economically, but only settled a very small portion of the land; an idea associated with postcolonialism

adversity: in literature, a theme frequently associated with characters that overcome obstacles like physical triumphs, to personal fears, societal barriers, or personal circumstances

alliteration: when the consonant sounds at the beginning of a series of words are the same, like the "g" sound in "goodness gracious"

allusion: an indirect or implied reference to a particular person, place, historical event, work or art, idea, or literary text

ally: a character archetype that fulfills a support role for the hero or protagonist of the narrative

ambivalence: in colonial terms, the phenomenon of the colonized being torn between the will of the colonizers and the resistance of the colonized; an idea associated with postcolonialism

analogy: a term for when a simile is extended across an entire work

anapest: a metrical foot of three syllables that follows an unstressed-unstressed-stressed pattern, example: interrupt

antagonist: an adversary of the protagonist in a text

archetype: the original "prototype" character or figure found in literature on which other similar characters are based; for example, the hero and the trickster

arena space: a stage that allows the audience to sit on all sides of the actors; very little room on stage for sets because they may block the audience's view

Ask Us!: a button on the UNCG Jackson Library webpage that enables a direct chat with the Library and/or librarians

assemblage: a collection of ideas and objects with situational but not necessarily permanent or inherent relationships to one another

assonance: the repetition of identical vowel sounds in words closely grouped together such as the long "o" sound in "slow going"

atmosphere: the emotional tone of a piece of writing created by elements such as diction and setting

authority: a term that relates to a source's author: requires assessment of the person, people, or organization responsible for a website; a necessary criteria for good research

autobiography: a long prose form that examines the story of one's own life

backstory: events and situations that occurred prior to the beginning of a work of fiction

beats: dramatic action subdivided into smaller units; a beat consists of exactly one cause and one effect

betrayal: the breaking of confidence; as a theme in literature, commonly seen as betrayal that occurs between one character and another, a character and him/herself, or a betrayal against an ideal, such as loyalty or perfection

bias: a term that relates to the content of a text; a source that only features one side of a story, calling into question the text's reliability

bildüngsroman: a story detailing a character's development or growth or coming of age

biography: someone's life story written by another person

blank verse: unrhymed lines of iambic pentameter

book review: a type of article that provides readers with a short overview of a book along with the reviewer's opinion of it so the reader can decide if he/she wants to read or buy it

burlesque: common subgenre of comedy; see *farce*

caesura: the punctuation that occurs in the middle of a line of poetry and emphasizes important elements in the text

cause and effect: something happens, which leads to something else happening, then something else happens in response (generally, until something happens that changes things in an inalterable way)

chapters: the division of a novel or other work of long prose into main sections

character analysis: a study of a character that explores who he/she is in relation to the narrative and discusses how he/she is presented both directly and indirectly in the text

cinquain/quintain/quintet: a five-line stanza

citation: a means for giving credit to the original author when quoted or otherwise used in a text; a citation builds credibility as an author because additional sources are shown as consulted, provides reader with a sense of the location of information, helps to avoid plagiarism

citation style: a formal citation method, generally tied to a professional field organization such as MLA, APA, or Chicago

class: as a theme in literature, relates to a system of divisions between people based on economic status or reputation

climax: the turning point in a narrative, when the intensity of the story's action has reached its highest point and brought the protagonist to the precipice of change

close reading: intense, targeted reading of a narrow passage of text that focuses on analyzing the literary elements in that particular section and how they contribute to the overall meaning both of the passage and the literary work as a whole

collage essay: a writer brings together many different and seemingly random ideas to create a new text

collection of poetry: a book that compiles multiple poems by the same author

colonial discourse: an idea associated with postcolonialism; communication focused on colonialism, most often creating a binary way of seeing the colonizers (representing the Occident) and the colonized (representing the Orient), a theory developed by Edward Said

colonial discourse analysis: an idea associated with postcolonialism; seeks to identify evidence of colonial discourse and its resultant effects in colonial and postcolonial settings

colonialism: the subjection of one population by another through the establishment of colonies; an idea associated with postcolonialism

comedy: often in reference to plays, this type of narrative is "an imitation of inferior people"; refers to both socially low-ranked people and morally corrupt people behaving badly

compare/contrast essay: uses similarities and differences to make a claim about literary works

complex tragedy: often in reference to plays, this type of narrative is caused by the main character's failings; depends on "reversal and recognition"

complication: a term that encompasses the struggle between opposing forces through a series of crises, which moves narrative action forward towards a climax

conceit: see *extended metaphor*

conflict: in literature, most often one character struggling against another, one character struggling against a group or society, or a character battling against nature

consonance: a type of sound imagery when the consonant sounds are similar or even identical and repeat throughout a line, sentence, paragraph, or other segment of a text

controlling metaphor: when a metaphor dominates and extends across the entire length of a work

cosmic irony: the discrepancy between individuals' designs for shaping their own lives and the designs of fate, the gods, or God

couplet: a two-line stanza; when the lines rhyme, it's known as an heroic couplet

creative nonfiction: a prose text in which literary devices are incorporated into a nonfiction narrative

cultural colonization: an idea associated with postcolonialism; the practice of replacing the cultural practices and beliefs of an indigenous people with European values, governance, and laws

cultural materialism: an idea associated with New Historicism; views culture as a social and historical product that is consumed, and it uses the study of literature to interpret the critic's current political culture

currency: a term that refers to an article or source's publication date; the more current an article is, the more likely it is to be viable as a source

dactyl: a metrical foot of three syllables that follows a stressed-unstressed-unstressed pattern, for example: dinosaur

deconstruction: analytical lens that views a text as not having a fixed meaning; the meaning of a text is determined by its reader

denouement: a term relating to the narrative arc of a text after the climax, which finalizes any unresolved issues of the conflict

dialect: the combination of words and pronunciations specific to a given region

diction: the use and choice of words and phrases in writing or speech

didactic: a text that presents the reader with a moral or lesson

discourse: refers to multiple ways of representing and writing about reality; the ways that ideas are articulated

discovery space: in staging, serves the same function as a proscenium arch by separating the audience from the actors or props it contains

disidentification: an idea associated with queer theory; term used to describe the way queer people of color have purposefully misused, or disidentified, with popular representations that do not explicitly include them

dramatic action: the series of cause-and-effect relationships that drive a play forward

dramatic irony: a type of irony established when the audience knows something a character does not; the gap between what a character in a text knows about his or her fate and what readers know

dynamic character: a character who experiences an epiphany after conflict, and as a result exhibits a permanent shift in perspective or attitude; the opposite of a static character

dystopia: narratives of imaginary societies, usually set in the future

emotional atmosphere: figurative language alerts the reader to the mood of the piece, governed by emotion rather than reason

end-stopped/end-blocked: when a line of poetry ends with a form of punctuation, such as a comma or a period

enjambed heroic couplets: a set of two lines that rhyme, with the idea continuing from the first line into the second without punctuation

enjambment: when an idea or phrase in a poem carries over from one line to the next without punctuation

epigraph: brief citation at the beginning of a literary work, alluding to other literary works and/or their writers

epilogue: a statement at the end of the novel, either to comment on the novel or to offer the reader a conclusion of sorts

epiphany: a sudden moment of insight or comprehension

essentialism: an ideology associated with feminist theory that maintains that femininity and masculinity are biologically rooted expressions

Eurocentrism: an ideology associated with postcolonialism that hinges on the assumption that European ideals and experiences are the standard by which all other cultures are to be measured and judged inferior

evidence: details or examples from a text that support an argument or claim

exposition: the segment of the narrative arc in which the character's problem or the conflict is exposed or revealed to the reader

extended metaphor: a figurative comparison that exists in multiple derivations for the duration of the text

fable: a short prose narrative that is didactic in nature

fairy tale: a fictional narrative that typically features supernatural or fanciful creatures as well as magic, charms, and disguises

falling action: a segment of the narrative arc that includes the various events and actions that occur immediately after the climax that lead up to the resolution; a plot's "loose ends" are tied up

fantasy: stories that take place in a nonexistent or unreal world, involving incredible characters

farce: often in reference to plays, this type of narrative tends to include deliberately over-the-top buffoonery

feminist theory: theoretical discourse centered around the feminist and post-feminist movements; focuses on questions of power and agency tied to women's roles in society

fiction: narrative that comprises imaginative characters and events, as opposed to actual happenings

figurative language: writing that has a metaphorical quality; not literal

figure of speech: see trope

first-person: point of view in which the narrator, speaker, or persona tells the story from his/her perspective, using the pronouns "I" and "we"

first-wave feminism: historical marker in the development of feminism defined by advocation for the recognition of women's legal status and the right to vote

flash fiction: an extremely short story, not surpassing 1,000 words: types include postcard fiction and short-short stories

flat character: any character in a text whose motivations and emotions are largely unknown, ultimately possessing a one-dimensional quality

foil: a type of character who contrasts the qualities of the protagonist, putting their differences on display

foot: any given combination of stressed and unstressed syllables in a line of poetry

form poetry: when a poem follows a historically contrived, recognizable pattern or displays consistencies from line to line, for example: ballad, sonnet, villanelle

formal essay: an essay form that can be characterized by its "logical organization" and "seriousness of purpose"

formalist: an author who chooses to write using traditional structural elements of form

forms: in literature, common structures and shapes

fourth wall: a fictional notion that in theatre, the audience is seeing the play take place through an invisible wall, and is therefore separate from the action of the play

free indirect discourse: when a narrator steps into the thoughts of a character

free verse: a type of poetry in which a poem creates its own structure through various elements such as internal rhyme, line breaks, and word choice

friendship: in literature, a theme that focuses on characters' friendly relationships with one another

gender: as a literary theme, generally addresses societal stereotypes and ideas of femininity and masculinity; in terms of critical theory, a person's choice of dress, behavior, and performance of either masculinity or femininity

genre: category of literature classified by style, form, and/or presentation of subject

GLBT: gay, lesbian, bisexual, and transgender/transsexual; also known as LGBT

gothic: a genre that centers on terror or suspense; sexuality, passion, and fear are often major themes

graphic novel: a narrative presented in primarily visual rather than textual format, employing a series of illustrated panels to convey the plot

heap: a dramatic term referring to the result or logical effect of a trigger

hegemony: the power of the ruling classes to convince other classes that their interests are the interests of all; an idea associated with postcolonial theory

herald: a character archetype that has a relationship to the hero, in that he typically calls the hero to action or indicates major changes that will happen in the text

hero: a character archetype that often endures great challenges to overcome personal and societal circumstances

heteronormativity: an ideology that is based on the construction of heterosexual relationships as not only the most valuable, but also the only most legitimate option for intimate relationships; associated with queer theory

historical novel: set in another time other than that in which it was written; reconstructs a past age

history play: a type of dramatic narrative characterized by fictional representations of historical events; often educational or patriotic in nature

homonormativity: in queer theory, an ideology that is based on the construction of homosexual relationships as legitimate option for intimate relationships, in contrast to heteronormativity

hybrid: a mix of novel types

hybridity: in postcolonial theory, the process by which new forms are created as a result of the interaction of colonizer and colonized

iamb: a metrical foot of two syllables that follows an unstressed-stressed pattern

iambic pentameter: the most common line of English poetry: five feet of unstressed-stressed syllables

ideology: a system of ideas ascribed to a group

image: the picture crafted by an author in a sentence, line, or paragraph; see *imagery*

imagery: language in a text that creates a picture by appealing to one or more of the five senses: sound, smell, taste, touch, and hearing

imperialism: the ideologically motivated and systematic settling of the globe to establish colonies that would be both politically and economically supportive of the empire; an idea associated with postcolonial theory

implied metaphor: when metaphors are not explicitly constructed with the "to be" verb

implied stage direction: stage directions embedded within the words spoken by the characters in a play

in medias res: a literary technique whereby the writer opens her story in the middle of the action

in-text citation: a means by which to attribute credit to research from another source; often a parenthetical notation that includes the author and the page number; should always be used with quotes

inciting incident: see *point of attack*

informal essay: an essay that can be characterized by the "personal element" as exemplified by humor, self-revelation and a non-argumentative quality of writing

interdisciplinary: utilizing the methods and research practices of multiple disciplines, including history, cultural anthropology, psychology, sociology, and economics, for example

internal rhyme: in poetry, rhyme that occurs from line to line not at the end but usually in the middle, and sometimes within parts of the words themselves

interpellation: in queer theory, the dynamics that situate a subject within already existing ways of thinking, an idea developed by Louis Althusser

interpret: the act of working to understand and analyze a text

interpretations: personal experiences that lead to connections in a text that help us relate and analyze the text

intersectionality: in feminist theory, a term that refers to the ways that different kinds of social categories and oppressions are present within each other

intertextuality: intentionally alluding to concepts, phrases, or forms from another work of literature

introductory paragraph: refers to a college essay: includes the author, title, genre, and era or specific date, when available, of the primary texts you are using in your argument, followed by a thesis statement

irony: a type of figurative language that refers to moments in a text that say one thing but mean something else, either in juxtaposition or opposition

juxtaposition: a term that refers to the identification of contrast between two ideas

legend: a hybrid genre that combines elements of fiction and nonfiction; grounded in realism and history

library database: searchable online collection of resources

limited perspective: when the reader only has access to one character's point of view, which is often biased

line: a row of words, as in a poem, the end of which is not created by the margin, but deliberately determined by the poet

linear plot: a narrative arc that follows a typical or traditional plot trajectory

literary canon: the traditional set of texts that academia values as important and influential

literary criticism: in research, scholarly works that provide an in-depth look at a text or a specific aspect of a text

Literary Reference Center: in Jackson Library, similar to the Literature Resource Center; provides full-text access to a variety of source types

Literature Resource Center: in Jackson Library, provides access to a significant amount of full-text content, including literature criticism, book reviews, author biographies, interviews, audio and video clips

loss: in literature, a theme often associated with grief following the death of a loved one

love: in literature, a theme that manifests as love lost, love conquering all, love as healing, unrequited or in another capacity

lyric essay: a form of personal essay; combines elements of the personal essay with aspects of poetry

lyric poetry: a type of poetry characterized as a meditation on a particular subject, the feelings, or the mood of the speaker

magician: a character archetype that uses the forces of the physical, and at times, the spiritual world to enact change or resolve conflicts

major theme: the central issue around which a literary work revolves, also known as a motif

martyr: a character archetype primarily associated with sacrifice; often in terms of willingly making a sacrifice for the greater good of the community or the hero

Marxist criticism: a critical movement founded on the political thinking of Karl Marx (1818–1883); associated with New Historicism

MEAL plan: a way of ordering components of a body paragraph for a scholarly essay in which the writer includes a sentence to support each aspect: **M**ain point in a paragraph, followed by an **E**xample from the text, supported by **A**nalysis of that example, which then **L**inks back to the essayist's main argument or thesis

memoir: a form of autobiographical writing, written in first person and similar to autobiography, that focuses on one main event in the author's life

mentor: a character archetype represented as an advisor or teacher that provides guidance to the main character throughout the text

metaphor: figurative comparisons that do not contain the words "like" or "as" and often use some variant of the verb "to be"

meter: rhythmical patterns in the lines of a poem

metrical variance: when poems do not adhere entirely (or at all) to a specific or traditional accentual-syllabic meter pattern

mimicry: the imitation of dress, language, and behaviors

minor theme: a pattern of recurring ideas that may only be briefly mentioned throughout a text; supplementary to the major theme

MLA citation: consists of in-text, or parenthetical, documentation in the essay itself, which corresponds to a full citation in the Works Cited page at the end of an essay

MLA International Bibliography: primary article database used for scholarly literature research; focuses on literature criticism

Modernist: a period of writing generally assigned to the late 19th through mid-20th century era, known for densely intertextual work and a shift away from traditional forms

monologue: in theatre, a speech delivered by an individual that is intended to convey his or her inner thoughts aloud, whether for him or herself or for the audience or another character

mood: the kind of emotional climate a work suggests through diction and tone, also referred to as atmosphere

mother: a character archetype, either a literal or metaphorical maternal figure who provides physical, emotional, and spiritual nurturing to other characters

motif: see major theme

motivation: an attempt to explain why a character performs any specific action in a play or narrative

multigenre: consisting of more than one genre, such as poetry and fiction

multimodal: compositions that combine multiple communication modes, such as text, image, speech, sound, and body language

multivalent: in queer theory, seeing the world as more than a series of binaries; having a range of interpretations, values, or meanings

myth: a traditional story about heroes or supernatural beings, often originating in oral culture and intended as an explanation for how things came into existence and how humans fit in with the world around them

mythology: group or collection of shared myths

narrative arc: five related stages of plot development: exposition, rising action, climax, falling action, and resolution

narrative mode: the way the narrator, speaker, or persona narrating the text expresses him or herself

narrative poetry: a type of poetry with the primary function of telling a story

narrator: the voice of the text, the persona or speaker telling the story

near rhyme/slant rhyme: close rhymes that incorporate similar consonant or vowel sounds; can act as a substitute for exact rhymes; e.g., "faith" and "breath"

neocolonialism: the continuation of colonial conditions under more indirect forms of control; an idea associated with postcolonial theory

New Criticism: a formalist approach to literature, prominent in the 1950s and '60s, which upheld the belief that a literary text could and should be studied without attention to the cultural or historical context in which it was produced

New Historicism: a popular critical approach to literary analysis that situates a literary text within its historical and cultural context, questioning how that context influenced the work as well as how the text shaped, altered, and interrogated the culture in which it was written

noble savage: a character archetype identifiable by intrinsic virtue and a lack of corruption from societal forces

nonfiction: work of prose based on real facts and information

nonfiction novel: actual events and real people presented in a novel-length narrative, using many of the techniques of fiction, such as flashbacks

novel: an extended, book-length prose narrative

novella: shorter than a novel and longer than a short story; long enough to be published on its own

Occident, the: the Western world/Europe; an idea associated with postcolonial theory

octave: an eight-line stanza in poetry

OED: *Oxford English Dictionary*; a good quality dictionary to define terms

onomatopoeia: when sounds mimic the action they are describing, such as "buzz" or "burp"

oral tradition: the vocal root of language, originating in songs

Orient, the: the Eastern world/Asia; an idea associated with postcolonial theory

Orientalism: the process by which Europe, through various disciplines such as anthropology and history, constructed an image of the "Orient"; an idea associated with postcolonial theory

outsider: a character archetype defined by marginalization; in a text this kind of character is alienated from or operates outside of society

paraphrase: in writing, to put into one's own words

parody: an imitation of another person or literary work's form or style

patriarchy: an idea associated with feminist theory: a system of male domination that oppresses women and is evident within a range of social phenomena

performativity: a term used in queer theory to describe the relationship of gendered and sexual expressions to power

persona: a role or mask through which the perspective of the speaker of the text is presented

personal essay: a short prose form less interested in argument, persuasion, and logic, and more interested in the communication of the essayist's personal experience

personification: figurative language in a text in which an abstract idea or inanimate object is given human qualities

perspective: point of view

plagiarism: intentional or unintentional act of representing the words of another as one's own in any academic exercise

play: a literary genre in which the story is acted out on stage and performed for an audience

plot: the main events of a work of literature such as a novel, short story, or play, deliberately chosen and arranged by the author to create a sequence of events intended to showcase a character, theme, or similar

plot: the deliberate and selective sequence of events that traces a character's struggle with a conflict or problem

poem: a text written in verse

poetic analysis: the close reading of a poem for literary elements like symbolism, figurative language, and sound imagery

poetic explication: the analysis of a poem; see *poetic analysis*

poetry: a literary genre written in verse

point of attack: the moment at which a play's principle conflict begins

point of view: perspective from which a story is told

popular source: magazine or newspaper articles; written for a more general audience

positionality: in feminist theory, one's personal relationship to power and oppression

post-feminist: a term used to imply that feminist movements have been so successful in generating gender equality that they are no longer necessary

postcard fiction: see *flash fiction*

poststructuralist theory: a mid-20th century theoretical lens that held that human knowledge is unstable because there is no way to avoid human systems of understanding in order actually to understand the unknowable; we are limited in terms of understanding by our humanity

power: in postcolonial, feminist, and queer theory, for instance; the ways in which people control and influence the actions and agency of others

preface: a statement at the beginning of a book

prewriting activity: brainstorming, diagramming, or outlining your ideas, for instance

primary source: original material that has not been filtered through interpretation or evaluation, such as a novel, poem, play, short story, interview, letter, or similar

problem paper: sets forth a problem you've noticed while you were reading a literary work, and offers up one or more solutions or responses to that problem based on textual evidence and sometimes secondary research

properties: any objects that appear onstage during a performance, also known as "props"

proscenium theatre: a physical space for dramatic performance that features a contained staging area, with the audience located entirely on one side of the stage

prose: the opposite of verse; any form of written or spoken expression that is not composed in metered language

protagonist: the main character of a narrative

protector: a character archetype that supports others in some capacity, whether through caregiving or helping others avoid danger throughout the text

pyrrhic: a metrical foot of two syllables, unstressed-unstressed

quatrain: a four-line stanza

queer theory: a theory that came about in response to challenges that scholars and activists were making to the ways that people understand gender and sexuality

race: as a literary theme, race focuses on differences or disparities between ethnic groups; common idea in postcolonial, New Historical, feminist and queer theories

realistic novel: a type of fiction that attempts to reproduce faithfully the surface appearance of life, especially that of ordinary people in everyday situations

reliability: in literature, the degree to which the narrator is trustworthy

repeated idea: a prominent idea that occurs throughout a text, see "theme"

resolution: the point in the plot when the problem is resolved, for better or for worse

revenge: as a theme, delves into the darker side of human ambition as one individual seeks to impose punishment upon another in response to real or imagined slights or injuries

rhetor: the speaker or writer of a text

rhyme scheme: the pattern of end rhymes found in a poem

rising action: a segment of the narrative arc that reveals how the character struggles with the problem; makes up the majority of the plot

romance novel: novels set in exotic locales, with fantastic events and idealized characters

round character: these characters are developed much more fully than their flat counterparts; the text offers insight to the inner workings—or emotional state, desires, and motivations

satirical essay: an essay form that employs exaggeration, ridicule, and irony to undermine and attack human vices and political folly

scansion: the act of marking metrical distinctions in a line or stanza of poetry

scholarly source: an academic, peer-reviewed, or refereed text; written both by and for scholars

science fiction: a narrative that relies on scientific principles that often have not yet been discovered

second-person: writing style defining texts where the narrator speaks directly to the reader, using the pronoun "you"

second-wave feminism: historical marker in the development of feminism defined by an emphasis on the rights of white women over the rights of women of color

secondary sources: a type of text that relies on numerous primary resources to provide context

septet: a seven-line stanza

sestet: a six-line stanza

set: the scenery in a play that is not part of the actual playhouse

setting: a physical place in which the action of a text takes place, as well as its time frame and cultural context; where and when a poem, play, or narrative takes place; can stand for more than just the literal location

sex: a person's biological identification, defined by genitalia, chromosomes, and other biological features; idea associated with queer theory

short prose: diverse category of texts including fiction and nonfiction; textual forms include myths, political speeches, riddles, short stories, personal essays, and fairy tales

short story: a brief fictional narrative in prose, shorter than a novella

short-short stories: see *flash fiction*

simile: a comparison between two dissimilar things using the words "like" or "as" in its construction

simple tragedy: often in reference to plays, this type of narrative revolves around events that simply happen to a character for no discernible reason

situational irony: in literature, the difference between what we expect in a given situation and what actually occurs

sketch: a short prose form with little interest in plot or story

social constructivism: in queer theory, the concept that ideas about sex and gender are created through various cultural rules and expectations

soliloquy: a speech that is generally not intended to be heard by others; employed as a way of communicating a character's internal struggle

sonnet: one of the most popular English poetic forms; fourteen-line poem in a fixed rhyme scheme; see Appendix for more detail

sound: the aural attributes of a word or words

sound imagery: musicality of diction, created by rhythmic and rhyming patterns

speaker: the voice, narrator, or persona, of a work

speaker: in poetry, performs the actions in the poem in conjunction with the worldview presented by the poet, but not synonymous with "author"

specificity of detail: the text on the page presents specific details that hint at a whole universe of meaning that isn't necessarily or explicitly stated by the narrator

speculative fiction: a type of fiction that takes current cultural and societal problems and hypothesizes their future ramifications

speech prefix: the way play texts identify the speaker, usually with the character's name, an abbreviated version of the name, or sometimes the character's function in the play

spondee: a metrical foot of two syllables, stressed-stressed

stage directions: unspoken sentences in a play text that tell the actor what to do in performance; for the reader, they describe something which physically occurs onstage

stanza: a set of lines in a poem that are intentionally grouped together

static character: a type of character that does not have a fundamental change in perception over the course of the text; the opposite of a dynamic character

story: the full sequence of events that affect the lives of the characters and extends before and after the plot of a narrative

stressed: a heightened inflection on a word or a specific syllable of a word, as noted in the dictionary

style: rules related to capitalization, spelling, hyphenation, and abbreviations; punctuation, including ellipsis points, parentheses, and quotation marks; and the way numbers are treated

subaltern: frequently an idea in New Historicism or postcolonialism; a person of inferior rank who is subject to the hegemony of the ruling classes; originated by the Marxist critic Antonio Gramsci

subject: as represented in queer theory, a being whose thoughts and beliefs about itself and others come from the society in which it exists

suggestion: using a few details to evoke a large, complex picture

surface reading: a preliminary, basic understanding of the plot of a text—the opposite of close reading

syllabic meter: when lines of poetry are devoted to a specific number of syllables

symbolism: a common method through which authors can communicate metaphorical ideas

symbols: objects, words, actions, events, or characters that represent something beyond the surface meaning of a text

syntax: the structure and arrangement of words on a page, such as grammar, capitalization, and punctuation

the Three Unities: the idea that a theatrical performance is consistent in time, action, and place, particularly a play in the Classical model

theatre-in-the-round: see *arena space*

thematic analysis: an essay that examines the presence of one abstract idea in multiple instances throughout the course of a literary work

theme: a prominent or recurring idea in a text; see *major* and *minor theme*

third-person: writing style defining texts in which the narrator is someone that is more removed from the story itself, using the pronouns "she," "he," or "they"

third-person limited: a writing style defining texts where the reader is only privy to what one character is thinking about the world, and the narrator is someone removed from the story using pronouns "she," "he," or "they"

third-person omniscient: when the narrator switches in and out of the heads of multiple characters, giving the narrator god-like knowledge of all events in the story

third-wave feminism: historical marker in the development of feminism that sought to widen the scope and potential of feminist thinking to include all groups marginalized by diverse forms of patriarchy

thrust stage: a performance space that allows the audience to sit on three sides of the playing space; the actors have "thrust" their way into the audience

title: the name by which a literary work is known; often a mini-thesis or introduction to a text, may also indicate an important image or phrase to which the author is explicitly directing the reader

tone: refers to the overall mood created by a piece of literature through elements such as diction

tragedy: dramatic genre; an imitation of events that evoke fear and pity

tragedy of character: dramatic genre; focuses on the pain of a specific person

tragedy of suffering: dramatic genre; focuses on society's emotional or physical suffering

tragic flaw: known as *hamartia* in Greek; the character trait that leads to the hero's downfall

tragic irony: dramatic irony when it is applied to tragedies

tragicomedy: a dramatic genre that denies cosmic order to world events; the audience is expected to find humor in the suffering and pain of others

transnational feminism: in feminist theory, an ideology that questions the role of power in relation to the production of nation-states and feminist movements within and across them

trapdoor: in drama, a physical element of the stage that allows actors to enter the space from either above or below; can often convey important information about characters

trickster: a character archetype often associated with mischief; goes against the expectations of others and sometimes breaks the rules to create conflict

trigger: a dramatic term referring to an action that causes something to happen; the precursor to a heap

triplet/tercet: a three-line stanza

trochee: a metrical foot of two syllables that follows a stressed-unstressed pattern

trope: a word or expression used in a figurative sense

truncation symbol: in online database searches, the symbol * used after a root word brings up anything that starts with that root

unity of impression: the short story always has as its focus a single, coherent emotional effect; noted by Edgar Allen Poe

unstressed syllable: a lesser inflection on word or a specific syllable of a word, as noted in the dictionary

Utopian: a perfect society

verbal irony: a term that describes the difference between what one says and what one means; sometimes the audience knows what makes a comment have another meaning (often opposite of the literal interpretation), whereas the recipient may not recognize the layered meaning

verse: poetry; writing with an emphasis on arranging words into a rhythmic pattern

villain: a character archetype that is considered a representation of evil; often provides contrast to the protagonist of a text

voice: refers to a piece of writing's narrative quality

warrior: a character archetype embodied by defenders of justice and figures of morality

Works Cited: a list of sources used within an essay that gives credit to the original authors; alphabetically listed

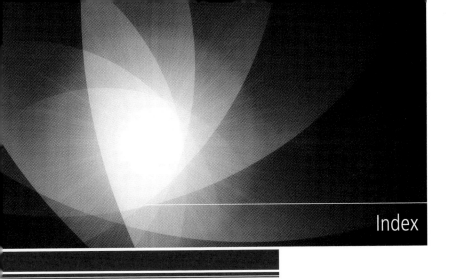

Index